Does God really exist?

That question arises sooner or later in every human mind. It haunts the believer in his hours of doubt, the non-believer no less in his.

Several years ago, a serious illness raised the question in acute form for Thomas E. Powers, a New York advertising man.

Powers had been, in his own phrase, a "liberal-scientific-humanist-atheist-agnostic." He was fairly sure there was nothing to religion, but in desperation he decided to test for himself its assertion that God is, and that his reality can be experienced by anyone who honestly seeks him.

"It worked."

In those two words, from the preface, is the essential message of an extraordinary book by Powers.

This is not a stuffy academic discourse on spiritual life. It is a powerfully-written handbook on how to find God, by a man who did so, to his own vast surprise.

Although the intellectual level of this book is always adult, and at times even scholarly, Powers writes in the breezy, uninhibited language of the advertising man.

He gets down to brass tacks on the first page.

"If you are in trouble or in some sort of crisis—if you seriously and quickly need to satisfy yourself that God exists—it can be done without a lot of skull-cracking or waste of breath.

"Here is how:

"*First*—Avoid like the plague all unnecessary argument and debate. Accept God as a working hypothesis. You can do this without straining your intellectual integrity, whatever your outlook on life may be. Sincerely ask him, if he exists, to help you and steer you.

"*Second*—Find and associate with a group of people who really do believe in God and who are working their belief in daily life. Try to find a group who are really doing this and not just talking about it.

"*Third*—Be open and truthful with these people about your situation, whatever it is, and follow the reasonable suggestions they make to you. Begin to train yourself as they are training and to do the things they are doing.

"*Fourth*—Keep an open mind and watch. The evidence of God's presence and influence will appear in your own life, possibly sooner than you expect."

This is what Powers calls the "emergency" approach to God. And of it, he confidently says:

"I do not merely hope and believe it works. I know it works."

The rest of the 352-page book is directed to "those who are not in an acute crisis, and who have time to make a more leisurely and extensive approach to the subject of God's existence than is possible in a tight pinch."

While these pages also are irradiated with the contagious conviction of first-hand experience, Powers does not rely primarily on personal testimony. He has obviously spent much time in recent years studying the classics of religious mysticism, and it is from this rich storehouse that most of the wisdom in his book is admittedly drawn.

Somewhere along his personal religious Odyssey, Powers became a Christian. But the signposts he has erected along the way to God are not all from the Christian workshop; the book also quotes copiously from Hindu, Buddhist, Jewish and Islamic scriptures, and from such "non-religious" sources as the famed psychiatrist Carl Jung.

"Although I am now a professing Christian," says Powers, "I find truth, get help, and take delight in other religions. . . .

"I must say that acquaintance with the teachings and the people of other religions has never lessened, but on the contrary has deepened, my devotion to Jesus Christ."

For those who are already tentatively or securely committed to religious faith, this book offers a guide toward deeper understanding of the spiritual life.

For those who do not believe in God, but who are troubled by what G.K. Chesterton called "the first wild doubts of doubt," it is a compelling invitation to a great experiment.

Louis Cassels
United Press International
July 26, 1959

Invitation to a Great Experiment

Invitation to a Great Experiment

EXPLORING THE POSSIBILITY
THAT GOD CAN BE KNOWN

Thomas E. Powers

New Expanded Edition

Crossroad · New York

1990

The Crossroad Publishing Company
370 Lexington Avenue
New York, NY 10017

Copyright © 1959, 1979, 1990 by The Queen's Work, Inc.

All rights reserved. No part of this book may be reproduced, stored in a retrieval system, or transmitted, in any form or by any means, electronic, mechanical, photocopying, recording or otherwise, without the written permission of The Crossroad Publishing Company.

Printed in the United States of America

Library of Congress Cataloging-in-Publication Data

Powers, Thomas E., 1911–
    Invitation to a great experiment : exploring the possibility that God can be known / Thomas E. Powers. —New exp. ed.
      p. cm.
    Includes bibliographical references and index.
    ISBN 0-8245-1049-6
    1. God—Knowableness. 2. Desire for God. 3. Happiness—Religious aspects—Christianity. 4. Trust in God. 5. Compulsive behavior. I. Title.
BV4501.2.P6 1990
248.4—dc20   90–33928
                                                                                     CIP

This book was originally published in 1959 as *First Questions on the Life of the Spirit* by Harper & Row. Subsequent editions—entitled *Invitation to a Great Experiment*—were published by Doubleday (1979) and East Ridge Press (1986). This new edition is a revised, updated, and expanded version of all previous editions.

Acknowledgments will be found on page 328, which constitutes an extension of the copyright page.

This is what you start with

This way of life is not something you merely read about and think about. It is something you do . . .

You start by learning a special technique with your alarm clock: You set it one hour earlier than usual, and when it rings you get up.

Do not underestimate (a) the importance and (b) the difficulty of this simple technique. It is important because it enables you to get what you absolutely need in order to get going on a new way of life—that is, *time*. Unless you make time for it, you will go nowhere. And if you are an alcoholic or involved with drugs or sick sex or some other kind of hard hangup, you can't afford through mere carelessness to lose your chance. So listen to this talk about the alarm clock, will you?

You set the clock one hour earlier than usual and get up. (See page 144.) It is *hard to do*. Be prepared for that.

You can see why. It is hard because at first you do not set a high value on it. If somebody were to pay you one hundred dollars for every morning that you got up an hour early, you would do it very cheerfully every day. This new way of life gives you something more valuable than a hundred dollars a day, but who is convinced of that in the beginning? Nobody. All you can do is catch a glimpse from somebody else's experience and hang on to that at first.

It is hard to keep the rule of getting up one hour early every morning in order to do the work, *but it can be done*. And after a while your own direct personal experience will show you that there is something even more terrific than money or sex to be had. After that it will be easier to get up in the morning and to do whatever else is necessary, because even in the face of great difficulties it is easy to do what you love.

I am not theorizing or guessing here but reporting to you out of actual practice. If you will hang in there and really use this hour in the morning, a basic change begins to take place in your relationship to yourself, to the people around you, and to God. *If you will merely do it*, something very big begins to happen. This way of life requires an investment of your time, your interest, and yourself. It pays off very large on the investment; but with no investment, nothing is possible. A great deal hangs on that hour in the morning.

What do you do with the hour? There is a lot of room for using your own judgment and following your own tastes, but it helps at the outset to follow some kind of schedule that has been worked out and found effective in actual practice by a number of people who have really been doing this thing. The following is such a schedule:

You divide the time into three periods of twenty minutes each. In the first period you *read*. In the second period you *pray or meditate*. In the third period you *exercise*.

For what to read, see pages 190 through 208. There is a *great* bunch of stuff to choose from. But remember that you are reading for know-how and not just fun. A lot of this literature is tremendously intriguing and fascinating, but all of it has a desperately serious underlying purpose: to communicate to you the reality of God and give you practical knowledge as to how to live from day to day.

From your reading you can learn how to get started in praying, meditating, and exercising. Soon you will be able to learn from, and also to help, other people, and that will really begin to change your life.

In conclusion, let me challenge you: Follow the above program faithfully for only one month. If nothing happens, if you don't feel that anything at all has taken place in yourself and your life, let me know, and I will eat six pages of this book on white or rye bread, whichever you specify.

Preface to the Second Edition

Don't worry, this is not an autobiography. Nevertheless, in order to get acquainted and to position us somewhat, I have to begin by telling you something about myself.

My father was a patient man, but he had his moments. In such a moment he once told me that I didn't have sense enough to come in out of the rain. I was impressed. In fact I was enlightened, if only briefly and partially. I did realize that what he was saying was in some way true. What I did not realize was that this strange truth was to become the story of my life.

It is the story of a lot of other lives, too. One of the chief features of the modern scene is that some very large number of people on the earth at this time do not know enough to come in out of the rain—in the sense that they fail, in spite of much science and much effort, to find refuge from the inclement weathers of life.

Lyndon Johnson is said to have said that being President is like being a jackass in a hailstorm: you just have to stand there and take it. And so it is with a great many today, not only our underprivileged and unfortunate but our most distinguished citizens as well. People are unable to find shelter from the drizzles of worry and boredom, the squalls of leaky emotion and blown vitality, and finally the great deluges of loss, dereliction, sickness of body and mind, and impending death. Nobody can stop these things, but there ought to be some kind of haven, and some way of making sense out of it all.

There ought to be, and there is.

The point of this book is that, after years of drenching and soaking and very near drowning, I at last *did* discover the way to come in out of these rains, and I have something to communicate about it. The way, although open to all, is no commonplace. Many who desperately need it and seek it are late in finding it, and many die without finding it. Help is always needed. Therefore, in this space and wherever else I can, I venture to share my own experience, strength, and hope with anyone who is able to pick up on it. There are far greater sources of help, of course, but sometimes a weak voice can be heard when a trumpet would overwhelm; and also one of the services that this source may render to you is to point the way to greater sources.

In 1940 I was insane and dying of a self-inflicted illness. I recovered, after all other efforts at recovery had failed, by giving my life up to God. If that sounds simple and rather sweet, believe me it was neither.

I fought against it tooth and nail for five years and yielded only when it became clear that there was no alternative. Thus, reluctantly and with a very imperfect idea of the amazing thing I was getting into, I entered the process which has historically been called the regenerative life, the path, but most often and universally all over the earth, the Way.

The present book was first published in 1959. It was intended as a *work book*, a manual for actually living, actually doing, actually working the regenerative life. The book incorporated nineteen years of working experience on my own part—plus the shared experience of several hundred contemporaries with whom I worked directly and some thousands of others with whom I was in touch occasionally or indirectly—plus my working contacts with the exceedingly rich lore of the regenerative Way, extending to the earliest times of our history, through books, music, architecture, art, and oral tradition.

My interest was, and is, in the actual *doing* of the work of the Way. I realize that theory is indispensable, but I am concerned with it only as it relates to practice. I want to know, and to share know-how, about how to get into the Way, how to find and relate to other people and all possible sources of help on the Way, and above all how to keep going on the Way—how to avoid falling away or drifting away.

The book was issued with the title *First Questions on the Life of the Spirit*. It was a clumsy and pedestrian label, but in spite of that handicap, the volume quickly began to find its way into the hands of

Preface to the Second Edition

people who were getting near to the Way or were already in the Way and working it. I began to hear from men and women all over the country, and eventually all over the world, who were using *First Questions* as it was intended to be used: as a work book.

Of all the group work using *First Questions* as a basis, none was as intensive, sustained, and effective as the group activity which finally centered down in Kansas City. There is always a prime mover in any particular vortex of this kind of work, and in the case of the Kansas City Project his name was Donald L. Campbell. Don, a six-foot-four Scotsman, had a remarkable capacity for communicating the excitement, the promise, and the working realities of the Way. Campbell started out in life in the undertaking business and then became an advertising agency executive, so you can see that he was on the move in a rather freewheeling way even before he got into the regenerative life. God only knows how a person like Campbell gets into the Way. Most people need a few illnesses or disasters to steer them in, but not this man. There wasn't anything drastically wrong with him, or his family either. He just got to thinking that there must be something more to life than undertaking and advertising.

Using *First Questions* as a work manual, Don sparked a regenerative-life group activity, first in the Western suburbs of Chicago and later in Kansas City and surrounding towns, that seems to me more real and more powerful than anything of its kind that I am aware of outside the major truth-centered and/or God-centered rescue movements such as Alcoholics Anonymous. Other *First Questions* groups have done similar work in areas as widely separated as Maine, Alaska, Texas, and New York. If you want to get the most out of this book—and especially if you are interested enough to seek out some friends and start a group—the experience of earlier pioneers may give you help and save you some headaches. See Appendix B, page 283.

First Questions is now reissued with a new title and with extensive additions which, I hope and believe, will be even more useful than some of the original material, because I have not been standing still during these succeeding thirty-one years but have been working more intensively and on a broader front than ever before.

The world has not been standing still either. What seemed only probable in 1959 now seems tolerably certain: that not just the sick and the insane but the whole human race is spinning toward some kind of imminent apocalypse. The regenerative life—the universal

Way to sanity, security, freedom, and eternal joy—now seems enormously more relevant to life in the twentieth century than when I wrote in the fifties. Indeed, the Way now seems more and more obviously to be the only port in the gathering worldwide storm.

No one can turn to God until he has satisfied himself, to some extent at least, with respect to the *reality* of God. And there is no way of doing this without investigating, without making trial, without testing. I would like to say something, therefore, about experiment as a necessity of the Way.

Experiment is the keynote of our entire cultural epoch. We have not been content to take anything on hearsay or traditional authority but have wanted to try everything out for ourselves, to experiment with it and prove it to our satisfaction.* We have experimentally explored practically everything conceivable. You name it—we have applied our techniques to it and have come up with some kind of reading on its reality. Experimentation is the genius of our age; we have experimented with everything within range of the human mind.

With one exception.

We have made no experiments upon God. The omission is striking. We have scientifically tested every imaginable datum, except the most elementary, most obvious, and most inescapable datum of all.

Why?

Are we so sure of God's unreality that we won't even take him as the basis of an experimental working assumption? I don't think so. I think that the most skeptical of us have uneasy feelings that there may be some fire behind all the religious smoke.

I think we do not seek God experimentally, scientifically, without fear or favor, *because we are afraid of what the result might be.*

If it turned out that God *is* real, and if we were to test and *prove* that reality, it would destroy our world. Our world is based on lies and violence, and these things are impossible—they simply melt and disappear—in the presence of the living God.

But our world seems to be coming apart anyhow, so the experiment of testing God's reality is a more possible thing for us now than it

---

*Modern natural science plays a critical role—both to help and to hinder—in the search for reality, for truth, and for God. See page 230, where Ernst Lehrs discusses a spiritual understanding of natural science, on the basis of Goethe's method of training observation and thought.

was when this book was first written. And it is something that can be done without waiting for any great agreement or backing among groups or nations. Any individual, anywhere, at any time, can begin the experiment.

If you are inclined to try it, I call to your attention one fact of immense importance. Very great guidance—very valid guidance—very practical guidance is available to you. Remember that the greatest teachers of the human race—Christ, Buddha, Moses, Muhammad, Krishna, Zarathustra, Hermes, Plotinus, Lao Tse—were not mere philosophers, not intellectual speculators, not logic choppers. And they were not speaking from somebody else's report. They were men who themselves had made the great experiment, with positive result. They knew the Supreme Reality by experiment and by experience. *And the Way that they teach is the Way of knowledge of God by experiment and by experience.*

T.E.P.

Note: In the matters under consideration in this book, your authors have been taught chiefly by four or five dozen basic schoolmasters—not gurus or rabbis but simply competent and highly respected teachers. The following are some of them:

In religion—
C. S. Lewis
George MacDonald
J. R. R. Tolkien
J. P. de Caussade
Malachi Martin
Jacques Ellul
The Pilgrim (and the Philokalia Fathers)
M. K. Gandhi
Frithjof Schuon (and the Sufi saints)
Israel ben Eliezer (the Baal Shem Tov)
Ko Hung (and the Taoist masters)

In philosophy—
Lev Shestov
Martin Buber
Irving Kristol
Robert Novak

Fyodor Dostoevsky
Jacob Boehme
St. Thomas Aquinas
Plotinus
Hermes Trismegistus

In natural science—
Ernst Lehrs
Guenther Wachsmuth

In history—
Will and Ariel Durant
Bruce Catton
William Manchester
Anne Catherine Emmerich
Mary of Agreda

In medicine—
Robert Mendelsohn
Norman Cousins
Berton Rouéché
David F. Musto
Samuel Hahnemann
Paracelsus
Hippocrates

In psychiatry—
Harry M. Tiebout
O. Hobart Mowrer
Thomas Szasz
C. G. Jung

In psychology—
Maurice Nicoll
Martin Gross

In magic (black and white)—
Arthur Machen
A. E. Waite
C. S. Lewis
George MacDonald

There is an Appendix in the back of the book called "A Sampler of Some of Our Schoolmasters' Teachings in the Lifesavers Way of Life," beginning on page 209, where you can get briefly acquainted with some of these people and their teachings if you wish.

Contents

THIS IS WHAT YOU START WITH	xi
PREFACE TO THE SECOND EDITION	xiii
INTRODUCTION	1

PART ONE
GOD IS AN EXPERIMENTALLY KNOWABLE REALITY. TRUE OR FALSE?

CHAPTER ONE
First Things First	7
In Case of Emergency	7
If You Qualify . . .	10
It Is Very Easy—and Very Hard	19

CHAPTER TWO
Toward Action: The People, the Books, and the Laboratory	22
Who Are the Right People?	22
What Are the Right Books?	29
Where Is the Laboratory?	46

CHAPTER THREE
The Ways to Knowledge	49
"With All Thy Mind"—the Way of Reason	49
"With All Thy Strength"—the Way of Faith	56
"With All Thy Heart and Soul"—the Way of Experience	61

PART TWO
IS THE EXPERIMENT A PRACTICAL POSSIBILITY?

CHAPTER ONE
What Do You Do?	77

The Alternatives	78
The Rules	80

CHAPTER TWO
The Practical Life Means Practice	86
The Practice of the Presence of God	87
The Practice of Ego-reduction or Dying Daily	94
The Practice of Watching	102

PART THREE
GOD'S WILL:
HOW TO KNOW IT AND DO IT

CHAPTER ONE
God's Will Is the Door. Prayer Is the Key	117
God Speaks Continuously . . .	120
But Who Can Hear Him?	122

CHAPTER TWO
How to Use the Key	127
The Practice of Abandonment	133
The Practice of Penetrating the Cloud	142
The Practice of Continuous Prayer	154
BIBLIOGRAPHY	171
SPECIAL BOOK LISTINGS	190

APPENDIX A
A Sampler of Some of Our Schoolmasters' Teachings in the Lifesavers Way of Life	209

APPENDIX B
The Lifesavers Way of Life	283
INDEX	323

Invitation to a
Great Experiment

Introduction

Osokin and the magician are both silent.

"What am I to do then?" says Osokin at last almost in a whisper.

There is a long pause.

"My dear friend," says the magician, breaking the silence, "those are the first sensible words I have heard from you since the beginning of our acquaintance. . . . You come here, you complain, and you ask for a miracle. And, when I can, I do what you ask because I sincerely wish to help you. But nothing comes of it. Try now to understand why nothing comes of it and why I am powerless to help you. Understand that I can carry out only your wishes, only what you ask for. I cannot give you anything on my own initiative. This is the law. Even what I am saying now I am able to say only because you asked me what you are to do. If you had not asked, I could not have spoken."

Ouspensky, *Strange Life of Ivan Osokin*

God can do anything, but "can do" is not "will do." He *will* do certain things, it appears, only in response to certain of man's doings. God evidently waits and watches for particular freely initiated actions on the part of man. One of these actions is the asking of questions.

And therefore questions are important in the search for reality. A smart man who "knows" so much that he has stopped asking questions can get way off base. A stupid or beaten or broken man who happens to be humble enough to ask real questions may be near to real answers.

Introduction

This is a book of questions. It is not exactly a book of answers. I am concerned with answers, of course, but I do not hope to give them, only to indicate them. The answers to the questions raised here would make a library, not a book. And the library would fall short of the real answers, because they are to be found in life rather than in libraries, and in the power and presence of God rather than in unregenerate "life."

The experiment of finding God is studied in this book under the headings of three key questions: (1) God Is an Experimentally Knowable Reality: True or False? (2) Is the Experiment a Practical Possibility? (3) God's Will: How to Know It and Do It.

Answers to such questions are not cheap; you have to work for them. But if you undertake this work seriously you find yourself being helped. And among the helps are people and books. One of the ways in which the present book may serve you is in suggesting how you can get in touch with people and work with them. Another aspect of this manual's possible usefulness to you is in suggesting other books which may be helpful. Throughout the following discussions of particular questions, related works and authors are indicated.

In a book of this kind the personal element is inescapable, and since responsibility for it should be taken, perhaps it will help for the author to identify himself briefly: I was born in Chadron, Nebraska, in 1911. At the age of twenty-nine I was a liberal-scientific-humanist-atheist-agnostic—a real omelet. I was an agreeable, witty, thin, and nervous fellow. I was doing very well in the advertising business. But at the same time I was suffering from a mentally and physically crippling illness which the doctors at last pronounced incurable. Doctors are a solemn lot anyhow*, and these doctors were not fooling. I had to believe them. Much against the grain of my whole outlook at that time, I was persuaded to seek help in the area of "spiritual experience." I didn't know what it was, and it sounded suspiciously like religion, but in desperation finally I was willing to try it.

It worked. The disease was arrested and eventually fully relieved. But the process went much further. Over a period of years, many problems, previously only half-realized, began to come to the surface and be corrected. A lively co-operation was necessary, but a Power greater than myself obviously was doing the job.

---

*Doctors and modern medicine have played a critical part—both to help and to hinder—in my recovery from that first illness and in my ongoing pursuit of the God-oriented life. My chief teacher in modern medicine has been a very stern but very fair schoolmaster, Robert Mendelsohn, M.D. See page 240.

Introduction

Just on the basis of facts in which I was profoundly involved, I had to drop my prejudices against God and the great cultural and psychological traditions ascending to God. There is no possibility of describing either the joy or the difficulties that came into my life when I saw that God is real and when I began trying to come into actual touch with that Reality. (Everyone and everything is of course in contact with God; the great turning begins to take place when the contact becomes in some degree *conscious*.)

Somewhere along the line I began trying to be a Christian. I am still trying. I am also strongly drawn to the truth in other great religions. I must say that acquaintance with the teachings and the people of other religions has never lessened, but on the contrary has deepened, my devotion to Jesus Christ. All men are children of one Father, and while it is perhaps inevitable that we should differ about his nature and names, it is a planetary shame and scandal that we get into murderous quarrels about such things.

Only one considerable point of disagreement occurred among my associates in the preparation of this work. We were not of one opinion about the advisability of including a wide variety of material pertaining to the many different religious and psychological systems of the world, as opposed to sticking more strictly to Christianity.

I am seriously impressed with the limitations and difficulties of including many diverse sources. One of my counselors posed this question: "If we are to consider Buddhism, Islam, Hinduism, and Christianity in the same view, are we not in danger of confusing and misleading readers? Are we not in for trouble if we begin to look everywhere for our light and push no tradition far enough to do more than confuse the one in which we are at home?"

I was so struck by the reality of these difficulties that I went some way to avoid them in the structure of this book. But I did not go all the way, for the following reason: it seems to me that there are very large numbers of our fellow citizens and fellow truth-seekers who are not at all "at home" in a religious tradition. These not-at-homers I venture, in all honor and with real affection, to call spiritual mongrels. They include many persons of deep spiritual devotion and considerable spiritual experience. I must confess my own position in this regard, for it will color this entire book, and I must briefly indicate my own viewpoint to which I intend to be faithful:

I am a member of the Christian community and cherish its interests, but I started out in the regenerate life as a mongrel, mothered and taught by mongrels. I have an essential kinship with the breed. I cannot disown it, and would not if I could. I am convinced that spiritual mongrels have an important work to do in the world, a work which may even have a certain deep relation to the core of Christianity: the brotherhood of man.

Although now a professing Christian, I am still a mongrel, in that I find truth, get help, and take delight in other religions, past and present, in nonreligious spiritual movements, and in religiously unlabeled spiritually oriented men. I do look everywhere for my light, and I do not find the process confusing but, on the contrary, illuminating and edifying. I believe that it is possible and necessary for many of us today in seeking the face of God to look not only high but low and not only at home but abroad. This outlook is rooted in deep conviction. I am stuck with it, and, if you read further, so are you.

I have written this book, and have suggested other books and sources, not only for my brother Christians but also for my brother mongrels. I am aware of the dangers of a too wide and therefore undisciplined interest in the various spiritual springs and streams of mankind. But I am also aware of what seem to me the even greater dangers of too narrow an interest. I am sure that readers may be misled at either extreme. While respecting the more restricted view, I am frankly on the broad side. Let the reader, if he is an at-home Christian and not a mongrel, beware.

In my own search, many people and many groups have given me help, much of which I am not in a position to acknowledge here. There is one group of spiritual pioneers on the earth at this time to whom I owe the most. They know who they are, and they know how much I owe.

Thomas E. Powers

Hankins, N.Y.
St. Patrick's Day, 1990

PART ONE

God Is an Experimentally Knowable Reality. True or False?

CHAPTER ONE

First Things First

Kindergarten is a strange place for an adult to arrive, as a student. But kindergarten is the only safe place and the only practical place from which to launch the kind of experiment that this book proposes.

There is no way to avoid touching upon matters in the beginning that may seem painfully elementary. A quick plunge into deep waters may produce unnecessary snorting and choking. A bit of prudent wading about in the shallows is indicated as a preliminary.

In Case of Emergency

If you are in trouble or in some sort of crisis—if you seriously and quickly need to satisfy yourself of God's reality—it can be done without a lot of skull-cracking or waste of breath. I know it can be done because I have seen many men and women, in real need, do it. Here is how:

First: avoid like the plague all unnecessary argument and debate. Accept God as a working hypothesis. You can do this without straining your intellectual integrity, whatever your outlook on life may be. Sincerely ask him, if he exists, to help you and steer you. Second: find and associate with a group of people who really do believe in God and who are working their belief in daily life. Try to find a group who are really doing this and not just talking about it. Third: be open and truthful with these people about your situation, whatever it is, and follow the reasonable suggestions they make to you. Begin to train yourself as they are training and do the things they are doing. Fourth: keep an open mind and *watch*. The evidence of God's presence and influence will appear in your own life, possibly sooner than you expect.

"Find and associate with a group"—I realize that this is more easily said than done. Nevertheless, it is possible.

And certain kinds of trouble make it easy. For example, if you are so fortunate as to be an alcoholic or a drug addict, you will find precisely the kind of group I recommend—one where the people are not merely talking about the work but doing it—in Alcoholics Anonymous or some of the therapeutic communities. If your trouble is gambling or neurosis or overeating, you will find the same kind of group opportunity in Gamblers Anonymous, Neurotics Anonymous, or Overeaters Anonymous.

But suppose you are not eligible for one of these communities. In that case I suggest you start looking in religion, your own if you have one, otherwise in other religions. There are churches where intensive, serious group work in search for God is being done—and where people are not merely talking about it but doing it. Granted, you will not find what you need in every church; religion is a very mixed scene today. You just have to look for the real thing until you find it. If you are a lazy looker or easily discouraged, please notice the heading on this section of this book. It reads: In Case of Emergency. Nobody in an emergency can afford to be lazy or easily discouraged.

If for whatever reason you cannot find a group to work with, you can start one. All you need is two or three people who are in the same boat you are in and who are serious enough to meet once a week and do some work on themselves in between meetings.

I don't want to make the problem of groups seem to be easier than it really is. It is relatively easy to start a group. To keep it going over a period of time is another matter, involving in most cases heavy resistance and serious difficulties. Nevertheless, it can be done.

Also I don't want to seem to be saying that you can't get anywhere without working in a group. You can do a lot for yourself by studying and applying what you learn in your own life from day to day. But sooner or later, no matter how successful you are in working on your own, you will come up against the need of working

An Experimentally Knowable Reality

with others. It is one of the laws of the game, and in an emergency it applies early on. See Appendix B, page 283.

This book does not build up to any kind of climax. We are not sneaking up on anything. We are exploring working principles and experience. Do not, therefore, underestimate the workable possibilities of the suggestion made here at the outset. I have firsthand knowledge of several thousand men and women of widely different ages and conditions who actually have taken this step and achieved radical success in it. I do not merely hope and believe it works; I know it works.

The description given here is bare bones only, but it is enough to make a start, if you are interested in working and not just reading. I write for a living, and I don't want to say anything that is bad for business, but I have to tell you that writing and reading about God's reality are not good unless there is a real solid chunk of work in the picture, too. Read about it all you want, but that is a waste of time unless you also work at it.

If you do make the experiment outlined above, you may find some of the stuff in these pages helpful as you go along. But above all do not become complicated or confused. The following material is intended for those who are *not* in an acute crisis in their development and who have time to make a more leisurely and extensive approach to the question of God's reality than is possible in a tight pinch. If your need for God is in the emergency stage, stay close to your friends who do believe in God and who are working their belief, and pull back to the simple terms of the experiment as indicated. There are never any real grounds for discouragement. In general, the greater your need, the easier it is to make a real contact with God.

(In case of extreme emergency: If you are in a hospital or are otherwise restricted, if you are cut off from ordinary human contacts and maybe even from books, or if perhaps you are so ill that you have nothing to hope for in this world, your situation is particularly favorable. For great things, indeed the greatest things, are possible between the undefended human heart and God. You are, or you can be if you choose, way ahead of most of the rest of us. You have nothing to learn from us. We could learn from you.)

If you really mean business in a critical period you can go a long way with no more knowledge than you get from reading and acting upon the suggestions in this first short section. That is the advantage of a crisis; it builds a fire under us; it gets us off our seats and into action. Crises, however, do not last. They present unusual difficulties and unusual opportunities, but the difficulties and opportunities pass. If you miss the tide one time, you have to wait until the next time, and nobody knows when that will be. But meanwhile you can make progress toward real answers if you want to. The effort is slower and more likely to peter out in normal times than in tough times, but it can be done.

So if you are not in a crisis, cheer up and read on. There is hope for you, too.

If You Qualify . . .

Is there a God? And can I enter into conscious contact with him? Unless the sanest element in the human race is crazy, real answers to these questions are possible. Not just intellectual answers but answers involving the entire man, answers that satisfy the intellect, the emotions, the instincts, and the deepest longings of the human heart. If you qualify, it is possible to reach such answers.

What does it mean, "if you qualify"? It means first of all trying to be honest with yourself and asking yourself some questions. The first question is "*Am* I honest?" And if the answer is a quick yes, you face the unpleasant fact that this answer is probably a lie. For the question of honesty is never that easy. Lying and self-deception are built into us deeply. An impressive majority of men are in some degree liars. This means not just phonies and sad sacks, but solid citizens, good family men, pillars of the community. And so it may include you. Of course only you would know. But *do* you know?

There is no concern at this point with philosophy or morals but only with a cool fact of experience that may be verified by anyone who will take the trouble—say, a week of alert observation—to notice how much plain and fancy lying he and his neighbors are doing. It will be seen more easily and clearly among the neighbors, of course, but with careful attention the same beast will be discovered in one's own back yard, too.

This is not to take a dim view of the human situation but to face a fact that must be faced, or no progress toward knowledge of God is possible. Unrecognized or unadmitted dishonesty obstructs the pursuit of any kind of knowledge. In the pursuit of God knowledge it is a fatal obstacle. Until the problem of honesty is sincerely faced, you are not qualified even to make a start toward finding real answers to questions about God's reality and availability.

Listen to the late Episcopal bishop of Pittsburgh as he cranks up and cracks this particular nail right on the head:

> Any religious movement or denomination that does not constantly seek to lead individuals to face the truth about themselves is not fulfilling its fundamental Christian responsibility. It is entirely possible to be an academic, or intellectual, or ritualistic adherent to the Christian Church and yet not be a Christian at heart. We can go further and say that it is possible to be a cardinal, bishop, dean, priest or minister in the highest ecclesiastical standing and still miss the point of practice of the faith: to "walk humbly before God," which means to be open to the truth about oneself, regardless of how much it hurts.
>
> Austin Pardue

That is a real cooking-type bishop. He understands what the boys in the beet fields are up against. What we are up against is the crude datum that God is truth. He has said so plainly through the mouth of Jesus of Nazareth and through many other mouths, ancient and modern.

God, as the Upanishad says, ". . . is found by veracity. . . . Falsehood turns from the way; truth goes all the way; the way is paved with truth." Every time you turn away from the truth, for whatever reason, you turn away from God. It is that simple. This is not a play with words. It is one of the facts of life. Truth is not only that which is known; it is also *the power to know;* it is the ability to see and understand. Therefore every time you tell a lie you throw sand in your own eyes. This is a law that anyone who wishes to may observe. These are kindergarten spiritual facts that you cannot skate around no matter how fancy a mental figure you may be able to cut.

Are you willing to raise the issue of honesty with yourself, really raise it and keep it raised, and to learn from other people who are also sweating out this elementary discipline? Are you willing, steadily and patiently and relentlessly over a long period of time, to look squarely into your own honesty and dishonesty, even when this involves painful discoveries and hard effort? If so, you are qualified in this area and may proceed. *But if you proceed without this qualification,* your subsequent efforts will lead not to real answers but to confusion, disputation, and high soarings followed by great crashes.

As sure as you are reading this page, unless you are alert to the necessity of rigorous honesty your efforts to study and work toward knowledge of God will run into subtle self-deceit, "holy" imagination, and other forms of pious blah. It is hard to believe when you are first told it, but take my word that this is the way it *always* works. People love to hear this God-seeking tune played soft and sweet on violins with dim lights and flowers, but the initial sound is more like somebody falling into the drums. The fact is that you have to be crudely, brutally, mercilessly honest with yourself even to make a pass at knowledge of God. Every man thinks he is an exception, and no man is. Unless you put yourself on the honesty carpet with the rest of the spiritual small boys, this flight never gets off the ground. (I hear you crying, and I am full of sympathy. In fact I am crying with you. This is my problem, too. The only comfort I can think of is that we have so much company.)

Note, please, that you are not required at first to *become* honest, in any permanent sense. Even a little research will show you that *becoming* honest is stubbornly elusive and probably will remain so for quite a while. No, all that is required is that you take a good hard look at your own honesty problem and go to work on it. You just *try* to be honest and keep trying. The effort is what counts, for a long time. To quickly say, "Now I am honest!" is kid stuff. To expect early results is to walk into an egotistical booby trap; it is to underestimate the problem and overestimate yourself. Progress comes from patiently trying, even in the face of little or no results. Real, practicing honesty is possible, but it is amazingly difficult. The actual accomplishment has to be slow, because when this mountain moves, the whole man and all his affairs move with it. You are working toward a spiritual avalanche here. It is well that you cannot hurry. The secret is to keep trying.

If you flinch from the discomfort of the effort, or get your dignity up, or fall for your own rationalizations (lies in defense of lies), you are defeated at the start. But, once past these initial blocks, the task of dealing effectively with the honesty issue becomes something that nearly anyone can do and do pretty well, with an increasing sense of enjoyment of the game. The only considerable group of noninstitutionalized people who appear incapable of progress in truth-facing and truth-telling is a class known as constitutional psychopathic inferiors, psychopathic personalities, or moral defectives. These folks are not insane in any ordinary sense, but it seems that they just haven't got it and can't get it in the honesty department, a condition which seems at first glance relatively harmless but which is finally more appalling and hopeless than many of the real psychoses.*

Actually, trying to be honest, while not as easy as the uninitiated suppose, is not at all grim slogging either. The attempt to be honest is an exhilarating challenge which, the moment it is accepted, releases powerful energies. There are apt to be explosions of laughter on the way. It is a relief and refreshment to the soul to drop the pose of being "an honest man," to admit kinship with the rest of the human race in this matter of lying and deceiving, and to begin calmly trying to catch the monkey at the monkey business.†

One attractive and plausible diversion that it is well to watch for and avoid on the way to honesty runs something like this: "I am now trying to live truthfully. Very well, I have a problem. I have been thinking about it a lot and I feel I *must* find an answer. Suppose I was living under a tyrannical government and my own son was a fugitive and was hiding in my house and the secret police came and asked me point-blank if he was in the house. Should I lie to save him?"

The reply to that one is that you learn by solving real truth problems, not fictitious ones. You can work up a fine moral sweat

---

* See *The Mask of Sanity* by Hervey Cleckley, M.D.

† Throughout this book references are made to "the monkey" and "the adversary." It will be clear from the contexts that we are dealing with the element best known historically as the devil. In deference to contemporary sharply split notions about the devil, no theological or morphological view is proposed here. As a matter of practical fact, however, there *is* a force, or congeries of forces, which operates within human psychophysical nature in a tricky, destructive, or malign way. "Monkey" and "adversary" are time-honored terms for designating this entity, whatever his shape, essence, and number may be. It would be much more convenient to ignore him, but nobody yet has succeeded in doing so. All that is achieved by evasive tactics is a change of names. If you are more comfortable with the modern labels, you may call him your subconscious, negative thinking, or what you will. The fact is, he's around, and it is a good idea to be aware of it.

by dreaming up these imaginary dilemmas or by agonizing over them in novels or on television. But that is not actually your problem, and it may distract seriously from reality by draining off energy and attention into a running moral soap opera. Your problem is to be truthful in the real situations of real life, not in your own or some author's imagination. Sure, you can learn from the experience of others, but you should observe where fiction begins and where it leaves off, and where it is helpful and where it is not.

In everyone's life there are real and powerful tensions between the requirements of truth and the requirements of love. These tensions create painful problems. *But in real life the problems are never insolvable.* Impossible truth-love tensions occur only in books or in imaginations. In real life you never have to choose between being really truthful and being really loving. It is often exceedingly difficult but it is never impossible to be both truthful and loving. In real life, that is. Try it and see.

And skip the imaginary gymnastics. They do more harm than good, even as a workout. Reality provides plenty of exercise. It is unnecessary and nearly always unwise to call upon the imagination in this connection. The reason why is interesting: in real life the factor of the grace of God is always present. In fiction, even good fiction, it is never present in the same way. And in poor fiction, which is what most of our imaginings are, grace is left out of account altogether, and so you create false problems. To exercise yourself with this sort of thing never is very helpful, and it can be a serious distraction from the real life work which is always at hand, awaiting only your attention.

Honesty is important in itself and also for two great by-products: (1) humility, called the queen of the virtues because it mothers all the rest and keeps them from corruption, and (2) the ability to be yourself.

It is practically impossible to achieve these two immensely valuable qualities by direct efforts. Attempts to be humble tend to be self-defeating or to produce caricatures of humility. Likewise with being yourself: if you deliberately set out to do it, you are likely to end up just putting on an act.

But regular work in practicing honesty automatically deflates pride and arrogance and thus produces a marginal increment of real humility. (If you look at the humility too hard, of course, or

An Experimentally Knowable Reality

rejoice in it too much, it is apt to evaporate. Look at it, if you must, out of the corner of your eye.) And finally, a man who is growing genuinely more honest and more humble does not have to struggle to be himself; it begins to come naturally. The relief in returning to oneself is almost incredible and sometimes almost insupportable. I know men who have wept when they felt it for the first time. The blessed, blessed freedom, the release and joy, of not having to maintain a front, not having to curry favor, not having to fool anyone! The clear, unshifting gaze and the steady nerves! This is worth working for!

Individual, personal work on oneself, trying to apply the principles of honesty and responsibility and fair dealing in the regular daily affairs of one's own life—this, of course, is basic. But without the further aid of a specific kind of group activity, the best efforts at self-honesty are likely to become slipshod, ingrown, and curiously blind after a time.

Why is special group work necessary? Because I can't see my own faults clearly, no matter how hard I try. In the right kind of group, I can get a look at myself through the eyes of others in a way that is deeply revealing and deeply releasing.

During the past few years truth-centered groups have become popular all over the country—a curious development with both good and bad aspects. These groups are usually called "encounter" groups or "inventory" groups, or, when they are extended over a day or two, "marathons."

The elemental power of these groups is great, and it comes from a single source: the truth. Unfortunately many of these groups do not adhere to the simple strengths of the process but soon find themselves involved in an increasing maze of devices, techniques, acts, stunts, tricks, and assorted embellishments that plunge the whole enterprise into mere gimmickry.

Your group discovers, let's say, that it seems good to sit around in a circle holding hands. Well, so far so good. Next, somebody suggests that it would go better if all were barefoot. So, okay. But then some cutie wants to hold the proceedings in pajamas, and another wants to add laurel wreaths for everyone, and one of the weightier brains perceives that it would be great with everybody in the nude. And so on. The details are now common and rather dreary knowledge. In this way a powerful and useful thing is turned into a childish game.

But don't let the game fool you. The thing in itself is clean, sane, and profound—and it is one of the essential tools of the spiritual life. It is not, as the gamesters would have you believe, new. It is very old. It is what the early Christians were doing in their meetings. It is what Gautama's people were doing in the sangha. It is what the Essenes did, and the Therapeutae, and the Desert Fathers, and the Hesychasts, and the Benedictines, and indeed every for-real spiritual group that ever existed.

This kind of honesty and openness is what was going on in the Oxford Groups—"absolute honesty" they were simple enough to call it—and this is what the founders of Alcoholics Anonymous picked up in the O.G. and incorporated into the first movement on earth that ever brought recovery to any considerable number of alcoholics.

The idea of rigorous honesty and openness in groups has spread throughout the land and finally become what many popular things become: a fad with a lot of foolishness overlaying its essential validity and power. But I repeat, don't let the fad fool you. There is something of the most fundamental importance in the work of small groups of people who agree to honor rigorously the principles of truth, openness, and responsibility in their lives and in their group work together.

I am talking about groups who work with the simple power of the principles, and without tricks, gimmicks, idiocy, or publicity. Do such groups exist? Indeed they do. They are relatively rare and hard to find, but they do exist. And if you can't find one you can found one.

When you have seen the necessity of trying to become honest with yourself, then another question can be asked: "Are you serious?" Serious, in this regard, does not mean devoid of humor. It means, "Are you in earnest? Are you sincere? Do you really need to get these answers about God, or are you just making talk?"

This God business is not a parlor game. Either, as the atheists think, there is nothing to it, or there is so much to it that it is no place for fooling around. Of course any amount of fooling around is

An Experimentally Knowable Reality 17

possible. But in this area, of all areas of inquiry, the mere conversationalist is particularly apt to get nowhere.

You can be more or less sincere in your attitude toward the basic God questions, and the deeper degrees of sincerity cannot be summoned by a snap of the fingers. If you are dying of cancer, for example, you are capable of much greater earnestness in facing the questions about God than is a well-fed, well-heeled, healthy, and happy citizen. But you cannot safely postpone your inquiry into the reality of God until the great crises of life and death are upon you. It is necessary to get on with it now, recognizing that the complacency that comes from temporary well-being and the "happiness" gained by separating your life from the life of suffering humanity are not helps but hindrances to sincerity in approaching the truth of God.

So, if your interest is not merely superficial but to some degree sincere, serious, and based on real need, you qualify in a further important respect.

Another question: "Are you willing to learn?" Many of us aren't. Sorry. But we really are not. After we get out of school and have learned our trade or business, we get out of the way of learning. We say we would like to learn about God. Well, maybe so. But also maybe we only want to get into some talk sessions and issue judgments and state preformed opinions on the subject. Maybe what we really want is not to learn, but merely to converse, to entertain and be entertained. This won't do, of course. With such a start there can be only the dreariest of vaporings about the questions of God.

Regardless of our physical age, there must be a certain youthfulness in the mind, an elasticity and eagerness retained or recaptured in spite of the burden of our years and our dignity and importance as men of the world. Otherwise the way to knowledge of God is shut up tight against us. We cannot begin to go through the needle's eye with our usual baggage of fixed ideas. Don't say, "I don't have them." We all do. Observe yourself inwardly for a week and see.

Somehow we must become young in mind and heart at the very beginning of this inquiry. Christ said we could not make the grade unless we turned and became as little children. Who can do that? Willingness to learn is no joke. Again, a quick answer in the affirmative is probably a lie. It is not that easy. But if after some real experimental work on yourself you are able to say, "Yes, I *am* willing to learn," you have added another indispensable qualification.

At this point it may seem that this is a blood, sweat, and tears approach, and to a certain extent so it is. "Are there," you may say, "no joys, no satisfactions?" Yes, there are great joys and great satisfactions. But if you are in such a hurry to get to the joys that you skip over the difficulties and ignore the disciplines, you arrive at no joys and no satisfactions, or worse, false joys and false satisfactions, ending in discouragement and even possibly in spiritual catastrophe.

The next question is: "Are you willing to work hard?"

Everyone understands and accepts the necessity of hard work in acquiring ordinary knowledge. If you want to learn, let's say, chemistry, you do not expect to get anywhere by holding a few conversations on the subject. And you do not just sit. Particularly you do not sit in your living room and expect to develop the laws and techniques of chemistry out of your own ruminations. No. If you really want to learn chemistry you get up off your chair and go to work. And you expect to work hard. You get in touch with people who have studied chemistry and practiced chemistry and submitted to the disciplines of chemistry and who consequently have some knowledge of chemistry. And you try to learn from them. You attend lectures. You take notes and study them. You get hold of the recommended books. Some of them may seem dry and difficult, but you dig into them anyhow because you know you must. You spend regular hours and long hours and lots of hours in the laboratory. And little by little you begin to know chemistry. Your knowledge is not final or complete, but it is real, effective, workable knowledge.

Now, does all this make you a hero? You know it does not. You know that everyone who learns chemistry (a few geniuses excepted) has got to learn it this way, by hard work. Everybody grumbles a little about this state of affairs but nobody seriously questions the fact of it.

And yet when we come to spiritual knowledge, learning about

An Experimentally Knowable Reality

reality, learning about God, a strange conceit and an even stranger sentimentality appear. More often than not the candidate imagines that *this* kind of knowledge can be poured into him like oil into a cruet, with no pain, no strain, no work, and certainly no *hard* work. This attitude, if it exists, is a considerable obstacle. It is based on the common assumption that since God is a loving Father, he must also be a silly old fool who would just as soon raise a brood of spoiled brats as a company of transcendentally competent, strong, gentle, brave, compassionate, free, and triumphant sons.

Whatever God may be, he is not some kind of chucklehead. It is a crude mistake to suppose that we may presume upon his paternity to expect him to suspend the laws of the universe or amend them hastily and miraculously in our favor just because we have lately deigned to become interested in him. Also we can hardly expect to seize the reins of divine power and go off on various kinds of health, wealth, and success drives in the first few years of our apprenticeship. There is a vogue for this sort of thing today, but it never gets anywhere over any period of time, because the Law is stern enough and tender enough to check it before it has gone very far. God is no doubt even more loving and kind and provident than anybody ever said he was. But at the same time, most fortunately for us, he is not a big boob whose leg we can pull for favors or whose pocket we can pick for material or spiritual perquisites.

Knowledge about God, and particularly knowledge *of* God, is not easier to come by than ordinary knowledge; it is harder. How could it be otherwise? Certainly there is such a thing as God's grace. And he does undoubtedly temper the wind to the shorn lamb. And he is the help of the helpless. And we cannot take one step in his direction without his prevenient mercy. And his yoke is easy and his burden is light. But at the same time no man may reasonably hope to come to knowledge of God without working harder than he ever worked in his life, without literally and painfully stretching every nerve, without grunting for it at least as heartily as he grunts for money.

It Is Very Easy—and Very Hard

There is no way around this paradox: the way is very easy and it is very hard. The logical mind wants to know which is true. The answer is that both are true, equally true, deeply true, and that there is no contradiction. Can this be? Yes, it can. One of the first bits of knowledge that our hard work will win for us is this: that while the logical mind has a very high place in the quest, it has not by any means the highest place. Transcendental wisdom, even the kind we encounter in spiritual nursery school, comes from a level at which the logical mind can only stutter and blink like an owl.

And since most of us today are heavily centered and identified in the logical mind, our first hard work will win for us not only a little knowledge but also a little humility, a precious advantage so early in the game.

So this is kindergarten. These are the qualifications you need to invoke and develop before you can go on safely toward real answers. In summary:

1. You've got to try to be *honest*. (Honestly, will you?)
2. You've got to be *willing to learn*. (Honestly, are you willing?)
3. You've got to *work hard*. (Honestly, now, will you?)

Even in this elementary stage, you must find other people who are doing this job and you must associate with them and work with them, helping them and accepting help from them. It is impossible to do it alone. This is no mere opinion; it is knowledge won from hard experience, from trial and error. Some of us have tried it alone. It doesn't work. Solitude is indicated in parts of the way, certainly. But no one yet has gone the whole route alone. Christ himself did not accomplish his assignment without human association, without forming a group, without working with people.

You've got to work with others, and you've got to sink yourself to the neglected level of simple honesty, of elementary truth-telling, staying patiently with it and working from there. Certain basic books along these lines may be consulted, the most basic of which is the Bible. Notice that the truth occupies a central position in the New Testament and especially in the Gospel According to St. John. The Fourth Evangelist's view of the truth ranges from the first description of God's appearance in human flesh, "full of grace and truth," to the showdown between the divine verity and the sophisticated ignorance of this world, expressed in Pilate's enigmatic question "What is truth?" See John 1:14, 1:17, 3:21, 4:24, 5:33, 8:40, 8:44, 14:6, 14:17, 15:26, 16:13, 17:17, 17:19, 18:37, 18:38.

In connection with realizing the importance of truth, an ac-

An Experimentally Knowable Reality 21

quaintance with M. K. Gandhi is suggested; his book *My Experiments with Truth* is a starting place; Vincent Sheean's *Lead, Kindly Light* is a good follow-up; try also Louis Fischer's biography *The Life of Mahatma Gandhi*.

We necessarily have had to beat the truth and honesty bushes so hard in this first chapter that the writer becomes involved here in a peculiar way. I fully expect to be caught in my own bear trap. Surely some person, wandering through this book, is going to find places where the truth is violated. The person will then say: "Powers, you preach but you do not practice. If you are such a steaming hot character in the truth department, why have you fostered a book with untruths in it?" So I hereby take refuge in a prior disclaimer. Most of the warmth which I experience in attempting to practice truth arises, not from the comforting radiations of success, but from the friction of repeated full-tilt running pratfalls. I cannot promise that the present writing will be devoid of untruth. I can and do promise that such untruth as it contains will be the result of ignorance or incompetence and not of intention.

The problem of finding the people, the books, and the laboratory facilities with which you will actually go to work now presents itself. We turn to that next.

CHAPTER TWO

Toward Action: The People, the Books, and the Laboratory

If you qualify at the kindergarten level already indicated—if you are willing to try humbly and stubbornly to be honest with yourself, if you are willing to swallow your grown-up pride and go to class again in the school of the spirit, if you are willing to give to this enterprise at least as much work as you would give to something important in ordinary life—then you are ready to move toward action. You will need three helps: (1) the right people, (2) the right books, and (3) a suitable laboratory or workplace.

Who Are the Right People?

They are the people who to some extent already know what you are seeking to know and who may be willing to help you and teach you. Do such people exist—people who really know the truth about God, people, further, who have direct knowledge of God?

Yes, they do exist. I testify that they do.

This is not merely a pious hope. It is a statement of fact, based upon my own and others' experience. Just at the point when the powers of darkness are at their strongest, the power of God is more than ever apparent. It has been so in my own case. God knows I've sunk deep enough in this life, into very black areas where I did not believe or see how it could possibly be true that there was any Spirit, any hope, any truth. And in that blackness messengers of light, people, came to me and said, "Look, God *is* true!" They didn't get it out of books; they were talking out of their own experience; they were people who had been in the same kind of darkness I was in.*

I see people who have *not* reached into the extremes of despair and nevertheless are awake and alert and have caught this good news and are helping others and being helped. I have great faith not just in the hope of this community but in the actuality of it. This wonderful thing permeates the world much more extensively than is believed by those who are not yet consciously involved in it. It transcends and overwhelms and soaks up the world's misery.

When you seriously set yourself to seek for the truth, the truth brings into your life men and women who have different degrees of authentic knowledge and who are able to pass it on to you, *if you are alert to the opportunity* and willing to receive what is offered. You have to be on the lookout for these people. They do not appear ringing bells and waving flags. Their real nature is hidden from the reach of careless scrutiny. They do not lightly disclose themselves. You might know one of them quite intimately in an ordinary life situation, say that of a business associate or even a brother or sister, and yet not know him at all from a deeper standpoint.

This is not a cloak-and-dagger operation; it is just the way it has to work if it is to occur in this world at all. At intervals and for special reasons a truth-bearing person permits his nature to be seen without veiling and without defense. And then there is apt to be a terrific hue and cry and a great outburst of worshiping and hating. The person so exposed often is injured or killed. So caution is necessary.

It is not that the spiritually awakened are not willing to witness, willing to help, and willing to sacrifice everything to those ends. They are aware of the sayings "Let your light so shine before men" and "He who does not confess me before men, him will I not confess before the Father." But they are also aware that there is danger of a useless and wasteful trampling under foot. They remember the counsel to be as harmless as doves *and* as wise as serpents. And they recall the admonition, repeated so many times, "Tell no man." The awakened, even the slightly awakened, have a keen respect for the ignorance, perversity, and violence latent in unregenerate human nature, and they are unwilling to provoke it except at their Lord's command.

In everyday life, therefore, you bump elbows with people who

*Psychiatrist Harry M. Tiebout, in 1946, recognized that this kind of "direct knowledge of God" was the X-factor that effected conversion in Alcoholics Anonymous. See page 244.

really know the truth of God, and yet you do not sense the opportunity that lies so close at hand unless your own hunger for real answers has come to life and begun to stir. Indeed, until you are hungry there is no more opportunity in the nearness of these people than if they were on the sun. The physical proximity of God-knowing men and women is more common than you think until you start looking. But their real and effective nearness to you is determined by other than physical laws. It depends upon their level of development (in which there are wide variations), upon the state of your own heart, and upon the sincerity, patience, persistence, and alertness of your search.

The great thing is that these people are available to you, and if you really try you can find them. The following is my own experience:

I started looking for answers about God when I was thirty-one years old. After many false starts, I had finally been working hard for four years and was beginning to get somewhere, when suddenly I had to move from New York to Chicago.

I thought to myself: "This is going to throw everything out of gear. At last I have begun to make real progress; I am in touch with people here in the East who know what the score is and who are giving me practical help; and now I have to go and live out in a new place where there will be nobody to steer me."

For about three months after I arrived in the Middle West, things were almost as bad as I had imagined them. I looked hard and I did find a number of people to work with, but there was nobody to give me the kind of help I needed most: contact with men of greater experience than I in the Way.

One day my wife said, "Look, we are going to have to join a church. The kids in this neighborhood are starting to make fun of our children because they don't go to church. And they are right. We've got to do something about it."

I had been "un-churched" for many years. I was brought up in a Christian home, but I threw it all overboard in my teens. Later in life, even after I came back to an interest in God and began actually working on it, I still had reservations and as a matter of fact a lot of resentments toward formal religion and church. But I could see that my wife was right. Our children weren't babies any longer and they needed some religion in their upbringing. The kids in the neighborhood had done us a favor.

A few days later my wife said, "The minister is coming to call this evening." I said, "The minister?" Then I remembered about our getting back to church, and I said, "Oh, sure, sure. I hope he won't stay long. I have some work to finish up." My wife said, "I hope he won't, too, because I am going to do some shopping with Aunt Kate."

Well, the clergyman came. He was a man about sixty years old. And he hadn't been in the house twenty minutes before I began to realize *that this man really knew something,* and that he could teach me. For a while I was stunned. I had never dreamed that a man of the cloth could help me, never even thought of the possibility. You can see how deeply my prejudice against religion ran.

My wife didn't do her shopping that night and I didn't get my work done. We talked with Father Holt (he was an Anglican priest) until late, and when he was gone I walked around saying to myself, "Well, I'll be damned." Shows how silly language can be. What I meant was, "How could anything so wonderful happen with so little warning?" Because I knew what subsequent months and years proved: that this man could help me.

Looking back on it now, I am still amazed and I still thank God for it. Father Holt not only knew about God; he knew God. He was exactly the man I needed at that point in my life to give me the help and encouragement and discipline and instruction I needed. I know it is easy to be superstitious and believe too much about this sort of thing; but you also can be negatively superstitious and believe too little. The truth, in my opinion, based on a considerable further experience and on the reports of others, is this: Once you really begin to go toward God, *the people you need to help you are brought to you,* often when you least expect them, for example when you've been trying hard and have failed and have almost quit trying.

This is just one man's story, of course, and it has its individual peculiarities, but it is characteristic of many others. It typifies in fact a perfectly reliable law of the way: the great law of A, S, K— Ask and you shall receive, Seek and you shall find, Knock and it shall be opened. It is a fact that your teachers and helpers in the path to God knowledge already exist. It remains for you to seek them out.

So you watch for these people. But when you find them they are sometimes not at all what you were looking for. It is by a miracle of grace that our human helpers-in-God come to us at last, because although we must look for them, we very often have wrong notions of what they should be. *The Philokalia*, the great book of wisdom of the Eastern Church, says that no one can know anything real about God unless he is willing to find and take his place in "the chain of saints." We make heavy weather of finding and taking our place because we have such strange ideas of what a saint is. We are looking for someone with folded hands and upturned or downcast eyes. Or if not quite such a plaster-cast image, then someone who is very "healthy"—or very "successful"—or very "good"—or nearly "perfect"—or at the very least a good churchman.

Yet when it really begins to happen we may find ourselves learning about God from a man with pimples and a bad temper who chews his gum too loudly. Indeed, it can be worse than that. We may have to learn from a recovered alcoholic, a reformed criminal, or an ex-whore. This sort of thing is not inevitable, of course; the conventionally outcast have no corner on the knowledge of God. (Some of them think they have and so fall into a kind of inverse snobbery, but it is not truly so.) Our teachers may turn out to be quite ordinary folk: an industrial executive, for example, or a traveling man from Scranton, or a housewife with three children and allergies. But the New Testament should have prepared us for the fact that just about anything can happen here and that the world's social and educational standards are not God's. Christ, you may have observed, often exercised a powerfully indelicate taste in his choice of friends.

A saint in the sense here considered is *anyone who is really looking for the Truth and who has already gotten somewhere on the Way*. And let us not be deceived any more by our expectation of words than by our imaginary previews of persons. The saint next to us in the chain, for example, may not use the word "God" very much. Possibly he is one who, with no great gifts otherwise, has somehow been captivated by the practice of truth-telling, who has been following it, and who really knows the ins and outs of this difficult and neglected art. This is not to say that churchmen, cler-

An Experimentally Knowable Reality

gymen, good pious laymen, and the like may not turn out to be among our helpers and teachers, too. They may. It is only to say that we must be prepared for a few surprises in the kind of people through whom the Truth chooses to speak to us.

This is a serious matter, because all except really sincere and really alert searchers will inevitably be put off, offended, by the people who could and would teach them. "Blessed is he who is not offended in me," said the Truth when he was presenting himself in the rural areas north of Judea in the person of a local carpenter up that way. Of course *now* the carpenter has a gilt-edge reputation. He came out on top in spite of a nasty turn or two, and so a lot of us cheer for him at a safe distance of two thousand years, and we soothe and flatter and tickle ourselves with pictures of how we would have recognized and accepted him if we had been there. And at the same time we freeze as rigidly as any Pharisee of old when the same Truth ventures to address us through a contemporary mouth in which the teeth are not straight or the breath is not sweet.

"But," says a conservative friend, "don't we have to be awfully careful about phonies here? Aren't there a lot of people who pretend to knowledge of God? Aren't there a lot of hypocrites and lunatics working the God pitch?"

Sure there are. But so what? This is only to observe that we are still operating in the human realm. Every human activity, the highest as well as the lowest, is crowded with con artists. Medicine has its quacks. The law has its shysters. Statecraft has its demagogues. Business has its pirates. Education has its crackpots. And so on and on. But still there *are* real doctors, legitimate lawyers, genuine statesmen, good businessmen, and capable educators. Likewise there are real and true knowers of the way to God. Yet here, as in every other concern involving mankind, "let the buyer beware." It cannot be otherwise.

The search for the people who can teach us is exciting, frustrating, bewildering, and immensely rewarding in friendships born of the love that has no price tag and seeks no return. This search requires of us a real hunger for the truth, a refusal to settle for anything but the truth no matter how it is disguised or hidden, and a willingness to suffer any pains for the sake of the truth—the qualities, in brief, of a true scientist.

In addition to our teachers, there are other people whom we need to seek out and associate with: folks who, like ourselves, are newcomers and know very little at first. We need the company of our peers as well as our superiors and elders on the Way. We need the help of those who are approximately in our own position, with whom we can share our experience, strength, and hope.

And there is still another group with whom we must enter into a working relationship. These are the men and women who are younger on the Way than we and whom *we* are able to help and to teach. Is this presumptuous? On the contrary, it would be presumptuous to assume that we could make progress without passing on what we have been given. In order to approach truth, we need not only helpers but those whom we ourselves can help. The relationships are informal and unfixed, of course, and the positions are quite apt to shift. No one need be surprised if his pupil someday becomes capable of teaching him, or if he himself becomes an instrument of instruction to someone who has been his mentor. Here we are dealing with, or rather being dealt with by, the Holy Spirit, and he has made it clear through all true tradition that he cannot be bottled up in our conventions, not even in our religious conventions, much less in our social conventions. So we need—*we just must have and cannot do without*—our teachers, our pupils, and our friends and fellow travelers in God.

"But," you say, "I am the shy and retiring type. All this talk about working with different kinds of people throws me way off. It simply is not the sort of thing I am good at."

Sorry. Objection not sustained. These are not ordinary relationships we have been talking about, and as a matter of experience the shy types do just as well in finding their proper associates in the pursuit of God knowledge as do the friendly and socializing types. This business of coming into contact with the right people, given real willingness and alertness on our part, is a matter that is engineered finally not by us but by guidance, by grace, by the Reality which we, however clumsily, are seeking. And the Reality in its working is not unduly facilitated by extroversion or outgoingness. Neither is it unduly hindered by shyness.

There are no good excuses for ducking this job, but you must observe yourself honestly and see what excuses you actually are making to yourself. There are no real reasons in anybody's temperament or circumstances for being put off, for being "offended." But there are a lot of very plausible phony reasons, and something—the adversary or the monkey or the subconscious or the you-name-it—*something* works very hard to make these poor excuses stick. You need only to look inward steadily for a little while to see the process at work.

The truth is that you can begin to get real answers, and you can begin to find the people who can help you, just as soon as you mean business and are willing to stop lying to yourself and go to work. But you must mean business. Otherwise the whole affair turns into just one more charade, one more thing with a lot of wind and words that go nowhere.

What Are the Right Books?

It is possible to get along without books. Knowledge of God was imparted to man and transmitted from one man to another for a very long time before books were invented. You *may* learn what you need to learn by having another person teach it to you by example and word of mouth only.

But that would be very unusual today. Teachers who can teach that way are now rare, and even they might not wish to eliminate the use of books entirely. In the last three or four thousand years written or printed documents have become such basic adjuncts to learning that if you can read at all it would be rash to overlook them. Books can strengthen understanding and faith, deepen prayer, give basis and structure for meditation, and sometimes even provide the spark that sets off the sunburst of enlightenment, as in the cases of Bucke, Pascal, Augustine,* and others.

There are four kinds of books about God and the path to God. The first kind are *bad* books, ranging from merely indifferent to really bad. They are either useless or harmful. At best they are a waste of time; at worst they may get you mixed up or lead you badly off the track. The second kind are *good* books. There are so many of these that their very number creates a special problem, which we will consider in a moment. The third kind are *great* books. It is necessary to know what these books are and where you

---

* R. M. Bucke, *Cosmic Consciousness*. Pascal, *Pensées*. St. Augustine, *Confessions*.

may find them, because they are basic tools in the work we are carrying on. Fourth and last (but first in importance) are the *greatest* books. They are in a class by themselves, and you should by all means know them and know how to use them.

When it comes to bad books, we have to face the fact that certain kinds of reading can do us definite and serious harm. There really are bad books and they really can hurt us. The trouble is, there are few hard and fast lines beyond which you can say that any book, as such, is bad. A book that may be useless to one man may be useful to another man. A book that may be harmful to nine hundred and ninety-nine men may be dangerous but still helpful and good for the thousandth man.

It depends on you whether a book is good or bad for you. And here *people* can help you; here the problems of "the right people" and "the right books" overlap. It helps greatly to talk over your current and prospective reading diet with friends who are somewhat ahead of you on the Way. Knowing you and your particular abilities and problems, they can suggest books which can be helpful and they can warn you off books that would be bad for you.

There is another and even more important source of help. From the very beginning, and continually as we go along, we should seek the direct influence of the Holy Spirit, the ever-present and all-pervading Spirit of Truth, in selecting and guiding our reading. *This influence is always available,* and only in a state of spiritual sleep or idiocy can we ignore it.

So the first step in seeking knowledge of God by means of books is to learn to smell out and avoid wrong books. A person does not need to be warned, of course, against such obviously bad books as the blind, banal, sentimental, and luxurious trash of all ages and the actual pornography which has become so accepted and so popular today, except as this kind of "literature" may be involved in any struggle he may be having with an actual hang-up. Certain books are so clearly out of order that they normally present no problem. The books you have to be on guard against fall into such groups as these:

—books that are over your head;
—books that start with the truth but lead into byways or blind alleys;
—books which may be good in themselves and useful to some

people but which are unsuited to your present needs and your present abilities to absorb and apply;

—books which are "smart," "intellectual," "clever," "bright," "scientific," but which really have no root in faith or experience, no heart, no sincerity, no truth.

These are general indications only. You have to develop know-how as you go along. It is quite impossible to make anything like a list of the "hundred worst books" or "five hundred spiritual stinkers." It is impossible in fairness to mention even a few titles and to say that these books always and under any circumstances would be harmful. You will not stub your toe too badly if you will only try to stay reasonably humble, reasonably alert to the actual dangers of the situation, and reasonably close to the sources from which help is available to you. You just have to keep awake, keep in close touch with your more experienced friends-in-God, pray to the Spirit of Truth for guidance, and go ahead cautiously, promptly putting aside books that turn out to be doubtful or definitely off base for you.

One more word of caution while we are doing some necessary negative thinking about books: even good books may be bad for you if you take them in the wrong way or at the wrong time. It is possible, for example, to get a swelled head from reading the Bible. Too much reading also is a bad habit, and in some natures it can become disastrous. It leads to garrulousness, to the confusion of wordiness with wisdom, and finally to pride and its chain of delusions. (The mentally lazy, of course, take cautions against overreading as an excuse not to do the reading they should do. The *shaitan*, the internal adversary who works continually against truth, can turn every truth to his own ends if you permit it.) But reading when it is God's will for you to be doing something else *is* spiritually a very deadly thing. This has been recognized from ancient times: "And further, by these, my son, be admonished: of making many books there is no end; and much study is a weariness of the flesh. Let us hear the conclusion of the whole matter: Fear God, and keep his commandments: for this is the whole duty of man" (Eccles. 12:12–13).

Father de Caussade, the great French Jesuit teacher of abandonment to God, sees the book problem very clearly. In *Self-Abandonment to Divine Providence*, in a chapter entitled "Reading and other exercises of piety only sanctify us in so far as they are channels of the action of God," he has this to say:

> The reading of a book arbitrarily chosen independently of God's Order is harmful to us; the Will of God and his Order give us grace which works in the depth of our hearts through the books we read as through everything else we do. Without God, books are but vain appearances and, deprived with regard to us of the vivifying virtue of his Order, merely empty the heart, through the very satisfaction they cause the mind. . . . A proud man who reads spiritual books from curiosity alone, averting himself in his reading from the Will of God, only receives the dead letter of what he reads in his mind and grows ever drier and more hardened. . . .
>
> If it is the duty of the moment to read, the book will effect this mysterious fulfillment (sanctification of the soul) in depths of the heart. If the Divine Will bids us abandon reading for the duty of actual contemplation of God, that duty brings to birth the New Man in the depths of our heart, whereas reading would be injurious and useless.

The following words of wisdom about books were spoken by Sri Ramakrishna, the nineteenth-century Hindu master. They are included in a chapter entitled "Religion is realization and not a matter of philosophical discussion":

> One day the late Keshab Chandra Sen of revered memory visited Sri Ramakrishna in the temple of Dakshineswara and put to him the question: "Many learned men read no end of sacred books; how is it then, that they remain ignorant in spiritual matters?" The reply was, "The kite and the vulture soar high up in the air, but all the time their eyes are fixed on charnel pits in search of putrid carcasses. The minds of the so-called learned scholars are attached to things of the world; hence it is that they cannot acquire true knowledge. What good could the reading of a vast number of sacred works do them?"
>
> Sri Ramakrishna used to say of *granthas* (books) that they were so many *granthis* (knots). In other words, mere reading of books, without discrimination and non-attachment, serves to increase one's arrogance and vanity, i.e., it multiplies the knots in one's mind. . . .
>
> He also said, "In the Hindu almanac it is recorded that the rainfall in Bengal will reach twenty adas. Wring the almanac, so full of rain-predictions, but not a drop of water can be got out of it. So,

An Experimentally Knowable Reality

also, many good sayings are to be found in the sacred books, but the mere reading of them will not make one spiritual. One must go through the practices enjoined in them."

Of course, these very warnings *against* books are solemnly and serenely printed *in* books by the sincere followers of the men who uttered the warnings. Obviously all this speaking against is only against the misuse of books. After everything possible has been said by way of caution, reading remains one of the very great aids, and usually one of the indispensable aids, on the Way.

Books are not the answer, *but they can lead to the answer.* The paradox of the useful uselessness of books in the spiritual quest is apparent in the following two incidents in the life of Ramana Maharshi.

On the one hand: one day a visitor asked the Maharshi, "Should I give up my business and take to reading books on Vedanta?" Replying, Sri Bhagavan said, "As for reading books on Vedanta, you may go on reading any number of them. They can only tell you, 'Realize the Self within you.' The Self cannot be found in books. You have to find it for yourself, in yourself."

On the other hand: describing experiences leading up to Sri Bhagavan's full realization, Arthur Osborne writes:

> The second premonition came soon after. This time it was provoked by a book. Again it was a wave of bewildering joy at perceiving that the Divine can be made manifest on earth. His uncle had borrowed a copy of the Periapuranam, the life-stories of the sixty-three Tamil Saints. Venkataraman (Sri Bhagavan) picked it up and, as he read, was overwhelmed with ecstatic wonder that such faith, such love, such divine fervour was possible, that there had been such beauty in human life. The tales of renunciation leading to Divine Union inspired him with awe and emulation. Something greater than all dreamlands, greater than all ambition, was here proclaimed real and possible, and the revelation thrilled him with blissful gratitude.
>
> From this time on the current of awareness which Sri Bhagavan and his devotees designate "meditation" began to awaken in him. Not awareness of anything by any one, being beyond the duality of subject and object, but a state of blissful consciousness transcending both the physical and mental plane and yet compatible with full use of the physical and mental faculties.
>
> Arthur Osborne, *Ramana Maharshi*

There are so many *good* spiritual books that nobody but a librarian can know even the names of a major portion of them. And those you can know about are still so numerous that it is easy to become confused. Because which of them is right for you, now? With only a limited amount of time for reading and with so many and so many kinds of books to choose among, how can you make even a start?

Here again you need the help of people who are a little ahead of you, who are experienced in spiritual reading, and who can recommend books that will fit your problems, and your particular lines of growth.

Great spiritual books stand out from merely good books by their profound influence throughout the centuries or by their special power in our own time. Most great books that we are able to recognize as such are older books; these are easier to identify as great because they have the witness of many years and much use and experience behind them. Yet not all of the great books are old. For example, Thomas Kelly's *Testament of Devotion,* written by a man who died in 1941, is probably a great spiritual book in the truest sense. Only future years can confirm its greatness, but it is possible now so to classify it. Not everyone, of course, would agree with this classification, and that reminds us that the line between "good" and "great" is not hard and fixed and there is room for plenty of difference of view.

Perhaps the best way to indicate what is meant by great spiritual books is to give a few examples: The works of Philo Judaeus, the *Enneads* of Plotinus, *The Philokalia* of the Eastern Orthodox tradition, the works of Dionysius the Areopagite, Shankaracharya's *Crest-Jewel of Discrimination,* the *Mathnawí* of Jalálu'ddín Rúmí, the works of Meister Eckhart, *The Divine Comedy,* the works of John of Ruysbroeck, *The Cloud of Unknowing, The Imitation of Christ,* the *Theologia Germanica,* the works of St. John of the Cross —such books are properly called great. You can think of many more offhand, but the whole list of presently available works is not large and might not exceed three or four hundred.

Every searcher should be on the lookout for great spiritual books and become acquainted with as many as possible. They provide solid food for the journey.

What are the *greatest* spiritual books? They are the sacred scriptures or holy writings of mankind. And they are, as we have said, in a special and peculiar class.

The number of these greatest books is very small. Among all the books of the world, they are a unique phenomenon. All of them are profound, difficult, often obscure and puzzling, not by any means "easy reading." Yet it is one of their strange qualities that they serve spiritual babes as well as they serve spiritual adults, and plain people as well as those who are called to scholarship. The holy scriptures are known, revered, read, studied, cherished, and absorbed at depth by men, women, and children of all kinds and classes in all times. They are the backbone of the spirituality of vast populations over great ages. These books have had an incomparable effect upon the mind and heart of humanity. We cannot afford to be ignorant of them.

No person, nation, or race is big enough to express fully the greatness of a true scripture. Only the passage of millennia and the testimony of countless redeemed lives can begin to bear witness adequately to the power and stature of a genuine sacred book. In the holy scriptures we find a reflection on our level of the *one* great Sacred Book, written in living words that penetrate all levels, by the Father of Lights himself. The *real* Word of God is indiscernible to merely human eyes and unendurable to merely human nervous systems. But we see something of it, and its very power is mediated to us in a strange and marvelous manner, in the greatest books, our sacred writings.

The following are very brief indications of some of the most important and most available of the greatest books.

First in interest for most Western men and women is the Bible. The word "bible" means simply "book." The Bible is "the Book" (although really it is a collection of books). The Christian faith is based upon the Old and New Testaments of the Bible. The New Testament is a group of writings about Jesus of Nazareth, the Christ, and his disciples. It consists of the Gospels, which tell of the life and teachings of Jesus and describe his death by crucifixion, his resurrection, and his ascension; the Acts of the Apostles, an account of the activities of the first followers of Christ Jesus; the Epistles, letters of counsel and doctrine written by Paul, James, Jude, Peter, and John; and a concluding prophetic book, the Revelation of John.

The Old Testament contains books that are held sacred in both Christianity and Judaism. These books deal with the Creation, the story of Israel in Egypt and the deliverance, the Law and the Prophets, Psalms and Proverbs, stories like Ruth and Esther, and great psychological and spiritual treatises like Job and Ecclesiastes.

The effect of the Bible upon mankind is quite incalculable. It has inspired Christianity and Judaism directly, and Islam indirectly, and the influence of the peoples of these faiths upon the rest of the world has been enormous. It is impossible to interpret the Bible's impact upon humanity in terms other than those of an immense spiritual power and a very great and critical revelation of Truth.

The Bible is the written wellspring of the spirituality of the Western world. To read the Bible, if only a little bit, daily and to meditate upon its message would seem to be a minimum discipline for anyone who hopes to understand the soul of Western man. For us who are Western men, it would be the minimum for a beginning in self-knowledge as well as in God knowledge.

After the Bible, the most influential book in the world is the Koran. It is the book upon which is founded the faith of Islam, one of the most widespread of the religions, embracing about one eighth of the world's population, distributed mostly in North Africa, the Middle East, and Asia. The Koran, which means "the reading," provides the canon of faith in the Islamic world, and also the textbook of ritual and the principles of civil law.

Islam means "submission to God," and a follower of this faith is called a Muslim, "one who submits." Muhammad is the Prophet of Islam, and it was to him, over thirteen hundred years ago, that God, in Muslim belief, made the revelations that are embodied in the Koran.

This book is held in great veneration throughout the Muslim world. It is described as "the glorious Koran, that inimitable symphony, the very sounds of which move men to tears and ecstasy." Pickthall, in introducing his translation, makes the point that the Koran truly exists only in Arabic, that it cannot in fact be translated, and that his "translation" is really only an attempt to present

An Experimentally Knowable Reality 37

the meaning of the Koran, and perhaps some of its charm, in English.

The Koran was given to Muhammad on various occasions when he was in a condition of ecstasy. The following account of his first illuminative experience is condensed (with some rearrangement) from Washington Irving's *Life of Muhammad* as quoted by Bucke.

> He was passing, as was his wont, the month of Ramadan in the cavern, endeavoring by fasting, prayer, and solitary meditation to elevate his thoughts to the contemplation of divine truth. It was on the night called by the Arabs Al Kadar, the Divine Decree. As Muhammad, in the silent watches of the night, lay wrapped in his mantle, he heard a voice calling him. As he uncovered his head, a flood of light broke upon him of such intolerable splendor that he swooned. On regaining his senses he beheld an angel in human form, who, approaching from a distance, displayed a silken cloth covered with written characters. "Read!" said the angel. "I know not how to read!" replied Muhammad. "Read!" repeated the angel. "I cannot read!" said Muhammad. The voice, more terrible now, commanded: "Read! In the name of the Lord, who has created all things; who created man from a clot. Read, in the name of the Most High, who taught man the use of the pen; who sheds on his soul the ray of knowledge and teaches him what before he knew not."
>
> Whereupon Muhammad instantly felt his understanding illumined with celestial light and read what was written on the cloth, which contained the decree of God, as afterward promulgated in the Koran.

India has been a deeply God-centered land since prehistoric times and is rich in sacred writings. Two works stand out as most honored and cherished in Hindu hearts generally, and these same two have been found helpful to Western seekers. First are the Upanishads, and the second is the Bhagavad Gita, although not necessarily in that order of importance. It would be very hard to say which should come first. The Upanishads are the older, so we shall consider them before the Gita.

The Upanishads are part of the Vedas, the part which deals with knowledge of God, as distinct from parts which deal with works: rules of conduct, sacrifice, ritual, and so on. The Vedas are the oldest scriptures of India; conservative Western scholars think they go back to about 1200 B.C., but Indian authorities put their origin very much earlier, perhaps as early as the fifth millennium before Christ.

The Upanishads, as part of the Vedas, share the prestige of the Vedas. In the Hindu view, the Vedas are eternal, without beginning. Their author is no man or men but the Lord himself. It is not, of course, the words of the Vedas which are thought to be eternal but the spiritual knowledge which the words express.

The Upanishads were actually put into writing for the first time a few hundred years before the time of Buddha (563-483 B.C.). But it must be remembered that these were sacred teachings before they were sacred writings; they were transmitted by word of mouth for many centuries before they were recorded. They were sung, chanted, spoken from sage to king, from husband to wife, from teacher to pupil, through a long line of illumined souls before they were written down.

If the Upanishads embody eternal knowledge, who were the men who penetrated to that knowledge and expressed it in terms that other men might hope to understand? They were the *rishis,* the seers who dwelt in the forests of ancient India. Their lives were devoted to the one great concern of knowing by experience (not just knowing about) the Supreme Reality immanent and transcendent in themselves and in the world around them, the Reality which has been called God in all generations but which these researchers most often call the Atman, usually translated as "the Self."

In the Upanishads the Self is not merely the exterior personal self of man, not just the phenomenal ego, but the Divinity pervading the universe and all things in it, including man. The essential Reality in man (Atman) and the essential Reality in the universe (Brahman) are identical. Both are One, and that One is the Self. And the great message of the Upanishads is *tat tvam asi,* "That art thou." This will seem blasphemous only if we make the error of taking "thou" to be merely the phenomenal ego. "That art thou" and "I and my Father are one" are equivalent statements. Both may be shocking statements for any man to make. (A certain Person, it will be recalled, so shocked his fellow men by taking this position that they executed him.) But the shock arises only if we mistake the surface ego or the mere body-mind for the true being of man. Here we are in deep water certainly, but these are depths which no man ultimately may hope to avoid.

The Upanishads say over and over again that the Self can be known. To know it is not easy, but it is possible, and life can never make sense until the Self *is* known. "Only when men shall roll up the sky like a hide will there be an end to misery, unless God has first been known," says the Svetasvatara Upanishad. Again and again the sharpest distinction is drawn between knowing *about* the Self and actually *knowing* the Self by transforming identification with it. This unitive knowledge is held up as the great aim of human life, failing which all other aims without exception are bitterly futile.

The Bhagavad Gita is a great spiritual poem which has been called "the Sermon on the Mount of Hinduism." The present value of the Bhagavad Gita is by no means confined to India and Indians. More and more Westerners are discovering that the Gita is an explicit and practical textbook on the technique of seeking God while working in the world. If you are sincerely pursuing truth, and if at the same time your duty places you in the midst of worldly obligations, you will find in the Gita a series of inspired instructions addressed directly to your problem. The central message is this: surrender your life to God; put God first; then do your duty whatever it is, but without attachment to the fruits of action; work, but surrender the results of work to God; work, but without desire for reward.

The divine teacher of the Gita recognizes that this is easy to say and hard to do. So he goes on to tell just how, in spite of difficulties, it can be done. Even so, it is easy to misunderstand the Gita's basic teaching; it is a common error, for example, to suppose that surrender of the fruits of action means that there will be no fruits. This is far from the truth. Hear what Gandhi says: "Again let no one consider renunciation to mean want of fruit for the renouncer. The Gita reading does not warrant such a meaning. Renunciation means absence of hankering after fruit. As a matter of fact, he who renounces reaps a thousandfold. The renunciation of the Gita is the acid test of faith. He who is ever brooding over results often loses nerve in the performance of his duty. He becomes impatient and then gives vent to anger and begins to do unworthy things; he jumps from action to action, never remaining faithful to any."

Chinese moral and social philosophy is summed up in the gentle wisdom of the scholarly sage Confucius. But the deepest essence of Chinese spirituality is expressed in a little book of 5,000 characters written 2,500 years ago. It is the Book of Tao, or the Tao Te Ching, traditionally said to have been composed by Lao Tse, who was born about 571 B.C. and whose name when translated means "ancient youth." He was a contemporary of Confucius and of the Buddha.

Very little is known about Lao Tse, and that little is in dispute among scholars. Ssu-ma Ch'ien says that Lao Tse was Keeper of the Imperial Archives or a sort of librarian at the Chou court. Legend says that he disappeared in middle life, although it is reported that he lived to a great age after his disappearance. He is said to have written the Book of Tao in a few hours to please a frontier guard as he was crossing the border on his way to retirement.

Some estimate of the importance of the Tao Te Ching may be made from Lin Yutang's evaluation of it: "If there is one book in the whole of Oriental literature which one should read above all others, it is, in my opinion, Lao Tse's Book of Tao. If there is one book that can claim to interpret for us the spirit of the Orient, or that is necessary to the understanding of characteristic Chinese behavior, including literally 'the ways that are dark,' it is the Book of Tao. For Lao Tse's book contains the first enunciated philosophy of camouflage in the world; it teaches the wisdom of appearing foolish, the success of appearing to fail, the strength of weakness and the advantage of lying low, the benefit of yielding to your adversary and the futility of contention for power. It accounts in fact for any mellowness that may be seen in Chinese social and individual behavior. . . . It is one of the profoundest books in the world's philosophy."

The word "Tao" is variously translated as "the way"—"a means"—"a doctrine"—"a principle." But it is more than these, much more. It is the ultimate Reality in which all attributes are united.

According to Kuan Tsu, Tao is "that by losing of which men die; by getting of which men live. Whatever is done without it fails; whatever is done by means of it, succeeds." It is the harmony of things, the way the universe works. It is, in fact, God. And therefore it is essentially indescribable and unutterable. "The Tao that can be told of is not the Absolute Tao." These are the first words of the Tao Te Ching.

The Book of Tao is full of paradoxes, and one wonders in the first place how the material came to be articulated at all, for "he who knows does not speak, and he who speaks does not know." And one hesitates to praise the book, for "true words are not fine-sounding; fine-sounding words are not true."

Among all the world's sacred writings, the Book of Tao stands out as gentle, motherly, profound, with a haunting nostalgia for a beatitude long forgotten yet ever at hand, resplendent with hints of the spiritual gold still buried in every man and indeed in every thing, and withal full of a strange sense of humor, a smile just starting—as if behind the enigma, behind the mystery and terror of human life, someone were gently laughing.

The reward for even a little knowledge of Buddhism is great, but it is not easy to achieve. Some of the difficulties are in Buddhism itself (which is logical and unsentimental, endlessly explicit, humorous, and very stern—all at the same time). And some of the difficulties we make ourselves. Ignorance of Buddhism is very thick today, and contempt for Buddhism is therefore common. Mention the Buddha and wearily, inevitably, you evoke a remark about Buddhists contemplating their navels, or a somewhat more serious but equally ignorant remark to the effect that the Buddha was an atheist.

This atheist business, however, is a good point of entry into Buddhist teaching. If ever a man knew God, it was the Buddha. Yet he patiently and flatly refused to talk about God all through a long lifetime of teaching. Why? Possibly because he saw with the clarity of perfect enlightenment how people hypnotize themselves and deceive themselves with words, particularly with key words like "God," and how talk about God lulls us into the pathetic assurance that we know something about God when we are actually in the darkest and deadliest ignorance of God.

Buddhism is shock treatment for conventional religious attitudes, for lazy piety, for pretense and deceit, for the "good" folks whose hypocrisy is lethal to the spiritual life but doesn't smell quite bad enough to be found out. (Christ, you will recall, also spanked this section of the human bottom with a very heavy hand.)

The man who became the Buddha was an Indian prince, born in 563 B.C., and known among Buddhists as Gautama Sakyamuni. He was intelligent, handsome, strong, and otherwise naturally well favored. He married happily at sixteen and spent his early manhood in comfort and luxury. At the age of twenty-nine, however, the bitter facts of worldly life had become so apparent to him that he renounced his family ties, left home, and retired to the forest, seeking Truth. After experimenting with extreme asceticism, he saw that the answer did not lie in that direction, and he thereafter developed his own way, later taught as the Middle Path. He finally attained full awakening and perfect enlightenment under the famous Bo tree, and thus he became a Tathagata: one who "has thus gone" —the last in a long line of Buddhas or Awakened Ones. He was thirty-five at the time of his Great Awakening and was at first reluctant to teach. Subsequently, however (he died at eighty), he was persuaded to teach a great deal, and from his influence have sprung streams of spirituality which to this day continue to water a large part of the earth.

A good example of Buddhist scripture for a newcomer to sample is the Dhammapada. Although its authorship and date are in dispute among scholars, it is quite certain that the words of the Dhammapada actually represent the teachings of the Buddha himself. It is a masterpiece of spiritual instruction and exhortation, a brilliant summary of the condition of unregenerate mankind, and a ringing call to snap out of the nightmare of ordinary life and to set out upon the journey to freedom and joy.

Buddhist sacred writings are divided generally into two groups: Theravadin (Pali) and Mahayana (Sanskrit), representing the two great divisions which have occurred in Buddhism. (Zen is a division of Mahayana. For Zen reading references see Suzuki listings in the bibliography.) Selections from Sanskrit, Pali, Chinese,

An Experimentally Knowable Reality 43

and Tibetan sources will be found in *A Buddhist Bible*, edited by Dwight Goddard.

The books described do not by any means include all the sacred writing available. For example, we have not covered the Persian Avesta, the Chinese Book of Changes, and others which are of very considerable interest and importance; but the ones discussed are outstanding in historical times and the ones most likely to be of practical use to a searcher.

Again, a word of caution is necessary. In spite of their immense value, you can trip over the holy books or get mixed up in unnecessary diversions because of them. People can abuse anything; they do abuse even the best and highest things; and our old friend the adversary is well known to quote scripture in the context of his own highly specialized interests. Therefore, not only in spite of, but often just because of, the power inherent in sacred writings, they are involved in everything from silly personal arguments to miserable and futile doctrinal squabbles. Regardless of clear warnings, the letter of scripture is still preferred to the spirit, the form to the essence, the necessary but deadly husk to the living and life-giving core.

Although holy scripture is in some ways the most difficult of all reading, from another angle it is the easiest of all, the safest of all, and the best of all. Most of us do well to include at least some scripture in our reading from the very beginning and to keep scripture as a kind of backbone to our further study, no matter how widely our interests range.

But note: Some persons cannot read scripture at all at first. It is too strong a dose. I give my own case for example: I got very far from God at one time, and it was several years after I turned toward the Light again before I could bring myself to read the Bible. In the meantime I could and did get great help from other, lesser, but more-to-my-measure books.

Scripture enthusiasts must be careful not to try to ram holy writ down anyone's throat. Some perfectly genuine little ones in Christ can be seriously offended in this way, a development which the Lord does not take lightly (Matt. 18:2–6). The sacred texts are just as wonderful as the keenest enthusiast thinks they are, but at the same time they are not everyone's cup of tea. And in these cases, help *can* come through other channels. The Spirit of God is not, never was, and never will be confined to any words, even the holiest words. If you forget this you may be rewarded with some poor results and with some handsomely deserved rebukes in your attempts to help your brothers-in-God—particularly your puffed-up or beaten-up brothers, your hardboiled-and-aggressive or scared-and-skittish brothers, your undereducated or overeducated brothers. Scripture is great. It is the tool of tools with which to learn about God. But it is also a fine instrument with which to make a fathead of yourself if you are not careful.

Read scripture if you possibly can, and keep on reading it. But you've got to know how. Here again friends can help. Talk over with them your Bible reading and your attempts to practice biblical principles in your life.

There are some basic considerations to be observed. First of all, no one, not even most saints, can read large sections of sacred writing at any one sitting. Really *read* it, that is. Of course, any eager beaver can, and many do, pass big chunks of scripture through their mental alimentary apparatus at one sitting and right out again, practically untouched, as in the case of all hastily ingested and excreted matters, by the assimilative processes. Cramming and bolting are not good practices with scripture. They nearly always lead to psychic indigestion, or, worse, to spiritual flatulence —a kind of gaseous and incontinent pride.

As a serious student you soon find out that in order to get the real good out of Bible reading you must take small pieces at a time and chew them thoroughly. And you don't jump right up and run around afterward. You have had a meal. You sit down and let it settle for a while.

Hit-and-miss, now-and-then scripture reading is better than no scripture reading, but only somewhat better. For best results you should read on a regular daily schedule which you follow as faithfully as brushing your teeth. There are many good printed schedules. The Episcopal Book of Common Prayer has a Bible-reading schedule or lectionary on page x. Certain editions of the Bible itself contain daily reading schedules. Or you may make up your own schedule.

Does holy scripture mean just the Christian Bible? That de-

An Experimentally Knowable Reality 45

pends on you. As a Christian you may wish to stick to the Bible exclusively for your scripture, not through any lack of sympathy or interest in other sacred writings or other religions, but because, as Ramakrishna has pointed out, it is better to dig one deep well than many shallow ones. This may be the part of wisdom for you.

On the other hand, most Christian denominations recognize that the Holy Spirit is not restricted to the Judeo-Christian writings, and that the highest Truth may express himself not only outside the Christian canon and Christian apocryphal works but outside the historical and formal Christian tradition entirely (although never of course outside the Christ who is all and in all [Col. 3:11]). So it is possible that you may extend your reading, not only safely but with great profit, to include such books as the Bhagavad Gita, the Tao Te Ching, the Upanishads, and others. Again no general rules can be laid down. These choices have to be made in terms of particular persons and actual circumstances.

Finally, a practical note: decide as you go along what books you need, and get those books. Don't say you can't get them. Borrow them from your friends or from libraries if possible; if not, buy them. "But this is expensive!" So it is. But if you were studying ballet or geology or dog training, you would get the books you need, somehow. A real student always manages to get hold of the books he needs, somehow.

People are funny about books. Even people who are hard up spend whopping big chunks of money on automobiles and television sets, but when it comes to fifty or a hundred dollars for some needed books, suddenly we are confronted with a howling impossibility. Here is an index of where the heart is and where the treasure is.

Get the books you want and need for your spiritual work. Buy them when you have to. If your bookstore doesn't have them, buy them from the publisher. If he is out of stock or the book is out of print, have one of the companies which locate books find what you want (see the New York *Times Book Review* classified advertising section for addresses of some of these companies).

One good way to tell if your spiritual quest has the minimum necessary kick and bite and drive is to ask yourself honestly whether or not you are too tight to purchase the essential tools. In a financial pinch it would not be good Christianity to steal the needed books, but it might be an encouraging sign for a Christian to think of the possibility. The point is to get the books, and if that takes money, get it up.

Where Is the Laboratory?

Anyone who starts out to find real answers to questions about God's existence and availability finds himself involved, not in a pleasant pastime, but in hard work. And anyone who does real work needs a workplace, a workshop, in the broadest sense a laboratory.

Fortunately a most amazing situation exists here. *Every man, woman, and child on this earth already has a perfect place in which to pursue the work of finding God.* Unfortunately very few realize that this is the situation, and even fewer take advantage of it. Many people have never heard of such a thing. Others, when they do hear of it, cannot see it or will not believe it. But it is true. You already have the perfect laboratory. It is large but portable; you can and do carry it around with you wherever you go.

This laboratory, this perfectly equipped workshop, is your own life: your body and mind; your exact circumstances, good and bad; your past, present, and future; your advantages and handicaps; your hopes and fears; your heart, lungs, glands, and brains; your hair and skin, hands and feet, warts and moles; your sensations, thoughts, and emotions. Everything that may properly be called you, everything that has gone, now goes, and some day will go to make up your life—this is your workshop, your laboratory. And it is ideally suited to the work of finding God and completely equipped for it.

If this is so, what about your weaknesses and shortcomings, your faults and failings, your pains and miseries, your depressions and frustrations? All of these are indispensable parts of your equipment. They are just as useful and necessary as your strengths, skills, abilities, successes, pleasures, joys, and attainments. Your bad qualities are no doubt bad enough in themselves, but in this work they are useful—provided you *work with them* and on them.

Good and bad depend on where you are going. On the way to God, part of your light and heat comes from burning your own garbage. Later on and at a higher level it comes from helping to burn

An Experimentally Knowable Reality 47

the world's garbage. Repudiations, dishonor, disgrace, physical torture, mental agony—the worst things, deserved and undeserved, which you may have to face—all are fuel for this fire. Christ gave us a hair-raising example of how it works. Nothing is lost. The bad things all are turned to good use in this laboratory.

The kingdom of God is within you. Really, now, what can that mean? Well, some of the meaning is not such a hidden matter after all. It can only mean that the answers you are looking for are within you—not in the South Seas or India or Italy or Tibet (unless you happen to go there and make them a part of you). Our Lord's words on this subject are quite explicit and quite clear. The answers—the real answers, the Great Answer himself and his kingdom—are within *you*.

It is of considerable importance, therefore, to understand what is meant by you in this case. Evidently it is not just your physical body. Human bodies have been drawn and quartered and otherwise cut up for centuries before modern autopsy brought some refinement to such procedures. And nobody has ever yet found the kingdom or any real hints to it in that way. The physical body is deeply involved in the search for spiritual answers, but obviously it is not you in the sense Christ means you when he speaks of the location of the kingdom. The pure in heart do not get that way by opening the thorax and sponging it out. And seekers for the kingdom do not physically explore their own viscera. Real clues, vital and essential symbols, can be found in the body, but not the answers themselves.

Well, then, what is meant by *you*?

You are *your whole life*, extended in and beyond time. It is something much greater than you suspect until you seriously begin to look into it. You are your body and mind and soul; you are all your associates and associations, all your experiences, pleasant and unpleasant, remembered and forgotten (but nothing *is* forgotten!). You are in truth a great whole within the Great Whole, of which the ordinary little "you" is only faintly aware at any one time. "You" have to enter *you* and go to work there.

Indeed, when a man asks himself, "Who and what am I?" he has raised the question of questions, and the full and ultimate answers lie not only in the heart of man but in the great heart of God.†

For immediate and practical purposes, however, it is enough to realize that you—the you in which the kingdom of God and the answers to the reality of God are to be found—are your whole self. You are your workshop. It remains only to go to work.

How you work is the next consideration.

† The question of one's identity, not just as a philosophical preoccupation but as a practical pursuit of real knowledge, is basic in the spiritual life. For further light on this question see Ramana Maharshi's *Self-Enquiry* and his *Who Am I?* These are in *The Collected Works*, edited by Arthur Osborne. Note also Radhakrishnan's *The Principal Upanishads*, pp. 73–78.

CHAPTER THREE

The Ways to Knowledge

> The first of all the commandments is, Hear, O Israel; The Lord our God is one Lord: And thou shalt love the Lord thy God with all thy heart, and with all thy soul, and with all thy mind, and with all thy strength: this is the first commandment.
>
> Mark 12:29–30

Who can hear this amazing and terrible commandment without a shocked realization of how far we are from being able to obey it? *And yet we can make a start.* We can make the first movement of love by turning our attention and our *interest* toward God. And we can do it in the ways he has indicated by enlisting (1) our minds, (2) our strength, and (3) our hearts and souls in this work. Let's see how it develops.

"With All Thy Mind"—the Way of Reason

Nearly all men reason about God. The unbeliever reasons against him, the believer reasons for him, but no one except an idiot can escape reasoning *about* him. The atheist least of all can avoid reasoning about God; his whole position depends on it. So there is no question as to whether we should or should not or will or will not reason about God. The only question is whether we will reason well or reason badly.

The ground where reason bears on the question of God is exceedingly well worked over.* Incalculable numbers of hours of debate have been devoted to the problem. There are mountains of books on the subject. The complexities, the difficulties, and the mere mass of material are immense. Would it not be better, therefore, just to skip this section entirely? Is not this whole problem of reasoning about God full of serious limitations at best and full of real booby traps at worst?

Yes, so it is. But we can't skip this section. We can and under some circumstances should postpone it, but we really cannot skip it. A normal man while awake can no more stop reasoning than he can stop breathing. He can stop briefly but not for long. In a few seconds or at most a couple of minutes he is breathing—and reasoning —again. If we are going to talk about God at all, we must reason. We may hope to get beyond reason, but not around it.

Reason, in the quest of God, is not an ass upon which we can ride and prance as in merely utilitarian pursuits. It is a lion on the path that must be faced. It is a sphinx whose questions we must answer, or go down to spiritual death. Reason is not a luxury with which we may or may not dispense; it is a necessity with which we must deal. If the questions of reason are not answered and the legitimate demands of reason are not met, reason will never stand still. And it is only when reason—pointing at last beyond itself—*does*

---

* Reasoning about the *existence* of God is a relatively modern phenomenon, occurring during the last two millennia, mostly in the West. The authors of the Old and New Testaments, for example, are not much concerned to prove that God exists. There is a reference in Psalm 14 to atheism, but it is regarded there simply as folly, not as a logical position and certainly not as a philosophical problem. Throughout the Gospels and Letters unbelief is not a problem of unbelief in God, but of unbelief in Christ's demonstration and teaching (Matt. 13:58, 17:20; Mark 6:6, 9:24, 16:14), unbelief in the promises, oracles, and plain revelations of God (Rom. 3:3, 4:20, 11:20; Heb. 3:19, 4:6), and unbelief in the Christian evangel (Acts 14:2; Rom. 11:30; Heb. 4:11). Only a few passages refer possibly to a rejection of God's very existence (Luke 12:46; Heb. 3:12). Not only the Bible but all of the great sacred writings of mankind take for granted the existence of a Supreme Being, either as a Supreme Person or Persons, or as a Supreme State of Being which transcends and includes all states of being, or both. Serious philosophical and theological efforts to develop "proofs" of God's existence appear in the West in the thought of Plato and Aristotle; they begin to take elaborate form around the time of St. Anselm and of St. Thomas Aquinas. The question of God vs. no-God reaches a kind of climax in the thought of Kant, and it emerges as the key underlying factor in the modern world political crisis.

An Experimentally Knowable Reality 51

stand still that the deep truth about God can begin to come to us.

Applying the honesty part of the program, could we agree that a large part of our desire to avoid reasoning arises out of laziness? Most of us are not yet intelligent enough and not yet enough in love with the truth to be afraid of reasoning. We are not put off by the real dangers of reasoning but by the fact that good reasoning involves hard work. (Bad reasoning, of course, is easy, and we do it all the time with no effort.) But good reasoning about any subject is a workout, and good reasoning about the largest of all subjects—God—is a real sweat-producer, inevitably.

So let's buckle into it and let's not mix it up. Remember, we are trying to get real answers to real questions; we are not playing games with words or amusing ourselves with ideas; we are not trying to prove that we personally are right or that some school or viewpoint is right. We are trying to find out what is the truth.†

Three general rules may help us; they are based on the experience of ordinary men like ourselves who have beaten these particular bushes before us:

Rule No. 1: Don't try to think or reason about God in a vacuum. The vacuum here is merely one's personal self. Heavily solitary thinking tends to be ignorant, self-centered, and sick thinking. Naturally we do a lot of thinking when we are alone, and that is fine up to a point. But somewhere along the line we need to mix our lone thinking with other thinking; we need to cook it in the fire of conversation and refine it in the discipline of reading and study.

Again, we need people and we need books.

Try to find a few persons, or at least one, who will take the time and trouble to talk with you. It does take time and it does in-

---

† Eugene Exman, in *The World of Albert Schweitzer*, reviewing the great doctor's stress upon the importance of thought, says: "Rational thought is important for its own sake and as it leads to a higher form which Schweitzer calls mystical thought. Pure reason can carry us only so far; to penetrate further, we must quiet the mind and await the insight for which reason has prepared us.

"This higher thought may contradict the expectations of logical, rational thought. Perhaps that is why men have often distrusted it. Actually the new insight may be a premise in support of which rational thought must build a new structure. Moreover, intuitive insight may include a larger whole than sense data can immediately verify—just as complete knowledge of H_2O must include awareness of ice and steam even though water be its present form recognized by the senses."

volve work. And it is better to do it on a regular basis than haphazardly. Thus you will find yourself working with a small group or a single friend or several friends individually. You should expose your ideas, questions, and problems freely in these conversations. Your friends should feel equally free to open their minds to you. Together you will be able to make progress toward truth that none of you could make alone.

Your discussions may blow up some storms. Sincere thinking about God touches the deepest part of us, and it is apt to trigger powerful feelings and stubborn prejudices. You will need all the good will, tolerance, forgiveness, and love of truth that you can muster. But if you are fundamentally sincere, if you really are seeking real answers to real questions, you can count on the fact that God's grace is greater than any troubles which can possibly arise during your studies and talks. This is an important promise, and you can prove by actual experiment that it is a true one.

Along with work with people you will want to be doing some reading. It does not make sense to try to think your way through the questions of God's reality without taking a look at what the rest of the human race has thought in the course of the centuries and is thinking today.* You can stimulate, nourish, and regulate your own mind, you can save yourself useless sweat, and you can avoid a lot of intellectual blind alleys by means of a well-chosen program of reading—sharing your insights with your friends-in-God as you go. Original thinking is great stuff and most of us assume that we are pretty good at it, but every man who tries to go this route entirely alone tends to repeat in his own thinking all the heresies and confusions that have ever existed. So our original thinking will move straighter toward truth if it is tempered by exposure to the best thinking that has already been done.

Rule No. 2: Don't get in over your head. In reasoning about the deepest things in life, this rule is a very simple but very important consideration. It just means that you take care not to get bogged down in conversations or books that are too complex or too difficult for your present degree of understanding (which you must estimate objectively and humbly).

Of course, there are times when the truth confronting you will require that you stretch your mind to the utmost. Often you will have to make hard efforts to study and digest some very tough ma-

---

*Philosophy itself—practical knowledge of reality and of God—is very difficult in our times. See page 226 where Hermes Trismegistus discourses on why this is so.

terial. But, following Rule No. 2, the minute you find yourself really in over your depth, you will cheerfully admit it and back up a bit.

Now and then you may have to back *way* up. One needs occasional vacations from hard efforts at serious thought. Reasoning at its best is cool and disciplined, but it can become a cold and dry process, and then it tends to starve other areas of the soul. Humility, honesty, and a sense of humor in good working order are needed to maintain one's balance. Which brings us to . . .

Rule No. 3: Don't lean exclusively or too heavily upon reason. It is very easy to do so, not only for eggheads but for us squareheads, thickheads, and boneheads, too. Even a modest ability to reason and a limited capacity to think can be giddy stimulants, and of course a really facile thinker may quite easily be led into a dead end by his specialty.

All of us, whether we are "clever thinkers" or not, must recognize the limitations of thinking. Note well, please, that we do not wish to value reason at anything less than its true worth. Let's give it everything it has got coming, which is a great deal. But at the same time may we remember that the spirit of our own times (the past three or four hundred years) has swung heavily toward idolizing reason. Men of today are terribly apt to assume that men, by taking thought, can probe the deepest secrets of the universe and call God himself on the carpet to give an account of his being and doing.

In sober truth, it simply is not and cannot be so.

The thinking faculty is limited, and there are places it cannot go. This fact has been recognized not only by saints and mystics but by thinkers and reasoners of every age, from Aristotle,* Augustine, Aquinas, Kepler, Leibnitz, and Kant to Poincaré, Planck, Carrel, Eddington, and Whitehead. It is not the real thinkers but the superstitious idolizers of the rational faculty who wander out into the deserts of mechanism, materialism, and positivism.

Reason has been regarded as a veritable goddess, as a divine faculty. It is obviously the distinctively human quality of mind, distinguishing human consciousness from that of the lower kingdoms. There can be no doubt as to its dignity and necessity in the human scheme; when reason is lacking, men quickly sink to bestial or insane levels. And yet this noble function is a curiously limited and

*See Lev Shestov on Aristotle and the limitations of modern philosophy, page 216.

finally inadequate instrument for attaining full knowledge of anything at all and especially of God.

You can reason about eating until your head aches, and never come near the kind of knowledge that one good mouthful of potatoes brings you. Reason may help you to eat properly, but it is no substitute for actual eating. Furthermore there are other and sometimes better ways of learning to eat (and to live) properly than reason; the instinctual, sensual, affective, and intuitive faculties must be involved and often given precedence over reason, or we die. And when it comes to knowledge of yet deeper matters—of the spirit of man and of the Supreme Reality—still greater functions must be allowed their due scope: prayer, contemplation, revelation, and unitive or integral cognition. Some worshipers of reason like to pretend that these deeper experiences are unimportant or unreliable or even that they do not exist; but this is very unreasonable.

"Oh," says the monkey, wearing his humble costume, "but these are *high* matters, beyond the concern of unpretentious and unassuming men (of which, of course, we are one)." On the contrary, it is exactly unpretentious and unassuming men (without any phony humility) who often have been most richly endowed and most profoundly exercised in these highest faculties of knowledge.

It is particularly necessary for us hard-pressed men of the twentieth century to reason clearly as to where we stand historically with respect to reason. A great cycle is coming full turn. In the past three or four hundred years reason has experienced one of its periodic elevations to a position as supreme arbiter of truth and judge of action in the affairs of men, all higher faculties being denied or lip-worshiped and effectively circumvented. And now we are having to realize that reason in the position of supreme Lord is in a false role. Reason is not thereby exalted. In practice it is debased and finally dethroned by the vital forces which it may have the intention to direct but lacks the sanction, the effective virtue and authority, to control.

Something very much like all this has happened before. It happened among our predecessors the Greeks. Hear what Will Durant says:

> The conflict between religion and philosophy had now seen three stages: the attack on religion, as in the pre-Socratics; the endeavour

An Experimentally Knowable Reality

to replace religion with a natural ethic, as in Aristotle and Epicurus; and the return to religion in the Skeptics and Stoics, a movement that culminated in Christianity. A like sequence has occurred more than once in history, and may be taking place today. Thales corresponds to Galileo, Democritus to Hobbes, the Sophists to the Encyclopedists, Protagoras to Voltaire; Aristotle to Spencer, Epicurus to Anatole France; Pyrrho to Pascal, Arcesilaus to Hume, Carneades to Kant, Zeno to Schopenhauer, Plotinus to Bergson. The chronology resists the analogy, but the basic line of development is the same. . . .

When a new religion [Christianity] took form out of the intellectual and moral chaos of the dying Hellenistic world, the way had been prepared for it by a philosophy that acknowledged the necessity of faith, preached an ascetic doctrine of simplicity and self-restraint, and saw all things in God.

In seeking psychological and spiritual truth, the *rational* must be given its full share of attention but the *superrational* no less so, for it is in the latter sphere that the deepest and most practical truths often lie. C. G. Jung has made a disciplined inquiry into these necessities. In his foreword to Richard Wilhelm's translation of the ancient Chinese oracular scripture, the I Ching or Book of Changes, Jung says:

The I Ching insists upon self-knowledge throughout. The method‡ by which this is to be achieved is open to every kind of misuse, and is therefore not for the frivolous-minded and immature; nor is it for intellectualists and rationalists. It is appropriate only for thoughtful and reflective people who like to think about what they do and what happens to them—a predilection not to be confused with the morbid broodings of the hypochondriac. . . . I have no answer to the multitude of problems that arise when we seek to harmonize the oracle of the I Ching with our accepted scientific canons. But needless to say, nothing "occult" is to be inferred. My position in these matters is pragmatic, and the great disciplines that have taught me the practical usefulness of this viewpoint are psychotherapy and medical psychology. Probably in no other field do we have to reckon with so many unknown quantities, and nowhere else do we become more accustomed to adopting methods that work even though for a long time we may not know why they work. Unexpected cures may arise from questionable therapies and unexpected

‡ The method of the I Ching is irrational, noncausal, in Jung's terminology "synchronistic."

failures from allegedly reliable methods. In the exploration of the unconscious we come upon very strange things, from which a rationalist turns away in horror, claiming afterward that he did not see anything. The irrational fullness of life has taught me never to discard anything, even when it goes against all our theories (so short-lived at best) or otherwise admits of no immediate explanation. It is of course disquieting and one is not certain whether the compass is pointing true or not; but security, certitude, and peace do not lead to discoveries.

Do use your reasoning capacity, but don't force it. If your brains get overheated, fall back on prayer, or take a walk, or both (it's a nice combination). The answers to questions about God, when they come, involve the whole man. Give reason its proper place in your search, no less, but *no more*.

It is a simple matter to sum up the limitations of reason as a God-seeking and truth-seeking faculty: Reason is always too cold, too late, and too external to touch the living truth itself. For example, one of the most skillful reasoners who ever lived was the author of the monumental *Summa Theologia* and *Summa Contra Gentiles*, the Angelic Doctor of systematic theology, Thomas Aquinas. How amazing and wonderful, considering this man's labor in the field of thought and his mastery of reason, is the experience that came to him near the close of his life (as reported by Reinhold in *The Soul Afire*):

> One day, the 6th of December, 1273, as he was celebrating Mass in the chapel of St. Nicholas, a great change came over him. From that moment onward he ceased to write or to dictate. . . . Reginald ventured to complain. "I can do no more," said his master. Reginald insisted. "Reginald, I can do no more; such things have been revealed to me that everything I have written seems to me rubbish. Now, after the end of my work, I must await the end of my life."

"With All Thy Strength"—the Way of Faith

No one can read the New Testament through seriously even once without realizing that faith is a quality upon which Jesus placed critical stress. He made amazing promises to those who shall have faith, and he spoke with a strange mingling of compassion and sharp rebuke to those without faith or with little of it.

An Experimentally Knowable Reality

What is this key quality? How may we examine ourselves for its presence or absence in our lives? And, lacking it in some degree, how can we fill our need for it?

Faith first of all clearly is not, repeat *not*, mere belief. It is not just every belief that is well-meaning and firmly or even heroically held. Millions of people during a certain period believed that a man named Hitler was a good leader for Germany. Many of them were entirely sincere, and they backed their belief with sacrificial action. But this belief *never was faith;* it was always delusion, because, as history has shown, it was *belief in falsehood,* and that is what, by definition, delusion is. It is a degeneration or perversion or caricature of faith, but it *is not faith* and indeed may be further from faith than simple unbelief.

Could we agree that *faith is the power to contact the truth, to recognize and accept the truth, and to trust and follow the truth when it is not yet perceptually evident or logically demonstrable.*

Faith is a homing instinct for the truth that transcends the sensual and rational functions. Faith is never blind. On the contrary, it is vision above the relative blindness of the lesser faculties. "Blind faith" is a contradiction in terms; there is no such thing. Blind belief, yes, but never blind faith.

The faculty of faith is used by everyone every day in the most ordinary activities. Without the exercise of faith no man would have the power to get up in the morning, eat his breakfast, and go to work. Indeed, in mental depression, when faith runs very low, a person may literally become unable to perform simple acts, such as eating and working. Note that *faith,* even at the ordinary levels of living, is directly and very practically related to *strength.* Peter (faith) is the brother of Andrew (strength).

Lack of faith or weak faith is a kind of illness. Faith is not a luxury in which "religious" or "spiritual" people indulge. It is a basic function of the human being, and when that function is in default the person eventually becomes unfitted for ordinary life, let alone spiritual life. When ordinary faith runs low, the strength merely to live runs low; when spiritual faith runs low, the strength to seek God runs low. When *faith* runs low, *strength* runs low.

So faith is not hard to understand. Just watch yourself for a few days and see it working in your own life. Everytime you sit down at the table and eat a meal you are exercising ordinary faith.

Your wife, you know, may be secretly fed up with your shortcomings and may be planning to poison you. It is perhaps a remote possibility, but still it *is* a possibility, and a sticky one. How to deal with the situation? You could hire a couple of operators to keep an eye on your mate, particularly while she is shopping and cooking. You might also hoist a few samples of the nutriment she is dishing up and send them out for chemical analysis. On the other hand, maybe the best way is just to go on believing in the dear girl's good will and trusting it. So you do this, and over the years her cooking does nothing worse than make you fat. This is *faith*. If, however, someday she does poison you, it will have been *delusion* after all. You see how important the difference is.

Everyone throughout life is sharpening his ability to distinguish between faith and delusion. Every healthy man goes on continually believing and trusting and trying to place his belief more in the true and less in the false.

Real trouble starts if you try to run away. The person who becomes frightened, withdraws from the game, and stops believing and trusting invariably falls into grave disorder of one kind or another; the kinds are legion.

Ordinary faith is easy to observe; it works hand in hand with the reasoning and perceiving faculties, and you use it every day. When you get into your car and drive off, you exercise faith in the manufacturer, in the man who recently changed the tires and relined the brakes, and in the local superintendent of highways. Every time you cross a bridge you demonstrate life-and-death faith in the engineers, builders, and maintenance men. Your whole day, and indeed your whole life, is a parade of acts of faith, spotted occasionally with mishaps which show where your faith has lapsed into delusion.

Spiritual faith is less common. Ordinary faith keeps us sane; spiritual faith leads us to peace and fulfillment. Ordinary faith illuminates ordinary life and keeps it from falling below the level of God's minimum intention for us, which apparently is that we do not become morally rotten or go crazy. Spiritual faith leads toward God's maximum intention for us, of which we see a forecast in the life of Christ. Evidently we really are intended to live in the same radiant freedom and beauty which Jesus demonstrated, transcending all the ills of this world, including the ill of death, and proceed-

An Experimentally Knowable Reality

ing to states of power and benignity and joy far beyond our present capacities to imagine or desire.

If anyone says he will settle for ordinary faith and that spiritual faith is a bit too rich for his taste thank you, there is a tough answer, rooted in hard experience: if you will not set your sights upon spiritual faith, upon the hope and promise God has put before us in the great religious traditions, you will not be able to remain for long in ordinary faith. Sooner or later you will fall below it into physical or mental illness.

How do you get faith? It is a gift, and you get it in the same way you get any gift. (1) You just find upon examination that you have it, willy-nilly, without asking or knowing where it came from. Or (2) you find upon examination that you have not got it; you recognize your great need for it; you have the elementary common sense to ask for it; and you get it. (Those who have it willy-nilly find that they do not have enough of it, so eventually they have to ask, too.) You get faith by asking for it.

Does anyone ask and not receive? No one. Of course a man may be merely playing with the idea of God in his still-proud mind, and he may "ask" in this mood and not receive, not because God is a slow giver but because evidently he does not enjoy dull games and does not encourage fools.

Anyone, however, who is ready to stop fooling around and really ask, really receives faith. How much? As much as he needs at the time. Usually, in any one dose, only a little bit. But this stuff is dynamite and a little does a big job, *if you use it*. How much more you get and how soon you get it depends on *how you use what you have already been given*. When a man is ready to receive faith, God usually draws him into association with those who already have it, and he catches it by a sort of benign contagion.

Faith and reason are not enemies, not contradictory, not mutually exclusive. It is a widespread modern heresy and superstition to believe that they are opposed and incompatible, and a very implausible and unreasonable superstition it is.

Reason and faith obviously are necessary to each other's health and strength and growth. Reason without faith becomes garrulous and thin and dry and finally cold and deadly. Faith without reason continually slips into delusion, exclusivism, fanaticism, and their attendant illnesses. In *The Supreme Path* "The Ten Errors" are listed; the first two are as follows: "(1) Weakness of faith combined with strength of intellect are apt to lead to the error of talkativeness. (2) Strength of faith combined with weakness of intellect are apt to lead to the error of narrow-minded dogmatism" (Goddard, *A Buddhist Bible*).

In a sound mind, faith and reason complement and correct and stimulate each other. Let them challenge each other by all means! Let the steel of reason strike sparks from the rock of faith. And let them encourage and support each other, too, as in the lovely, sane words of the old hymn: "Faith, our outward sense befriending, makes our inward vision clear."

Indeed the wholly imaginary "quarrel" between faith and reason occurs only in the minds of men who do not have faith, who do not understand faith, and who do not recognize the nature of the poverty from which they suffer. On the other hand, those who have faith but are weak in the appreciation and exercise of reason are equally unfitted for the pursuit of verity. The balance which alone qualifies one to eat the strong meat of truth is found in the mind in which both reason and faith are well developed and in right relation. *True faith* is never hostile to reason and, although transcending reason, often makes powerful use of it. *True reason* is strongly governed by faith and is to be sharply distinguished from the corrupt and undisciplined "reason" of the merely curious or monkey mind.

> True reason, such as man had in the beginning, cannot be had or acquired by any man who has not first been purified and become passionless. . . . None who are wise in words ever had true reason, because, from birth, they let their reasoning powers be corrupted by unseemly thoughts. The sensory and prolix spirit of the wisdom of this age, so rich in words, which creates the illusion of great knowledge but actually fills one with the wildest thoughts, has its stronghold in this prolixity, which deprives man of essential wisdom, true contemplation and the knowledge of the one and indivisible.
>
> St. Gregory of Sinai

But faith as a spiritual quality—as the sail which we raise to the ever-blowing wind of God's grace, as the means whereby we are able to love God with all our strength—is far more than the capacity to *believe* the truth or even to *know* the truth. Above all, faith is the power to *trust* the truth, to bet our lives on it, to leave all and follow it.

Faith is the world-shaking and world-redeeming power of *loving confidence in God*. It cannot be faked or imitated, and its presence finally is unmistakable: those who have it are simply willing to dare all and lose all for God. And often they *are* heavy losers. But wisdom is justified especially in these children, for they find all in God eventually, and that is so great a thing that this poor old world can hardly bear the dazzling truth to which they witness: the truth that God *is real* and that *he can be known*.

It is no good arguing about God. It is no good trying to persuade persons who don't believe in God to believe in God. Even Christ did not make this effort. It is no great thing after all to believe in God. The devil believes in God. Evidently something more is required. And this is where we all balk.

It is said that God cannot be comprehended, but shall we therefore assume that God cannot be apprehended? Obviously God cannot be comprehended. But what follows? Neither can the ocean be comprehended. But it is still possible to jump into the ocean, to be drenched by the ocean, to swallow mouthfuls of the ocean, to come out dripping with the ocean and smelling of it.

To *merely* believe in God can be a greater disaster than not believing. Much talk about God winds up talking all around God. There is really very little to discuss. If you know enough about God to know that God *is*, you know all you need to know of that kind of knowing. The rest is a plunge.

That plunge takes us beyond reason, beyond faith, into spiritual experience.

"With All Thy Heart and Soul" —the Way of Experience

> Have you had any spiritual experience, as yet? Time is flying. Don't waste another moment.
>
> Brahmananda

Now we come to it. This is the key word and the key way: experience. You can tell a key term by the heat it generates, and "spiritual experience" is a hot one.

Let us observe the heat first: a very large group of earnest and learned people today is convinced that spiritual or religious experience has no basis whatsoever in reality. They say that it is all fantasy, hyperbole, poetry, wishful thinking. Another large group believes that spiritual experience is real enough in a way, but that it is also pathological, varying from crackpot to actually insane.

A detached observer could hardly fail to remark that both of these groups, although they are agile rationalizers, are not very valuable witnesses, because they pass judgment upon a kind of experience which they themselves invariably have not had and which they take rather scrupulous care to avoid.

Certainly there is such a thing as psychosis with religious content. Some of the insane do kick up a fuss about religious and spiritual things, but they also fuss about parents, children, politics, food, and sex. Shall anyone really take this fussing as an indication that there *is* something inherently insane about parents, children, politics, food, sex—or religion? A severely disturbed mind simply is apt to hurl its subject into the areas of deepest human concern, namely: parents, children, politics, food, sex, and religion.

Spiritual experience, more than any other kind of experience, should be open to searching criticism and rigorous evaluation. But to try to dismiss it, without direct contact or participation, as unreal or abnormal is the mark of a mere quibbler in this field. And it is far too important a field for time to be wasted in word-mincing, logic-chopping, and beating around the verbal bushes on the fringes of the subject.

One of the keenest inquiries into these pseudo-intellectual and pseudo-medical objections is to be found in William James's *The Varieties of Religious Experience* (pp. 3–26). But if you wish really to satisfy yourself as to the verity, sanity, and value of spiritual experience, don't brain it around too much in advance, even with William James. Debates in this area are a dissipation of precious energy. First go get instruction and follow the instruction that leads to actually having spiritual experience. Then read the intellectual pro and con books if you will. (They will be more interesting in that case and yet less detaining, because you will be moving on to other and far more interesting books.) The great thing is that *spiritual experience is real, and it is attainable*. Many sources testify to this, the central fact of human life:

An Experimentally Knowable Reality

There is a great experiment possible in this life and there is a great crown of the experiment, but in the nature of things it is not to be bought cheaply, for it demands the whole man.

A. E. Waite

And as he journeyed, he came near Damascus: and suddenly there shined round about him a light from heaven: And he fell to the earth, and heard a voice. . . .

Acts 9:3–4

There is a man I know who was carried out of himself in Christ, fourteen years since; was his spirit in his body? I cannot tell. Was it apart from his body? I cannot tell; God knows. This man, at least, was carried up into the third heaven. I can only tell you that this man, with his spirit in his body, or with his spirit apart from his body, God knows which, not I, was carried up into Paradise, and heard mysteries which man is not allowed to utter.

II Corinthians 12:2–4

As regards this state and as regards its gifts, even at the early stages, I testify that the Divine in the universe answers to the Divine in man. . . . A life which is tuned to the keynote of the eternal mode knows of the things that are eternal. It knows very soon that it is not on a false quest. . . . If we say that there is something which is, as it were, ineffable in the world above, we need not think it unattainable in respect of ourselves: it may be an untrodden field of our consciousness. . . . The normal personality does not cognize this supernal part of being, but we must not be deceived by the idea that their separation is on account of a distance in space; it is because of the restriction of self-knowledge in the normal state. . . . If we be faithful to the aspiration, the realization will be true to us. It may come like a thief in the night, at a point where we least expect it: the Gate of Glory opens and we see that God has his throne in the highest part of our nature. . . . The records tell us that there is an experience of unity possible to the soul of man. The testimonies concerning it are everywhere; and, when every allowance has been made for the distinction of national mentality, for modes of metaphysical thought and the diverse helps or hindrances of official religious belief, the testimony is always the same.

A. E. Waite

At times a man rests on his bed, and it appears to his family as though he were asleep, but he spends this hour in solitude with his

> Creator, blessed be He. That is a high rung, that he beholds the Creator at all times with the eye of his insight, as he sees another man. And consider this: if you persevere in a pure thought, then the Creator also looks at you, as a man looks at you.
>
> Martin Buber

> Know for certain that God can be reached—that his spiritual form can be seen and it is possible to talk to him.
>
> Brahmananda

This matter of experience is crucial. Very many men and women are inwardly called to seek the answers about God. Relatively few of them arrive at real answers, full answers, utterly satisfying answers, undeniable and life-transforming answers. But these are the only kinds of answers worth having.

Why do so many thus fail?

Because they stop short. They stop short at reason or they stop short at faith. And neither reason nor faith, nor reason and faith together, is enough. Reason and faith are means. *God himself is the end.* And the means, blessed and wonderful in themselves, become deadly obstacles if they are mistaken for ends. People and books can help, but they cannot do the job for you. You will never get the answers you are seeking until God unmistakably gives them to you. And the answers are not words only, not thoughts only, but God himself, directly experienced. All original religion, all scripture, every voice that ever has spoken with authority on this point, agree: in order to know the truth of God one must win through to *one's own experience of God.*

> Who has not tasted, does not know. Who has not eaten is not satisfied by conversation with him that has eaten. Who has not drunk, his thirst is not quenched by the narration of him that has drunk. Who has not experienced, the experience of another does not profit.
>
> Bar Hebraeus, *Book of the Dove*

> A clear vision of the Reality may be obtained only through our own eyes, when they have been opened by spiritual insight—never through the eyes of some other seer. Through our own eyes we learn what the moon looks like; how could we learn this through the eyes of others?
>
> Erudition, well-articulated speech, a wealth of words, and skill in

expounding the scriptures—these give pleasure to the learned, but they do not bring liberation.

A sickness is not cured by saying the word "medicine." You must take the medicine. Liberation does not come by merely saying the word "Brahman." Brahman must be actually experienced.

A buried treasure is not uncovered by merely uttering the words "come forth." You must follow the right directions, dig, remove the stones and earth from above it, and then make it your own. . . . Pure truth . . . can be reached by meditation, contemplation, and other spiritual disciplines such as a knower of Brahman may prescribe—but never by subtle arguments.

Shankara, Crest-Jewel of Discrimination

If reason has led you to see that God may indeed be real and available, and if faith has led you to further insight and to putting your conviction into practice, sooner or later you will begin to have spiritual experience. How soon depends on several things: your *need* for it, your *desire* for it, the sincerity and persistence of your *practice*, and the unpredictable and unfathomable action of the grace of God. Nevertheless, if you are faithful, it will come.

Caution: the adversary, the monkey-mind inside each of us which works against man's coming to knowledge of God, plays his cards very adroitly when the question of one's own actual experience arises. The monkey, having failed to keep one out of spiritual life entirely, tries by every possible device to block the issues of direct experience. He works feverishly to keep things on the level of reason and faith. He hates these faculties but greatly prefers them to the (to him) deadly possibility of *experience*.

His arguments run something like this: "Sure, spiritual life is great stuff and we are all for it, of course. But humility is the thing, isn't it, and not getting too big for our britches? We've done a lot of thinking about God, and we should continue to do a lot more. And we *have* got faith; see what a difference it has made in our life! So let's not go overboard on this experience angle. It's all right for saints, no doubt, but we are a good comfortable long way from that. Thinking and believing, and of course lots of good works, are plenty good enough for us. And they have the merit of being safe. Once you get to seeing or feeling or actually experiencing these things, who knows where it will end? People did consider this man Christ to be crazy, you know, and look at the nasty mess he and some of his friends finally got into. . . ." And so forth and so forth and so forth. There is something in each of us which balks hard at our opening ourselves to the direct touch of Reality and will fight cleverly and persistently to prevent it.

In the face of all the false humility, the monkey's chattering, and the coward's whistling, the scripture says, calmly and plainly enough: "Taste and see that the Lord is good," and "Blessed are the pure in heart, for they shall see God." The aim of every great religion is direct experience of the Divine. Such experience is not something tacked on to religion as a bonus for a few honor students. On the contrary, *spiritual experience is the target to which the heart of everyone without exception is directed.* It is recognized that many will miss the mark, but all are called to shoot at it. Furthermore, those who seem to miss do not finally miss. We see very little of the whole human life in the short period between birth and death. Vast possibilities open up at death and beyond.*

Everyone, therefore, is encouraged to press forward—as humbly and prudently as you please but at the same time ardently and with high hope—toward the great realms of direct spiritual experience where reason is illuminated and transcended and where faith is transfigured in the living Light of the Divine Reality. That Light is not far removed from ordinary men. Spatially it is not removed at all. We, unknowing, are immersed in it continually. It is our very life. Only a film of hypnotic ignorance prevents our seeing, feeling, *knowing* the Light for what it is. *And the film can be removed.*

As the Light of spiritual experience begins to dawn on the horizon toward which our life is moving, the adversary rushes forward with another stop-the-cruise effort. "Wait," he cries, "this is utterly uncharted sailing. This may be great, but it is the great abyss. This *really is* the unknown!"

Well, boo! right back at him. Again the truth is quite the contrary. The way to God *is* charted. The way of reason is well charted; the way of faith is very well charted; and the way of experience is wonderfully and gloriously charted.

Naturally, you have to know that there *are* charts. You have to know how to find them. And you have to learn how to read them and follow them. Your course in spiritual experience will be guided from three sources: first, books. As experience begins, you find that reading takes on a new and very different character. You are no

---

*See especially Arthur Machen (page 278) for an understanding of healing as an aspect of spiritual experience.

An Experimentally Knowable Reality

longer reading for instruction, for correction, for direction—comparing your own data with those of others who have gone this way before you. You use a book now the way a chemist or a doctor or a dietician uses a book—for practical, working reference. Or, even more wonderfully, as you read you may find yourself able to aim not only to know the truth of God but actually to taste it. "When one is reading," says St. Bernard, "let him seek not so much learning as savor." Thus reading can, under grace, become directly related to spiritual experience.

The second source of guidance is people. One of the discoveries that accompanies the beginning of your own spiritual experience is the happy realization of how many other people have had actual experience, too. You ask yourself, "How could I have failed to notice this before?" The answer, of course, is simple enough: People who have had genuine spiritual experience are often reticent about it. If they do not know it at first they soon learn that this kind of experience, as we have said, is a hot potato in our society—widely regarded as at best eccentric, at least fantastic, and at worst pathological. So people of real and sustained and developing spiritual experience are not quick or loose talkers. On the other hand, they are willing to share their knowledge with anyone whom they recognize as a sincere seeker of God and certainly with one who has himself begun to pass into direct experience.

The third source of guidance is the action of the presence of God upon one's own inner mind. ". . . You have by the grace of God, the desire for spiritual knowledge. . . . Now you must strive to win the grace of your minds . . ." (Brahmananda). We may say that at a certain point God himself begins to direct the experiencer into yet deeper and fuller levels of experience, and to encourage and correct him.

> Howbeit when he, the Spirit of truth, is come he will guide you into all truth. . . .
>
> John 16:13
>
> And all thy children shall be taught of God.
>
> Isaiah 54:13

Naturally an uncooked ego can make a fine mess out of things if it attempts to improvise this condition of inner illumination or to manipulate it after it has genuinely come. All sorts of inflations are possible: "illuminism," silly flights, and paranoid twists. Not pretty! And many seekers become involved, at some time and to some extent, in this kind of aberration. A little sincerity and simple honesty, however, soon break it up, and no real harm is done in most cases. Indeed the subject often is humbled and enlightened and, when he has had his spankings, proceeds onward with better ability to keep his feet on the ground as experience deepens. A real casualty, a prolonged inflammation of the ego, is possible; but it is quite rare and nearly always involves a character which was fundamentally unstable from way back. If you have anything like ordinary common sense you can receive intuitive guidance from God with great benefit and without upset. All you have to do is check your intuitions against what you learn from authentic books and genuinely experienced people, be willing to be corrected at all levels, including the intuitive, and you will find yourself getting along very well.

Spiritual experience is a development in many ways comparable to physical growth. Although some of the factors are inscrutable, the process is an orderly and reliable one. It moves along well-established lines by well-marked stages.* In the spiritual tradition of the Western world these stages are indicated as follows:

1. *Awakening:* This is an experience in which the person for the first time, or at least for the first time in adult life, becomes unmistakably aware of the living presence of God in himself and in the universe. This experience may be gentle and gradual; or it may be abrupt and in the nature of a drastic upheaval. A genuine awakening has a profound effect upon the life, and it leads, except where there are unusual obstructing elements, to the succeeding stages.

2. *Purgation:* The person continues to experience the presence of God, it may be strongly or it may be faintly, and usually with

---

* The phenomenon of spiritual awakening, sometimes called conversion, is a special consideration in itself. The three "ways" which follow awakening—the purgative, illuminative, and unitive—are a deeply traditional Christian scheme of understanding spiritual experience. The terms go back to Dionysius the Areopagite (Pseudo-Dionysius), that "anonymous, mysterious, monastic genius" who, writing probably in the fifth century A.D., "taught the foremost Christians for ten centuries both in the East and in the West, for nearly every great medieval scholar made use of his writing and his authority came to be almost final" (Introduction to *The Mystical Theology*, Shrine of Wisdom edition).

An Experimentally Knowable Reality

many interruptions. The Presence acts upon the man, as St. John of the Cross says, like fire upon a wet log. It "cooks" the spiritual, psychic, and physical natures, exposing and driving out weaknesses and impurities. Conscious awareness of what is happening and cooperation with the action of grace are of great importance, and to a considerable extent they determine the length of time one remains in purgation.

3. *Illumination:* When purgation is well along in its work and the mind and body are beginning to come free of obstacles to the presence of God, the consciousness begins to be illuminated from within by a Light which is both intellectual and affective. The person knows and feels things he could not know or feel before. Difficult and obscure points with which his understanding formerly struggled now are clearly and easily comprehended. There is a considerable ability to know and to carry out God's will and to help others. And the life is increasingly flooded with joy.

These major stages overlap, and there are phenomena of flash-back and flash-forward. For example, at the time of awakening a person may spend a few hours or even a few days in an illuminated condition. On the other hand, having won through to illumination as a fairly steady state, one may find oneself dropped back into purgation for a while. These temporary and necessary returns to the purgative condition must be distinguished from a profound purgative state, called the "night of the spirit," through which one passes when the illuminative is developing into the final or unitive phase of experience.

4. *Union:* There comes a time when the experience of God goes beyond the subject-object relationship, and a transforming mergence, marriage, or union occurs. This fulfillment is largely beyond description in our language. It involves relationships so sacred that, in Paul's words, "it is not lawful for a man to utter" the knowledge of them he may have. Certain kinds of music are much more successful than words in giving hints of the triumphant reality of the unitive state. We beginners are well advised not to fash ourselves unduly with such matters; it is easy to become psychically overstimulated and either frightened or ambitious from hearing about them too much.

On the other hand, it is good even for very new beginners to have some realization of the staggering and glory-drenched heights to which God has called man and to which some men and women have already been raised. It is good to know that the invitation to move in this direction is extended to everyone, and that the meanest of us can, if he will, start the journey right here and right now.

To *begin* is the great key. The idea of "heights of glory" is all very well and all very true, but it is true in a sense we cannot well understand in advance. The point to remember, cling to, and never forget is that experience of God begins right here and now, down in the midst of this common, ordinary, everyday life. Sooner or later there will be flights to the heights. But it is wrong to overwork the imagination about them; doing so, we go on miserable pseudo-flights and gravely stunt our true spiritual growth.

The first utterly valid experience of God is the experience of everyday *truth*, of *common honesty* and *common decency*. Cling to this, work at this, be faithful in this, and the gates of glory will swing open—not yet on high, but here, now, on this still frightfully unredeemed earth. Meet God where he meets you—here, now. Don't be concerned about moving up. Sit down in the lowest seat. Have your experience of God in the place where you are. Let him take care of the moving up; then it will be in safe hands; not otherwise. God can be found, experienced, known, wherever you make your bed, even in hell. Find him where you are, today.

It is of critical importance that spiritual experience be not taken in a woolly and thoughtless way. If it is, great confusion can result, particularly right at the point where some actual experience has occurred but has not been understood or has been feebly and improperly understood. A common confusion of this kind arises *when the experience of awakening is assumed to be the whole of the regenerative process*. The man who has just begun the journey thinks he has reached the end of it. Thomas Bromley, in London in 1710, wrote a most helpful comment upon this crucial point (condensed, with italics supplied, from *The Soul's Progress in the Work of the New Birth,* quoted by A. E. Waite in *The Secret Tradition in Alchemy*):

> Regeneration greatly concerns us in its initiation, progress and consummation. The *beginning* of the work implies that first change of the soul when the frame of the will is swayed God and Heavenward. In its *progress* it is the growth and motion of the soul from

An Experimentally Knowable Reality 71

the image of the earthly toward the image of the Heavenly. In its *end* it is the bringing forth of the perfect and complete image of God in our humanity. When we attain this we are complete in Christ, wholly new-born, and made fit to see and enjoy that Eternal Kingdom which has been prepared for us from the beginning of the world. Regeneration then in its full latitude is that transforming quickening work of God's Spirit which begins, carries on and completes God's image in us. But in the ordinary acceptation [the term "regeneration"] is used for the first change of the soul toward God in Christ; and I find too much weight laid upon this first work, as though it were the complete new birth. Hence many rest upon and have a continual eye to it, though they feel their chariot-wheels stand still.

We do need guidance in our experience of God, and holy scripture is the best of all written sources. The Bible is a book of God experience from beginning to end—from the experiences of Adam, Enoch, Abraham, Jacob, Moses, Samuel, David, Elias, Isaiah, Daniel, and many other Old Testament seers to the experiences of Jesus Christ, and of Paul, Peter, John, and many other apostles and disciples. There is a common obstacle to the application of the Bible in our own quest of God experience. It is the notion that the great meetings with God which happen over and over again in the Bible are confined to remote times or to people who are very different from ourselves. The notion is unfounded. And once this block is removed the Bible becomes a very practical guidebook in the realities we are seeking personally to contact.

Finally: beware. For it is all true, after all. God does exist. And once there is any sincere seeking, *experience may come at any minute.* And then we may find ourselves reacting like the actor who was supposed to be shot in the second act, and whose line was "Help! I'm shot!" But one night a real bullet somehow was put into the pistol instead of the customary blank, and he delivered his line with new emphasis: "Help! I *am* shot!"

Far from being a dream figure or a merely psychological entity, God is the Reality of reality. And that Reality is vivid, intense, and dangerous. Yes, plainly, dangerous. All scripture is quite blunt on this point, and so is the testimony of God-realized men and women everywhere. God is the most solicitous of Fathers, tenderly aware of the teardrop on the infant's cheek, but he is also Lord of the flaming caldrons of deep heaven. He is love, but he is also law. The heart of his compassion lies between mercy on the right hand and severity on the left.

Let no one who may be attracted to the search for God by the feeble witness of this present book complain, if he is knocked about or burned in the process, that he was not warned. I do not compose the warnings; I merely call attention to them. They are sounded in every age. They are obviously not intended to discourage the timid, who are in fact tirelessly and ingeniously coaxed by God's love. No, but the warnings are there simply to tell the rash, the foolish, and the perverse, if they will hear it, *that God is real*, that it is dangerous and futile to hide from him, but that it is also dangerous to come into his presence without due preparation.†

† Let's face it. Contact with God can unhinge a person. That is why preparation is so stressed in every true teaching. The contact may be utterly real, entirely valid, and still throw the mind out of gear. There may be actual psychosis with religious content, *or* the man may be completely sane and yet so altered, so much the vehicle of authentic and powerful spiritual influx, that his associates are frightened and distressed (Jesus, St. Paul, St. Francis of Assisi, Chaitanya, Muhammad, George Fox, Sri Ramakrishna, and the apostles on Pentecost Day are examples of the latter condition). The state of people who are touched by God in this way is traditionally recognized in Islam and in India, where they are protected and honored at all levels of society. This seems more clear-sighted than our handling of the problem in the West, where the God-intoxicated person is simply thrown in with the run of psychotic cases and left to flounder there. This sort of thing happens more often today than you would know if you were not in contact with it. I am intimately acquainted with a number of cases. It happens right along: these people get a real touch of the Spirit; it knocks them off their trolley for a while (or, while they remain quite sane, their behavior is so changed that they are deemed insane); they wind up in psychopathic wards where doctors, whose philosophy includes no provision however remote for the realities involved here, fumble around trying to classify them; and finally they are set loose again when their harmlessness becomes apparent and they begin to recover their balance, which they nearly always do spontaneously after a while.

The problem of derangement incidental to spiritual awakening needs practical study by men who are qualified to make such studies. These cases, as mankind's birth struggle deepens in the next few years, will probably increase. This is not necessarily a bad sign. Instances which are considered insane but which, like those of Paul, Ramakrishna, etc., turn out to be genuine awakenings, should be distinguished from cases of out-and-out psychosis. Genuine insanity, with hatred, suspicion, hostility, and ego-inflation, should not be identified with the condition of God-struck people who are certainly confused and perhaps psychically shocked and paralyzed, but in a benign and harmless way, and whose prognosis is one of far better than normal maturity and scope in this life if they are handled not necessarily skillfully but just without too much blundering. St. Francis, George

An Experimentally Knowable Reality

Friend, how comest thou in hither not having a wedding garment? . . . Then said the king to the servants, Bind him hand and foot, and take him away. . . .

Matthew 22:12-13

It is a fearful thing to fall into the hands of the living God.

Hebrews 10:31

Jung puts it beyond all possible doubt that the experience of God, which brings God home to us as a living quantity and not merely as an object of faith in the sense that we acknowledge or subordinate ourselves to a traditional dogma, is an extremely dangerous and terrible thing. Psychically, it claims the whole man, and it is a fatality which may land him in greater spiritual distress and disaster than many of the purely outward circumstances we so dramatically call "fate." . . . When the experience of God is a real living thing, it touches us to the quick, and time and strength are needed in order to come to terms with it. In moments like these we feel the perils and ambiguities of life not only in the surrounding world, not only in our bodies, but in our very souls; then they are as close to us as they possibly can be, are as dangerous and terrible as they possibly can be, and in certain circumstances are also as rapturous as they possibly can be.

Hans Schaer, *Religion and the Cure of Souls*

And not only the unknown depths of reality but outer conditions and men, too, become a menace to the God-seeker: ". . . Yea, the time cometh, that whosoever killeth you will think that he doeth God service" (John 16:2). And yet, at the very same time, if we are willing to develop sincerity, willing to work, and willing to learn: there is nothing to fear. The most broken, the weakest, and the

---

Fox, and company, as history abundantly has proved, were *not* psychotics; they were cases of real or seeming derangement incidental to religious or spiritual awakening; *psychosis with religious content is something else again;* it would seem very important to distinguish the two. And even in the latter cases, not only a great healing but a great advance in the whole life can take place if they are treated with religious and spiritual insight. (See Boisen, *Religion in Crisis and Custom.*)

Spiritual experience is real. Sometimes it comes on gently and gradually. But sometimes it is like grabbing hold of, or being touched by, a high-voltage wire. If you are in any way really prepared, all goes well in spite of the power of the experience. But today this kind of contact is coming closer and closer to large numbers of people who are not at all prepared. We really should find out what is happening here and learn how to handle it properly.

most undefended of persons are exactly those who have the least cause for anxiety in approaching God:

> Blessed are the poor in spirit . . . they that mourn . . . they which are persecuted . . . [Matt. 5:3, 4, 10]. Come unto me, all ye that labour and are heavy laden, and I will give you rest [Matt. 11:28]. Are not five sparrows sold for two farthings, and not one of them is forgotten before God? But even the very hairs of your head are all numbered. Fear not therefore . . . [Luke 12:6–7]. Peace I leave with you, my peace I give unto you . . . [John 14:27]. In the world ye shall have tribulation: but be of good cheer; I have overcome the world [John 16:33].

The sentimental seekers after a soft berth with God and the angry thunderers of anathemas both can find plenty of references to quote in support of their positions, but both have to quote sharply out of context, for both are very far from the most veritable and most universal descriptions of the Way to God. These truest indications are always paradoxical: the Way is easy and hard, joyful and full of terrors, ecstatic and suffering, sweet in the mouth and bitter in the belly, offering both a cross and a crown.

C. S. Lewis has touched upon this truth in introducing a book of selections from the writings of his teacher George Macdonald. Referring to Macdonald, Lewis says:

> I dare not say that he is never in error; but to speak plainly I know hardly any other writer who seems to be closer, or more continually close, to the Spirit of Christ Himself. Hence his Christ-like union of tenderness and severity. Nowhere else outside the New Testament have I found terror and comfort so intertwined. The title "Inexorable Love" which I have given to several individual extracts would serve for the whole collection. Inexorability—but never the inexorability of anything less than love—rings through it all like a refrain; "escape is hopeless"—"agree quickly with your adversary"—"compulsion waits behind"—"the uttermost farthing will be exacted." Yet this urgency never becomes shrill. All the sermons are suffused with a spirit of love and wonder which prevents it from doing so. Macdonald shows God threatening, but (as Jeremy Taylor says) "He threatens terrible things if we will not be happy."

PART TWO

Is the Experiment a Practical Possibility?

CHAPTER ONE

What Do You Do?

Getting down to practical, day-to-day details, how do you follow the ways to God? What, specifically, do you *do*? That depends on you and circumstances.

If you have latitude in your choice of a way of life, that is, if you are not closely bound by duties, and if you are of a certain temperament and vocation, you may enter one of the several possible situations in which the way to God is mapped out in detail and with the authority of much successful experience.

For example, you may become an Anglican Benedictine monk; or you may become a Roman Catholic Trappist or Carmelite; or you may place yourself under the direction of a Hindu *guru*; or you may become a Buddhist *bhiksu*. There are many such possibilities. If you choose one of them, your procedure, inwardly and outwardly, is clearly explained to you. Your task is to find your way upon a plainly marked and well-trodden path. Directors, techniques, books, and associates—all are provided. The problem of your relationship with the world and its duties is largely solved at the outset, or the manner of its solution is definitely indicated. A wealth of appropriate material is at your disposal as you set about the practice of the spiritual life in earnest.

But there are many men and women who sincerely want to seek God who would say that none of the above kinds of ways is practical for them. By which they mean that they cannot discharge the duties of a householder, a father or mother of a family, and at the same time follow the established ascetic, monastic, or yogic ways to God.

The Alternatives

What then? Must the householder give up the idea of finding God or put off the quest until circumstances change? Not at all. As a householder, particularly in this day and age, you *can* find your way to God right in the midst of your immediate surroundings, however "unspiritual" these may be at the start. Perhaps as you go along you will alter your circumstances considerably, but it is not necessary to abandon the life and duties of a family man or woman; these are not barriers to real spiritual progress.

There is authority for this conclusion. Christ himself founded no monasteries, ordained no priests, and called most of his immediate servants from among laymen and householders. And he said that not only common people but whores and politicians would enter the kingdom of God, and that they would get in before the professed religious unless the latter stopped playing big shot and got down to earth with the rest of the human race. You, as a family man or woman, with all the duties and limitations inevitable in that state, have as good a chance as anyone to receive the *charisma*—holy, saving power and wisdom—and to go on to full regeneration. All you have to do is abandon yourself before God, ask for the gift, and act in its light.

And this evidently is a universal offer. If your outlook is receptive to Eastern spiritual teachings, you will find the same point emphasized there. Among the great Hindu teachers, for example, our near-contemporary Sri Ramakrishna repeatedly assured those who consulted him that the life of the householder is not incompatible with God-realization; see *The Gospel of Sri Ramakrishna*, particularly Chapter 4, "Advice to Householders"; Chapter 20, "Rules for Householders and Monks"; Chapter 22, "Advice to an Actor"; and Chapter 31, "Advice to Ishan."

Founding figures in our main spiritual traditions—Jesus, Buddha, Muhammad, Lao Tse, Sri Rama—were laymen who lived and taught in the world; three of the above were married. The Christian tradition, prolific in ecclesiastic and monastic developments, at the same time is full of laymen who faithfully and successfully have followed the way to God, from Simon Bar-Jona through Francis of Assisi to Therese Neumann.

St. Francis de Sales, himself a priest and Doctor of the Church, was deeply concerned with the spiritual direction of men and women who were devoted to giving their lives to God in the midst of worldly duties and occupations. His book *Introduction to the Devout Life*, a masterpiece of counsel for just such people, grew out of casual notes of instruction and advice which he wrote to Mme. de Chamoisy, a cousin by marriage who had placed herself under his spiritual care. Another great churchman who was a specialist in the direction of God-seeking men and women in the world was Fénelon, Archbishop of Cambrai; his wonderfully sane, practical, and loving letters are as alive and helpful today as when they were written and first read in seventeenth-century France.

Among the Eastern teachings which are of value to householders seeking God, none is more helpful than the Bhagavad Gita. The Gita teaches karma yoga, i.e., nonegotistical action and service in the world, leading to experiential knowledge of Reality and thus to salvation and liberation.

In our own time there has appeared a system that is intended specifically to enable men and women in the world, "good householders," to achieve spiritual change and to reach higher levels of consciousness. This teaching is called "the fourth way" (as distinguished from the ways of the fakir, the yogi, and the monk). The doctrine of the fourth way claims not to be new but to be an expression in contemporary terms of a universal spiritual "work" which always had existed. "The fourth way" and "the work" in the context indicated here are equivalent terms.

This system has evolved from the influence of two men and their followers and commentators. The first is G. I. Gurdjieff, an extraordinary and highly enigmatic person, who is regarded by some who knew him well as an authentic saint, by others as an eccentric if not a villain or a black magician, but by none as a neutral or uninteresting character. Gurdjieff brought to the West the knowledge of the principles which were developed in the teaching of the fourth way.

A Russian named P. D. Ouspensky studied and worked with Gurdjieff for a number of years beginning in 1915. Subsequently, in a series of lectures and personal teachings, he made possible the first widely published statements of the fourth-way system. Ouspensky, trained as a mathematician, journalist, and philosopher, was a disciplined and audacious thinker. He was also a serious, a relentless, and in a certain cool way a heroic seeker for truth. Before his meeting with Gurdjieff he already had produced one of the most penetrating and revolutionary of modern essays in thought, a book entitled *Tertium Organum*. The lines of inquiry opened up in this work were followed further in a later book, *A New Model of the Universe*. Ouspensky's books which stem from his work with Gurdjieff and which are concerned specifically with the fourth way are *In Search of the Miraculous, The Psychology of Man's Possible Evolution,* and *The Fourth Way,* all published after his death in 1947. Ouspensky's collaborators and followers include Maurice Nicoll, who wrote *Psychological Commentaries on the Teaching of Gurdjieff and Ouspensky,* and Rodney Collin, who wrote *The Theory of Celestial Influence* and *The Theory of Eternal Life*.

The Rules

Spiritual awakening and growth in God are possible in ordinary life. But they come only to men and women who deeply long for the *truth,* who find and follow the *rules,* and who do the necessary *work*. These three—(1) the truth, (2) the rules, and (3) the work—are the ladder to success. We have already considered the place of truth in the quest for God. It is alpha and omega. Simple honesty, which any child can understand (but few children and fewer adults can practice), leads straight to the goal. By practicing honesty you win the grace of the Spirit of Truth. Then God himself, the Holy Ghost, becomes your inner teacher, the guide who takes you to your Lord and King. And he in turn enables you to understand the rules and do the work.

What about the rules? They are clearly stated in the great sources accessible to all: the Old Testament, the New Testament, the Bhagavad Gita, the Yoga Sutras, and the Buddhist scriptures. They can be epitomized so as to be readable in just a few minutes. It is assumed, however, that no one will take the brevity of the ensuing summary as grounds for underestimating the depth, sublimity, and binding necessity of the rules. Whoever takes the rules lightly or foolishly or fails to take them at all disqualifies himself not only for spiritual life but finally for any kind of life at the human level.

The following is a boil-down of the rules in contemporary terms:

A. *The Decalogue:*
   1. First things first. Avoid idolatry: i.e., do not put lesser values above higher values or any love above the Supreme Love. This is a very hard rule to follow.
   2. Do not kick sacred things around. Do not invoke God or use his name unless you are aware of what you are doing and unless you mean business.
   3. Do not ignore basic cosmic rhythms and laws. There are, for example, cycles of activity and rest which have their roots in Divine Nature itself and cannot be violated with impunity by anyone, because no one can exist outside that Nature. Man's health and sanity depend on understanding and reverently accommodating his life to the profound implications of such traditions as the Sabbath.
   4. The home, and particularly the relationship with father and mother, is a sacred institution. It reaches to the heights and depths of man's soul. It is the great analogue of man's relationship to his Creator. It is to be protected and honored.
   5. Do not murder.
   6. Do not commit adultery.
   7. Do not steal.
   8. Do not lie about your neighbor.

   9 and 10. Do not covet your neighbor's wife or goods.

B. *The precepts of Christ (New Testament):*
   1. (Quoted by Christ from the Law of Moses): Love God with your whole heart, soul, mind, and strength and your neighbor as yourself. Another hard rule to follow.
   2. If you want to enter into eternal life, keep the commandments.
   3. Repent, i.e., change your attitude, your outlook, your way of life, your mind; go beyond your present state, transcend yourself (Greek *metanoia: meta,* "change" or "beyond"; *nous,* "intellect," "mind," "understanding").
   4. Wake up. Snap out of it. Pay attention. Watch (Greek *gregoreite*).

5. First things first: Leave all, sell all, and follow Christ (the Lord, the truth, the way). Deny yourself, observe and bear your unregenerate nature every day, and follow Christ.
6. Resist not evil; do not retaliate.
7. Do not be angry.
8. Do not touch a woman illegitimately, even in your mind.
9. Live one day at a time. Do not worry about tomorrow. Do not worry about food and clothes.
10. Pray always, and do not faint, do not collapse.
11. Heal the sick, cleanse the lepers, cast out devils, raise the dead.
12. Do not murder.
13. Do not commit adultery.
14. Do not steal.
15. Do not lie.
16. Honor your father and mother.
17. Be poor, and poor in spirit. (Let go of material *and* spiritual possessiveness.)
18. Mourn. (Let suffering and loss do their full work in you.)
19. Be meek (Greek *praos*, "disciplined," "trained," "non-resentful," "gentle," "tractable," "teachable").
20. Be hungry and thirsty after wisdom, justice, right knowledge, skill in the way.
21. Be merciful.
22. Be a peacemaker.
23. Be pure in heart.
24. Be perfect (Greek *teleios*, "complete," "undivided," "unlimited," "finished," "mature," "integral") as God is perfect.
25. Love your enemies; pray for anyone who abuses you.
26. Endure persecution and calumny cheerfully.
27. Believe and trust in God as your Father, hallow his name, seek his kingdom and his truth, ask him for what you need, knock at the door of God realization.

C. *The essence of the Bhagavad Gita:* Be devoted to God above all other interests. Work without craving for results or rewards.

D. *Pre-yogic moral disciplines* (Compiled from Gandhi, Vivekananda, Mees, Prabhavananda):

Is the Experiment a Practical Possibility? 83

The five yamas (cardinal vows):
1. Harmlessness (non-violence, non-killing, non-resentment, meekness, *ahimsa*).
2. Truthfulness (non-falsehood in thought, speech, and actions, *satya*).
3. Non-stealing (not taking more than needed, not wasting).
4. Continence (refraining from illicit sexual experience, in thought, word, and deed, *brahmacharya;* further: restraint of all waste and leakage in the vital nature).
5. Non-possession (non-covetousness, giving up the sense of ownership, becoming "poor" and "poor in spirit").

The five niyamas (casual vows):
1. Purity (bodily cleanliness, outside *and* inside; mental cleanliness; regulation of diet, reading, and associations).
2. Contentment (non-worrying, non-fretting, non-striving, equanimity, even-mindedness).
3. Austerity (conserving energy and directing it toward the spiritual goal, *tapas,* training).
4. Study (reading and meditating on the scriptures and other works leading to God).
5. Devotion to and surrender to God.

E. *Buddhist guiding principles* (extracted and condensed from "Summary of Buddha's Dharma"; Buddhist writings; Goddard, *A Buddhist Bible*):

The Four Noble Truths:
1. The universality of *suffering.*
2. The *cause* of suffering rooted in desire.
3. By ending desire, suffering comes to an *end.*
4. The *way* to end desire, and hence to end suffering, is to follow the Eightfold Noble Path.

The Eightfold Noble Path:
1. Right ideas.
2. Right resolution.
3. Right speech.
4. Right behavior.
5. Right vocation.

6. Right effort; following the ideals of
   a. unselfish charity,
   b. sincerity and fidelity in keeping the precepts,
   c. humility,
   d. zeal and perseverance,
   e. tranquillity and one-pointedness.
7. Right mindfulness.
8. Right *dhyana* (attention, meditation, concentration, rapture).

The Ten Bodhisattva Stages:
1. Gladness and joy.
2. Purity and peace.
3. Effortless patience.
4. Effortless energy.
5. Higher consciousness (*samadhi*) while retaining touch with this world.
6. Self-mastery and unshakable confidence.
7. The "turning about" from which one never again recedes.
8. Transcendental powers and utter acceptance.
9. Perfect wisdom and compassion, directed to the emancipation and enlightenment of the world.
10. Complete identification with the Great Truth Cloud; perfect integration with all lives.

F. *The seven things to avoid,* the capital sins (Christian tradition):
   1. Pride.
   2. Greed.
   3. Lust.
   4. Anger.
   5. Gluttony.
   6. Envy.
   7. Sloth.

G. *The root trouble* against which all the rules are directed is *egotism* (exaggerated personal self-sense), giving rise to a condition variously termed craving, desire, lust, thirst, clinging, sticking, attachment, infatuation, delusion, beguilement— English: concupiscence; Greek: *epithumia;* Sanskrit: *moha;*

Is the Experiment a Practical Possibility? 85

Pali: *tanha;* Russian: *prelest;* modern American: "To hell with you, Jack. I've got mine."

The above survey of the rules is of course not complete, but it is carried far enough to indicate what the outstanding principles are, as stated in the main sources, and to show how they overlap, agree, supplement, and confirm each other. There is no substitute for consulting the sources themselves and really absorbing what they have to tell you.

For help in understanding the rules themselves, their truth and significance on the one hand and their utility and practice on the other hand, four work books are suggested (one Roman Catholic, one Anglican, one Hindu, and one Eastern Orthodox Christian): *The Spiritual Life* (a treatise on ascetical and mystical theology) by Adolphe Tanquerey; *The Warfare of the Soul* by Shirley C. Hughson; *How to Know God* (the yoga aphorisms of Patanjali), translated and with commentary by Prabhavananda and Isherwood (pp. 95–173); and *Unseen Warfare* (the *Spiritual Combat* of Lorenzo Scupoli, edited by Nicodemus of the Holy Mountain and Theophan the Recluse).

The *work* consists of the practical application of the rules in daily living. Spiritual work far exceeds any other kind of work in interest and meaning, in challenge and difficulty, and in real accomplishment and fulfillment; it is the subject of our next chapter.

CHAPTER TWO

The Practical Life Means Practice

Practice in the spiritual life is the thing that separates the men from the boys. Lots of people today as always are ready to talk about it and hear about it; relatively few are ready actually to do it. But hearing without doing is impractical: i.e., it doesn't work. This is a hoary old truth, but some of us still manage to elude it.

> Whosoever heareth these sayings of mine, and doeth them, I will liken him unto a wise man, which built his house upon a rock. . . . And every one that heareth these sayings of mine, and doeth them not, shall be likened unto a foolish man, which built his house upon the sand. . . .
>
> Matthew 7:24, 26

Questions as to whether seeking God is practical, i.e., whether it can be done at all by a mere mortal, are usually raised by men and women who have not yet really tried it, or who have tried it a little and found that it pinches pretty hard in the comfort or pleasure or self-esteem department.

Anyone who has begun to practice in full earnest will tell you that seeking God is practical enough in any circumstances, but that it is indeed very difficult. Of course it is also difficult to build skyscrapers, raise mink, or play a good game of golf, and there are plenty of people doing those things. The fact is that men, even more than ants and bees, stubbornly make their way over and under and through all kinds of difficulties on the way to objectives in which they *really believe* and which they *deeply desire*.

People balk at spiritual life not because of difficulties but because they are still asleep to the reality of it. They do not really believe in it (although they may be pious "believers"), and they do not really want it. The awakening to the reality is a gift of God; all we can do is pray for it. But when it comes, when a man gets a whiff of the joy of returning to God, it draws him far more strongly than money or sex or power. He then no longer talks of difficulties but quietly gets on with the work.

How do you work? *You start right where you are* and apply the rules in your own daily life. Whoever you are, wherever you find yourself, this is a big order. But fortunately there are several simple, proved, time-honored practices which help to clarify and channel the work as it proceeds and to make its accomplishment entirely possible for anyone who really means business.

The Practice of the Presence of God

Nicholas Herman of Lorraine was a big, clumsy man whose life was turned to God as a result of looking at a tree.

> He told me that God had done him a singular favor, in his conversion at the age of eighteen. That in the winter, seeing a tree stripped of its leaves, and considering that within a little time the leaves would be renewed, and after that the flowers and fruit appear, he received a high view of the providence and power of God, which has never since been effaced from his soul. That this view had perfectly set him loose from the world, and kindled in him such a love for God that he could not tell whether it had increased during the more than forty years he had lived since.
>
> *The Practice of the Presence of God*

Like certain men of Galilee in old times, Nicholas Herman was ignorant and uneducated. He was humble enough to enter a monastery, hoping "that he would be made to smart for his awkwardness." He was admitted as a lay brother among the barefooted Carmelites in Paris in 1666 and thereafter was known as Brother Lawrence. He was the monastery cook. From the uneventful life of this uncomplicated person there developed, almost by accident, one of the most influential and helpful of all books on the practical search for God.

The Practice of the Presence of God consists of conversations with Brother Lawrence recorded by M. Beaufort, Grand Vicar to the former Cardinal de Noailles, and letters written by Brother

Lawrence himself, with no thought that they would ever be published. Emanating from a monastery, these spiritual counsels have been of greatest help to God-seeking men and women in the world.

The practice of the Presence of God can be done anywhere by anyone who is not dead, crazy, or asleep. It is direct; it is simple; it involves no theological or intellectual difficulties; it produces genuine spiritual power; it really works. (It does not work as well or as often as it could and should, but that is a curious question which we shall examine below.)

The appeal, the great practical value, and the wide popularity of Brother Lawrence's technique will be found to cut across denominational and interreligious lines. The practice of the Presence is praised and studied by Catholics and Protestants alike and has won considerable attention among devoted people outside the Christian tradition.

What is the practice? How do you do it? You can find out by reading the book. But do not be deceived by its simplicity. Do not read it and be charmed by it and put it aside as so many do. Read it slowly, a little bit at a time, daily for six months. And practice it daily. Only by doing it can you begin to know *what* the method is and *how* to do it.

You will notice that the practice of the Presence of God consists of three stages. The first is *recollection*. Brother Lawrence teaches us simply to remember—not as philosophy but as living realization in the midst of our ordinary occupations—what is the true state of affairs: God is everywhere. We are continually in his presence. We know this, and yet we do not know it. We alternate between very brief periods of faintly remembering it and very long periods of utterly forgetting it. The practice of the Presence begins with remembering more often and more vividly and forgetting for shorter periods and less completely.

> . . . acquire a habit of conversing often with God, and forget Him the least you can.
>
> Let it be *your business* to keep your mind in *the Presence of the Lord*. If it sometimes wanders . . . the will must bring it back in tranquillity.
>
> Let us thus think often that our only business in this life is to please God, and that all besides is perhaps but folly and vanity . . . let us begin in earnest; let us repair the lost time. . . .

Is the Experiment a Practical Possibility? 89

> One way to recall the mind easily in time of prayer . . . is *not to let it wander too far at other times* . . . being accustomed to think of Him often, you will find it easy to keep your mind calm. . . .
>
> That useless thoughts spoil all; that the mischief began there, but that we ought to reject them as soon as we perceive their impertinence to the matter in hand or to our salvation, and return to our communion with God.

The second stage in Brother Lawrence's way to God is *conversation*. The first and second stages overlap; they are given in sequence here only for convenience. Recollection of the Presence and conversation with God are mutually supporting acts.

> That we should establish in ourselves a sense of God's Presence by continually conversing with Him. That it was a shameful thing to quit His conversation to think of trifles and fooleries.
>
> That in order to form a habit of conversing with God continually, and referring all we do to Him, we must at first apply to Him with some diligence. . . .

Conversation, like recollection, seems simplicity itself—when you are merely reading about it. When you actually practice it, you discover that the simplicity is real all right but that it is a surface beneath which lie a great depth and a great power.

Recollection of the Presence and *conversation* with God together represent a critical turning point in the inner life of man. Nearly anyone can remember God and converse with him, now and then. But when you are able to do it more often, and then still more often, a tremendous event is taking place in the soul. This is still a beginner's stage, but it is the *beginning of the true life in God*. Father Reginald Garrigou-Lagrange has written of this experience with wonderful clarity in his synthesis of the spiritual life, *The Three Ages of the Interior Life:*

> As soon as a man ceases to be outwardly occupied, to talk with his fellow men, as soon as he is alone, even in the noisy streets of a great city, he begins to carry on a conversation with himself. If he is young, he often thinks of his future; if he is old, he thinks of the past, and his happy or unhappy experience of life makes him usually judge persons and events very differently.
>
> If a man is fundamentally egotistical, his intimate conversation with himself is inspired by sensuality or pride. He converses with

himself about the object of his cupidity, of his envy; finding therein sadness and death, he tries to flee from himself, to live outside of himself, to divert himself in order to forget the emptiness and the nothingness of his life. In this intimate conversation of the egoist with himself there is a certain very inferior self-knowledge and a no less inferior self-love.

He is acquainted especially with the sensitive part of his soul, that part which is common to man and to the animal. Thus he has sensible joys, sensible sorrows, according as the weather is pleasant or unpleasant, as he wins money or loses it. He has desires and aversions of the same sensible order; and when he is opposed, he has moments of impatience and anger prompted by inordinate self-love.

But the egoist knows little about the spiritual part of his soul, that which is common to the angel and to man. Even if he believes in the spirituality of the soul and of the higher faculties, intellect and will, he does not live in this spiritual order. He does not, so to speak, know experimentally this higher part of himself and he does not love it sufficiently. If he knew it, he would find in it the image of God and he would begin to love himself, not in an egotistical manner for himself, but for God. His thoughts almost always fall back on what is inferior in him, and though he often shows intelligence and cleverness which may even become craftiness and cunning, his intellect, instead of rising, always inclines toward what is inferior to it. . . . The intimate conversation of the egoist with himself proceeds thus to death and is therefore not an interior life. . . . The interior life is precisely an elevation and a transformation of the intimate conversation that everyone has with himself as soon as it tends to become a conversation with God.

(1) Recollection of God and (2) conversation with God, as taught in the simple, uncomplicated, authoritative terms of Brother Lawrence, represent an outlook and a technique which lead to the third and culminating stage of the practice of the Presence, the condition of (3) sustained awareness.

When you reach this point, your own efforts become so blended with the grace of God that you who once had to swim so hard now find yourself drifting with the current of God's love and you who tried with such difficulty to walk toward God now find yourself upheld and carried, constantly, steadily, by an ever-present Power. Knowledge of God and communion with God in the stage of sustained awareness are spontaneous, effortless, and rarely

Is the Experiment a Practical Possibility? 91

interrupted. The Presence is known and communed with under all kinds of circumstances.

That with him the *set* times of prayer were not different from other times; that he retired to pray, according to the directions of his Superior, but that he did not want such retirement, nor ask for it, because his greatest business did not divert him from God.

He is now so accustomed to that *Divine Presence* that he receives from it continual succor upon all occasions. For above thirty years his soul has been filled with joys so continual, and sometimes so transcendent, that he is forced to use means to moderate them, and to prevent their appearing outwardly.

That he had so often experienced the ready succor of Divine Grace upon all occasions, that from the same experience, when he had business to do, he did not think of it beforehand; but when it was time to do it, he found in God, as in a clear mirror, all that was fit for him to do.

There is a special power and appeal in Brother Lawrence's book. Many people are afraid of the spiritual life because it seems difficult and remote. Brother Lawrence presents it as easy and immediate.

. . . Spend the remainder of your life only in worshipping God. He lays no great burden upon us; a little remembrance of Him from time to time; a little adoration; sometimes to pray for His Grace, sometimes to offer Him your sorrows, and sometimes to return Him thanks for the benefits He has given you, and still gives you, in the midst of your troubles. He asks you to console yourself with Him the oftenest you can. Lift up your heart to Him even at your meals and when you are in company; the least little remembrance will always be acceptable to Him. You need not cry very loud; He is nearer to us than we think.

To be with God, there is no need to be continually in church. We may make an oratory of our heart wherein to retire from time to time to converse with Him in meekness, humility, and love. Every one is capable of such familiar conversation with God, some more, some less. He knows what we can do. Let us begin, then. Perhaps He is just waiting for one generous resolution on our part.

Is it possible that Brother Lawrence was mistaken? Hardly. The power of the man and his work, the purity and authority of his words, are too great. But if the practice of the Presence of God is so easy and so effective, why is it that more people do not follow it through to the stage of sustained awareness as Brother Lawrence himself did? *As a matter of actual fact, not many do.* But why don't they?

Getting down to contemporary cases, here is what we find: The practice of the Presence *is* easy to try. Let's say you are one of the many people who try it, and you find to your delight that in a few days you are making undoubted and exhilarating progress. And then . . . then . . . several months later you wake up and find that somehow, somewhere, you have dropped it completely and forgotten all about it. It is not consciously abandoned. No decision is made. The great adventure simply peters out, and you cannot tell for sure just where the stream disappeared in the desert.

But you are intrigued. You remember the joy of those few days when it was working so wonderfully and so easily. So you try it again. And again it works very well! You are thrilled. You resolve to be more alert and not to lose it again. Days go by, great days. And then . . . then . . . the strange drama is repeated. You come to, and you realize that you have not been practicing the Presence of God for weeks.

Some good comes from these sporadic and unsustained experiences in Brother Lawrence's technique. But the fact remains that they fall short of the thing Brother Lawrence is talking about, and they are distressingly in the majority.

Why?

First, probably because the ease and simplicity of the practice of the Presence are only a part of the picture. The practice is a long ladder. Its feet are comfortably planted at the easy levels where all may climb. But the upper rungs rise into clouds of glory. As the apostles did at the Transfiguration, you are apt to fall asleep in this rarefied atmosphere; and then you fall off the ladder.

The great quality, therefore, in practicing the Presence is the persistence to try again and again. Do not be discouraged when, time after time, you undergo the humiliating experience of falling asleep spiritually and simply forgetting that God is here and that we may converse with him always. This kind of sleep lies close to the root of the fall of man; it is embarrassing; but the difficulty is made bearable by the realization that you share it with the rest of the human race.

Is the Experiment a Practical Possibility? 93

Anyone who wishes seriously to study and practice Brother Lawrence's way should read Gerald Heard's two essays on the subject, entitled "Notes on Brother Lawrence's Practice," in *Vedanta for the Western World*.* With his combination of scholarship and spiritual insight, Heard shows that there is much more than meets the casual glance in *The Practice of the Presence of God*. Without wishing to detract from the appeal and comfort and usefulness of the book, he points out that it can be understood and successfully followed only after penetrating study of its content and meditation upon its real meaning.

> . . . That method [the practice of the Presence], though the description of it has been popular, has owed its popularity not to the fact that it is really simple or rudimentary but because we have felt sentimental about a pretty title and a charming old man. . . .
>
> The first thing that a careful study of these four conversations and fifteen letters discloses is that though the language is so simple, often even conventional, yet they contain far more specific information than the easy rapid reading suggests. . . . We find that this is not at all a beginner's book. . . . The system is simple because it is advanced. This is not a spiritual child speaking with unreflective simplicity. This is a man at the end of an intense, never-remitted struggle of a dedicated lifetime, having won to that consummate ease, that master's power to extemporize in any mode, which comes only to those who, at the top and climax of their form, having achieved all particular controls, now have such perfect command of expression and apprehension that every event becomes precisely that opportunity which allows fresh, unexhaustible creativeness to be exhibited.

Who is right—the people who see in Brother Lawrence and his way a direct, unconfused, and wonderfully easy method of living the practical life in God, or Gerald Heard, who sees in Lawrence a man very far advanced in sanctity and in his practice an expert's, not a novice's, technique?

Both views may be true. So many ordinary people have been attracted to the practice of the Presence and greatly helped by it that we must agree with the enthusiasts who praise it as one of the great and basic spiritual practices. At the same time, so many give up serious attempts really to follow it after a few trials that we

---

* Isherwood, *Vedanta for the Western World*, pp. 396–98.

must also conclude that Gerald Heard is to be thanked for reminding us that the simplicity of this attractive, easy-to-try practice hides a master's way to the highest perfection.

For this very reason, however—just *because* it combines comfort and encouragement for the beginner with the scope and scale of deepest spirituality—it is a peculiar treasure of counsel in the quest for God. Let no one be put off by the paradoxical extremes of its range. Let the beginner be fed by its simplicity and clarity. And let the more mature seeker drink of its hidden springs. And let them respect and honor each other, so that the one will not be embarrassed by his novice's position or the other inflated by his own progress.

For the average person just starting out on the living of the life in God, Brother Lawrence's practice is a thoroughly sound guide, a perfectly possible and practical method to follow, containing a built-in challenge and test of his sincerity and his capacity to keep going when the practice would lead him into really deep awareness of the beloved Presence.

The Practice of Ego-reduction or Dying Daily

If God is so real and so near, why do we not see him and feel him? Why are we not constantly aware of him? What stands in the way?

That which stands in the way is an amazing thing, indicated by one of the shortest words in our language: "I."

I stand in my own way. The obstacle is nothing but what arises from the ordinary experiences of "I," "me," "mine." The terms most commonly used for this condition are "ego" and "egotism."

"Ego" is just a Latin word that means "I." In some modern systems of psychology it is used to designate the conscious individual. In spiritual teaching, however, the meaning is quite different: the "ego" there is universally recognized as *the root of selfishness*. "Egotism," as a spiritual term, is not enlightened interest in oneself. It is a blind, narrow, and destructive obsession with the cravings and drives of the merely personal self. Egotism is a pampering of the lesser self at the expense of the true Self. It is "Saul" getting in the way of Christ. It is the individual arrogantly and foolishly pitting himself against the universal, the child against the parent, the human against the divine.

The ego is the self-centered brat in you. If you can't find him in yourself, it does not mean that he isn't there; it just means he has you hoodwinked.

Egotism leads to ignorance, sin, sickness, suffering, spiritual sleep, and spiritual death. The fall of man is a fall into egotism. The regeneration of man is a salvation from egotism. The eclipse of God —and the consequent loss of wisdom, health, and truth—comes from one thing only: egotism. The troubles of the world, *all of them*, come from one thing only: egotism. Your own troubles, whatever they may be, come from one thing only: egotism. No man can hope to deal with himself, let alone the world, let alone God, until he understands egotism. The job is to know (1) what it is, (2) how to reduce it, and (3) how to get rid of it.

You do not come to understand the ego, and most certainly you do not reduce it, by hearing words about it—even the wisest words. You begin to understand the ego by looking for it in yourself—by recognizing it and holding it under steady scrutiny in yourself, by struggling against it and separating from it in yourself, and finally by entering into the death grapple with it in yourself.

The final step—killing the ego—is beyond human strength (but not beyond human co-operation). The hand that strangles the snake at last is the hand of God, curiously and wonderfully united with your own hand. The first steps, however—watching for the enemy, recognizing him, and struggling against him—are well within the capacities of anyone who has seen the necessity of the encounter and is ready for work.

The first real glimpses of the ego in yourself are easy to recognize. They are accompanied by acute pain and a desire to run and hide somewhere. The recognition of your own egotism arouses embarrassment, shame, shrinking, and a sharp inclination to turn away from what is being perceived. But it is very important to persist, because this is *the* route to spiritual reality.

Ordinarily you cannot find God by a direct effort. The indirect effort of ego-reduction in most cases is the quickest and straightest way to the goal. For, as Meister Eckhart has said, when the false self is eliminated, God rushes into the soul as air into a vacuum. It is his nature to do so. As soon as you make room for him, there he is! And room is made by reducing and finally dissolving the ego.

"Where is the dwelling of God?"
This was the question with which the Rabbi of Kotzk surprised a number of learned men who happened to be visiting him.
They laughed at him: "What a thing to ask! Is not the whole world full of His glory?"
Then he answered his own question:
"God dwells wherever man lets Him in."

Martin Buber

Like all great movements in the truth-seeking life, ego-reduction is a paradox. It is very straightforward and simple, and very tricky and difficult, all at the same time. The best way to begin work on it is to begin. For example: you wake up this morning and something inside you says: "Let's turn the alarm off and catch a few more winks. We've got fifteen minutes before we absolutely *have* to get up." Another inner voice says: "Better get up now, take things easy, and get off to a good start for the day." You take the counsel of the first voice, oversleep forty-five minutes, bolt your breakfast, miss your first appointment, lie to the boss, and don't snap out of your snit till nearly noon.

This is a typical, ordinary egotistical mess. You must study this sort of thing in yourself and see where the ego enters in and how it keeps the stew cooking.

A man under grace sees that this state is not "normal" and not "harmless," even if indeed it is "what everyone is doing." When egotism enters, precious energy is captured and curdled. The light of the intelligence is dimmed. The vitality is bled off into futile and destructive directions. The emotions are quickly poisoned. The life runs downhill. While it lasts the man is moving away from the kingdom of God and toward physical and mental illness, which may be more or less delayed in crystallizing out or may be checked by counterforces.*

"Normal life" consists of spells of acute egotism relieved by periods of natural grace and good will, during which some healing and restoration take place. Spiritual life begins when you see the deadly nature of this situation, the precarious and dangerous balance involved, the constant liability to degeneration into the worst

---

*On the question of *normal* vs. *sick*, see Martin Gross, "The Psychological Society," page 270.

Is the Experiment a Practical Possibility? 97

kinds of trouble, and the absence of any real security or hope for the future. At this point you see that *what the spiritual guides of humanity have always said is true:* the only way out is to face the ego in ourselves, submit to its reduction, and co-operate finally in its being rooted out. This procedure is at the base of every religion, and most certainly the Christian religion.

Ego-reduction requires intelligence and the grace of God right from the beginning. Courage and willingness to suffer are needed, but they are not enough. You have to learn how to work along with it as the job is being done. It is a skilled operation, and the skill can only be acquired slowly, by actual experience, by trial and error.

Certain phrases that are used to describe the practice must be taken in the right way. "Destroying the ego" and "killing the snake" must not lead to acts of self-persecution or self-violence, on the physical *or* mental level. The ego must not try to amputate itself. God is the surgeon. At the same time we must do our part, and do it sanely, without foolish excesses: ". . . Fasting and other forms of self-restraint . . . are needed for subduing the desire for sense objects, which however is rooted out only when one has a vision of the Supreme. The higher yearning conquers the lower yearnings" (*The Gita According to Gandhi*). Union of the lower with the Higher Self "is not for the man who overeats, or for him who fasts excessively. It is not for him who sleeps too much, or for the keeper of exaggerated vigils. Let a man be moderate in his eating and his recreation, moderately active, moderate in sleep and in wakefulness" (Prabhavananda and Isherwood, *Bhagavad-Gita*).

The following extracts bearing on this aspect of the process are from the notebook of a person who has been working on the ego problem for some time:

> A particularly helpful and instructive dream: September 7, 1956. I am a member of a troupe of traveling actors. One of our troupe turns out to be a terrible liar and murderer. Several other members of the troupe and I decide that we must kill the murderer. We make many attempts to do so, and we have many fierce struggles with him, but he always escapes. He begins to impersonate the other members of the troupe so successfully that, in the attempts to kill him, we are in danger of killing each other. Once, trying to kill the liar, I almost kill my best friend.
> This dream seemed to me to be of extraordinary significance for

my life. I take it to mean that although the ego is a liar and a murderer, he cannot be eliminated by trying to use his own methods against him, i.e., by killing him or using violence against him. Not only does it not work, but it may do harm to the true individual (the dearest friend). The ego is really eliminated only when it is dissolved in truth. Neither arguments nor tricks nor hounding will do the job. It takes real spiritual experience and the opening of the whole being in the truth-atmosphere.

It is important to *paralyze or dissolve the ego*. If the ego is only injured or maimed, it is subject to all kinds of inflations, depressions, distortions and explosions; these set up repercussions at the personal level, and it is a very bad show all around.

The ego is an actual psychic structure; it is a sort of king-structure which holds a lot of other structures together. It may be literally paralyzed or dissolved; *or* it may be only hurt or crippled. *The distinction here is critical.* A dissolved ego permits enlightenment and healing of body and mind. A crippled ego results in mental and/or physical illness. (Remember Ramakrishna's snake that had caught the frog and could neither cough it up nor swallow it? A very *exact* figure of the botched ego-killing job that results from clumsy spiritual disciplines or ignorant medical practices.)

Do not confuse the psychophysical aggregate, the body-and-bodymind, with the ego. It is *not* the ego, although it is the place where the ego arises, where the ego is entrenched, where the ego hides. The ego is only a stubborn and diseased self-notion which carries on a fugitive and precarious existence built upon an ignorant but powerful and persistent confusion of the psychophysical organism with the immortal individual. The ego is simply dissolved at the first full whiff of real truth. *But it may re-form.*

There are two kinds of real death which the ego can undergo: (1) small deaths, which are complete but temporary, and after which the ego re-forms, and (2) the Great Death, the final sacrifice and irrevocable dissolution which precedes and permits ultimate salvation and full entry into the Kingdom of God, of which Christ's death is the great example.

The psychosomatic organism is not an illusion. *But the ego, the normal self-notion,* quaintly and humorously *is* a complete illusion. The whole egotistical show is a tempest in a teapot. You can keep it boiling and bubbling exactly as long as you like. But for a man to live anything but the spiritual life is just silly. The ego-centered life is far beneath the real dignity of man and not at all commensurate with the real intention for man. Not everyone, of

Is the Experiment a Practical Possibility? 99

course, is meant to live a professed religious life, but, in whatever occupation, all are meant to live a spiritual life, a truth-centered life, a God-centered life.

One secret of successful ego-reduction is to realize as a fact that there are two selves in man, a greater and a lesser. When the lesser self presses its claims too far, we may speak of a true self and a false self, or even of a good self and an evil self.

These two selves are referred to in the New Testament as the first Adam and the second Adam, the old man and the new man, the earthly Jerusalem and the heavenly Jerusalem, the natural body and the spiritual body. "Plato, again, continually reminds us that there are two in us, and that of these two souls or selves the immortal is our 'Real Self'" (Coomaraswamy, *Hinduism and Buddhism*). In Eastern teaching the personal or lesser self is called the *jiva* and the Divine Self is called the *Atman*. The relationship is described in a famous statement in the Mundaka Upanishad:

> Two birds, companions who are always united, cling to the self-same tree. Of these two, the one eats the sweet fruit and the other looks on without eating. On the self-same tree, a person immersed (in the sorrows of the world) is deluded and grieves on account of his helplessness. When he sees the other, the Lord who is worshipped, and his greatness, he becomes freed from sorrow.

Paul's teaching is alive with the realization of the two selves. "I live, yet not I, but Christ liveth in me." And, speaking as the personal man diminishing as the Divine Man takes over the life, he says, "I die daily." This is perhaps the best short statement on record of what ego-reduction actually feels like. The lesser self is not destroyed in this process. Only its arrogance, its ignorance, and its sense of separateness are destroyed. But these factors are so rooted in the vitality that their elimination is experienced literally as death itself.

The death of Jesus and his perfection in Christ is the great historical and traditional example of the redemption of the personal "I" in the Son of God, the salvation of the individual man in the Universal Man. Christ took our nature upon him, and our nature is egotistical to very near the core. The temptations in the wilderness all are appeals to egotism: "Enjoy wealth and power!" "Be a great world figure and leader!" "Amaze and conquer people's minds by

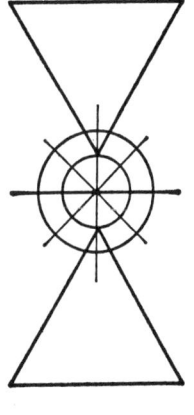

The ego stands between the Divine (expressed in the active triangle of beauty, goodness, and truth) above and the human (the instrumental triangle of intellect, emotion, and sensation) below. This is the prepared sacrifice, the cup, the cross.

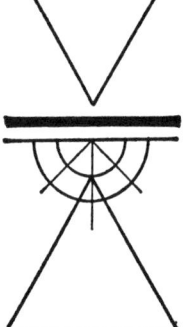

When the man turns away from his Creator, the ego splits, hardens, and inflames the lower principles with a false light, false freedom, false movement. "Saul" persecutes Christ. This is "egotism," the sacrifice spilled, the cup defiled, the cross refused.

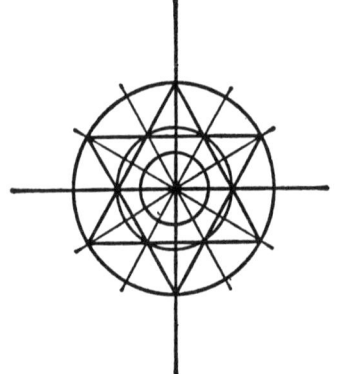

When the ego surrenders itself to God, the Divine nature penetrates the human, "Paul" receives Christ, and the man is made whole. This is salvation, the cross accepted, the sacrifice accomplished, the Holy Grail, the White Stone, the New Name.

spectacular demonstrations, and test God's patronage at the same time!" "Serve your own appetites by supernatural means!"

Christ's earthly life is a constant struggle against the more and more rarefied egotism in the humanity, culminating in the agony of prayer in the garden, "Let this cup pass from me," and the cry from the cross, "Why hast thou forsaken me?" The entire Christian demonstration is a complete triumph over egotism, the final and utter submission of the humanity to the Divinity, the death and resurrection of the lower nature in the Highest, the passion, transfiguration, and perfection of the flesh in the Logos.

The "I" in man—the sense of being and the power of identity—is the principle which stands between the lower and the Highest. In a "normal" man this ego is pulled both ways. It is attracted to the Christ—the truly good, truly beautiful, and truly true Being—above. At the same time it is constantly tempted to a separate and ignorant service of the lower principles of intellect, emotion, and sensation.

The ego is capable on the one hand of rising to an experience of the One who named himself to Moses as "I AM" and who proclaimed to certain later Hebrews, "Before Abraham was, I AM." On the other hand the ego may fall to saying "I am" on its own part, separate and away from God. Thus it identifies with the psychophysical organism, binds itself to the transient and the perishable, gains perhaps the whole world but loses its own soul.

The lesser natures, intellectual, emotional, and sensual—find their true orientation only in a life surrendered to God. When these lower elements draw the ego into separate and selfish experience, they lose their proper power and dignity, debase the "I" (their natural lord), and lose contact with the Supreme Ruler. The "I" so debased is the "self" which must be denied, the "ego" which must die daily, in the Christ-centered life. Ego-reduction is nothing but the daily and hourly remembrance of the great central fact of spiritual life: "I . . . yet not I, but Christ. . . ."

The great Western treatise and "how-to" book on ego-reduction is the *Theologia Germanica*. This "spiritual noble little book," as Luther called it, addresses itself directly, charmingly, and with great practical wisdom to the task of solving the ego problem.

> What did the Devil do else? What was his going astray and his fall else, but that he presumed to be also somewhat, and would have it that somewhat was his, and somewhat was due to him? This pre-

sumption, and his I and Me and Mine, these were his going astray and his fall. And thus is he to this day.

What else did Adam do but the same thing? It is said: It was because Adam ate the apple that he was lost and fell. I say: It was because of his arrogating something to himself, because of his I, Mine, Me, and the like. Had he eaten seven apples, and yet never arrogated anything to himself, he would not have fallen; but as soon as he arrogated something to himself, he fell, and would have fallen if he had never bitten into an apple. . . .

Now when a man rightly knows these things in himself . . . he does not arrogate anything to himself, and the less he arrogates things to himself, the more perfect does his knowledge become.

The author of the *Theologia Germanica* is not known. He calls himself a "Frankfurter," a "Teutonic Knight," a "priest." Whoever he was, he probably wrote in the second half of the fourteenth century. Certainly he was greatly influenced by Meister Eckhart and John Tauler, and his book is strongly identified with the Rhineland mystics who called themselves "Friends of God."

The practice of the Presence of God as taught by Brother Lawrence and the practice of ego-reduction as taught by the *Theologia Germanica* are complementary and mutually interdependent experiences. If you practice the Presence you will find, as a corollary, that your ego is being reduced. If you work at dissolving the ego, you will find that the presence of God consequently becomes more real to you.

The practice of ego-reduction is facilitated not only by the practice of the Presence of God but also by a number of other disciplines. Several of these will be discussed in a later chapter: the practice of abandonment to the will of God, the practice of penetrating the cloud, the practice of continuous prayer. And there is a most interesting and powerfully helpful procedure—the practice of *watching*—which is the subject of our next section.

The Practice of Watching

What, could ye not watch with me one hour?

Matthew 26:40

One of the best ways to sustain progress on the way to God is to discover key words and find out what they really mean. One key

Is the Experiment a Practical Possibility? 103

word is the term which in the New Testament is translated "watch." It occurs over and over again, in the Gospels, the Acts, the Letters, and the Apocalypse.

It is easy to miss the tremendous meaning of this word "watch." Christ Jesus commands us to "watch and pray," and we say, "Sure, sure, I know, prayer is very important." And we do spend some time trying to learn to pray, but we tend to slide right over the command to watch, assuming that we know what it means and that it is not essential anyhow. The fact is that we cannot pray well until we have first learned to watch. Not by accident does the command to watch come ahead of the command to pray. And not by chance is the double command, "watch and pray," repeated so often and in such crucial settings. A spiritual fact of the greatest importance is involved here, and it is well worth while finding out what it is.

In order to understand what "watch" means, we must first know that there are in the earth roughly four kinds of people: (1) those who are spiritually *dead*, (2) those who are spiritually *asleep*, (3) those who are spiritually *awake*, and (4) those who are spiritually *alive*. Notice that these terms describe *spiritual* conditions. A man may be physically alive and spiritually dead ("let the dead bury their dead") and physically awake and spiritually asleep.

It is a critical mistake for any of us to assume that we are spiritually alive. The best of us, with very few exceptions, are not even spiritually awake. We spend a large part of our time in spiritual sleep, with only occasional flickers of awakening; and rarely if ever do we experience moments of real life.

The *spiritually dead*, of course, are those who have unwittingly or deliberately severed all conscious contact with their Creator and are busy spending the capital they took with them when they left the Father's household. The end of this kind of "life" is death in the deepest sense, unless one has the good fortune to come to in the hogs and husks stage and start back home, where, in God's incredible softheartedness, a warm welcome is always waiting. I myself am a witness from the dead, having spent some years in that condition.

Spiritual sleep is the state of those who have not lost their faith, who are not sunk in deliberate and enjoyable evil, who perhaps practice their religion seriously and try hard to live right—but who at the same time have only a mental and theoretical knowledge of God, who are hopeful but dry, and who spend long periods in effective forgetfulness of what they really do know. This forgetting is the chief characteristic of spiritual sleep.

If you are *spiritually awake,* you see and know God directly, just as directly as "normal" people know the air they breathe, the food they eat, and the solid earth under their feet. God is as obvious to an awakened man as sunshine is to the rest of us. The *how* of this can be understood only in the awakened state. It is possible for awakened men to pass some of their knowledge down to those in the sleeping state, but only under great limitations and in a severely modified form. The best favor which the awakened can do for the sleeping is to tell them, not what the awakened state is like, but how to awaken.

None of the tasks of human life can be understood, much less accomplished, in the state of spiritual death. A spiritually dead man, if he has a glimmer of insight left, can only hope and pray to come alive. (But when his prayer is answered he finds himself not yet in spiritual life but in spiritual sleep, with still a long way to go.)

A man's real problems can be dimly apprehended, and with hard effort painfully and partially resolved, in the condition of spiritual sleep. The objective of the sleeping man, however, must be not to dream better dreams but to wake up. For it is only in the awakened state that—with a crashing joy as of Beethoven's music—the problems are fully met and the great meanings and the triumphant solutions come pouring in.

What would it be like to be a man who is *spiritually alive?* We cannot say. There are examples, but we look at them as at direct sunlight and are dazzled or blinded. Jesus Christ was such a man. He represents a reality which profoundly shocks and upsets the ordinary personal consciousness. In order to teach us sleeping men, Christ has to stoop to the level of spiritual awakening, and from there instruct us, because this is all that most of us can endure. As an awakened man who healed and helped people, he was popular. But when he stood up in his full stature and his quality of spiritual *life,* the rocks split, the elements sprang to obey him, and the Light of Glory streamed from his very garments. The three men who were chosen to witness his transfiguration were overcome by— sleep! People who heard him speak from his depths were not at-

Is the Experiment a Practical Possibility? 105

tracted but turned away: ". . . This is an hard saying; who can hear it?" The temporal and religious authorities of his own time could not and did not tolerate him. And after two thousand years our scholars, having failed to explain him, now spend much of their time trying to explain him away. Let's face it: we earth men are not pining for spiritual *life;* we are afraid of it. And properly so, because we are not yet awake.

What has all this to do with "watching"? We are coming to that.

From a practical, working standpoint, the critical relationship is that between spiritual sleep and spiritual awakening. Now put yourself in the position of a real spiritual teacher. He is in the awakened state, looking upon our present humanity, and what does he see? He sees even the best men and women wandering around in the state of spiritual sleep. *What would be his first command to such people?* Would it not be the command, "Wake up!"? And this is exactly what it is in the New Testament; this *is* the meaning of the word which is translated "watch."

"Watch" is not an inaccurate translation, but it is a seriously inadequate one. The Greek word is *gregoreite,* and it does indeed mean "be vigilant, pay attention, be watchful," but it also and more fundamentally and far more significantly means, "wake, wake up, keep awake." A perfectly good modern equivalent of the original meaning would be the command "Come to! Wake up! Snap out of it!" The word "watch" conveys the true meaning only if we read it as a sharp warning given to a sleepwalking man who is about to step off the edge of a building—"*Watch!*"

This one word is loaded, and it handsomely repays some digging. *Gregoreite* is the imperative form of *gregoreuo,* which comes from the root *egeiro,* a word rich in meanings, all of which relate directly to the great turning point in our life which would occur if we began to obey the directive: "Watch! Wake up!" These are the meanings: to awake, to take up, to lift up, to raise up, to rise again, to stand, to rouse from sleep, to rouse from sitting or lying, to rouse from disease, to rouse from death, to rouse from obscurity, to rouse from inactivity, to rouse from ruins, and to rouse from nonexistence.

There is real spiritual dynamite and an entire spiritual discipline packed into this one command, "Watch!" The discipline we shall examine in just a moment. The dynamite is in this, that *if we can hear it and obey it* this command will effectively change our lives and launch us—*really*, not just sentimentally or theoretically—on the way to God's living truth and to God himself.

What is the first sign that a spiritually sleeping man has heard the command "Wake up!"? It is that *he realizes he is sleeping*. He may not awaken right away, but he knows briefly that he is not awake. For just an instant he sees himself, not through a haze of ignorant imagination and self-deception, but in the aurora of truth. Such moments of realization are short and infrequent at first, but they are precious almost beyond estimate, because they signify not only that light has penetrated our darkness but that light *has been received*; it has pierced through into our awareness; it has revealed, however fleetingly, our own true condition, our own state; it has shown us not yet where we are going but where we are and where we can start from. Thus in responding to the Christian command to watch, we simultaneously and inevitably also respond to the classical command, "Man, know thyself!"

Why does the command to watch precede the command to pray? Because otherwise we pray in our sleep! Any prayer is better than no prayer, but obviously awakened prayer is incomparably better than sleeping prayer.

Here is the explanation of whole lifetimes of "religious" and "spiritual" efforts which seem to achieve almost nothing. Some of us do not go anywhere because we are always getting ahead of ourselves. We press on to high school, whereas the knowledge we really need and could use, the power that could transform our lives, is still in kindergarten. We "pray" (and "read" and "worship" and "meditate") before we have learned to wake up. And so we pray and worship and meditate in spiritual sleep, and of course it is unsatisfactory, and finally it may become a tragic self-deception and frustration. We are perhaps better off than if we did not pray or worship or meditate at all, but at best we are spinning our wheels.

The cure for all this is clear. It is to embrace the terribly simple principle of first things first—swallow our spiritual pride, abandon our pretenses and our play-acting, go back to low school, and pray God to teach us what it means to wake up, to come to, to snap out of it, to *watch!* (Hypocrites anonymous, rally round! Take notice! Let us be sure not to misunderstand: it is not somebody else who has to do all this. It is I, me, myself—just this smug little personality with my own dear name attached to it. That is who has to see himself and his own real status before the face of Christ.)

If we do succeed in having moments of first-degree awakening, what are we to watch? We are to keep an eye on *ourselves*—objectively, dispassionately, uncritically, and above all, honestly. Honest self-watching is the discipline that is included in this commandment of Christ, concurrent with the repeated shocks of self-awakening.*

A wonderful thing follows immediately. We are able to pray! Now—truly, urgently—we can pray because we know and feel our need. Watching produces keen, *felt* experience of our own spiritual poverty. And this is the first beatitude, the basic blessing, upon which rests the foot of the ladder of bliss. When we actually (not theoretically or sentimentally or "piously") wake up and watch ourselves, we feel our great need for God's help as keenly as a starving man feels hunger, and we are able sincerely to ask for the food which will salvage our lives. Awakening and watching mean not just a change of mind but a change of state—*metanoia*. Nothing high yet, but clear and true.

I must speak here of my own experience with watching. I think it is perhaps impossible merely in books, in writing, to convey a real working knowledge of how to begin and pursue this basic practice. I think you need to come into personal, learning relationships with other people who know from experience what this great command means and how to do it. I am sure that when you pray to be brought into contact with such people you are always heard. My own instructors were a variety of people in many different stages of spiritual growth. They had the common denominator of admitting their own great need for God's help, of rigorous self-honesty, of willingness to watch themselves patiently and steadily and without blinking. And slowly, with reluctance and pain, I began to learn from them this lifesaving art.

A man who has been given the grace to begin the practice of watching sooner or later acquires the extended grace of beginning to see himself as an objective person. *He begins to see himself as he would see another man.* And in this way his self-watching becomes impartial, cool, penetrating, accurate. He is neither so easy on himself nor so hard on himself as he used to be. Regarding himself, he acquires a mother's heart and a surgeon's hand. He enters into him-

*See Maurice Nicoll on honest self-watching, false personality, and self-love (page 262).

self and at the same time rises above himself. From this viewpoint, and only from this viewpoint, the work of co-operating in his own regeneration can be carried on.

Watching is a particular extension of the practice of the Presence: I observe Tom Powers in the light of the truth that whatever he feels, thinks, says, and does is felt, thought, said, and done in the presence of the living God. If you are able to do this—nothing more, just this—for any length of time, an amazing and powerful change takes place in your feeling, thinking, saying, and doing. You do not try to manipulate these functions. You don't change them. You simply observe them, and *they change*—wonderfully. Try it and see.

The practice of watching occupies a basic position in the universal spiritual teaching, and so it occurs in many traditions both within and without the Christian framework. It is known by different names, referring to the same essential practice. It is central, for example, in Buddhism. Recall that Christ's command means both "watch!" and "awake!" Then note that "the Bodhisattva is an 'awakening being,' or one of 'wakeful nature'; the Buddha is 'awake' or 'The Wake.'" In Zen Buddhism, the key word *satori* indicates a "sudden awakening." Original Buddhism itself is called "the Doctrine of Awakening." And one of the fundamental disciplines within the doctrine corresponds exactly to the Western discipline of "watching," in its aspect of viewing one's own person as an objective entity: ". . . one strives first of all for achievement of what is known as *ñāna-dassana,* the vision which comes from knowledge, having as its object one's own person, in its totality. It is . . . a liberating . . . carried out by contemplation of oneself . . . as if one were another person or thing" (Evola, *The Doctrine of Awakening,* p. 218).

In the Jewish spiritual tradition, watching is referred to within the scope of the key word *kavanah.* Abraham Heschel (in *God in Search of Man*) interprets it as follows:

> What is meant by the term kavanah? In its verbal form the original meaning seems to be: to straighten, to place in a straight line, to direct. From this it came to mean to direct the mind, to pay attention. . . . Kavanah, then, includes, first of all, what is commonly called *intention* . . . the state of being aware of what we are doing. . . . In this sense, kavanah is the same as atten-

Is the Experiment a Practical Possibility? 109

tiveness. . . . Kavanah is attentiveness to God . . . direction to God, and requires the redirection of the whole person. It is the act of bringing together the scattered forces of the self.

The practice of watching plays a prominent part in the psychology of Ouspensky and Gurdjieff, where it is broken down into two disciplines, "self-observation" and "self-remembering." The former is a way of watching oneself as an objective person; the latter is a technique of touching a higher level within oneself; both work together toward awakening from spiritual sleep. (See Nicoll's *Commentaries.*)

The Eastern Christian saint Nicephorus the Solitary speaks of watching as "guarding the mind," "attention of the mind," or just "attention," and describes it in these terms (italics supplied):

> [Nicephorus first quotes St. Simeon]: Have you understood, brethren, that there exists a certain spiritual method swiftly leading whoever follows it to passionlessness and the vision of God? Are you convinced that the whole of active life is regarded by God as nothing but leaves on a tree which bears no fruit and that every soul which has no guarding of the mind will labour therein in vain?
>
> [Then the followers of Nicephorus put this request to him]: We have learned . . . that there exists a certain doing which speedily frees the soul from passions and by love unites it to God. . . . But we beg you to teach us what is attention of the mind and how to become worthy to acquire it. For this work is quite unknown to us.
>
> [And Nicephorus responds]: . . . I shall try as far as is in my power to show you what attention is and how, God willing, one can succeed in acquiring it. Some of the saints have called attention the safekeeping of the mind, others—the guarding of the heart, yet others—sobriety . . . and others again by other names. But all these names mean the same thing.
>
> [And in the same tradition, St. John of the Ladder says]: Sitting on high, *observe, if only you know the art,* and you will see how and whence, how many and what kind of robbers are trying to enter to steal the grapes. When the sentinel gets tired, he gets up and prays, and then sits down once more and again resumes his work with new courage.
>
> [Further, still in the Eastern Christian group, St. Isaac says]: . . . Every sentient being changes times without number and every man alters hourly. . . . His trials, day by day, have special power to make him wise in this, if he *watches over himself* with

sobriety; so that, among other things, he may *observe himself* with his mind and learn what changes his soul undergoes every day, how it departs from meekness and its peaceful disposition and is suddenly thrown into confusion, and what unspeakable danger threatens him at such times.

The Philokalia

To awaken and pay attention is to stop living heedlessly, to stop drifting. When you have begun to watch, you are no longer wholly driven by pleasure, sucked under by habits, or carried away by dreams. You are now able to use the God-given and God-contacting faculty of *attention* as a power to edge your life toward its fulfillment. Attention is the key which lies ready at hand and yet is steadily ignored by most of us.

A man of the people one day asks the bonze Ikkyou: "Bonze, will you write for me some maxims of high wisdom?"

Ikkyou took up a brush and wrote a word, "Attention."

"Is that all?" said the man, "won't you add a few more words?"

Ikkyou then wrote twice: "Attention. Attention."

"All the same," said the disappointed man, "I don't see much depth or subtlety in what you have written there."

Ikkyou then wrote the same word three times.

Slightly irritated, the man said: "After all, what does this word 'Attention' mean?"

And Ikkyou replied: "Attention means attention."

Benoit, *The Supreme Doctrine*

Alas, the practice of watching, like the practice of the Presence of God, is easy to begin—and easy to drop.† A good exercise in es-

† Watching, like the practice of the Presence, is superficially easy and fundamentally difficult; it seems to be a novice's technique but is really a master's way. The novice *can* attempt it with real success, but he should not be deceived thereby into imagining that he has plumbed the possibilities of the practice. The beginner should not be dismayed at the immense ranges opened up by watching; neither should he be inflated by his early successes; rather should he be led on humbly over months and years of patient effort toward real mastery.

Some idea of the scope of self-knowledge into which the practice of watching leads can be gained from the works of Hubert Benoit, who has made psychological studies specifically along these lines. Dr. Benoit is not easy to read, but if you have been attempting to watch for some time, you may find his views exceedingly helpful, because he discusses exact techniques for observing oneself at real depth. The following excerpt is from *The Supreme Doctrine:*

"In practice this work should entail inner gestures repeated, but short and

tablishing oneself in watching, in learning its meaning and feeling its importance, is to turn to those places in the New Testament where the practice is stressed and use them as a basis for meditation. Notice that the command to watch is given in situations of urgency, of testing, of trial. But it must be carried out constantly in order that one may be ready for the trials. Observe that there is danger of crucial wrong turnings and grave loss if one does not watch. See how difficult, in spite of its simplicity, it is to watch. And see how watching is connected with the Lord's coming, with the actual experience of God, and with the capacity to sustain that experience. Note particularly Matthew 24:42–43; 25:13; 26:38, 40, 41; Mark 13:33–35, 37; 14:34, 37–38; Luke 12:37, 39; 21:36; Acts 20:31; I Corinthians 16:13; Colossians 4:2; I Thessalonians 5:6; Hebrews 13:17; I Peter 4:7; Revelation 3:2–3; 16:15.

Christ calls to us: *Gregoreite!* snap out of it! so that we will revive enough to reach out for our true life and the Power greater than ourselves who can lead us to it.

If by some rare grace we manage to glimpse what Christ is revealing to us, if we begin to see that we are really and literally asleep, we may experience a brief moment of awakening and with it a shock. For the awakened man briefly sees the terrible problem: sleeping men, even if they know they are asleep, do not know how to awaken.

Clear instructions have been given to us on this critical point, but we find them exceedingly difficult to understand or to follow. Christ in the Gospels, the Buddha in the Sutras, Sri Krishna in the Gita, give plain directions which, if followed, would lead to full spiritual awakening—but not one man in a hundred thousand picks up on it.

---

light. It is not a question of laboriously dwelling upon it as though there were something to seize. There is nothing to seize. It is a question of voluntarily noting, as in the winking of an eye, instantaneous and perfectly simple, that I am conscious of myself . . . in that second . . . I succeed instantaneously or not at all; if I do not succeed at all I will try again later (this may be a few seconds later, but the gesture should be carried out at one go). It is to my interest to make this gesture as often as possible, but with suppleness and discretion, disturbing as little as possible the course of my dualistic inner life; I have to interrupt the consciousness that I habitually have of my dualistic life by a 'break' that is clean, frank, instantaneous, but without doing anything which modifies it directly. The normalizing modification will be carried out by the Absolute Principle through the instantaneous 'breaks' produced by this inner work."

All of the great religions contain these instructions, but they tend to get lost in the conventional way people take religion. Fresh, contemporary statements out of actual experience are urgently needed. One such is by G. I. Gurdjieff. The practice which Gurdjieff called self-observation is pure *gregoreite*, and Gurdjieff was able to present it in terms that are not easy but at least possible for a contemporary Western man to get hold of:

> To begin self-observation and self-study it is necessary to divide oneself. A man must realize that he indeed first of all consists of *two men*.
>
> So long as a man takes himself as one person *he will never move from where he is*. His work on himself starts from the moment he begins to feel at first *two men* in himself. One is passive and the most it can do is to register or observe what is happening to it. The other, which calls itself "I," is active, speaks of itself in the first person, and is in reality only an invented, unreal person. Let us call this invented person in a man A.
>
> When a man understands his helplessness in the face of A, his attitude towards himself and towards A in him ceases to be either indifferent or unconcerned. Self-Observation becomes observation of A. A man understands that he is not A, that A is nothing but the mask he wears, the part that he unconsciously plays and which unfortunately he cannot stop playing, a part which rules him and makes him do and say a thousand stupid things, a thousand things which he would never do or say himself. If he is sincere with himself, he feels that he is in the power of A and at the same time he feels that he is not A. He begins to be afraid of A, he begins to feel that he is his enemy. No matter what he would like to do, everything is altered and intercepted by A. A is his enemy. A's desires, sympathies, thoughts, opinions, are either opposed to his own views, feelings and moods, or they have nothing in common with them. And at the same time, A is his master. He is the slave, he has no will of his own. He has no means of expressing his desires because whatever he would like to do or say would be done for him by A. On this level of self-observation a man must understand that his whole aim is to free himself from A. And since he cannot in fact free himself from A because he is himself, he must therefore master A and make him do, not what the A of the given moment wants, but what *he* himself wants to do. From being the master, A must become servant.
>
> *The first stage of work on oneself consists in separating oneself*

from A mentally, in being separated from him in actual fact, in keeping apart from him. But the fact must be borne in mind that the whole attention must be concentrated upon A, for a man is unable to explain *what he himself really is*. But he can explain A to himself, and with this he must begin, remembering at the same time that he is not A.‡

A modern man, intending to obey Christ's command *gregoreite*, would need to study these precise directions carefully and execute them faithfully. What is involved is something simple to do but easy to forget. Do not be led off into theorizing or arguing about it. Just do it.

If you will go ahead and do it, and keep doing it, you will find that it works. Self-observation really does produce moments of awakening and periods of freedom from the bad dreams of resentment, self-pity, despondency, anxiety, boredom, and the lot.

One caution needs to be kept in mind constantly. A big danger is that we will fall into *imagining* that we are self-observing when we are not. Maurice Nicoll, one of Gurdjieff's commentators, writes:

> Many of you think that Self-Observation consists merely in noticing that you feel moody, that you feel unwell, that you feel negative or bored or gloomy or depressed and so on. Let me assure you that this is *not* Self-Observation. Self-Observation begins with the establishing of Observing "I" in your own inner world. Observing "I" *is not identified* with what it observes. When you say: "*I* am feeling negative," you are not observing yourself. You *are* your state. You are identified with your state. There is nothing distinct in you that is standing outside your state, something that does not feel your state, something that is independent of it, and is looking at it, something that has a quite different feeling from your state. If you say: "*I* wish *I* were not negative," this is quite useless. It is "I" speaking the whole time. You are taking yourself as one mass. You are not dividing yourself into two, which is the beginning of Work on yourself. You are not saying: "Why is *it* negative?" but "Why am *I* negative?" You are taking *it* and *you* as the same. Try to understand what it means to divide yourself into two—an observed side and an

‡ This and the next quotation are from *Psychological Commentaries on the Teaching of G. I. Gurdjieff and P. D. Ouspensky* by Maurice Nicoll (London, 1964: Vincent Stuart).

observing side—and try to feel the sense of "I" *in the observing side* and not in the observed side.

There is amazing power in the practice of watching. You cannot appreciate it, and indeed you can hardly believe it, until you experience it. When the personal self is watched, it reacts as a small child with both hands in the forbidden cookie jar who suddenly realizes that someone is observing him; the child simply and sheepishly withdraws. Likewise, when the eye of truth is open, without any great tension or struggle much stubborn mischief just ceases. This is *not* brought about by picking on oneself; it is done by a simple, clear, uncritical but unsparing glance within.

The mere act of watching, of patiently and calmly and honestly observing oneself, brings peace and inner healing which no amount of guilt or chagrin or self-castigation can begin to accomplish. Watching is not faultfinding or internal henpecking. It is simply—watching. When it is done right, it produces results. If there are no results, you just have not learned how to do it yet. You must be at least slightly awake to do it at all. And you have to try it yourself over a considerable time before you begin to realize how great the results can be.

The man who watches also dies daily, because the ego can thrive only in the dark; when observed, it begins to shrivel like a spider in a flame. The watcher finds himself, furthermore, practicing the Presence of God, because he sees his true relationship to God, keenly feels his need for God, and prays for the supplying of that need. He prays inevitably, by reflex, as a drowning man says "help" and a bee-stung man says "ouch"—and with the same elementary sincerity.

And finally the watching man finds himself behaving with wisdom and love in personal, family, business, social, and political situations. Not by overdependence on theories but rather by the direct power of truth, he begins to know what to do and *to be able to do it.*

PART THREE

God's Will: How to Know It and Do It

CHAPTER ONE

God's Will Is the Door. Prayer Is the Key

Do you want to succeed in life? Do you want to be really happy? Do you want to find the highest adventure, the greatest wealth, the utmost growth, and the most wonderful fulfillment possible for you?

It is very simple to attain these goals: just *know* the will of God and *do* it. If God exists at all, he sees what our greatest good is, beyond our fondest hopes and dreams; furthermore he is able to bring us to that good. So it is only a matter of discovering his will and carrying it out. The will of God is the door to our heart's desire.

Alas! as an answer this is too simple. It is a true answer. It is what we all have to do. But how do you know God's will, and how do you do it? If we stay in the realm of mere philosophy we can chirp along making rather bright noises about this great question. Talk is cheap and pleasant. If we buckle down, however, and begin to do some experimental work, several tough but reliable and interesting facts emerge:

Fact number one is that in our normal state we do not know the will of God and *cannot* know it. Self-deception on this point, even the most "well-intentioned" self-deception, is among the surest ways to abort the second birth.* To know and to do the will of God quite simply is to live in paradise. And that is where, in our

---

* Loose imagination miscalled vision, pigheadedness miscalled faith, and undisciplined notions about the will of God combine to produce what is known as "illuminism," the watchword of which runs something like this: "I've got the inside track, boys. God has spoken to me. Clear the way. Here I come!"

usual condition, we do not live. We are fallen from there, not in some "old biblical" and remote sense, but strictly, technically, immediately, and effectively. Jacob Boehme, a man who knew these things from direct experience, puts it this way: "*What, and where is Paradise, with its Inhabitants?* We have hinted . . . that it is in this world, yet as it were swallowed up in the Mystery; but it is not altered in itself, it is only withdrawn from our sight and our source [property, or sense]; for *if our eyes were opened, we should see it* [italics supplied]. Nay, God in his Ternary is with us; how then should Paradise be lost? We have lost its source [property, or working] and fruit in the outward life, as the devil lost God, when he wilfully exalted himself as a haughty spirit, and would be lord; so it is with us" (*The Forty Questions*, p. 297).

Now don't get excited and don't go away. If you have not been schooled and drilled in honesty, you will never face this condition. You will just go on forming pretty good notions of what the divine intention for you may be and pretending and "believing" that these notions are the will of God. In other words, a kind of self-deceit on the subject will be translated (with the monkey's help, of course) into a kind of "faith."

But let's back up a bit. A sincere person cannot help making the *best possible estimate* of what God wills for him. It is right and highly necessary to do so, if one is merely to live sanely, let alone grow toward truth. So far so good. But it usually goes farther, and here is where the trouble starts. The estimate of God's will—which is the closest we can come to the truth—is taken for certainty. If there are any doubts, they are smothered by "faith." The enlightened guess—which is the best we can do—is taken for knowledge. You can practice this kind of deceit on yourself without really noticing what you are doing, or you can half-notice and actually congratulate yourself on your "power of belief." A lot of this monkey business goes on today; there are even teachers of the art. But it is the devil's own gambit, and God help you if you don't find a way out of it.

Here is the place where a man who really means business in the quest of truth must rigorously stop kidding himself. He must sternly rid himself of such moonshine. Concerning God's will for you, make the best estimates and the most enlightened guesses you

God's Will: How to Know It and Do It 119

possibly can. Your physical, mental, and spiritual health depend on your doing so. But do not tell yourself that this is *knowing*. Test and find the truth for yourself in your own life: except for rare moments of inspiration or exaltation, an ordinary man does not know and cannot know the will of God.

A further and more difficult point: Even if we knew it for sure, we are normally incapable of doing the will of God. We may and must approximate doing it. But actually and fully do it? No. In the problem of doing as in the problem of knowing, it is equally easy and equally dangerous to pretend.

Pause. Consider. If you were able for just one hour to do the will of God you would begin abruptly to behave very much like Jesus Christ. You would give sight to the blind, heal the sick at a glance or touch, raise the dead, and do other things just as great. People for miles around would be thunderstruck. No, no. We ordinary men do not do the will of God. We do not often come close to doing it. Let us never imagine that we do. Let us at least refrain from any such dreadful flattery of ourselves. Good Lord! millions of us can't even stop lying or masturbating or backbiting or overeating for a few days or weeks on end; other millions, sunk in such miseries, don't even hope or try to break out. And yet we have quick and easy courses for knowing and doing the divine will!

Can you face this? *Can you feel it?* It bears repeating: our greatest need is to know and to do the will of God. At the same time the most striking fact of our present life is that we do not know it and we cannot do it. Realization of this state is a salutary shock. It is a sharp taste of the first beatitude: spiritual poverty. It is the way, and the only way, to real prayer. "Thy kingdom come" ceases to be a bored and mumbling little recitation and becomes a cleansing agony of spirit. "Thy will be done" is lifted up from a dumb and fearful acceptance of a bleak unknown to a passionate hunger and search for the one thing needful.

Furthermore, once you move out of the region of sentimentality and dream religion, once you come to grips with this terrible situation of man's position and God's will, the more interesting it becomes. For example, how very odd it is that we do *not* know the divine intention, for it is the sober truth that God is not far from us and he is not silent to us. . . .

God Speaks Continuously . . .

Look, really look, at a seascape, a field of corn, or a city lot full of rubbish. Look and (even in the disorder) see the law, the beauty, and the indelible significance. See the meaning within meaning, even in the foam and the soil and the trash.

The attempt to explain away the universe as an idiot's delight has been made and has failed. You may take an idiot's-eye view if you choose, but that does not change the cosmos. And a chastened, truly modern science will no longer support you. It is now obvious that this present world and this present power are at once the expression and veil and crucifix of a Higher Power.

In the most ordinary things, God confronts us. All children (except very sick children and perhaps even they) know this. You do not need to know the word "God" to know the truth of it; little children are alive with it, and to it. The bulk of the human race in nearly all eras has known it. We are living in one of those fortunately rare times when very many adults have forgotten it. Perhaps that is why, in a teaching addressed particularly to this age by One who entered deeply into its pain, we are commanded to turn and become as little children.

You do not need books and laboratories for this (although indeed they may help). But just go and look at the trees. How could they *be*, by accident? Take up a handful of summer soil and see the tiny lives moving in it. Sit before a clump of marigolds and watch the bees industriously, ecstatically, wisely, and efficiently working them over. And then notice the birds . . . ah, God, the birds! . . . no wonder that in the language of heaven to speak of a bird is to speak of a spirit.

There is no harm in analyzing the trees and the bugs and the birds if we would only *see* them first. Our young children see them, but we do not. We see shadows, and we exhaust our lives classifying and arguing and actually fighting about shadows. And the shadows grow harder and colder and deader, and they assume meaningless and chaotic forms, and finally it is a hideous dream which confronts us, which we blasphemously call reality.

All nature is enacting God's will and singing God's song, and not only every beautiful creature but every lump of garbage is

God's Will: How to Know It and Do It

pregnant and bursting with holy significance, but we do not hear it and we do not see it. God help us. Can we not find the grace at least to admit our so painful and so obvious blindness? Do please help us. Merely to admit our helplessness is the beginning of redemption. In mercy, carry us that far if we cannot or will not walk to it!

God confronts us everywhere. "That which is before you is it in all its entirety and with nothing whatsoever lacking."† This is not "mysticism" or "pantheism" or any other special cuss word which some academic toe dancer may wish to hang onto it. It is the truth. And therefore it is a fit subject for religion and science and common experience. ". . . The One is totally, infinitely present in all particulars."‡ This is not an abstraction but a statement of tremendous, empirical fact. "Wherever there are two, they are not without God, and wherever there is one alone I say I am with him. Raise the stone and there thou shalt find me; cleave the wood and there am I."* This is not something you can swallow up in classifications and name-callings. It is the staggering but simple truth, which the humblest man can prove to his own utter satisfaction, if he will. His ego will be shattered in the process, *but he will know the truth.*

God confronts us everywhere. If we even faintly know it, life is full of meaning, satisfaction, and joy. If we do not know it and will not probe it, life is full of frustration, misery, and idiocy. I did not learn this from books (although certain books clearly tell of it§). I learned it from living it, both ways. I have been a self-appointed, frustrated, miserable idiot in this very life. I wouldn't mind so much having reached that state if it weren't so unnecessary. But God's mercy is inexhaustible: when the idiocy gets bad enough, it becomes the seed of its own cure. One is reminded of the toast attributed to Gurdjieff and spoken presumably in his imperfect English: "Here's to hopeless idiot! When he knows he is hopeless idiot, he is no longer hopeless idiot."

God confronts us everywhere. The whole universe as it changes from moment to moment is a perfect expression of the will of the Unchanging. It is a complete and lucid statement of the will of God, faultlessly adapted to the understanding of every creature—

† Hsi Yun, *The Huang Po Doctrine*, p. 23.
‡ Huxley, *Heaven and Hell*, p. 37.
* "Sayings of Jesus," Dunkerley, *Beyond the Gospels*, pp. 133 ff.
§ Among the most notable are the books of C. S. Lewis. See page 210, where Lewis is talking about what life is like when you get off the planet.

from the man to the star to the atom to the squirrel on the fencepost. Everything that happens to you, good or bad, is a messenger of God's will for you. Your whole life is a consummately articulated script of God's will for you.

Since it is so obvious, since we are surrounded at all times and immersed in a great, coherent, beautiful, and unfailing expression of God's will for us, since God speaks without ceasing to the human heart, telling it what he wishes and intends, why do so few understand it, even a little bit, and why do even fewer do it, even a little bit? Here is a mystery.

God confronts us everywhere, and he is not silent to us. He speaks. God's voice—the thundering, crashing, sparkling, warning, encouraging, and pleading symphony of God's Word—is sounding down all the aisles of creation, from high heaven to the remotest sinks of outer darkness, without interruption. It is sounding right where you are and right where I am at this very moment. God speaks continuously. . . .

But Who Can Hear Him?

On this earth, very few men can hear him. It is a wonder that God speaks, and it is an almost equal wonder that we are deaf to him. It is not "hope" or "faith" but cruel and deadly foolishness to deceive ourselves on this point. Thank God the heart of humanity is stirring in its sleep. Many today are yearning, seeking, praying, watching, and listening. But how many truly *hear* that Voice and how many truly *do* his will? Few, very few. Let us be ready to give our lives that their number may increase!

Far from hearing God's voice, far from knowing what God's will *is*, not one man in a thousand has even an adequate rational idea of what the will of God *may* be and how it *may* operate in human affairs. To clear one's mental sights is a minimum move if the subject is to be touched at all. One of the very best ways I know to begin to do this is to study Leslie Weatherhead's brief but powerful book called *The Will of God*.

If you have never thought it out, the question of God's will can be painfully confusing, and in a personal emergency or tragedy it can arise suddenly as a fierce and insistent challenge. We all know, vaguely, that nothing can happen outside the scope of God's will.

God's Will: How to Know It and Do It   123

Does he, then, will that bombs fall on helpless and harmless little babies? that men die in slow and futile agony of battle wounds, cancer, and alcoholism? Does he will that people burn to death while trapped in wrecked automobiles and airplanes or drown wretchedly in sunken railway coaches? Does he intend that our insane asylums be filled to overflowing?

"Not my will but thine be done," said Jesus, and we know the sequel. Was it really the deliberate and coolly calculated will of the omnipotent God that this good and blameless man be shamefully and brutally tortured to death? That is what the story seems to be telling us. Is there some mistake? Is God himself after all some kind of bloodthirsty monster? The question, if it presents itself seriously, is a horror too great to be borne; it threatens one's sanity quite directly. From it, men turn to atheism with profound relief.

Clear, unevasive, and unsentimental answers to such questions are desperately needed. The answers must be rooted not only in scholarship but in experience. Dr. Weatherhead's remarkable book *The Will of God* takes us into the area of such answers. God's will, he says, bears upon human beings in three different aspects: (1) God's *intentional will*, that is, his original plan, including his intention to create man as a free being; (2) God's *circumstantial will*, that is, his revised intention in the face of evil circumstances with which free men are free to confront him; and (3) God's *ultimate will*, that is, the triumphant outcome of his over-all plan, in spite of, and often by means of, the very evil that opposed it.

Here is a view that smells to me of the truth, a welcome odor in a field of inquiry where, particularly in our time, the savor of truth often has been lost in the unfaced terror of a terrible question. If Leslie Weatherhead's thesis is sound, we really need not play ostrich with the obvious facts of evil. We need not embrace the evil of lying to ourselves about evil, of pretending against the voice of our whole soul that evil does not exist. Neither need we accept the outrageous alternative that the good God actually approves of men's torturing themselves and other men. God's full will, his three wills taken and understood as one, includes all the facts of life in a love that *is* absolute: absolutely good and absolutely true. "All," as our Lord said to the Lady Julian, "*is* well." The ultimate and utterly satisfying understanding of the sublimity of God's holy will must await the meeting of our souls with the Uncreated Light. But such explanations as Leslie Weatherhead's help us to keep clear heads while our hearts are being opened.

Meanwhile, for working purposes, let us take our places where the vast majority of us belong: among those who do not yet *know* but who are only able to yearn, seek, pray, watch, and listen. Let us humbly and frankly face our exile, our inability to hear our Father's Word, and our impotence, if we did hear it, to obey it. We need solid foundation for our hope, our encouragement, and our final triumph in God. Let us seek such undergirding in a present effort to understand our present failure, our amazing refusal to receive the King of the Universe into the councils of our hearts.

This is the fall of man we are talking about. It is not a gag, and it is not an "old tribal belief." It is the bones and bowels of the human problem. And it is not solved by brash excursions into certain kinds of self-hypnotism mislabeled "faith." It is also not solved by cross-less Christianity, by biblical emasculation masquerading as biblical scholarship, by logical positivism and materialism masquerading as science, or other kinds of modish whistling in the dark.

But we mustn't quarrel about these things, either. Even the best-intentioned religious and scientific disputes in our time can be nothing more than folly. We do not (perhaps fortunately) have time to argue with each other. The only real hope for a solution must lie in opening ourselves—spirit, soul, and body—to what the Eternal is now telling us and eternally has been telling us. The way out for mankind, and for every individual, is not in more bright ideas but in listening to God. If we won't do that, of course there will be consequences. Our freedom is real, and so is our responsibility.

The glorious and terrible fact is that God's will is in exquisite reciprocal relationship with the will of man. Evidently he wants it that way and will not have it otherwise. He has arranged it so that our redemption depends not alone on him but on our co-operation with him. A right relationship with God can arise only out of this root. There is no use trying to ignore him; on the other hand it is no good trying to play him for a patsy; furthermore we cannot blame him for withholding blessings or permitting disasters. All of our cute little tricks with him are beginning to appear about as bright and attractive as a stubborn case of paranoia. We know better than

God's Will: How to Know It and Do It

this; he has given us the power of knowing better; we cannot even claim his pity.

Obviously, even so, he does pity us. But his mercy is inexorable. What happens to the human race and to particular men is up to him all right, but he puts it right back up to us. It still depends on what we do and what we do not do—as a species, as nations, as families, and as little frightened individuals under the covers at night.

Maybe we had better start watching, praying, and listening real hard. It is getting late.

In the end, as C. S. Lewis has pointed out, there are only two kinds of men: those who say to God, "Thy will be done," and those to whom God says, "*Thy* will be done." A child of God may well pray for many things, for his everyday needs—"give us this day our daily bread," for example. But prayer that remained in this area alone would be dangerous, because if we actually have advanced to the point where our requests are beginning to be granted, and if at the same time we are not wise enough to know what is really good for us, we are in for trouble. We must include in our asking, as the great prayer does, things even nearer to the deepest human necessity—the power, for instance, to cancel moral indebtedness and to have our own debts canceled.

But the ultimate and only wholly safe refuge is found in the greatest request and the greatest gift of all: *the power to receive God's intentions and to be ruled by them.* This is the answer to everything. "Thy kingdom come, thy will be done." Or, as the salvaged alcoholics say—they who have known in their very blood the hell of separation from his holy order and the incredible joy of return —"[We] sought through prayer and meditation to improve our conscious contact with God, as we understood Him, *praying only for knowledge of His will for us and the power to carry that out.*"

Our situation, then, with regard to God's will (the door to all happiness) and prayer (the key to the door) is simple but difficult. The facts we need to keep in mind are few but inescapable:

Our failure to know and do God's will arises not because he does not give knowledge and strength but because we have lost the capacity to receive. Two revolutionary steps lead from the life of the spiritually dead to the life of the living: (1) *realization that we have lost the capacity* to know and do the will of God and that life is fruitless without it, and (2) *asking* with humility and courage and a sufficient awareness of desperate need *that the capacity be restored* to us.

This kind of asking constitutes the very metal of the key: the life of prayer. And that is our next consideration.

CHAPTER TWO

How to Use the Key

What is prayer? It is the simplest and most wonderful thing in the world. It is an infant cuddling with his Mother. It is a child talking with his Father.

In some systems this talking is called "low prayer." "Middle prayer" occurs when the child speaks to his Father of the needs of other children. And in "high prayer" the child is rapt beyond personal concerns and immersed in pure worship and adoration of the living flame of Love which is his Source and Goal.

But let us not go beyond low prayer too soon, or indeed ever. Our Lord, the night before he died, used low prayer. It is well not to lose the capacity to be just a child talking to his Father. For all our high flights, there are moments in life, perhaps the greatest moments, when we are returned to being just a child talking to his Father. Please, Father, don't let thy gifts of glory ever make us forget our eternal childhood in thee.

Prayer is the most wonderful and beautiful thing in the world. But like everything else which is entrusted to men, its beauty shines through a cloud of confusion and distortion.

"Prayer" is like "love," a great word that is burdened almost to death by loads of free and easy talk on the subject. Many a man who goes in for seeking God soon finds himself talking, often with exhilarating glibness, about high states of "prayer" and about the great power of "love." (I personally have been in this bag up to my ears, so I am level with the other offenders and not looking down my nose at anyone.) In the midst of certain kinds of cocksure talk about "love" and "prayer," however, I feel a deep uneasiness. For the fact is that prayer and love are profound and sacred mysteries about which most of us know very little and can do even less. The little we can do is immensely important, but it is still little. "Optimistic" and "positive" feigning to the contrary is not really healthful but, since wholeness depends on truth, eventually is sickening.

The confrontation of this situation is unpopular; the writer, therefore, had better stay in the first person, which is the only sound place to be in difficult discussions, stop talking about the "other offenders," and describe his own experience. I do notice that many persons are involved in eager, well-meaning, and largely unconscious pretense in the key areas of prayer and love. But a far more disturbing observation is that I myself am not able to stay out of this charming and mutually seldom criticized daisy chain. Like a lot of other eager beavers I have learned what I *ought* to be doing in prayer and love, and what the great saints and God-lovers *have* done in prayer and love, and the temptation to talk as if I were at least in ninth or tenth grade in these subjects is almost irresistible. Indeed, sometimes it *is* irresistible.

But occasionally the Self-Existent visits me in his marvelous and little-appreciated quality of *geburah*: rigor, severity. And then it is brought home to my reluctant attention where Tom Powers really stands in these matters. And I see, quite apart from any monkey-play of pious inferiority or phony humility but very simply as the truth, that in the practice of prayer and love I am in subkindergarten. (I will not speak for anyone else, but I will say that I do not feel lonely here. I have company.)

I am a beggar and a clodhopper when it comes to prayer and love. In my normal state, that is. There *are* periods when the grace of God moves through me and I become for the time a vessel of love. Again, the Holy Spirit acts and I become a channel of prayer. But this is not my love or my prayer. I am entirely conscious, indeed unusually conscious, while all this is going on. But afterward it is very hard to bear true witness to what happened, because ego elements intrude in spite of good intentions. Perhaps the truest thing that can be said is that *only God prays* and *only God loves*. In my worst times I am miserably divorced from prayer and love. In my middle times I hopefully grope toward loving and praying.

And in my best moments I am caught up in real love and real prayer—not mine, but his.

I do not wish to confuse things which are beautifully simple, to make easy acts difficult, or to make vinegar out of the wine of God's truth. I recognize that love and prayer are as natural and spontaneous as breathing—for the pure in heart. But for myself, and for many another yet-unpurified seeker, there is a need to crouch low going through these great doors, just because the spirit of hypocrisy insinuates himself in such subtle ways where prayer and love are concerned. *Mephistophel,* the corrupter-liar, is very active right here. Wouldn't you be, with his assignment?

In approaching a discussion of prayer I must come at it from this conservative angle because prayer, in its lowest form, is as high as God. Either it reaches to God or it isn't prayer. And so it breaks out beyond heaven and sinks lower than hell. It is more intimate than sex and more necessary than eating. I can't help this. I didn't invent prayer. It is just the way it is. Every fool who prays knows this.

I cannot avoid flying high in speaking of prayer, and so I want to be well anchored at the start at least. I do hope constantly to remember who provides the air and the wings and the heart for such flights and to remember that without grace I am quite incapable of prayer. Finally, I hope that my limitations as a commentator on prayer may be divested of any mock "humble" aspects and appear clearly as just what they are—facts, which may be useful to other men, similarly limited.

All right, so prayer is the key. Before talking about how to use it, may we examine the key itself just briefly:

It is an ancient key, as old as mankind and possibly very much older, and being a gift of God it is purest gold. But before we can use it we have to clean it off and brush it up a bit, for it is smeared with the adversary's rancor and smudged with human perversity and weakness. Prayer and purity are necessarily related.

And so we need to say a word about *morals:*

This, of course, is another twentieth-century hot potato. The puritans love it excessively, and the libertines hate it excessively, and between the two an ordinary mortal is inclined merely to skip it.

But no skipping is possible here, if we are to consider prayer at all. The science of right and wrong (morals) must accompany the science of divine access (prayer). Observe why: genuine prayer, even the most rudimentary kind of prayer, is an approach to the divine Life, and therefore to sacred power (*mana*, *Kraft*, virtue). If the approach is right, prayer is the greatest of all human activities. If the approach is wrong, prayer is literally and very seriously dangerous. For the divine Life is real, and sacred power *is* power; and such things are not given to nitwits, unless the nitwits insist, and then they may wish they hadn't. Holy virtue immemorially has been surrounded by specific safeguards, to ignore which is folly. If you touch but the hem of the garment of Truth, you touch and draw into yourself his living sap, his sacred Life-stream. This is not a pious fiction. It is more real than electricity.

Any prayer at all is better than no prayer, and generous fools sometimes may succeed where the stingily prudent fail, but let us not be deceived for all of that: there are right and wrong ways to approach God, and we are sternly cautioned to learn what they are and to observe them in our practice. "Friend, how comest thou in hither not having a wedding garment? . . . Bind him hand and foot, and take him away." (Matt. 22:12–13.)

In an emergency you can and should forget the hygiene and pray just as you are, even if you are right in the trough with the pigs. But otherwise certain preparations for prayer should be made. The most obvious of these is that you should clean yourself up morally before you pray. Nothing complicated or obscure is suggested. Just clean up in the simplest possible sense. Specifically: so far as you are able, stop lying, stop cheating, stop deceiving, stop guzzling, stop gorging, stop loafing, and stop fornicating. Stop envying, judging, and condemning. Stop wallowing in self-pity, self-hatred, and self-concern. Stop hating or fearing your fellow men. Unless you are delirious or deranged, you know what you are doing and which of these little pastimes are on your list. It is not a philosophical matter at all. These things, spiritually considered, are dirt. Prayer is a movement toward holiness (wholeness, oneness, integrity, health). And dirt and holiness do not mix. It is not the holiness which suffers in an improper contact, it is the dirt. If you touch the holy in an unduly dirty condition, you are liable to be burned. I know. I've been there.

But now here is something for all of us to remember always: if

God's Will: How to Know It and Do It 131

a man waited to approach God until he had perfectly cleaned himself up, he would never pray at all. Because it is not in our power to accomplish our own purification. Again, the situation is very simple. We are required to clean up *as much as possible* before turning to God. As always, something remains to our responsibility, and on that the whole wheel of grace turns; we must do our part.* *Then* we go to him, and we are warmed in his fire, certainly never burned beyond our capacity to endure, if we have done an honest cleanup job in preparation.

Out of prayer, and out of the warmth and the benign burning, comes the capacity for further cleansing; this permits deeper prayer; and thus God and man co-operate in the basic redemptive phase of purgation, which nobody—note: *nobody*—escapes. God is Author and Lord of love, and he is by no means above loving whores. But they end up washing his feet in their tears.

Prayer is the key to the will of God. Prayer is easy and simple; it is also deep and difficult. This is a typical paradox of the way to God; and like all such mysteries it is also a very practical fact. The first motions of prayer are humbling to the rational mind, because we would not have to pray at all if the rational mind were as competent as it sometimes thinks it is. Nobody really understands prayer, so that he could analyze it and explain it. And yet everyone, for his own direction, has to understand as well as possible.

There is no end to the ways in which one may speak of prayer. It may be said, for example, that prayer is a holy instinct, a holy art, and holy breath.

Prayer obviously is an instinct, the deepest of all. The act of praying, of calling for help, for life, for sustenance, for love and understanding and guidance, is built into us far below the level of language and conceptual thought. It is in our very cells. It is in our vegetable, animal, and infantile natures, which we never lose no matter how old and sophisticated our minds become. A sudden upset is apt to throw us back to these levels at any time. And this is gain, not loss, if it enables us to recover the primitive capacity of the creature to seek help from its mother the universe and its Father the Spirit of the universe.

The whole creation up to the human level is one vast orchestration of need and fulfillment, hunger and food, seeking and finding. This is not yet the language of religion but of existence. If

*See O. Hobart Mowrer, page 254, on the place of sin in modern religion and modern psychiatry.

man has lost the feeling of his participation in the universal prayer life at that level, it is because egotism has cut him off from nature as well as from God. But he *can* recover, because prayer is in his very bones, and it is apt to find its voice whenever the person's outer shell is scratched. If the shell is actually *cracked*, the voice sounds loud and clear. Sometimes a light tap will break the personal shell, and the instinctual prayer is heard easily and sweetly. Sometimes, particularly nowadays, a real whack is required. For emphasis, I give an extreme example:

I know a man who went off his rocker in early middle life and was given shock treatment. (He is a nice man who since has fully snapped back and today is as healthy in the head as anybody and maybe more so than many; so I guess his report, strange as it is, may be trusted.) As I said, he broke down and was given shock. This was in the pioneering days of shock treatment; he was getting it (without premedication) with Metrazol, and it was rough.

One day they had not quite matched the dosage to his increasing physical tolerance for the drug, and he began to go into shock in full consciousness. Several times he passed out but then returned to the body consciously, still in the shock. Once, on the edge of returning to consciousness, he heard someone screaming. "God!" the cry went. "God! . . . Help! . . . God help me! . . . God! . . . God! . . . God! . . ." For a while the man wondered calmly and objectively who was doing the screaming. Then his focus changed, and suddenly he knew that it was *he himself* who was screaming.

Afterward, when he had a chance to think it over, the man was surprised, because he was a cast-iron atheist and had been for many years. He realized then for the first time, and upon further observation and reflection very much more so, that there are levels of being at which no man is an atheist. He saw that atheism is a phenomenon strictly confined to people who do not know their own depths.

The above is an example of low-low prayer, and it really is built into every one of us, deep, deep down. Prayer in the most literal sense is an instinct.

Prayer also is an art. When we have recovered our animal-vegetable instinct for prayer (which is apt to restore our health and to give us a considerable measure of release from neurotic self-concern), we are ready to advance to the specifically human levels of prayer, to the *art* of prayer, properly so-called. Nothing fancy is indicated here. It is just the threshold where, consciously and with full human rationality and freedom, we reach out to contact and offer ourselves to the Higher Power who broods above us and within us, to be "a reasonable, holy, and living sacrifice" unto him.

There are no rules of prayer in the sense of stiff regulations or sharp do's and don'ts. But over the centuries a lot of major and minor artists in prayer have left us a rich legacy of records of their experiments, their trials and errors and achievements, their discoveries and surprises, their techniques and their soarings above technique. This literature constitutes a gold mine of wisdom for our encouragement and instruction in learning the art of arts.

Beyond instinct and art, prayer is breath. Beyond intentional training, as its flower and fruit, there is the life of spontaneous aspiration, receiving and reciprocating continuously the love of God and mediating it to the creation, rising above personal self-consciousness as a sort of higher instinctual octave in which the rationality and self-direction of the human nature are transformed in a greater Intelligence and greater Guidance. Prayer now is as steady as the heartbeat and the breath, but with full and joyous conscious participation. It is indeed the synchronization of the human breath and the Holy Breath. Prayer at this level is not learned from books or from people, but from the Holy Spirit of God himself.

Prayer is the key both to the human heart and to the Heart of God. In the use of this precious key there are three great traditional practices, and every child of God who is groping his way back toward his Father's house should know them.

The Practice of Abandonment

How can you clear the way to true prayer? At any moment shock or emergency may clear it spontaneously and abruptly (but temporarily). But otherwise two steps are indicated: (1) a moral cleanup, which we have already considered, and (2) a surrender to God, a giving up of the self-direction of your life and affairs and abandoning them to the divine will and the divine providence. For convenience, we can call this act just "surrender" or "abandonment."

Surrender seems to be a firm and indispensable prerequisite to any real spiritual progress. Many balked or bogged-down attempts to realize God can be traced back to failure or refusal to surrender.

Abandonment or surrender is a definite, technical, critical phase of the truth-seeking life. If you want to work with it, you must first understand what it is and then realize that it is not only important but inescapable as a condition which permits real, living, breathing, knowing contact with the Higher Consciousness. In brief, if you want to get to God, you've got to surrender.

So what is surrender? It is a giving up of the egotistical, self-centered notion that I, just as I am, can direct and run my own life effectively and well. Surrender or abandonment is preceded by a keen appreciation that without conscious co-operation with the Higher Power I do not properly know how to eat, to sleep, to work —and most certainly I do not know how to love or pray or rejoice in life.

This realization is not cheap, and, particularly for people with good animal health and a medium to large bank roll, it is exceedingly difficult to grasp at the working level, that is, at the point where it becomes a moving force and not just a pious notion. It is true that nobody can live his life well for a single day without intentional contact with God. But people who are "doing all right" in this world find it hard to believe, to know, and to *feel* this truth.

What can be done about it? First of all, you must be alert to a certain kind of event which varies greatly from person to person but which no life is without: crises, disasters, tragedies, injuries, and illnesses. These are great aids in the process we have been considering. A major aspect of their significance in the human moral and spiritual economy no doubt lies in just this peculiar power to help in abandonment to God.

When these things come, you are wasting your life if you do not seize them as means to bring you to surrender at the feet of the Lord. The harder it is to take, the more powerful is the potion. It is necessary to refuse the false anodynes of whining and self-pity, to reject the gall of cursing and complaint, and to gaze steadily through the darkness toward the ever-present Light. But *then* when the scalding cup of pain or loss is drunk right down, it takes you into the Presence as nothing else can.

Of course disasters and illness are not to be self-induced or

God's Will: How to Know It and Do It   135

self-sought. In many a soul there is a monkey-governed twist, usually buried but still often effective, which draws the person toward sickness and accident for wretched and weirdly egotistical reasons of its own. Do not say too quickly that you could not be guilty of this; you may be; it is a very common condition. The probe of truth must be thrust right into this stinking boil. Any tendency in yourself toward fraudulent illness or tricked-up tragedy should be faced, watched, and strictly denied influence in the heart or mind or body. You will never know the redemptive power of real pain unless you have rejected phony pain. The true cross is the straight road to the Highest, but false crosses are about the meanest and most injurious kind of pretending, conscious or "unconscious," to which a human being can stoop. If you must play-act, do not do it at this level. It is not just bad theater; it is a travesty of the deepest revelation of truth that this earth has yet received. Do not dare to provoke or improvise the most terrible of all mysteries. Leave the cross alone until it is given to you. *Do not fake suffering.* It is the gateway to God. The Father on his sapphire throne expects his own anointed Son—not some miserable ham.

Suppose you are not in any difficulty. Suppose you *are* "doing all right" in this life. Suppose you are not caught in false suffering and the aid of genuine suffering is denied to you for the present. Suppose at the same time you do see the necessity for surrender to God and abandonment to his will and providence. Suppose you are willing to surrender, so far as you can be willing in spiritual sleep (which is where most of us are, remember?). Where do you go from there?

Well, if your experience is like a lot of other people's, you lock yourself in the bedroom or bathroom or wherever you have decided to experiment with conversation with That which is above you, and you say something like this: "Hello. Are you there? I'm feeling well, thank you, and actually doing rather well, it seems (correct me if I'm wrong). But I've been hearing about a thing called surrender. It makes sense to me, and I want to try it. I see that it probably would be good for me, and that it may be necessary in any event. Please make me understand it and give me the grace to do it, or begin doing it."

Then when you emerge from prayer, during the rest of that day you try to *get out of the driver's seat.* Try to let God run your life and you go along for the ride. The secret is just to remember to do it. The actual attitude and act are not so hard, but we are heavily prone to forget. Patiently and with good humor in spite of failures, make the effort to remember. Make little quick prayers for the grace to remember. It is simple but tricky. Just remember—to remember. You cannot realize how much hangs on remembering until you try it. But first you've got to remember to try it.

The monkey really hates this business and will inevitably counterattack on two fronts, first with a tweezers and later on with a wrench. His first tweezer touches, in the phase in which you are trying to remember to surrender, are so light and so deft that you have to be an old campaigner to notice what is actually going on. All a neophyte can observe is that, somehow, in spite of good intentions, he is forgetting to surrender. Automatically, with no conscious knowledge of how it happened, again and again he winds up in the driver's seat and running his own life like a fire engine. So he tries again to surrender, and again, but less often as time goes on.

After a while, when he does remember his original intention, he may feel a faint discouragement and distaste for the effort involved. Somewhat later it may occur to him that the whole idea is probably unsound. "After all, why wind up throwing your life to the winds and acting eventually perhaps like a spineless dope. . . . A man does need to have at least some of the control of his own affairs in his own hands. . . . It's only natural. . . . Responsibility is something we all have to remember" etc., etc., etc. By this time, of course, the end of the enterprise is in sight. The monkey wrench never appears at all, and soon Jocko will feel safe to sheathe the tweezers until the next nasty little threat to the kingdom of ego arises, if it ever does.

Maybe you think this is a jolly overportrayal. On the contrary, it is taken right from life, my own and others'. And, again, it is much more likely to happen to you than you can possibly realize until you yourself really try to surrender.

What is the proper strategy in such a case? I say it is not just to go on making harder efforts and kicking yourself for a chump when you fail. The ground needs to be reconnoitered on an empirical basis. And what do we find? Those whom the adversary succeeds in tricking right out of the game are the *loners*. So the secret lies not only in more determined efforts but in more determined

God's Will: How to Know It and Do It

efforts *plus* constant association with other people who are making the same effort. Here you really need the group, the *ecclesia*, to lift you up and carry you on. You need pretty regularly to swap experience with other laborers on this particular section of road. You need, also, occasional contact with journeymen who are further along, who are in veritable contact with the Master, and who can reflect his know-how back into this rocky stretch in which the ego is first learning to let go and let God.

Maybe you are remembering that wrench and wondering when the monkey uses it. He brings it to bear if and when the tweezers fail. If you succeed over any considerable period of time in remembering to surrender, if you really do begin to get out of the driver's seat, if the attitude of abandonment begins to become habitual and to involve the heart—then the infernal little chum begins to clobber you with the wrench. That is to say, he drops the subtlety, steps out in the open, and confronts you directly with his own special version of an old production called "Frank and Fearful Possibilities." The lines go something like this: "What! Are we to have *no* part in the government of our very own life—*none at all?* Does God wish to destroy our *integrity?* Having given us the innate and sacred thirst for freedom, does he now propose to make a *puppet* of us? Is he after all a God of *slaves?* Are we finally to have no privacy, no choice, no adventure, no noble individual and personal striving? Is all to be swallowed up in this ghastly 'surrender'? It's a swindle and a shame. To hell with it. We won't have it, that's all. We will just forget all about it and get back to normal, back to sanity, back to real life. . . ."

This kind of concern—whatever the language in which it may appear—is a heavy-handed attack against our progress toward full abandonment, and it is likely to strike home not only in the mind but in the deep emotional nature. Something very profoundly rooted in the primordial part of every human being fiercely and passionately does not wish to surrender to anybody or anything. Particularly it does not wish to be subordinate to a "God" in which it does not believe and which it regards as a piece of pious idiocy (if it is under the sway of Ahriman, the devil of obscuration and materialism) or a God whom it knows to be real but whom at the same time it loathes and execrates as a cosmic and eternal enemy (if it is under the rule of Lucifer, the devil of pride and false light).

The monkey aspect finally is seen to be an amiable and misleading disguise. The real face of the enemy is a death's-head, and it is mortally opposed to the surrender of this life into the hands of its Creator.

In order to press firmly on toward effective and sustained abandonment, you must remember first of all to practice the art, and then you must be prepared to persist in the face of a determined and prolonged enmity, entrenched deeply within yourself. The opposition is so heavy just because the lines here are clearly drawn and the stakes are high. And the adversary knows it.

Fortunately in this crucial area there is available today a written work (published as two books) which mediates to the life of him who reads, understands, and receives its message the most authentic and workable wisdom of God.

I wish I could tell you that these two little books (*Self-Abandonment to Divine Providence* and *Spiritual Letters* by J. P. de Caussade) are easy to read and to follow, but at first I did not find them so. Some beginners do, and some do not. The books were recommended to me by a friend whose insight I greatly respect, and therefore I tried earnestly to study them and to practice what they teach. But I got almost nowhere; perhaps it would be correct to say really nowhere at all. And after some months I gave up and put this particular source into my suspense account, intending to return to it later. A considerable period of time ensued, during which my search for truth ran along other lines.

Then suddenly I found myself in the midst of one of the worst difficulties of my life. It involved my family and my marriage, and both my physical and emotional natures were so influenced that my mind was clouded and literally numb—at a time when, perhaps as never before in this lifetime, I needed to think clearly; a great deal depended on it. For some time I was quite unable to read, although at the same time I felt a keen need for the help certain kinds of reading can bring. And then one day I found myself reading *Self-Abandonment*, and not only reading it but drinking into my soul the precious light it has to give.

I could read no other book during the time my trouble lasted (and it continued over some months), but I could and I did regularly read *Self-Abandonment*. Never, never before had I even half-realized the power of a holy man of God to reach out over the centuries and across the oceans and to give to a modern man, so far separated from him in the flesh, his blessing of living knowledge, living courage, living love.

The full name of the man into whose debt I have so deeply entered in this way is Father Jean Pierre de Caussade. He was a Jesuit, living in France from 1675 to 1751. The writings in which his greatest work is embodied are two collections of letters, incomplete and incorrectly copied, of counsel and encouragement addressed to a few Visitation nuns.

Before you decide that you could not receive help from so unlikely a person, do yourself the favor of sampling him. He is one of the men who have made me practically, unsentimentally, and utterly sure of the communion of saints.

Please don't be put off by the fact that Caussade writes in the style of another century or (if you are a Protestant) that he is a member of the Roman Church. Don't mind that he is not a clever or amusing writer. As a matter of fact he writes very well, but he is overwhelmingly an influence, not at all an entertainer. He is a rare genius in understanding and communicating the art of surrender. Be patient in opening yourself to him. If you can receive him, he is a tremendous teacher. I wish there were more like him, but it seems to me that, in this great specialty of abandonment to God, in the West and East he stands alone. All men of God know and teach abandonment, but I have encountered none who teaches it so singlemindedly, with such passion and flame, and yet with such clear common sense and practical concern. Maybe I am partial to this man. Read him yourself and be my judge.

Father de Caussade is quoted twice already in this present book. I will not quote him further. I would not rob you of the joy, the profit, and perhaps the blessed and strengthening difficulty of reading his great words in his great books themselves. I will only say in summation: if you wish to surrender your life to God, read Caussade. Do what he tells you to do. Find and work with your friends in God who also are entering the deep, sweet, swift current of abandonment. Keep it up. Do not be discouraged. Of all ways, this way leads most directly to true prayer, and to the Goal of prayer.

The heart of Caussade's teaching is in what he calls "the sacrament of the present moment." It is not necessary, he says, to know the will of God in advance but *to accept it,*[*] to abandon yourself to it as it unfolds in your life *from moment to moment*. Ordinarily we get all mixed up about the will of God because we are straining to know it either in advance or in retrospect. We want to know what it is going to be two weeks from now or tomorrow or five minutes from now. Or we brood and scratch over what it might have been yesterday or five years ago or in 486 B.C. We jump and bounce around like fleas in a windstorm, while the thing we are seeking and forever missing lies in the calm eye of God's *present* intention for us. The human mind continually and obsessively and indeed pathologically runs behind or ahead of the point where the will of God actually may be contacted and accepted, if not "known." We crave forecasts and enjoy rehearsals. We want elaborate descriptions and blueprints of God's will, whereas he steadily and faithfully gives us his whole will in the living moment.

This makes complete sense if you will take the trouble to think it through. To state it properly is easy. But to grasp and hold it is exceedingly difficult, because it is encapsulated in a stubborn illusion and a stubborn habit of thought to the contrary. Hard-won flashes of the truth of the magic of *now* are likely to disappear as mysteriously as they appear.

Caussade's method is a combination of "watching," i.e., continual awareness of your own life, moment by moment, and the practice of the Presence of God, i.e., unwavering attention to God's grace and his will as they bear upon you from moment to moment—plus a patiently and diligently repeated act of abandonment to the divine providence, in the exact circumstances of your daily life, from moment to moment.

The secret—and it is a great one—is in focusing upon the present moment. Caussade's gift lies in himself realizing, and then in transmitting to us, a single tremendous insight: the truth that once you are centered in the present moment, the sacrament of surrender becomes simple, easy, joyful. It is not a burden and not a

---

[*] How can you accept something you don't know and don't understand? It's easy. You do it all the time. You breathe and you eat, but do you really *know* air? and do you *understand* food? Of course not. If acceptance did not naturally and continually precede full knowing, none of us could live the day out. What Caussade recommends is as simple and sensible as eating a steak. You don't require a laboratory analysis in advance. You just have a good look at it, take a good sniff of it, and then you sink your teeth into it.

God's Will: How to Know It and Do It

drudgery; it is a leap, a shout, a kiss, a dance. It is not "ideally" so but actually and literally so. And it is so not for healthy and rich folks only but also—and perhaps especially—for the inadequate and the undistinguished.

If you are looking for an easy way to God, this is it. The ease lies not in the absence of pain or trouble but in the fact that pain and trouble and everything else are caught up into the deluge of God's love and mercy from moment to moment. You don't have to be a spiritual giant to do this; all you have to do is remember, from moment to moment. You may not do it very often to begin with, but do it as often as you can; that is absolutely all that is required.†

Believe me, a miracle takes place every time you succeed in entering the present moment and surrendering. The "doing" of it is quite possible for anyone. To sustain it, however, is frankly not easy. We forget. Or we lose the blessed simplicity necessary to enter into a simple grace, and begin again automatically and thoughtlessly to seek complicated "solutions" that are going to help us, when? . . . tomorrow!

But abandonment must be practiced, and can only be practiced, *now*. We must ask God what he wants of us *now*. We must ask him for what we need *now*. We must open our eyes and our ears and our hearts to what he is telling us *now*.

Experiment with this in your life, now, today, beginning with this moment. Do not juggle words about it or get into inner arguments about it. That is just exactly the monkey's dish. He has a great assortment of "reasons" why so simple and effective a practice as abandonment to God from moment to moment "won't work." It "excludes foresight," of course, and it "cuts out memory," and it "leaves no place for planning." (Ah, planning! *That's* what we need more of, isn't it?) Let this kind of talk run on inside yourself if you want to, but try to see how much captious gibberish

---

† We must beware of misunderstandings at the extremes of such practices as self-abandonment. Because it is so easy at the beginning extreme, let us never forget that at the other and final extreme abandonment is the greatest of all difficulties. Not just the practice of surrender as a discipline but the utterly effective, final, and irrevocable self-abandonment of the spirit into the hands of the Father—the act which Christ Jesus accomplished upon the cross—this is beyond our view at this time. All prayer, all spiritual life, leads toward it, but it is beyond the scope of the present discussion. (See Jean-Nicolas Grou, *Manual for Interior Souls*, Chapter LXIII, "On Entire Abandonment.")

is mixed up in it. And inner debates, even without the gibberish, never yet brought anybody to God.

If you will postpone the grand analysis and get on with the *practice*, you will find that, as the moments of self-abandonment to God's will flow into hours, and as the hours flow into days, foresight and memory are not lost or weakened. They are clarified, rather, and they find their proper places as servants, not tyrants. They are not forever getting in the way now. They do not bug you so much any more.

Abandonment to God *is* prayer, and it is also the great preparation for other kinds of prayer: "the practice of penetrating the cloud," for example.

The Practice of Penetrating the Cloud

Nearly all men live in a cloud of ignorance of God. "Penetrating the cloud" is a term which describes a certain kind of prayer: broadly speaking, it is prayer done in *time specifically set aside* for the purpose.

There are ways of praying throughout the day in the midst of other activities, and there are even ways of praying continuously. But the particular kind of prayer which is practiced in specially reserved time every day occupies a position of central importance in the way to God, and very few can get along without it.

You must learn how to practice penetrating the cloud, but even before that you must *find the time* for it.

Further, you must continue without interruption to find the time for it. A few days or weeks of this practice will do you no harm, but they probably won't do you much good, either. The practice of penetrating the cloud must become like eating your meals, sleeping, or going to the bathroom. When the time is at hand every day, you just do it, period. Unless you can put it on that basis (and everybody can who really wants to), you are merely stirring around in the cloud, not practicing the penetration of it.

Time must be set aside at least five days a week and preferably six. (You may want to take a seventh-day rest, even from this blessed kind of work.) Morning is best for most people, although evenings will do, and any time of day is all right in a pinch. It should be done at the same time every day; a few lapses on this point are permissible, but not many.

How much time every day? At least ten minutes to begin with. That is my own estimate of the need; opinions vary widely; one of the most experienced men I know says you cannot do much in less than half an hour. Ten minutes obviously is less than a good working minimum, but it is a *possible* time for anyone, and it will serve to get things going and keep them going. For a starter, it is not presumptuous and not a strain, and nobody can lie his way out of the daily appointment on the plea that it is too much for him. It seems to me that in many cases these advantages outweigh the admittedly grave disadvantages of so short a time.

An old man who was teaching me started me out at this level. He instructed me in what he called the "wedge system." Said he: "Ten-minute periods faithfully and regularly held every day are far better than half-hour sessions held occasionally or in spurts. When the ten-minute wedge is firmly inserted in your daily routine (and this might take six months or a year), then you can drive it in a little further, maybe expanding the time to fifteen minutes—later to twenty—later to thirty—and so on, up to what your real capacity for daily practice of this kind turns out to be. It is wrong to lag, but it is no good trying to be a saint overnight, either."

When I first began to listen to this man, he questioned me about my habits of prayer. "How long do you go?" he asked. "About two hours at a stretch," I said, trying with a great effort to appear modest. (It was true. I was less than twelve months out of a moral and physical collapse in which I had been floundering for years. But I had been reading books, and I am inclined to excess, and I *was* practicing, at that time, two hours at a clip.)

My old spiritual father looked at me narrowly.

"You do this every day?" he said.

"Well, no," I said.

"You do it for a few days and then skip a few days?" he said.

"Yes," I said.

"And sometimes you skip a few weeks, perhaps?" he said.

"That's the way it goes," I said.

"Ten minutes a day for you," he said. "No less *and no more.*"

Thank God I found my way into the old man's hands. In another few months I probably would have blown some fuses or soured myself on prayer forevermore, the way I was going. The point is, to begin with a time period which is not beyond your ability to sustain, however humble and indeed however humiliating that period may be. If you want to be a star performer, fine; but take it easy, at least at first. There are real heroes in this game, and it is a good thing to emulate them, but it is also possible to get something like a spiritual hernia. If the ten-minute beginner's time really is too easy for you, by all means increase it, but not too much and not too fast. On the other hand, after a while if you are not succeeding in keeping the ten minutes clear at least five days a week without fail, drop back to five minutes. Find out what time you *can* keep, and *keep it*. Then you are on the way, not otherwise.

Now a word about the place in which you practice. So far as possible it should be the same place every day. It would not serve our purpose here to go into the reasons why, but it does make a difference. (If you are traveling, you just do the best you can on the road, using whatever places are available, and try to stay to a regular place at home.) A bedroom is fine. A bathroom will do. The room should have a door with a lock or bolt, if possible. Again, this is not the occasion to develop the rationale, but it makes a difference to work in a room secured against accidental intrusion. A certain animal level of the mind remains distractingly alert unless it knows it won't be watched or butted into from the outside. Why waste time trying to argue with it or reassure it, when you can so easily just lock the door?

How do you use the time? That depends. There are many sources of instruction in the art of penetrating the cloud. Using them as little or as much as makes sense, you've got to find your own way, or rather, the application of the one Way in your particular case. Some common knowledge along these lines, arising out of my own experience and the experience of those who have shared their lives with me, may be of interest here. The following discussion, of course, is directed to the problem of the householder, the man or woman in the world. The science of penetrating the cloud is very highly developed in certain religious communities and particularly in enclosed orders. On the other hand, as William Temple has pointed out, God is by no means exclusively or even preferentially interested in the formally religious affairs of the world. The monk in his oratory may *or he may not* have clearer access to the ear of

God than the father of a family locked in his bedroom for a few minutes before rushing off to his day's work.

The attitude, the mental and emotional set, with which you approach and enter your daily period of prayer is important. You have put aside a time for a meeting with God. Either it is that, or it is nonsense. If the President of the United States agreed to meet with you and to give special consideration to your personal, family, and vocational needs, you would come up to the meeting with your face washed, your attention well focused, and your heartbeat stepped up. In prayer, either you are meeting with the Executive and Sovereign Monarch of the Universe, or you are kidding yourself. Make up your mind which it is. And try to let the truth sink home, even as you approach prayer. Try to get out of the area of lukewarm half-knowledge and half-belief; it is almost worse than no knowledge and unbelief. Either you are a silly fool muttering to himself, or you are entering into an interview with the omnipotent God. This hasn't anything to do with your spiritual status or capacity. It is just a cold-turkey question with a cold-turkey answer. Either you are talking to Papa or you aren't. If you are, go in on your toes.

The first consideration, when your time has come around and you have entered your room and locked the door, is what to do with the body.

There are a number of possibilities. You may want to walk around for a while at first, just to get loosened up. This is a good time to stretch and yawn a bit, to break up tensions. And sometimes it is good to pray standing. Prayer while standing upright has a long traditional background, and in certain conditions nothing is the equal of it.

Kneeling, of course, has a profound effect upon both body and soul. For me, kneeling was a crisis in my return to communion with God. Over many years I had lost my faith completely, and for a while even after I began trying again it was exceedingly difficult for me to pray at all. Then I got to the point where I could pray, but I could not bring myself to kneel. At last I slid out of bed where I had been trying to pray one cold February night, and I actually *did* kneel—and it made a great diffcrence. It broke something down inside me. After so long a struggle to rule in my own place, it was an act of profound significance to put myself finally in this position before God—the attitude of a servant before his liege Lord. It spoke more powerfully in my soul than any words I could have uttered. It took me at once below and above my proud mind. It not only moved me, it moved the Lord himself toward me. I don't have to guess about this. I know.

So the physical position you take in prayer is not a matter of indifference; it is something worth reverently experimenting with. Standing up, kneeling, and lying down are positions of great utility in certain states of mind and heart. But each of them has its disadvantages, too. Standing or kneeling over any considerable period of time usually induces a degree of fatigue and discomfort which is distracting. Praying while lying down is peculiarly useful if you are ill or injured. Some of the very greatest prayers, the prayers of the dying, are uttered in this position. Ordinarily, however, lying-down prayer is apt to go very well for a while but then to merge ever so gently into sleep. This is not a bad way to end the day, but it is not suited to the regular attempt consciously to enter and to remain in the presence of the living God.

The physical disposition which seems best suited to sustained work in practicing the penetration of the cloud is sitting. Just plain old comfortable sitting down. With certain qualifications, however. Sitting must not be confused with its cousin, lounging. That is one position which is definitely contra-indicated. You would not lounge in an important business interview; do not lounge in the presence of the Creator. Sit as comfortably as possible, but do not slump, sag, twist, lean, crouch, coil up, or collapse. We get into these contortions so often that they actually come to seem comfortable; but if you try to stay in one position for more than a minute or two, as you must in prayer, you will find that any of the varieties of lounging certainly are not comfortable; indeed, they are very soon unendurable.

You may sit in a chair or cross-legged on a folded blanket on the floor. Sit bolt upright, with the spine straight and the head floating lightly on top like a pumpkin balanced on a pole. Then, while remaining bolt upright, deliberately relax. *It can be done.* Relaxation need not involve wilting. Straight does not mean stiff. There is a golden mean between the ramrod and the dishrag. Quite easily, by a simple and direct effort, you can achieve real relaxation while simultaneously sitting up as straight as a string. Just try it, and see.

The upright, relaxed, sitting position—with the hands resting on the thighs or folded in the lap, and (if you are in a chair) with the feet about three to six inches apart and flat on the floor—is wonderfully comfortable. It takes some learning and some getting used to, of course. You must learn particularly how to relax the muscles of the face, back, and neck. But the position is amazingly easy and invigorating when achieved, and you can remain in it for considerable periods of time with little attention, little effort, little fatigue, and therefore with little distraction. At the same time the very physical attitude tends to keep the mind awake and alert. For these reasons it is ideally adapted to the practice in which, by deliberate effort, you intend to present yourself—body, soul, and spirit—at the court of the Great King.

Now something needs to be said about breathing. When you are sitting right and the mind is released somewhat from overconcern with the physical frame, the attention is likely to be drawn to the breathing. Ordinarily we pay little or no attention to breathing, unless we have to run for a bus or something and the laboring and aching lungs then force us to notice. But in prayer, when the body is quiet and the mind is alert, the breath is apt to become prominent in the field of awareness.

Do not try to ignore it. Without considerable training, it is impossible to do so, and it is not necessarily desirable to do so. At the same time, do not deal with the breath foolishly or recklessly. Right at this point certain things may be done which are powerfully effective, i.e., which will produce quick and striking and real results, but which for that very reason are exceedingly dangerous unless they are done under the direct guidance of an experienced and competent instructor. There is a delicate and intimate connection between the instinctive rhythm of the breath and the total instinctive balance of the body. Whoever deliberately assumes control of the breath had better know what he is doing.

Specifically: *do not do any "breathing exercises," do not manipulate, direct, "control," or play any tricks at all with the breath,* unless you are in immediate, personal, and responsible touch with someone *who really knows what needs to be known* about the relationship of the human breath to the entire human body-and-mind.

You can do the following with complete safety. When the breath calls attention to itself, give it what it asks: attention. Give it all the time it wants, too; do not be in a hurry to move on to something else. Observe the breathing. Let the mind dwell upon it, and *in it*. This in itself has a soothing and balancing effect upon the whole organism. Quietly, calmly, noncritically, and nonmanipulatively, notice the breath. Observe it in the nose, in the throat, in the lungs, in the head. Observe how it penetrates to parts of yourself you never suspected it would; indeed, on a subtle level it fills the entire body. All you are doing is noticing the breathing. You are merely paying attention (for once). Without directing it, *allow* it to become quiet—peaceful—steady—unhurried—quiet—peaceful—steady—unhurried—quiet—peaceful—steady—unhurried. . . .

You may combine your first prayers with your breathing. You may say "Thy kingdom come" on the in breath and "Thy will be done" on the out breath, for example. Or you may repeat the name of God calmly a number of times on the in breath and say "Bless me . . . bless me . . ." on the out breath. If this is a possible thing for you, the Spirit of Truth quite clearly will teach you your own best ways of doing it.

Even this elementary degree and amount of inner working may open the way to marked changes in you. Already there may occur, at a certain point, a definite change of consciousness. It may be something rather like the opposite of going to sleep, a gentle but pronounced kind of awakening. It may be accompanied by joy. It may induce tears. There are a number of ways in which it may come; to describe them in too much detail would not help and might hinder by suggesting something which, if it is to come at all, should come of its own motion and the motion of grace. If this does happen, and if you are unprepared for it, you may find yourself retreating hastily. But there is no cause for alarm. You have done nothing wrong or bad in this attempt at communion, nothing unauthorized by the laws of God, man, or common sense. There is nothing to be upset about. You have just succeeded a little bit, that is all. It is quite safe to go on praying. God surely will guide and protect you.

At the same time it is well to take the changes which may occur in prayer very seriously. Either prayer goes nowhere (I wonder if it ever does go just nowhere?), or it goes toward the great deeps, the ocean of psychic and spiritual life upon which every personal life floats. One need never be uneasy in sincerely approaching God, but

God's Will: How to Know It and Do It 149

it is a good thing for the mind to be somewhat prepared for what may happen. This is a razor's edge. If there is too much mental preparation, it leads to guessing games, pseudo experiences, and a shameful kind of egotism. If there is too little preparation, you may be unduly and unnecessarily frightened when things really do begin to happen in prayer.

There are ways of briefly covering the ground in advance, and they may help in this connection. After having made your preparations and before actually beginning to attempt any movement toward the deep contact, you may address yourself to the Holy Spirit in some such terms as these:

"I am about to begin to pray again, but as usual I really do not know what I am doing. I have read books and talked to men, but I am still ignorant and a fool, now possibly more than ever. And at the same time, although I can talk glibly about my attraction toward you, when the Light begins to appear I am a coward. When the Door begins to open I am afraid. I have withdrawn, you know how many times.

"Now take pity on me again. In my deepest heart I do seek you, and I want you regardless of consequences. Let me die if necessary in the act of seeking which is about to take place. On the other hand, let me not ignorantly injure these instruments, this body and mind, which you have put under my care and control.

"Guard me against my timidity and lack of courage on the one side and my rashness and blind irresponsibility on the other. Be my guide and my strength against these enemies within. And by thy grace, let me confidently and easily and with childish trust now enter into prayer."

If no changes in your mental, physical, or conscious state occur, that is fine and perfectly normal, too. Progress in prayer does not depend on their happening or on their not happening. If they do not happen, be of good cheer and proceed without them. Some masters of prayer regard this as the more auspicious way.

If changes do occur, proceed with caution but without worry or fear. You cannot choose which of these ways you will go. Temperament and many other factors enter in. Go the way God leads you. Do not be discouraged by lack of "results," and do not be afraid when results appear.

Spiritual awakening, in or out of prayer, is one thing; psychic phenomenalism, in or out of prayer, is something else again; the two may be related, and they may be quite unrelated or even opposed. There are no hard and fast formulas for distinguishing them; you need to rely heavily and directly on the inner Spirit of Truth.

In certain natures there may be physical or mental phenomena, visions or monitions for example, even quite early in the practice. Your attitude in the face of such happenings must be quietly but firmly neutral. You must turn immediately to the Supreme Guide with some such words as these: "I wish neither to accept nor to reject these things for their sake or for my own sake. I want only the truth. If what is occurring here is of the truth, let me receive it, and please help me in receiving it. If it is any other kind of intrusion, let it be removed at your pleasure, and show me how to bear myself toward it while it remains, or if it recurs." Such a prayer never falls on empty air. The Lord will direct you in terms that are right and effective for you. You can count on it.

Visions and such things *may* be messages or messengers from God; or they may be a kind of trash—or worse. They may bring true enlightenment and encouragement; and they may lead off into the bogs and sloughs of the lower psychic realms—*where egotism flourishes as nowhere else in all the worlds,* where truth and falsehood are jammed together in one vast suet pudding, where the psychic and the spiritual are hopelessly confused, and where the life of prayer quickly may be sucked down to death, drowned in silly and ghoulish parodies.

Complete protection against these dangers, however, is always at hand. If you cling sincerely to honesty and humility, and if you turn quietly and constantly to the ever-present Light of Light for help, then visionary and phenomenal experiences need not trouble you, by their presence or by their absence. You may be helped by reading St. John of the Cross in this regard (*The Complete Works,* Vol. I, pp. 143–58).

Now may we return to the actual details of practice. To begin the period of prayer, sometimes a few minutes of reading, in the Bible or other basic work, are helpful. The saying of a favorite prayer or two is a good way to get started, the Lord's Prayer, for example, or the Twenty-third Psalm, or the Collect for Purity ("Almighty God, unto whom all hearts are open, all desires known, and from whom no secrets are hid, cleanse the thoughts of our hearts by

God's Will: How to Know It and Do It 151

the inspiration of thy Holy Spirit, that we may perfectly love thee and worthily magnify thy Holy Name. . . ."), or the Serenity Prayer ("God grant me the serenity to accept the things I cannot change, courage to change the things I can, and wisdom to know the difference").

When the body is composed, when the breathing is easy and steady, and when the mind and breath are in harmony, you can say such prayers in a way not ordinarily possible: slowly, a phrase at a time, with long, calm pauses in between, during which new and wonderful light is apt to break out from the old familiar words.

We have stayed close to the common, ordinary, strictly kindergarten aspects of the kind of prayer which may be called the practice of penetrating the cloud. But do not for that reason underestimate the power and the possibilities in such an approach. If you do your part in it, your life is highly apt to be revolutionized. If—say, for a couple of years—you will do no more, but also no less, than the simple everyday practice outlined in this chapter, if you will faithfully do the elementary work, take the elementary precautions, and observe the elementary rules, expanding your daily time as you are able, then your guidance into deeper and higher regions of communion with God will be very sure and *very* competent, because it will come unmistakably from God himself.

A book like this present one can do little more than to give you hints on getting started and to suggest other and more detailed sources for your immediate and future consideration. Actual progress will be very much a matter between you and God.

One final word of caution: You sometimes hear talk of "making the mind a blank" in prayer. This is impossible. The true mind already is a blank, a void, a virgin. But the blank is normally filled with objects, with phenomena, with images—in medieval terminology, with "creatures." Those who speak of making the mind a blank actually are talking, often quite ignorantly and nearly always prematurely, about the advanced, technical, and difficult stage of spiritual training known in both the West and the East as "detachment from sense objects" and in the Rhineland school and in other schools of Christian teaching as "leaving imagery" or "leaving the creatures." It does not mean that you make your mind a blank, and it does not mean that you leave your wife or your dog or your automobile and go away somewhere. It means something quite else.

152   *Invitation to a Great Experiment*

When the time comes to do it, by grace you will know how to do it.

You must leave the creatures, sure enough, but *you can do it too soon* and you can get yourself terrifically worked up and continentally confused in the attempt, unless the Spirit is leading you directly, or unless you are in touch with experienced compeers and teachers. Read what the *Theologia Germanica* says on the subject (Chapter XIII, entitled "How a man often casts aside imagery too soon"):

> Tauler says: There be some men at the present time who take leave of imagery too soon, before truth and knowledge have shown them the way thence; hence they are scarcely or perhaps never after able to understand the Truth aright. For such men will follow no one, hold fast to their own understandings, and desire to fly before they are fledged. They would fain mount up to heaven in one flight. . . .

When it is time to go to high school, unmistakable signs will appear. Meanwhile just plug along with the kids in grade school. It is safer and surer and better all around. Remember that you cannot normally make your mind a blank, in prayer, sleep, meditation, or any other condition. Indescribable states most certainly may be reached, but not blanks. Even deep sleep, trance, anesthesia, and coma are not blank areas in the life, as often popularly assumed. They are states of which the ordinary man retains no memory. There are men who know how to enter and leave such states with intact memory, and they report something *very much other* than a blank.

The "void" (*sunyata*) of Buddhism, the "Unqualified Absolute" (*Nirguna Brahman*) of Advaita Vedanta, and the "divine darkness" of the deepest and most orthodox of Christian mysticism‡ —these are simply terms which cannot possibly be understood, and can hardly fail to be actively misunderstood, by an unprepared and inexperienced person. There is nothing snobbish about this. It is just a plain fact. It is very much the part of wisdom to leave such considerations humbly and reverently aside until some years of training and actual practice in prayer have been lived through. Nothing is accomplished by mental groping and flights of speculation on the margins of such abysses of Reality, and much harm is

‡ See St. Dionysius (Dionysius the Areopagite), the *Mystical Theology*.

God's Will: How to Know It and Do It 153

done if the heart is filled with hopes and horrors that have no basis in the Truth.

Do what you can do with your mind, especially in prayer. You *can* learn to entertain such "creatures"—i.e., such impressions, thoughts and ideas—as by God's will are appropriate and ordained for your present condition. You can learn to see, honestly and steadily, what phenomena do as a matter of fact habitually occur in your particular mind. You can learn to distinguish your true friends from your actual enemies and to extend hospitality to the one and to deny your consent and your vitality to the others. *This* is the inner work for a long time. This is not yet knowledge of God, but it is knowledge of the road to God.

And some day, when the road is clear and the time has come to enter the naked ignorance, stripped of its phenomenal rags, you will be strong and humble and ready for the task. *Then* you may probe out beyond the mind, stabbing with the heart's primordial fire of love into that "cloud of unknowing" which lies between the fallen human being and the face of Almighty God.

I shall not speak of that task here. Certain documents, and certain people, are available, and exceedingly well able, to help you when your time comes. For all I know, of course, you may be ready now. In that case it needs only to say that the books which can help you are well known. There are many, but you may note particularly the works of Poulain, Augustine Baker, Teresa of Jesus, John of the Cross, Walter Hilton, and John of Ruysbroeck.

There is one book which addresses itself (indeed, by its very title) so directly and with such skill and power to the deeper phases of the kind of prayer we are considering that it is worth special attention and study. It is also worth quickly putting aside if you find that it does not suit you at present. Put it aside so that you may come to it again by grace at the time when it *will* be useful for you.

I would hate to steer anyone off who could possibly profit from reading *The Cloud of Unknowing*. But at the same time I take the unknown author's warning, which is set down at length in the Prologue, very seriously. He repeatedly "charges" and "beseeches" the reader—"in the name of the Father and of the Son and of the Holy Ghost" and "by the authority of charity"—to leave the book alone unless you are going to take the time to read it "all over," as he says.

In other words, we are warned that this is not a book for spiritual posy-sniffers or pious dabblers, and that such may be harmed by it. And I agree and entirely believe that *indeed they may be harmed by it.* I would echo the old author in saying earnestly to anyone: "Leave this book alone unless you understand what area of life it is dealing with, and unless you utterly mean business in that area."

The writer of *The Cloud* has a specific list of the kind of characters who should lay off: "Fleshly janglers, open praisers and blamers of themselves or of any other, tellers of trifles, ronners [gossips] and tattlers of tales, and all manner of pinchers [niggardly or greedy types], cared I never that they saw this book." Now maybe you don't fit in any of those quaint old categories, but try this one on for size: ". . . neither they," he says, "nor any of these curious, lettered, or unlearned men."

Here the word "curious" is the key. If it is curiosity—"spiritual," psychological, literary, academic, artistic, vulgar, or any other kind of mere curiosity—that has brought you to *The Cloud of Unknowing* and not a deep heart's hunger for the invisible and inscrutable God, then you have come to the wrong book. So says the man who wrote it, and again I entirely agree.

The Practice of Continuous Prayer

There *is* a way of praying continuously. Not absolutely continuously at first—for not only the in-working of the Holy Spirit but a lot of practice on our own part is required—but continuously for considerable lengths of time, even in the beginning. As you gain proficiency, it is possible in this way to pray for a whole day at a time, without interfering with your duties, but on the contrary with a great gain in light and strength for duties. And finally, I am reliably told and I believe, this practice leads to a point where prayer is absolutely continuous, uninterrupted even by the most demanding occupation or by sleep.

> It would be a misunderstanding of the whole matter if we supposed that the occupations of life are a hindrance to this sort of prayer. On the contrary they are, or at least often may be, our way of practising it and there is a kind of prayer which is rightly named the prayer of action. . . . If an animal action such as eating or

God's Will: How to Know It and Do It

drinking does not interrupt the continuity of prayer, it is still less likely to be interrupted by the labors of body or mind or of any kind of domestic affairs or by the duties of our occupations. There is nothing in any of these concerns in themselves to distract the heart from its union with God, nothing to arrest the actions of the Holy Spirit or the soul's inward conformity with it. That is an understatement; indeed all these things tend to unite us more closely to God and to maintain the hidden communion of the Holy Spirit and the soul.

Grou, *How to Pray*, p. 82

So here is something that starts conveniently low and rises very high indeed. Imagine the revolution that would be accomplished in a life in which prayer had become absolutely continuous! This development is frankly way ahead of most of us, but the practice that leads there starts from where we are, wherever that may be. Furthermore, this is something which no Christian can afford to ignore, because it is commanded to him—not recommended but commanded by clear precept—by the Lord, Christ Jesus himself. Père Grou, a real authority, leaves no doubt at all on that score:

This section on continual prayer requires, both for its own sake and for the consequences which flow from it, to be treated with great care and read with attention.

Men ought always to pray, says the Gospel, *and not to faint* (Luke 18:1).

Let us weigh these words. *We ought:* it is a precept and not a counsel; it concerns a matter of obligation and not a counsel of perfection. If we fail in this we are sinning more or less seriously. *We ought:* it is a general duty which concerns all Christians. It is said not only for ministers of the Church, not only for those who are consecrated by religious vows, but for all those who profess to believe in the Gospel and to follow it as their rule of conduct, whether they live in the world or are withdrawn from it. *Men ought always to pray:* not only to have a fixed time for prayer and not allow a day to pass without prayer, but to make prayer our continual practice, never suspended or interrupted.

That these words: *to pray always*, must be thus understood is shown by what follows: *and never faint*. The Gospel commands us first to pray unceasingly and then forbids us to cease doing so, thus uniting these two ways of expressing one precept. You will not find in all Scriptures a precept which is laid down in stronger or more definite terms.

But this precept, if we understand it as applying to vocal prayer, or even to that form of mental prayer which we call meditation, is plainly impossible. So those who do not recognize any other kind of prayer, have thought themselves justified in restricting the obligation to certain fixed times. No doubt they would be right were there no other way of praying to God, except by the lips or by the application and concentration of the mind.

But the words of the Gospel take us further and might have opened their eyes to the necessity of allowing another kind of prayer, of such a nature that every Christian can practice it unceasingly.

What kind of prayer is this? It is the essence of prayer, the only kind that attracts God's attention and which gives value to all the other kinds, in a word the prayer of the heart. This prayer can continue without interruption, as no other can.

Ibid., pp. 79–80

What the French Roman Catholic master of prayer here calls "prayer of the heart" is designated also by that identical term in a great Christian tradition of which Père Grou hardly can have had any direct knowledge: the Hesychast tradition of the Eastern Orthodox Christian Church.* We shall hear more of that, and of how the Hesychast "prayer of the heart" has been brought down to modern times, in a moment.

Meanwhile, at the outset, I would like to describe in the simplest possible terms one of the most powerful of the methods of inducing and co-operating with continuous prayer of the heart, namely, *japam* or repetition. The very simplicity of this way is for many people the chief obstacle to its serious practice. The sophisticated modern mind often cannot bring itself to admit that anything as simple as repeating the name of God could be effective in life, let alone life-transforming.

Repetition of a name of God, or of a short phrase incorporating a name of God, is basically all you do in this practice. How you do it makes an immense difference, but still that is all you do.

* Indeed, Père Grou seems to be entirely unfamiliar with the Hesychast *method* of attaining continuous prayer of the heart, repetition of "the Prayer of Jesus," and I think we may assume complete nonacquaintance on his part with the Eastern Christian *practice* in this kind of prayer.

Any beginner can use this method with real effect, real results, real benefits. And yet the same method is useful to the proficient approaching the radiant mountaintop of consciously beholding God's very face. I never heard of a method of prayer which covers such a range—which can be practiced in such a potpourri of life conditions by such a variety of persons—with such power and authority on all levels.

We observed before the desirability in some natures of a weekly one-day rest from the practice of penetrating the cloud. Nothing like a vacation from prayer itself was indicated, but only a rest from a specific kind of work in prayer. But no such rest is necessary or desirable in the practice of prayer of the heart. By grace and without forcing it, the nearer it comes to absolutely continuous prayer the better.

Inevitably and immediately, the mind raises questions and objections to *japam* or repetition of God's name. May I say right away that few of the objections are valid, and all of the questions can be fully and satisfactorily answered. We shall see, as we go along.

There is one book which describes—simply and basically and workably—this universal practice of prayer in its deeply traditional Christian form. That book is *The Way of a Pilgrim* (and *The Pilgrim Continues His Way*). Let me first bear witness briefly to my own experience of this great book and this great way of prayer and to the experience of my friends in God who know this blessing, too. Then I shall let the Pilgrim speak for himself, and shall refer you further to the other sources which are qualified to describe this prayer and to instruct you if you are willing to learn it.

I first read *The Pilgrim* twenty-five years ago, and since then I have read it again and again and have practiced the method of prayer it teaches. It has been a great power for good in my life. No book, not even the Bible itself, has been of more practical help to me. Nowhere have I found such clear insight on how to "pray without ceasing." Many friends of mine have had similar experiences with it.

The Abbot of St. Michael's Monastery at Kazan discovered the manuscript of *The Way of a Pilgrim* in possession of one of the monks at Mount Athos. He made a copy of it, and this was printed at Kazan in 1884, the year of the Abbot's death. The name of the author of *The Pilgrim* is not known; all we know is that he was a Russian pilgrim, and in his narrative he tells of his experiences as he wandered about from one holy place to another in Russia and Siberia, evidently in the period after the Crimean War of 1853 and prior to the Liberation of the Serfs, which occurred in 1861. He tells how an old monk, his *starets* or spiritual teacher, taught him the method of prayer which he calls "the Prayer of Jesus." He describes the prayer as follows:

> The continuous interior Prayer of Jesus is a constant, uninterrupted calling upon the divine Name of Jesus with the lips, in spirit, in the heart, while forming a mental picture of his constant presence, and imploring his grace, during every occupation, at all times, in all places, even during sleep. The appeal is couched in these terms: "Lord Jesus Christ, have mercy on me." One who accustoms himself to this appeal experiences so deep a consolation and so great a need to offer the prayer always, that he can no longer live without it, and it will continue to voice itself within him of its own accord.

Specific instructions are given as to how to develop this prayer within oneself, and the objections which inevitably arise in the skeptical mind are met and answered:

> Many so-called enlightened people regard this frequent offering of one and the same prayer as useless and even trifling, calling it mechanical and a thoughtless occupation of simple people. But unfortunately they do not know the secret which is revealed as a result of this mechanical exercise; they do not know how this frequent service of the lips imperceptibly becomes a genuine appeal of the heart, sinks down into the inward life, becomes a delight, becomes as it were, natural to the soul, bringing it light and nourishment and leading it on to union with God.

This type of prayer, of course, is not confined to Christianity. In Hinduism it is called *japam* (recitation of the divine Name) or *Ramanama* (repetition of the Lord Rama's Name). *Ramanama* was the mainstay of the spiritual life of Mohandas Gandhi. To a question by a missionary friend whether he followed any spiritual practices, Gandhi said:

> I am a stranger to yogic practices. The practice I follow I learnt in my childhood from my nurse. I was afraid of ghosts. She used to say to me: "There are no ghosts, but if you are afraid, repeat

Ramanama." What I learnt in my childhood has become a huge thing in my mental firmament. It is a sun that has brightened my darkest hour. A Christian may find the same solace from the repetition of the name of Jesus, and a Muslim from the name of Allah.† All these things have the same implications and they produce identical results under identical circumstances. Only the repetition must not be a lip expression, but a part of your very being. . . . One should pour one's soul into it. . . . The Mantra becomes one's staff of life and carries one through every ordeal . . . it is my constant support in my struggles.‡

Gandhi, Ramanama, pp. 5, 6, 11

† The repetition of the Name is a basic discipline in Islam, as in most of the great religions of humanity. Carl Vett reports the ensuing bit of conversation, following his introduction to a Muslim teacher by a friend called "the Bey": " 'Very successfull' said the Bey as we left. 'It almost seems that you have roused the old man's interest. . . . What kind of impression would it have made on you, if the master had had you do nothing but repeat the name of Allah out loud five thousand times a day? And that is one of the commonest exercises for a beginner' " (Vett, *Dervish Diary*, p. 55).

‡ A description of the power of repeating God's name occurs in the work which Gandhi regarded as "the greatest book in all devotional literature," the Ramayan of Tulasidas:

"Install the luminous gem in the shape of the divine Name . . . on the threshold of the tongue at the doorway of your mouth, if you will have light both inside and outside, O Tulasidasa.

"Yogis (mystics) who are full of dispassion and are wholly detached from God's creation keep awake (in the daylight of wisdom) muttering the Name with their tongue, and enjoy the felicity of Brahma (the Absolute), which is incomparable, unspeakable, unmixed with sorrow and devoid of name and form. Even those (seekers of Truth) who aspire to know the mysterious ways of Providence are able to comprehend them by muttering the Name. Strivers (hankering after worldly achievements) repeat the Name, absorbed in contemplation, acquiring superhuman powers. . . . If devotees in distress mutter the Name, their worst calamities of the gravest type disappear and they become happy. . . . The glory of the Name is supreme in all four Yugas [ages] and all the four Vedas, particularly in the Kali age [the dark or iron age, the present age] in which there is no other means of salvation.

"Even those who are free from all desires and absorbed in the joy of devotion to Sri Rama have thrown their heart as fish into the nectarine lake of supreme affection for the Name. . . .

"(Not only in this Kali age, but) in all the four ages, at all times (past, present and future) and in all the three spheres (viz., heaven, earth and the subterranean region) creatures have been rid of grief by repeating the Name. . . . In this terrible age the Name alone is the wish-yielding tree, the very thought of which puts an end to all the illusions of the world. . . . In Kaliyuga neither Karma (action) nor Bhakti (devotion) nor again Jnana (knowledge) avails; the Name . . . is the only resort.

"The Name repeated either with good or evil inclinations, in an angry mood or even while yawning, diffuses joy in all the ten directions" (*Sri Ramacharitamānasa*, Tulasidas, pp. 40, 41, 45, 46).

The Prayer of Jesus as given in *The Pilgrim* actually is the principal means to union with God in the Hesychast tradition of Eastern Orthodox spirituality. Frithjof Schuon (in *The Transcendent Unity of Religions*) says:

"This method [Hesychasm] has been handed down, through the Desert Fathers, in a direct line of descent from primitive Christianity . . . all the forms of Hesychasm are derived with strict traditional fidelity from something that existed in Christianity at the beginning . . . it is the Hesychast Tradition, from the Desert Fathers to the 'Russian Pilgrim,' which undoubtedly represents in its most unaltered form the inheritance of primitive Christian spirituality, that which properly can be called 'Christ-given.'" If there is any possibility that this tremendous statement is true, it deserves the electrified attention of every Christian.

The great book containing the treasured writings of the centuries of this tradition is *The Philokalia,* mentioned again and again by the Pilgrim. The *Philokalia* writings specifically indicated in *The Pilgrim* are found in a volume entitled *Writings from the Philokalia on Prayer of the Heart.* See also *Early Fathers from the Philokalia.* See further *On the Prayer of Jesus* by Bishop Ignatius Brianchaninov.

The practice of continuous prayer of the heart (achieved by means of repetition of the Prayer of Jesus, or of the name of Allah, or by the name of a Bodhisattva, or by *Ramanama*) is taught or recommended by many of the major spiritual teachers of the world,* including, in or near our time, Sri Ramakrishna and Sri Ramana Maharshi. *The Gospel of Sri Ramakrishna* contains many references to the power of repeating the divine Name. Brahmananda, a direct and beloved disciple of Ramakrishna and a tremendous teacher in his own right, strongly urged *japam,* repetition of the Name, upon the young aspirants in his charge:

> The mind rules the senses. Therefore it must be controlled. . . . Always be on your guard until you have transcended the mind. . . .

---

* For an example of the Buddha's teaching of the power of uttering the name of the Bodhisattva Avalokitesvara, see *Samantamukha Parivarta,* "the Lotus of the Good Law," the twenty-fifth chapter, known as "The Kwannon Sutra" (Suzuki, *Manual of Zen Buddhism,* pp. 30–32). In Mahayana Buddhism *Nembutsu* is "a ceaseless invocation to Amida Buddha" and is markedly stressed in the Jodo sect.

God's Will: How to Know It and Do It

> Plunge yourself deeply into the practice of japam and meditation. The mind is gross and feeds on gross objects. But as japam and meditation are practiced, the mind becomes subtle and learns to grasp subtle truths. Practice. Practice. See for yourself if there is really a God.
>
> <div align="right">Brahmananda, <i>The Eternal Companion</i>, pp. 142-43</div>

Prabhavananda, who knew Brahmananda directly, and who edited *The Eternal Companion,* comments upon Brahmananda's teachings of *japam* as follows:

> In his teachings, Maharaj [Brahmananda] lays great stress on the value of japam.
>
> Japam may appear monotonous and mechanical when not accompanied by meditation. Nevertheless, it has a good effect. If one persists, the monotony will break, and the presence of God will be felt. Through japam, an inner joy and sweetness will arise which will help the aspirant to devote himself more and more to the practice of the Presence of God.
>
> Ibid., p. 223

And further, in his commentary on the sutras of Patanjali, Prabhavananda gives one of the clearest and most cogent expositions of the power of repeating the Name:

> People who have never tried the practice of repeating the name of God are apt to scoff at it: it seems to them so empty, so mechanical. "Just repeating the same word over and over!" they exclaim scornfully. "What possible good can that do?"
>
> The truth is that we are all inclined to flatter ourselves—despite our daily experience to the contrary—that we spend our time thinking logical, consecutive thoughts. In fact, most of us do no such thing. Consecutive thought about any one problem occupies a very small proportion of our waking hours. More usually, we are in a state of reverie—a mental fog of disconnected sense-impressions, irrelevant memories, nonsensical scraps of sentences from books and newspapers, little darting fears and resentments, physical sensations of discomfort, excitement or ease. If, at any given moment, we could take twenty human minds and inspect their workings, we should probably find one, or at most two, which were functioning rationally. The remaining eighteen or nineteen minds would look more like this: "Ink-bottle. That time I saw Roosevelt. In love with the night mysterious. Reds veto Pact. Jimmy's trying to get my job.

Mary says I'm fat. Big toe hurts. Soup good . . . , etc., etc." Because we do nothing to control this reverie, it is largely conditioned by external circumstances. The weather is cloudy, so our mood is sad. The sun comes out; our mood brightens. Insects begin to buzz around us, and we turn irritable and nervous. Often, it is as simple as that.

But now, if we introduce into this reverie the repetition of the name of God, we shall find that we can control our moods, despite the interference of the outside world. We are always, anyhow, repeating words in our minds—the name of a friend or an enemy, the name of an anxiety, the name of a desired object—and each of these words is surrounded by its own mental climate. Try saying "war," or "cancer," or "money" ten thousand times, and you will find that your whole mood has been changed and colored by the associations connected with that word. Similarly, the name of God will change the climate of your mind. It cannot do otherwise. . . .

Mere repetition of God's name is, of course, insufficient—as Patanjali points out. We must also meditate upon its meaning. But the one process follows naturally upon the other. If we persevere in our repetition, it will lead us inevitably into meditation. Gradually, our confused reverie will give way to concentrated thought. We cannot long continue to repeat any word without beginning to think about the reality which it represents. Unless we are far advanced in spiritual practice, this concentration will not be maintained for more than a few moments; the mind will slip back into reverie again. But it will be higher kind of reverie—a reverie dominated by sattwa rather than by rajas or tamas. And the Name, perpetually uttered within it, will be like a gentle plucking at our sleeve, demanding and finally recapturing our attention.

Patanjali, *How to Know God*, pp. 58–61

At what is perhaps a considerable risk of confusing the subject, I have included references to continuous prayer of the heart (as aided by repetition of the name of God) from many different places and times. It seems to me that the risk is justified, in order to bring out the important fact that, in historical times, this is one of the most widespread, most practical and helpful, and most seriously practiced of all forms of prayer. From the Desert Fathers in the West and the devotees of Rama and Avalokitesvara in the East, the practice of the repetition of the Name has come down recently through *The Pilgrim* to becoming in our day a prominent subject in

God's Will: How to Know It and Do It 163

two stories by J. D. Salinger in *The New Yorker* magazine. God works in mysterious ways indeed.

May I conclude these references by sharing briefly with you a few experiences of my own with this kind of prayer of the heart.

Until I read *The Pilgrim* I had no idea that any such prayer existed, much less that it would be a possibility for me. I had encountered references to "*japam*," "chanting God's name," "repeating the *mantram*," etc., etc., in Eastern teachings, but they were just words and phrases as far as I was concerned. They all seemed to me to refer to practices that were local, special, and frankly a little bizarre—you know, fine for those Hindus but not for me. I didn't tumble at all to what they were talking about, and certainly I never guessed what a mine of grace I was skipping over so lightly.

But then I came upon *The Pilgrim*, and although at first I did not suspect the full power and depth of the Prayer of Jesus, nor did I then realize the place it occupies historically and traditionally in Christianity, still I did recognize right away that there were real possibilities in this kind of prayer, and I set out to explore them. (Only much later did I begin to see the connection between the Jesus Prayer and similar practices throughout the spiritual life of humanity as a whole.)

I began experimenting with "Lord Jesus Christ, have mercy on me" (or "Lord Jesus Christ, have mercy on us," if I had someone else in mind), said silently and inwardly, on a train commuting to New York City five days a week. There was about a twenty-minute run between my home town of Chappaqua and the change-engines stop of North White Plains, less than halfway to the big city, and in that period I began to work the prayer every commuting day.

At first it was odd and difficult and clumsy, and I soon saw that I was trying too much at a time, so I cut it down to the stretch between Chappaqua and Hawthorne, about ten minutes.

Then it went rather well for a while. Of course I encountered the early kind of difficulties that everybody else does. I worried quite keenly, for example, that the other commuters would notice what was happening and that they would be powerfully confirmed in an impression that a real live nut got on the train every morning along with the solid citizens at Chappaqua. But I carefully said the prayer inwardly and with no motion of the face or lips; so the only thing unusual was that I was sitting up straight and otherwise unoccupied. As a matter of fact lots of people doze or gaze absently about on a train. Nobody of course paid the slightest attention to me. By holding an open book or newspaper on my lap I felt my disguise to be complete, and I proceeded without further concern on that score.

The next development, as the prayer was going on, was that one of my crew of inner voices began to point out that our Lord has cautioned us against *vain repetition* (this voice was one of the pious, scripture-quoting members of my crew). I had the grace, however, to see the wisdom of another inner voice (one of the work gang), who called attention to the fact, which was quite obvious as soon as observed, that whether the repetition was vain or not turned upon an interesting point: it depended upon whether I was able to keep my attention even faintly on the words and to realize even a very little bit what they mean.

At times, in spite of all efforts, the repeating of the phrase would sink out of the circle of fully conscious attention and thus into the realm of vain repetition. *But not quite.* It was not entirely vain. Because as long as it kept going, as long as I did not forget it entirely and drop it, even the mechanical repetition served finally to pull the attention back, and the prayer immediately arose for a time above the vain level. It was indeed, as Prabhavananda says, "like a gentle plucking at the sleeve." And therefore I realized early in the game the really quite remarkable value of the practice even at its humblest, least esteemed, and most criticized level.

Then there were times, rare at first and brief, when the prayer rose, of its own momentum or of a hidden momentum, to a kind of peak, where it seemed right on the point of breaking out into some kind of light, right on the edge of another kind of knowing and feeling. This happened in every case spontaneously, never when I was pushing or struggling with the practice in any way, or when I was strenuously hoping for a rise or a break in it. Whenever I tried to direct the prayer toward such a peak, the exact opposite or nothing at all occurred. It just kept on at the ordinary level or sank to an even duller plane than usual. I soon saw that the peaks cannot be promoted or manipulated in any way. They come, I am now

God's Will: How to Know It and Do It

very certain, as a result of grace, and so do other and deeper involvements of the prayer. The quantity, as Bishop Brianchaninov points out, is somewhat within our choice and control. The quality is not.

Of course there were many ups and downs and hiatuses, but the ten minutes in the morning finally were going so well that I added a similar bit on the train coming out in the evening. The run from Grand Central to 125th Street is a hair short of ten minutes, and so it suited the need very nicely.

Then, when it felt as if I had solid bases in the two periods, morning and evening, I experimented with extending the time. It was much easier to do so successfully in the morning than in the evening (I think that this was simply a matter of available energy and the fatigue threshold). At the end of a year I was able occasionally to maintain the prayer with good attention all the way from Chappaqua to New York. The first time I did so, I got off the train in Grand Central in such a state of inner joy that I had to stop the repetition and pray: "God, please help me to get my feet down on the ground; I've got a day's work to do."

There is nothing much worse than getting into athletic feats in prayer or endurance contests with yourself or anyone else. But in this particular kind of prayer it *is* helpful, with no thought of setting any records, to extend the periods of practice gradually up to what you are fully capable of, and then to accustom yourself to being in this continuous prayer as you go about your daily affairs. Abbot Chapman's observation is profoundly true: "The more you pray, the better it goes." I think that my early attempts with the Prayer of Jesus represent about an average beginning experience, which any serious experimenter would find himself able to duplicate or exceed quite easily.

It seems hardly possible when you have just heard about it and are trying to figure it out, but when you actually get to doing it you find that you are able to keep the prayer going in the midst of all kinds of activities, including sometimes even hard mental work.

Repetition of the prayer while walking is excellent. I found also that it went very well while mowing the lawn. It works fine, too, while driving a car, particularly on longish trips. (Note to the National Safety Council: I testify that this practice positively does not interfere with proper attention to the serious business of driving; on the contrary: the back of the mind of everyone who drives a car is filled with random thoughts, more or less chaotic, more or less angry or fearful or otherwise sour-emotional, and more or less distracting; but the back of the mind of one who repeats the Jesus Prayer is occupied with a calming, steadying influence which clarifies rather than obstructs the outer attention and assists rather than hinders one in any such occupation as driving a car.)

There are many occasions during the day that are particularly suited to establishing prayer of the heart: times when you are waiting for an appointment, when you are walking from one building or place to another, when you are doing routine chores of any kind, such as brushing your teeth or washing the dishes. I found that the quiet hours spent on a trout stream were a perfectly wonderful time for it. Mealtimes of course are ideal, because they present opportunities to combine the prayer with the essentially sacramental and holy acts of eating and drinking.

Times of illness and difficulty are specially suited to repetition of the Name. The place of this practice in healing is a very important one. It is indeed one of the greatest aspects of the prayer, but it is a large subject in itself and I cannot develop it here (See Gandhi, *Ramanama*).

You might think that mixing prayer with the daily life in this way would tend to induce woolly or abstracted or slightly dissociated states, but the exact opposite is true: The practice of continuous prayer of the heart makes one much more alert and awake in all his faculties and much better able to do work of any kind. I realize that it is hard and perhaps impossible to visualize in advance how this could be so, but I assure you, from my own experience and that of many others, that it *is* so.

In order even to begin to experience the validity and authority of the Prayer of Jesus, it is necessary to say it "in the heart." You should take the trouble to understand what is meant by the "heart" in this context. It involves the physical heart, but something very much beyond that, too. *The Pilgrim* gives clear instructions for bringing the prayer into the heart. I would say that this phase in the development should be undergone at first in quiet and undistracting circumstances, because when the prayer actually does enter the heart there are repercussions throughout the whole being. One of the best simple modern expositions of what the "heart" is in

God's Will: How to Know It and Do It 167

universal spiritual teaching, and what its powers and functions are, is given in Austin Pardue's *Create and Make New* (particularly pp. 17–39).

Continuous prayer of the heart, *in* the heart, is like the practice of the Presence of God, the practice of watching, and the practice of abandonment, in that it is easy to start and difficult to maintain. But that difficulty seems to be a characteristic of all of the really basic movements of the truth-seeking life. I guess it is just the part that is left to our own volition; and for most of us volition toward God is a frail element which needs tender nursing and plenty of patient, unhurried, undiscouraged exercise.

I am going to close with something I've been avoiding all along: a scale or map of the territory covered by prayer.

I am uneasy about systems and maps of prayer (although some of the greatest men of prayer have used them), because they sometimes tend to intimidate beginners and to inflate premature proficients. Further, they tend to give a mechanical and academic dress to something which should be fresh and natural and uncalculated. "Systems" of prayer sometimes provide not a ladder but a series of artificial hurdles between the praying man and the Reality to whom he prays.

On the other hand, a good map does enable you to see the ground in which you are working and to confirm and guide your own experience within a rational, empirical, and traditional framework. One of the simplest and most useful maps I know is compiled from all traditions but follows, in its structure and terms, the view of prayer held in Russian and Greek (Eastern Orthodox) Christianity.*

You will observe that the practice of continuous prayer by means of repetition of the Name takes one from the vocal, through the mental, to the cordial level, and from the Prayer of Attention right up into the Prayer of Grace, that is, from the place in which you are your own man to the place in which you are God's man. This is a tremendous transition. Note the critical distinction between the Prayer of Attention and the Prayer of Grace. In the one, *quantity* is involved, and that is up to you. In the other, *quality* is involved, and that is up to God.

And so, as my last word in this book, I would like to make some observations as to how one may bear oneself in this transi-

A MAP OF PRAYER

I. The PRAYER of ATTENTION

... within our control and initiative.

- A. VOCAL prayer: Talking with God. Petitions: "low prayer." Intercessions: "middle prayer." Thanksgivings. Spoken group prayer. Sung prayer. Liturgical and congregational prayer. Spoken repetition of the Name.

- B. MENTAL prayer: Meditation. Quiet prayer. Attention of the mind to God. Unspoken repetition of the Name.

II. The PRAYER of GRACE

... *not* within our control and initiative.

- C. CORDIAL prayer: Preternatural clarity and truth. Warmth. Joy. Rapture. Bliss. Unction. Tears. Fire. Ecstasy. *Bhakti*. The Love of God. Compassion (leading to) service (leading to) sacrifice. Prayer of the heart: repetition of the Name in the heart.

- D. TRANSCENDENTAL prayer: Direct realization of God. Living Light. Literally beyond all description.

tional area, this crucial flash point between one's own action and the action of the Grace of God:

The Prayer of Attention, in all its varieties and ranges, is *within our voluntary control* (unless we are willingly in the grip of vice, in deliberate hatred, or in some other deadly sin or God-eclipsing condition). If we set ourselves to it we can pray a great deal—even four or five hours a day—just by deciding to do so and sticking to it. God has put this area of prayer within the range of our effective choice and implementation to a very considerable extent. Few of us exercise the amount of effort and do the amount of work we could do in the Prayer of Attention. The chief problem is to find the time and, even when there is the time, to remember to do it. Mainly it is a problem of remembrance, because, as we have seen, there are ways of praying even in the midst of business. A very busy man, *if he remembers*, will find himself doing a remarkable amount of the Prayer of Attention in the interstices of his daily affairs, even if they are extremely crowded. The point is that the Prayer of Attention is up to us, except in states of deadly separation.

The Prayer of Grace on the other hand is *not* within our voluntary control. *It cannot be attained by us.* The Prayer of Attention clears the way and prepares the ground for the Prayer of Grace, but *it is not at all the cause* of the Prayer of Grace. To bear this in mind is of the greatest importance. Unless we do a lot of the Prayer of Attention we shall probably have very little or none of the Prayer of Grace. And yet, no amount of the Prayer of Attention will *result* in the Prayer of Grace. There must be an erasure of any and all thoughts of cause and effect that arise here. *The Prayer of Grace is always the gift of God.* You may strive and struggle in the Prayer of Attention. You must not strive or struggle in or for the Prayer of Grace. Ask for it, yes. But do not grasp for it. Ask and wait.

Don't get tired asking and don't get tired waiting. And when it does come, it is to be welcomed in the deepest possible gratitude. We never know how we are going to behave when the Prayer of Grace comes to us. I have often withdrawn in fear. I felt that God was giving me something I was afraid to receive and requiring something of me that I was afraid to give. Such reactions are normal enough, and with time and continued grace they are outgrown. The ideal attitude is to relax in perfect trust and let God have his way with you. But at first this may not be possible. Just do the best you can. He understands.

In addition to strengthening and cleansing joy, the Prayer of Grace always brings with it a subtle and wonderful guidance. If we are alert to this and if we will give ourselves up to it, then we are beautifully led and taught how to receive the comfort and bliss. When this type of prayer is well developed (which usually takes some time), then God himself becomes the man's teacher, and he needs to rely less and less on exterior counsel, while remaining humbly open to it at all times.

In the meantime, as always, there are dangers to be guarded against. Every advance in spiritual life, in addition to its advantages, brings difficulties and perils that must be surmounted. This is outstandingly true of the advance into the Prayer of Grace.

One danger, which we have already looked at briefly, is that the man, hearing about the Prayer of Grace or actually having tasted it, will try by various methods to induce it. This is futile, because, as we have seen, the prayer by its very nature is a gift. And the striving leads to psychic indigestion or worse. The ego, which is by no means amputated yet, at this point may become subtly but seriously inflamed by these clear tokens of God's encouragement and approval, and the *persona* may begin to strut and preen itself in hidden and tricky ways in the light which God has introduced into the soul. No man may say, "Oh, that could never happen to me." It could happen to anyone and has happened to many. On the one hand we must be alert and humble; on the other hand we must not fall into scruples. (1) A *childlike trust* in God and (2) a *cheerful willingness* to see secret faults in ourselves and to be corrected by the Truth in the areas of our deepest experience—these two attitudes are our refuge and protection against all danger when the Prayer of Grace is starting.

You cannot force God. But by surrendering, by seeking to penetrate the cloud of your own ignorance, and by trying to pray continuously, you can break your heart for him—and he does not remain unmoved at that. With all your work and sweat you cannot cause anything to happen—but a great deal does happen. Nobody is ever going to figure it out, but that is the way it is.

Bibliography

Books indicated throughout the text are listed here in alphabetical order. The approximate "weight" of each book is indicated by notations ★, ★★, or ★★★ immediately following the listing: ★ means light reading; ★★ means medium reading; ★★★ means heavy reading.

Please use caution in interpreting these marks. They are intended as a rough index of ease of reading, but they must be applied with discrimination. It would be a misuse of this device, for example, if you were simply attracted to the easy books and repelled by the difficult ones. Some of the not-so-easy works may be among the most useful and enjoyable of all books for you. The Bible, for instance, is marked ★★★ because, like all sacred writing, it *is* difficult to understand thoroughly. But at the same time it is of the greatest practical value even to people who are not used to hard reading.

On the other hand a single ★ does not mean that the work so checked is frivolous or shallow; it just indicates a book that treats its subject in an elementary way or in terms that are quite easy to comprehend. For instance, Brother Lawrence's *Practice of the Presence of God* is marked ★ because it is easy reading; nevertheless it is a profound spiritual treatise, as you may discover for yourself by reading it over four or five times a year and experimenting with the practice it suggests. So take these ★s, ★★s, and ★★★s with a grain of salt and an eye to your own particular situation. Used that way, they should serve you without misleading you.

For a listing of books grouped according to special purposes, see Special Book Listings beginning on page 190.

Albert the Great, St. *Of Cleaving to God*. London, 1954: Mowbray. ★★.
Alcoholics Anonymous. Anonymous. New York, 1955: Alcoholics Anonymous World Services. ★.
Alcoholics Anonymous Comes of Age. Anonymous. New York, 1957: Alcoholics Anonymous World Services. ★.
Aquinas, St. Thomas. *Basic Writings*. Edited by Anton C. Pegis. New York, 1945: Random House. ★★★.
———. *Summa Contra Gentiles*. Translated by Anton C. Pegis. 4 vols. Notre Dame, Inc., 1975: University of Notre Dame Press. ★★★.
———. *Summa Theologiae*. 60 vols. New York, 1976: McGraw-Hill. ★★★.
Aristotle. *The Basic Works of Aristotle*. New York, 1941: Random House. ★★★.
The Art of Prayer: An Orthodox Anthology. Compiled by Igumen Chariton of Valamo. Translated by Kadloubovsky and Palmer. London, 1966: Faber. ★★★.
Ashton, Joan. *Mother of All Nations: The Visitations of the Blessed Virgin Mary and Her Message for Today*. San Francisco, 1989: Harper. ★.
Attar, Farid al-Din. *Muslim Saints and Mystics*. Translated by A. J. Arberry. Boston, 1973: Routledge and Kegan Paul. ★★.
Augustine, St. *The City of God*. Edited by Vernon J. Bourke. New York, 1950: Doubleday. ★★.
———. *Confessions of St. Augustine*. Translated by Rex Warner. New York, 1963: New American Library. ★★.
Aurobindo, Sri. *The Life Divine*. New York, 1949: The Sri Aurobindo Library, Inc. ★★★.
Austin, Lou. *You Are Greater Than You Know*. Winchester, Va., 1955: The Partnership Foundation. ★.
Baker, Ven. Father F. Augustine. *Holy Wisdom*. Wheathampstead, Herts, England, 1964: Anthony Clarke Books. ★★★.
Baly, Denis. *The Geography of the Bible*. New York, 1974: Harper and Row. ★.
Bar Hebraeus. *Book of the Dove*. Translated by A. J. Wensinck. Leyden, Holland, 1919: E. J. Brill. ★★★.
Beevers, John. *Storm of Glory: The Story of Therese of Lisieux*. New York, 1977: Doubleday. ★.
Benoit, Hubert. *The Supreme Doctrine*. New York, 1968: Penguin. ★★★.
Bernard, Theos. *Hatha Yoga*. New York, 1950: Weiser. ★★.
Bernard of Clairvaux, St. *On the Song of Songs*. Translated by Kilian Walsh. Kalamazoo, Mich., 1976: Cistercian Pubs. ★★★.
Bhagavad Gita. Of special value because of Gandhi's great personal demonstration of the Gita's teaching is *The Gita According to Gandhi*.

Ahmedabad, India, 1946: Navajivan Publishing House. ★★★. Gandhi himself considered Arnold's the best English translation:

———. *The Song Celestial*. Translated by Sir Edwin Arnold. London, 1948: Routledge and Kegan Paul. ★★★.

Other translations:

———. *Bhagavad-Gita, The Song of God*. Translated by Prabhavananda and Isherwood. Hollywood, Calif., 1973: Vedanta Press. ★★★.

———. *The Bhagavadgita*. Translated and with commentary by S. Radhakrishnan. New York, 1948: Harper. ★★★.

For interpretation and study:

———. *Essays on the Gita*. By Sri Aurobindo. New York, Sri Aurobindo Library. ★★★.

———. *Talks on the Gita*. By Vinoba Bhave. London, 1960: George Allen and Unwin. ★★★.

———. *The Yoga of the Bhagavat Gita*. By Sri Krishna Prem. London, 1938: Watkins. ★★★.

Bible. The best-known English Bible is the Authorized or King James Version, the classic Protestant version ordered by James I of England in 1611, ★★★. Consult such publishers as Harper, Nelson, Oxford, and The American Bible Society (all in New York) for various editions available. Roman Catholic Bibles include the Douay-Rheims version, a translation from the Latin Vulgate dating from 1582 and 1609 (New York, 1914: P. J. Kenedy & Sons), ★★★. There are several new Catholic translations of the Bible into modern English, including the Knox Bible, translated by Monsignor Ronald Knox (New York, 1956: Sheed & Ward), ★★★, *The Jerusalem Bible* (New York, 1966: Doubleday), ★★★, and *The New American Bible* (New York, 1970: P. J. Kenedy & Sons), ★★★. There are also a number of Protestant translations of the Bible into modern English, including the Revised Standard Version (New York, 1952: Nelson), ★★★, *The New Testament in Modern English* (Translated by J. B. Phillips. New York, 1958: Macmillan), ★★★, *The New English Bible* (New York, 1970: Oxford University Press), ★★★, and *The New International Bible* (Grand Rapids, Mich., 1978: Zondervan), ★★★.

For reference: *The Scofield Study Bible* (New York, 1945: Oxford), ★★★. *The Westminster Study Edition of the Holy Bible* (Philadelphia, 1947: Westminster), ★★★. *Strong's Exhaustive Concordance of the Bible* (Nashville, Tenn., 1981: Abingdon), ★★★. *Young's Analytical Concordance to the Bible* (New York: Funk & Wagnalls), ★★★.

Boehme, Jacob. *The Aurora*. Greenwood, S.C., 1960: The Attic Press. ★★★.

———. *The Forty Questions*. Translated by John Sparrow. London, 1911: John M. Watkins. ★★★.
———. *Mysterium Magnum*. Translated by John Sparrow. 2 vols. London, 1924: Watkins. ★★★.
———. *The Signature of All Things*. Greenwood, S.C., 1960: The Attic Press. ★★★.
———. *The Way to Christ*. London, 1964: Watkins. ★★.
———. See also Franz Hartmann.
Boisen, Anton T. *Religion in Crisis and Custom*. New York, 1955: Harper. ★★.
Bossuet. *Letters of Spiritual Direction*. London, 1958: Mowbray. ★★.
Bowden, Guy. *The Dazzling Darkness*. London, 1950: Longmans. ★★.
Brahmananda, Swami. *The Eternal Companion*. Compiled by Swami Prabhavananda. Hollywood, Calif., 1944: Vedanta Press. ★★.
Brianchaninov, Bishop Ignatius. *On the Prayer of Jesus*. London, 1953: Watkins. ★★★.
Brother Lawrence. *The God Illuminated Cook: The Practice of the Presence of God*. Hankins, N.Y., 1975: East Ridge Press. ★.
Buber, Martin. *Eclipse of God*. New York, 1957: Harper. ★★.
———. *For the Sake of Heaven*. New York, 1969: Atheneum. ★★.
———. *Hasidism and Modern Man*. New York, 1958: Harper. ★★.
———. *I and Thou*. New York, 1970: Scribner. ★★★.
———. *The Legends of the Baal-Shem*. New York, 1969: Schocken. ★★.
———. *Tales of the Hasidim*. 2 vols. New York, 1973: Schocken. ★★.
Bucke, Richard M. *Cosmic Consciousness*. Secaucus, N.J., 1970: Citadel. ★★.
A Buddhist Bible. Edited by Dwight Goddard. Boston, 1970: Beacon. ★★★.
Bulwer-Lytton, Sir Edward. *Zanoni*. Blauvelt, N.Y., 1971: Rudolf Steiner Publications. ★★.
Bunyan, John. *Pilgrim's Progress*. New York, 1970: Dutton. ★★.
Burns, John, with three other recovered addicts. *The Answer to Addiction*. New York, 1990: Crossroad/Continuum. ★.
Carrel, Alexis. *Prayer*. London, 1947: Hodder & Stoughton. ★.
———. *The Voyage to Lourdes*. New York, 1950: Harper. ★.
Catherine of Genoa, St. *The Treatise on Purgatory*. Westminster, Md., 1946: Christian Classics. ★★.
A Catholic Dictionary. Edited by Donald Attwater. New York, 1961: Macmillan. ★★.
Catton, Bruce. *This Hallowed Ground*. New York, 1955: Doubleday. ★.
Chapman, Dom John. *Spiritual Letters*. Edited by Dom Roger Huddleston. New York, 1935: Sheed & Ward. ★★.
Chesterton, G. K. *The Everlasting Man*. New York, 1953: Dodd, Mead. ★.
———. *St. Francis of Assisi*. New York, 1957: Doubleday. ★.

Bibliography 175

———. *St. Thomas Aquinas: The Dumb Ox.* New York, 1956: Doubleday. ★.
The Choice Is Always Ours. Edited by Dorothy Berkley Philips, Elizabeth Boyden Howes, Lucille M. Nixon. Wheaton, Ill., 1975: Theosophical Publishing House.
Cleckley, Hervey. *The Mask of Sanity.* St. Louis, 1964: Mosby. ★★.
The Cloud of Unknowing. Anonymous. Edited by Evelyn Underhill. London, 1946: Watkins. ★★.
———. Edited by Abbot Justin McCann. London, 1952: Burns Oates. ★★.
———. Translated by Clifton Wolters. New York, 1968: Penguin. ★★.
———. Translated into modern English by Ira Progoff. New York, 1957: Julian Press. ★★.
———. Shortened version in modern English. New York, 1948: Harper. ★★.
Collin, Rodney. *The Theory of Celestial Influence.* New York, 1954: Weiser. ★★★.
———. *The Theory of Eternal Life.* New York, 1974: Weiser. ★★★.
Collins and Lapierre. *Freedom at Midnight.* New York, 1980: Ballantine. ★.
Common Prayer, The Book of. (Episcopal.) New York, 1928: Church Pension Fund. ★★.
Confucius. *Analects.* Translated by Arthur Waley. New York, 1966: Random House. ★★★.
———. *The Wisdom of Confucius.* Translated and edited by Lin Yutang. New York, 1948: Modern Library. ★★★.
Coomaraswamy, Ananda K. *Am I My Brother's Keeper?* Plainview, N.Y., 1947: Books for Libraries. ★★.
———. *Buddha and the Gospel of Buddhism.* New York, 1964: Harper. ★★★.
———. *Hinduism and Buddhism.* Westport, Conn., 1971: Greenwood Press. ★★★.
Cousins, Norman. *The Anatomy of an Illness.* New York, 1979: Norton. ★.
Cranston, Ruth. *The Miracle of Lourdes.* New York, 1955: McGraw-Hill. ★.
Daily, Starr. *Release.* New York, 1942: Harper. ★.
Dante. *The Divine Comedy of Dante Alighieri.* Translated by Dorothy L. Sayers. 3 vols. New York, 1974: Penguin. ★★★.
Daumal, René. *Mount Analogue.* Translated by Roger Shattuck. San Francisco, 1952: City Lights. ★★.
Davenport, Russell W. *The Dignity of Man.* Westport, Conn., 1973: Greenwood Press. ★★.
The Dead Sea Scriptures. Translated and edited by Theodore M. Gaster. New York, 1956: Doubleday. ★.
De Caussade, Jean Pierre. *on Prayer.* Translated by Algar Thorold. London, 1949: Burns Oates. ★★★.

———. *Self-Abandonment to Divine Providence*. Translated by Algar Thorold. Rockford, Ill., 1985: TAN. ★★★.

———. *Spiritual Letters*. Translated by Algar Thorold. London, 1948: Burns Oates. ★★★.

Dechanet, J. M. *Christian Yoga*. Westminster, Md., 1972: Christian Classics. ★★.

DeHartmann, Thomas. *Our Life with Mr. Gurdjieff*. New York, 1972: Penguin. ★.

De Laredo, Bernardino. *The Ascent of Mount Sion*. New York, 1952: Harper. ★★★.

De Molinos, Michael. *The Spiritual Guide*. London, 1907: Methuen. ★★★.

De Sales, St. Francis. *Introduction to the Devout Life*. Edited and with introduction by Thomas S. Kepler. Cleveland, 1952: World. ★★.

The Desert Fathers. Translated by Helen Waddell. Ann Arbor, Mich., 1957: University of Michigan Press. ★★.

The Dhammapada. Translated by S. Radhakrishnan. New York, 1974: Oxford. ★★★.

Dionysius the Areopagite. *The Mystical Theology and the Celestial Hierarchies*. Nr. Godalming, Surrey, 1961: The Shrine of Wisdom. ★★★.

———. *Theologia Mystica*. Translated by Alan W. Watts. West Park, N.Y., 1944: Holy Cross Press. ★★★.

———. *On the Divine Names and the Mystical Theology*. Translated by C. E. Rolt. New York, 1940: Macmillan. ★★★.

Dunkerly, Roderic. *Beyond the Gospels*. New York, 1957: Penguin. ★★.

De Nouy, Lecomte. *Human Destiny*. New York, 1947: New American Library. ★★.

Dostoevsky, Fyodor. *The Brothers Karamazov*. New York, 1957: New American Library. ★★.

———. *The Idiot*. New York, 1935: Random House (Modern Library). ★★.

Durant, Will and Ariel. *Caesar and Christ*. New York: Simon & Schuster. ★★.

———. *The Life of Greece*. New York, 1939: Simon & Schuster. ★★.

———. *Our Oriental Heritage*. New York: Simon & Schuster. ★★.

Eckhart, Meister. *Meister Eckhart: A Modern Translation* By R. B. Blakney. New York, 1941: Harper. ★★★.

———. *Meister Eckhart*. Translated by C. de B. Evans. 2 vols. London, 1947 and 1952: Watkins. ★★★.

———. *Breakthrough: Meister Eckhart's Creation Spirituality in New Translation*. Translated and with commentaries by Matthew Fox. New York, 1980: Doubleday. ★★★.

———. *Meister Eckhart and the Rhineland Mystics*. By Jeanne Ancelet-Hustach. New York, 1957: Harper. ★★★.

Ehrenfeld, David. *The Arrogance of Humanism*. New York, 1978: Oxford. ★★.
Ellul, Jacques. *Apocalypse: The Book of Revelation*. New York, 1977: Seabury. ★★.
———. *The Betrayal of the West*. New York, 1975: Seabury. ★★.
———. *The Judgment of Jonah*. Grand Rapids, Mich., 1971: Eerdmans. ★★.
———. *The Meaning of the City*. Grand Rapids, Mich., 1970: Eerdmans. ★★.
———. *The Subversion of Christianity*. Grand Rapids, Mich., 1986: Eerdmans. ★★.
———. *The Technological Society*. New York, 1964: Knopf. ★★.
———. *Violence*. New York, 1969: Seabury. ★★.
Emmerich, Anne Catherine. *The Dolorous Passion of Our Lord Jesus Christ*. Hawthorne, Calif., 1968: Christian Book Club. ★★.
———. *The Life of the Blessed Virgin Mary*. Compiled by Clemens Brentano. Rockford, Ill., 1970: TAN. ★★.
———. *The Life of Christ*. Edited by The Very Rev. Karl E. Schmoger. 4 vols. Fresno, Calif.: Apostolate of Christian Action. ★★.
———. See also Schmoger, The Very Rev. K. E.
The Essential Gandhi. Edited by Louis Fischer. New York, 1962: Random House. ★.
Evans, Sebastian. *The High History of the Holy Graal*. Greenwood, S.C., 1969: Attic Press. ★★.
Evans-Wentz, W. Y. *The Tibetan Book of the Great Liberation*. With commentary by C. G. Jung. New York, 1954: Oxford. ★★★.
———. *Tibet's Great Yogi: Milarepa*. New York, 1951: Oxford. ★★.
Evola, J. *The Doctrine of Awakening*. Translated by H. E. Musson. London, 1951: Luzac. ★★★.
Faber, Frederick. *Self-Deceit*. Wallingford, Pa.: Pendle Hill. ★.
Fedotov, G. P. *A Treasury of Russian Spirituality*. New York, 1948: Sheed & Ward. ★★.
Fenelon, Francois. *Christian Perfection*. Minneapolis, 1975: Bethany Fellowship. ★★.
Ferm, Vergilius. *Religion in the Twentieth Century*. Westport, Conn., 1948: Greenwood. ★★.
Fischer, Louis. *The Life of Mahatma Gandhi*. New York, 1962: Macmillan. ★.
Fosdick, Harry Emerson. *The Meaning of Faith*. New York, 1950: Association Press. ★.
———. *The Meaning of Prayer*. New York, 1962: Association Press. ★.
Fox, George. *Journal*. New York, 1924: Dutton (Everyman's Library). ★★.

Francis of Assisi, St. *St. Francis of Assisi: The Legends and the Lauds.* Edited by Otto Karrer. New York, 1948: Sheed & Ward. ★.

———. See also G. K. Chesterton; *The Little Flowers of St. Francis.*

Freud, Sigmund. *The Future of an Illusion.* New York, 1975: Norton. ★★.

———. *Basic Writings.* Edited by Dr. A. A. Brill. New York, 1938: Random House (Modern Library). ★★★.

Gandhi, M. K. *An Autobiography: The Story of My Experiments with Truth.* Boston, 1972: Beacon. ★.

———. *Ramanama.* Ahmedabad-14, India, 1949: Navajivan. ★.

———. See also Bhagavad Gita; Collins and Lapierre; Louis Fischer; Vincent Sheean.

Garrigou-Lagrange, Rev. R. *God: His Existence and His Nature.* 2 vols. St. Louis, 1934: Herder. ★★★.

———. *The Three Ages of the Interior Life.* 2 vols. St. Louis, 1947: Herder. ★★.

Gaucher, Guy. *The Story of a Life: St. Therese of Lisieux.* San Francisco, 1987: Harper. ★.

Geoffrey of Monmouth. *History of the Kings of Britain.* Translated by Sebastian Evans. New York, 1958, Dutton. ★★.

Gilson, Etienne. *The Christian Philosophy of St. Augustine.* New York, 1960: Random House. ★★★.

———. *The Christian Philosophy of St. Thomas Aquinas.* New York, 1960: Random House. ★★★.

———. *History of Christian Philosophy in the Middle Ages.* New York, 1955: Random House. ★★★.

Ginzberg, Louis. *The Legends of the Jews.* 7 vols. Philadelphia, 1909: The Jewish Publication Society. ★★.

Goethe, Johann Wolfgang Von. *Faust.* Part I. Translated by Alice Raphael. New York, 1930: Jonathan Cape and Harrison Smith. ★★.

———. *Goethe's Faust.* Parts I and II. Translated by Albert G. Latham. New York, 1910: Dutton (Everyman's Library). ★★.

Gollancz, Victor. *From Darkness to Light.* New York, 1956: Harper. ★★.

———. *A Year of Grace.* New York, 1955: Penguin. ★★.

Govinda, L. A. *Psychological Attitude of Early Buddhist Philosophy.* New York, 1970: Weiser. ★★★.

Grimm, George. *The Doctrine of the Buddha.* Mystic, Conn., 1973: Verry. ★★★.

Gross, Martin L. *The Brain Watchers.* New York, 1962: Random House. ★.

———. *The Doctors.* New York, 1966: Random House. ★.

———. *The Psychological Society.* New York: 1978: Random House. ★.

Grou, Jean-Nicholas. *How to Pray.* Greenwood, S.C., 1964: Attic Press. ★★.

———. *Manual for Interior Souls.* London, 1952: Burns Oates & Washbourne. ★★.

———. *Spiritual Maxims.* Springfield, Ill., 1961: Templegate. ★★.

Bibliography

Guardino, Romano. *The End of the Modern World*. New York, 1956: Sheed & Ward. ★.

Guénon, Réné. *Man and His Becoming According to the Vedanta*. London, 1945: Luzac. ★★★.

———. *The Reign of Quantity*. London, 1953: Luzac. ★★★.

Gurdjieff, G. I. *Beelzebub's Tales to His Grandson*. New York, 1973: Dutton. ★★★.

———. *Meetings with Remarkable Men*. New York, 1963: Dutton. ★★.

———. *Views from the Real World: Early Talks of Gurdjieff*. As recollected by his pupils. With a foreword by Jeanne De Salzman. New York, 1973: Dutton. ★★.

———. See also Rodney Collin; Réné Daumal; Thomas De Hartmann; Maurice Nicoll; P. D. Ouspensky.

The Haggadah. Illustrated by Arthur Szyk. Jerusalem: Massada Press. ★★★.

Hahnemann, Samuel. *The Chronic Diseases*. Philadelphia, 1896: Boericke & Tafel. ★★★.

———. *The Life and Letters of Dr. Samuel Hahnemann*, by Thomas Lindsley Bradford, M.D. Philadelphia, 1895: Boericke & Tafel. ★★★.

———. *Organon of Medicine*. Philadelphia, 1897: Boericke & Tafel. ★★★.

Hall, Francis J. *Theological Outlines*. New York, 1961: Morehouse-Barlow. ★★★.

Hartmann, Franz. *The Life and Doctrines of Jacob Boehme*. Blauvelt, N.Y., 1977: Rudolf Steiner Publications. ★★★.

———. *Paracelsus: Life and Prophecies*. Blauvelt, N.Y., 1973: Rudolf Steiner Publications. ★★★.

Heard, Gerald. *Is God Evident?* New York, 1948: Harper. ★★★.

———. *Is God in History?* Hollywood, Calif., 1950: Vedanta Press. ★★★.

———. *Training for the Life of the Spirit*. Hankins, N.Y., 1975: East Ridge Press. ★★.

Heller, John H. *Report on the Shroud of Turin*. Boston, 1983: Houghton Mifflin. ★.

Hermes Trismegistus. *Hermetica*. Translated and edited by Walter Scott. 4 vols. Boston, 1975: Shambhala. ★★★.

———. *The Fathers of the Church: The Apostolic Fathers*. Edited by Ludwig Schopp. New York, 1947: Christian Heritage. ★★★.

Heschel, Abraham. *God in Search of Man*. New York, 1966: Harper. ★★.

Hilton, Walter. *The Stairway of Perfection*. New York, 1973: Doubleday. ★★★.

Hordern, William. *A Layman's Guide to Protestant Theology*. New York, 1957: Macmillan. ★★.

Hsi Yun. *The Huang Po Doctrine of Universal Mind*. Translated by Chu Ch'an. London, 1947: The Buddhist Society. ★★★.

Huang Po. *The Zen Teaching of Huang Po*. Translated by John Blofeld. New York, 1959: Grove Press. ★★★.

Hughson, S. C. *Contemplative Prayer*. West Park, N.Y. 1935: Holy Cross Press. ★★.
———. *The Warfare of the Soul*. West Park, N.Y., 1942: Holy Cross Press. ★★.
Huxley, Aldous. *Heaven and Hell*. New York, 1971: Harper. ★★★.
———. *The Perennial Philosophy*. New York, 1970: Harper. ★★★.
The Hymnal of the Protestant Episcopal Church in the United States of America, 1940. New York, 1940: Church Pension Fund. ★.
Ignatius of Loyola, St. *St. Ignatius' Own Story*. As told to Luis Gonzales de Camara. Translated by William J. Young. Chicago, 1956: Regnery. ★.
The Imitation of Christ. Variously attributed to Thomas a Kempis, Tauler, and others. Whitford translation. Edited by Edward J. Klein. New York, 1941: Harper. ★★.
Inge, William R. *Christian Mysticism*. New York, 1956: Living Age (Meridian). ★★.
———. *Mysticism in Religion*. Chicago, 1948: University of Chicago Press. ★★.
———. *The Philosophy of Plotinus*. Westport, Conn., 1968: Greenwood Press. ★★.
———. *The Platonic Tradition in English Religious Thought*. Folcroft, Pa., 1977: Folcroft Library Editions. ★★.
Iyengar, B. K. *Light on Yoga*. New York, 1973: Schocken. ★★.
James, William. *The Varieties of Religious Experience*. New York, 1958: New American Library. ★★.
John of Ruysbroeck. *The Spiritual Espousals*. Translated by Eric Colledge. New York, 1953: Harper. ★★★.
———. *The Adornment of the Spiritual Marriage, The Sparkling Stone, The Book of Supreme Truth*. Translated by Dom C. S. Wynschenk. London, 1951: Watkins. ★★★.
———. *The Seven Steps of the Ladder of Spiritual Love*. Translated by F. Sherwood Taylor. London, 1944: Dacre Press. ★★★.
John of the Cross, St. *The Complete Works*. Edited by E. Allison Peers. Translated by P. Silverio de Santa Teresa. 3 vols. Westminster, Md., 1945: Newman. ★★★.
Johnson, Raynor C. *The Imprisoned Splendour*. New York, 1953: Harper. ★★.
Julian of Norwich. *Revelations of Divine Love*. Translated by Clifton Wolters. London, 1973: Penguin. ★★★.
Jung, Carl G. *Answer to Job*. Princeton, N.J., 1972: Princeton University Press. ★★★.
———. *Psychology and Religion: West and East*. New Haven, 1938: Yale University Press. ★★★.

Bibliography 181

Keller, Helen. *My Religion*. New York, 1973: Swedenborg Foundation. ★★.
Kelly, Thomas R. *A Testament of Devotion*. New York, 1941: Harper. ★★.
Ko Hung. *Alchemy, Medicine and Religion in the China of AD 320: The Nei P'ien of Ko Hung*. Translated and edited by James R. Ware. New York, 1966: Dover. ★★★.
The Koran. Of the English translations of the Koran, that of Pickthall was considered best by a man well qualified to judge, one who had perhaps a greater stake in understanding Islam than any non-Muslim who ever lived, Mohandas Gandhi: *The Meaning of the Glorious Koran*. (Translated by M. M. Pickthall. New York, 1953: New American Library.) ★★★.

———. Since Gandhi's death Abdullah Yusef Ali has provided a new edition, showing the Arabic text together with English translation, and commentaries: *The Holy Qur'an*. (Lahore, 1977: Sr. Muhammad Ashraf.) ★★★.

———. *The Koran Interpreted*. A. J. Arberry. London, 1955: George Allen & Unwin. ★★★.

Kristol, Irving. *America's Continuing Revolution*. Washington, D.C., 1975: American Enterprise Institute. ★★.

———. *On the Democratic Idea in America*. New York, 1972: Harper & Row. ★★.

Lamb, George. *Brother Nicholas*. New York, 1955: Sheed & Ward. ★.
Laotse. *The Wisdom of Laotse*. Edited and translated by Lin Yutang. New York, 1958: Random House. ★★★.

———. See also Tao Te Ching.
Lecaro, Cardinal. *Methods of Mental Prayer*. London, 1957: Burns Oates. ★★★.
Lehrs, Ernst. *The Language of the Clouds*. Spring Valley, N.Y., 1987: St. George Publications. ★★.

———. *Man or Matter*. Spring Valley, N.Y., 1986: Anthroposophic Press. ★★★.

———. *Spiritual Science, Electricity, and Michael Faraday*. London, 1975: Rudolf Steiner Press.

Lewis, C. S. *The Abolition of Man*. New York, 1972: Macmillan. ★★.
———. *The Chronicles of Narnia*. 7 vols. New York, 1950: Macmillan. ★.
———. *George MacDonald: An Anthology*. New York, 1987: Macmillan. ★★.
———. *God in the Dock: Essays on Theology and Ethics*. Grand Rapids, Mich., 1989: Eerdmans. ★★.
———. *The Great Divorce*. New York, 1973: Macmillan. ★.
———. *Mere Christianity*. New York, 1973: Macmillan. ★★.
———. *Out of the Silent Planet*. New York, 1965: Macmillan. ★.
———. *Perelandra*. New York, 1973: Macmillan. ★.

———. *The Screwtape Letters*. New York, 1961: Macmillan. ★.
———. *That Hideous Strength*. New York, 1973: Macmillan. ★.
———. *Till We Have Faces*. Grand Rapids, Mich., 1974: Eerdmans. ★.
Lin Yutang. *The Wisdom of China and India*. New York, 1942: Random House. ★★★.
Lings, Martin. *Mohammad*. Rochester, Vt., 1983: Inner Traditions. ★★.
The Little Flowers of St. Francis. Translated by Raphael Brown. New York, 1958: Doubleday. ★.
MacDonald, George. *At the Back of the North Wind*. New York, 1989: Words of Wonder. ★.
———. *The Gifts of the Child Christ*. 2 vols. Grand Rapids, Mich., 1973: Eerdmans. ★.
———. *Phantastes* and *Lilith*. With an introduction by C. S. Lewis. Grand Rapids, Mich., 1964: Eerdmans. ★★.
———. *The Princess and Curdie*. New York, 1973: Penguin. ★.
———. *The Princess and the Goblin*. New York, 1973: Penguin. ★.
Machen, Arthur. *Tales of Horror and the Supernatural*. New York, 1948: Knopf. ★★.
Maharshi, Ramana. *The Collected Works of Maharshi*. Translated by Arthur Osborne. New York, 1972: Weiser. ★★.
———. *The Spiritual Teaching of Ramana Maharshi*. With an introduction by Carl G. Jung. Berkeley, Calif., 1972: Shambhala. ★★.
———. See also Arthur Osborne.
Manchester, William. *American Caesar*. Boston, 1978: Little, Brown and Co. ★.
———. *The Last Lion*. Boston, 1983: Little, Brown and Co. ★.
Maritain, Jacques. *Approaches to God*. New York, 1954: Harper. ★★.
———. *Saint Thomas and the Problem of Evil*. Milwaukee, 1942: Marquette University Press. ★★.
———. *Three Reformers: Luther, Descartes, Rousseau*. New York, 1970: Apollo. ★★.
Martin, Malachi. *The Decline and Fall of the Roman Church*. New York, 1981: Putnam. ★.
———. *Hostage to the Devil*. New York, 1979: Harper. ★.
———. *The Jesuits*. New York, 1987: Simon & Schuster. ★★.
———. *Rich Church, Poor Church*. New York, 1984: Putnam. ★.
———. *Vatican*. New York, 1986: Harper. ★.
Martin, P. W. *Experiment in Depth*. Boston, 1955: Routledge and Kegan Paul. ★★.
Mary of Agreda. *City of God*. 4 vols. Washington, N.J., 1971: Ave Maria Institute. ★★.
Mendelsohn, Robert S., M.D. *Confessions of a Medical Heretic*. Chicago, 1979: Contemporary Books. ★.

———. *Dissent in Medicine*. Chicago, 1979: Contemporary Books. ★.
———. *How to Raise a Healthy Child . . . In Spite of Your Doctor*. Chicago, 1984: Contemporary Books. ★.
———. *Male Practice: How Doctors Manipulate Women*. Chicago, 1981: Contemporary Books. ★.
———. *The People's Doctor Newsletter*. Evanston, Ill., 1973 to 1988: The People's Doctor Newsletter, Inc. ★.
Merton, Thomas. *The Seven Storey Mountain*. New York, 1948: Doubleday. ★.
Miller, Basil. *George Muller: Man of Faith and Miracles*. Minneapolis, 1981: Bethany Fellowship. ★.
Morality and Mental Health. Edited by O. Hobart Mowrer. Chicago, 1966: Rand McNally. ★★.
Mowrer, O. Hobart. *The Crisis in Psychiatry and Religion*. Princeton, 1961: Van Nostrand. ★★.
———. *The New Group Therapy*. Princeton, 1965: Van Nostrand. ★.
———. See also *Morality and Mental Health*.
The Mysteries. Papers from the Eranos Yearbooks. Edited by Joseph Campbell. New York, 1955: Pantheon. ★★★.
Nicoll, Maurice. *Living Time*. Boston, 1984: Shambhala. ★★.
———. *The Mark*. Boston, 1987: Shambhala. ★★.
———. *The New Man*. New York, 1972: Penguin. ★★.
———. *Psychological Commentaries on the Teaching of Gurdjieff and Ouspensky*. 5 vols. Boston and London, 1984: Shambhala. ★★★.
———. *Psychological Commentaries on the Teaching of Gurdjieff and Ouspensky*. Index to Volumes One through Five. Compiled by The Gurdjieff Society of Washington, D.C. Boston, 1989: Shambhala.
Nigg, Walter. *The Heretics*. New York, 1979: Knopf. ★.
———. *Warriors of God*. New York, 1972: Knopf. ★.
O'Brien, John A. *The Faith of Millions*. Huntington, Ind., 1974: Our Sunday Visitor. ★.
Osborne, Arthur. *The Incredible Sai Baba*. New York, 1972: Weiser. ★.
———. *Ramana Maharshi and the Path to Self-Knowledge*. New York, 1954: Weiser. ★★★.
———. *The Teachings of Ramana Maharshi*. New York, 1971: Weiser. ★★★.
Ouspensky, P. D. *The Fourth Way*. New York, 1971: Random House. ★★.
———. *In Search of the Miraculous*. New York, 1971: Harcourt, Brace, and World. ★★★.
———. *A New Model of the Universe*. New York, 1971: Random House. ★★★.
———. *The Psychology of Man's Possible Evolution*. New York, 1974: Random House. ★★.
———. *The Strange Life of Ivan Osokin*. New York, 1973: Penguin. ★★.

———. *Tertium Organum*. New York, 1970: Random House. ★★★.

Paracelsus. *Paracelsus: Selected Writings*. Edited by Jolande Jacobi. London, 1951: Routledge & Kegan Paul. ★★★.

———. See also Franz Hartmann.

Pardue, Austin. *Create and Make New*. New York, 1952: Harper. ★.

———. *Prayer Works*. New York, 1950: Morehouse-Gorham. ★.

Pascal, Blaise. *Thoughts: An Apology for Christianity*. Edited by Thomas S. Kepler. Cleveland, 1955: World. ★★.

———. *Pensées*. Translated by A. J. Krailsheimer. London, 1966: Penguin. ★★.

For study and interpretation:

———. *The Clue to Pascal*. By Emile Cailliet. Philadelphia, 1943: Westminster. ★★.

Patanjali. *How to Know God: The Yoga Aphorisms of Patanjali*. Translated by Prabhavananda and Isherwood. Hollywood, Calif., 1953: Vedanta Press. ★★★.

Philo. *Works*. 11 vols. Cambridge, Mass.: Harvard University Press. Loeb Classical Library. ★★★.

The Philokalia. *Writings from the Philokalia on Prayer of the Heart*. Translated by Kadloubovsky and Palmer. London, 1951: Faber & Faber. ★★★.

———. *Early Fathers from the Philokalia*. Translated by Kadloubovsky and Palmer. London, 1954: Faber & Faber. ★★★.

The Pilgrim. *The Way of a Pilgrim*. Translated by R. M. French. New York, 1965: Seabury. ★.

Plato. *The Dialogues of Plato*. Translated by Benjamin Jowett. New York, 1953: Oxford. ★★★.

Plotinus. *The Enneads*. Translated by Stephen MacKenna. London, 1969: Faber & Faber. ★★★.

———. *The System of Plotinus*. By the editors of the "Shrine of Wisdom." London, 1924: Shrine of Wisdom. ★★★.

Poulain A. *The Graces of Interior Prayer*. Translated by Lenora L. Yorke Smith. St. Louis, 1950: Herder. ★★★.

The Practice of the Presence of God. See Brother Lawrence.

Pythagoras. *The Golden Verses of Pythagoras*. Translated by Fabre d'Olivet. New York, 1975: Weiser. ★★.

The Quest of the Holy Grail. Translated by Pauline Matarasso. Harmondsworth, Middlesex, 1969: Penguin. ★★.

Radhakrishnan, S. *History of Philosophy, Eastern and Western*. 2 vols. London, 1952: George Allen & Unwin. ★★★.

———. *Recovery of Faith*. New York, 1955: Harper. ★★.

Bibliography

Ramakrishna, Sri. *The Gospel of Sri Ramakrishna.* Translated by Swami Nikhilananda. New York, 1969: Ramakrisha-Vivekananda Center. ★★.
Ramayana. A telling of the story of the Ramayana in simple English prose, by Mrs. Shudha Mazumdar. Bombay, 1953: Gita Press. ★★.
Read, David H. C. *The Christian Faith.* New York, 1956: Scribner. ★.
Reinhold, H. A. *The Soul Afire.* New York, 1944: Pantheon. ★★.
Richard of Saint-Victor. *Selected Writings on Contemplation.* New York: Harper. ★★★.
Robertson, A. T. *A Harmony of the Gospels.* New York, 1950: Harper. ★★★.
Rolle, Richard. *The Fire of Love.* New York, 1971: Penguin. ★★★.
Rosten, Leo. *A Guide to the Religions of America.* New York, 1955: Simon & Schuster. ★★.
Roueché, Berton. *The Medical Detectives.* New York, 1980: Times Books. ★.
Sacred Sex. Edited by Thomas R. White. Hankins, N.Y., 1975: East Ridge Press. ★★.
Schaer, Hans. *Religion and the Cure of Souls in Jung's Psychology.* New York, 1950: Pantheon. ★★★.
Scheffler, Johannes (Angelus Silesius). *The Cherubic Wanderer.* Translated by Willard R. Trask. New York, 1953: Pantheon. ★★.
Schimberg, Albert P. *The Story of Therese Neumann.* Folcroft, Pa., 1937: Folcroft. ★★.
Schmoger, The Very Rev. K. E. *The Life of Anna Catharina Emmerich.* Fresno, Calif., 1968: Maria Regina Guild. ★★.
Scholem, Gershom. *Major Trends in Jewish Mysticism.* New York, 1961: Schocken. ★★★.
Schroeder, Eric. *Muhammad's People.* Salt Lake City, 1955: Wheelwright. ★★.
Schuon, Frithjof. *The Transcendent Unity of Religions.* New York, 1953: Pantheon. ★★★.
———. *Understanding Islam.* New York, 1972: Penguin. ★★★.
Schweitzer, Albert. *The World of Albert Schweitzer.* By Erica Anderson and Eugene Exman. New York, 1955: Harper. ★.
Scupoli, Lorenzo. *Unseen Warfare.* (*The Spiritual Combat* and *Path to Paradise* edited by Nicodemus of the Holy Mountain and revised by Theophan the Recluse.) Translated by Kadloubovsky and Palmer. Crestwood, N.Y., 1978: St. Vladimir's Seminary Press. ★★★.
Shankara. *The Crest-Jewel of Discrimination.* Translated by Prabhavananda and Isherwood. Hollywood, Calif., 1978: Vedanta Press. ★★★.
Sheean, Vincent. *Lead, Kindly Light.* New York, 1949: Random House. ★★.
Shestov, Lev. *All Things are Possible & Penultimate Words and Other Essays.* With an introduction by Bernard Martin. Athens, Ohio, 1977: Ohio University Press. ★★★.

———. *Athens and Jerusalem.* Translated and with an introduction by Bernard Martin. Athens, Ohio, 1966: Ohio University Press. ★★★.
———. *Doestoevsky, Tolstoy, and Nietzsche.* Translated by Bernard Martin. Athens, Ohio, 1978: Ohio University Press. ★★★.
———. *In Job's Balances.* Translated by Coventry and Macartney. With an introduction by Bernard Martin. Athens, Ohio, 1975: Ohio University Press. ★★★.
———. *Kierkegaard and the Existential Philosophy.* Translated by Elinor Hewitt. Athens, Ohio, 1969: Ohio University Press. ★★★.
———. *Potestas Clavium.* Translated and with an introduction by Bernard Martin. Athens, Ohio, 1968: Ohio University Press. ★★★.
Smith, Margaret. *Readings from the Mystics of Islam.* London, 1959: Luzac. ★★.
———. *The Way of the Mystics: The Early Christian Mystics and the Rise of the Sufis.* New York, 1978: Oxford. ★★.
Sorokin, Pitirim. *The American Sex Revolution.* New York, 1960: Dutton. ★★.
———. *The Crisis of Our Age.* New York, 1957: Dutton. ★★.
———. *Forms and Techniques of Altruistic and Spiritual Growth.* Millwood, N.Y., 1954: Kraus Reprint Company. ★★★.
———. *The Ways and Power of Love.* Boston, 1954: Beacon. ★★.
Standen, Anthony. *Science Is a Sacred Cow.* New York, 1958: Dutton. ★★.
Steiner, Rudolf. *Cosmic Memory.* San Francisco, 1981: Harper. ★★★.
———. *The Gospel of St. John.* New York, 1940: Anthroposophic Press.
———. *Knowledge of the Higher Worlds and Its Attainment.* New York, 1942: Anthroposophic Press. ★★★.
———. *Life Between Death and Rebirth.* New York, 1968: Anthroposophic Press. ★★★.
———. *The Road to Self-Knowledge and the Threshold of the Spiritual World.* New York, 1938: Anthroposophic Press. ★★★.
———. *Occult Science.* New York, 1950: Anthroposophic Press. ★★★.
Stevenson, Robert L. *Dr. Jekyll and Mr. Hyde.* New York, 1972: Dutton. ★★.
Suso, Henry. *The Life of the Servant.* Translated by James M. Clarke. London, 1952: James M. Clarke & Co. ★★.
Suter, John Wallace, Jr. *The Book of English Collects.* New York, 1940: Harper. ★★.
Suzuki, D. T. *The Essence of Buddhism.* London, 1947: Buddhist Society. ★★★.
———. *Introduction to Zen Buddhism.* New York, 1964: Grove. ★★★.
———. *Manual of Zen Buddhism.* New York, 1960: Grove. ★★★.
———. *Mysticism: Christian and Buddhist.* New York, 1957: Macmillan. ★★★.

Bibliography

———. *Outlines of Mahayana Buddhism*. New York, 1963: Schocken. ★★★.

Sweetser, Wesley D. *Arthur Machen: A Biography*. New York, 1964: Grosset & Dunlap. ★.

Szasz, Thomas. *The Myth of Mental Illness*. New York, 1974: Harper. ★.

———. *The Myth of Psychotherapy*. Syracuse, 1988: Syracuse University Press. ★★.

———. *The Therapeutic State*. Buffalo, N.Y., 1984: Prometheus Press. ★★.

Tanquerey, Adophe. *The Spiritual Life*. New York, 1960: Desclee & Co. ★★★.

Tao Te Ching. (The Book of Tao.) By Lao Tse. *The Way and Its Power*. By Arthur Waley. London, 1943: George Allen & Unwin. ★★★.

———. *The Way of Life, Lao Tzu*. By R. B. Blakney. New York, 1955: New American Library. ★★★.

   For study and interpretation:

———. *The Parting of the Way*. By Holmes Welch. Boston, 1957: Beacon. ★★★.

———. See also Laotse.

Tauler, John. *The Life and History of the Reverend Doctor John Tauler of Strasbourg: with Twenty-five of His Sermons*. Translated by Susanna Winkworth. New York: Eaton & Mains. ★★.

Teresa of Avila, St. *Complete Works*. Edited by E. Allison Peers. 3 vols. New York, 1973: Doubleday. ★★★.

———. *The Life of Teresa of Jesus: The Autobiography of St. Teresa of Avila*. Translated by E. Allison Peers. New York, 1973: Doubleday. ★★★.

———. See also William Thomas Walsh.

Tertius. *The Chronicles of Brother Wolf*. City of Oxford, 1952: Mowbray. ★.

Theologia Germanica. Anonymous. Translated by Susanna Winkworth, revised according to the Bernhart version. Introduction by Joseph Bernhart. New York, 1949: Pantheon. ★★.

———. *The Theologica Germanica of Martin Luther*. Translated by Bengt Hoffman. New York, 1980: Paulist Press. ★★.

Therese of Lisieux, St. *The Autobiography of St. Therese of Lisieux: The Story of a Soul*. Translated by John Beevers. New York, 1957: Doubleday. ★★.

———. See also John Beevers; Guy Gaucher.

Tolkien, J. R. R. *The Hobbit*. New York, 1974: Ballantine. ★.

———. *The Lord of the Rings Trilogy*. (*The Fellowship of the Ring; The Two Towers; The Return of the King*.) New York, 1965: Ballantine. ★.

———. *The Silmarillion*. Boston, 1977: Houghton Mifflin. ★★.

Tolstoy, Leo. *What Men Live By*. New York: Peter Pauper Press. ★.

———. *Why Do Men Stupefy Themselves?* Hankins, N.Y., 1975: East Ridge Press. ★★.

The Torah. Philadelphia, 1962: Jewish Publication Society. ★★★.

Toynbee, Arnold. *A Study of History*. 12 vols. New York, 1954: Oxford. ★★★.
Trochu, Francis. *The Curé d'Ars*. Rockford, Ill., 1977: TAN. ★.
Twain, Mark. *Personal Recollections of Joan of Arc*. Hartford, Conn., 1980: The Stowe-Day Foundation. ★.
Underhill, Evelyn. *Mysticism*. New York: Dutton. ★★★.
———. *The Spiritual Life*. New York, 1936: Harper. ★★.
Upanishads. *The Principal Upanishads*. Translated and with commentary by S. Radhakrishnan. New York, 1953: Harper. ★★★.
———. *The Ten Principal Upanishads*. Translated by Shree Purohit Swami and W. B. Yeats. London, 1938: Faber. ★★★.
———. *The Thirteen Principal Upanishads*. Translated by R. E. Hume. London, 1931: Oxford. ★★★.
———. *The Upanishads*. Translated and with commentary by Swami Nikhilananda. 3 vols. New York, 1956: Harper. ★★★.
———. *The Upanishads, Breath of the Eternal*. Translated by Prabhavananda and Manchester. Hollywood, 1947: Vedanta Press. ★★★.
For interpretation and study:
———. *Brahma-Sutras*. Translated and with commentary by Swami Vireswarananda. Mayvati, Almore, 1948: Advaita Ashrama. ★★★.
———. *Self-Knowledge*. By Shankaracharya. Translated and with commentary by Swami Nikhilananda. New York, 1946: Ramakrishna-Vivekananda Center. ★★★.
Van Paassen, Pierre. *Visions Rise and Change*. New York, 1955: Dial. ★★.
Vedanta for the Western World. Edited by Christopher Isherwood. Hollywood, Calif., 1978: Vedanta Press. ★★.
Vett, Carl. *Dervish Diary*. Los Angeles, 1953: Knud K. Mogensen. ★★.
Voss, Carl Herman. *The Universal God*. Cleveland, 1953: World. ★★.
Wachsmuth, Guenther. *The Etheric Formative Forces*. New York, 1932: Anthroposophic Press. ★★★.
———. *The Evolution of Mankind*. Dornach, Switzerland, 1961: Anthroposophic Press. ★★★.
Waite, A. E. *The Hidden Church of the Holy Graal*. London, 1909: Rebman. ★★★.
———. *Lamps of Western Mysticism*. New York, 1923: Knopf. ★★★.
———. *The Secret Doctrine in Israel*. New York: Occult Research Press. ★★.
———. *The Secret Tradition in Alchemy*. New York, 1926: Knopf. ★★★.
Walsh, William Thomas. *Our Lady of Fatima*. New York, 1954: Doubleday. ★.
———. *Saint Teresa of Avila*. Rockford, Ill., 1987: TAN. ★★.
Watts, Alan. *The Supreme Identity*. New York, 1972: Random House. ★★★.

———. *The Way of Zen*. New York, 1974: Random House. ★★★.
The Way to Higher Consciousness. Edited by Meredith Murray. Hankins, N.Y., 1975: East Ridge Press. ★★.
Weatherhead, Leslie. *The Will of God*. Nashville, Tenn., 1975: Abingdon. ★.
West, John Anthony. *Serpent in the Sky: The Higher Wisdom of Ancient Egypt*. New York, 1979: Harper. ★★.
Wilhelm, Richard. *The Secret of the Golden Flower*. With commentary by C. G. Jung. New York, 1962: Harcourt, Brace, & World. ★★★.
———. *The I Ching*. Rendered into English by Cary F. Baynes. 2 vols. New York, 1950: Pantheon. ★★★.
William of St. Thierry. *On Contemplating God*. London, 1955: Mowbray. ★★★.
Williams, Charles. *All Hallow's Eve*. New York, 1969: Avon. ★★.
———. *Descent into Hell*. Grand Rapids, Mich., 1973: Eerdmans. ★★.
———. *The Greater Trumps*. New York, 1969: Avon. ★★.
———. *Many Dimensions*. Grand Rapids, Mich., 1970: Eerdmans. ★★.
———. *The Place of the Lion*. Grand Rapids, Mich., 1973: Eerdmans. ★★.
———. *Shadows of Ecstasy*. Grand Rapids, Mich., 1973: Eerdmans. ★★.
———. *War in Heaven*. Grand Rapids, Mich., 1972: Eerdmans. ★★.
A Woman Clothed with the Sun. Edited by John J. Delaney. New York: Doubleday. ★.
The World's Great Religions. By the editors of *Life*. New York, 1957: Time Inc. ★★.
Zimmer, Heinrich. *Philosophies of India*. New York, 1951: Pantheon. ★★★.
The Zohar. *Zohar, the Book of Splendor* (selections). Edited by Gershom Scholem. New York, 1949: Schocken. ★★★.
———. *The Zohar* (the whole work). 5 vols. Translated by Sperling and Simon. London, 1949: Soncino Press. ★★★.

Special Book Listings

The following books are grouped according to the special purposes to which they are related; note text page references.

These groups of books do not constitute a suggested schedule or diet of reading; taken as such they might produce indigestion. Each group, rather, is a kind of book cafeteria from which you can select what suits your appetite. You are responsible for your own diet. Titles representing widely different viewpoints are included—orthodox and unorthodox, Western and Eastern, ancient and modern. This broad scope is indicated because of the variety of the spiritual needs of individuals today. It is assumed that from the cafeteria offering you will choose such books as may meet your particular requirements. It is assumed further that you will not confuse yourself with incompatible mixtures but will simply pass over books which do not fit your background, are out of phase with your spiritual orientation, or are outside the range of your present interests.

BOOKS RELEVANT TO THE WAY OF REASON
See pp. 49–56.

Two books, one Protestant and one Catholic, are suggested as bridge books between philosophy and the more specifically theological viewpoints. The first is Elton Trueblood's *Philosophy of Religion,* an excellent outline and examination of the possibilities and difficulties of thinking one's way toward the reality of God. The second is the beautifully disciplined and boiled-down study entitled *Approaches to God* by the great Catholic scholar Jacques Maritain.

This little book covers the various philosophical approaches to God, with major emphasis naturally on a philosophy which is fundamental in Catholicism, that of St. Thomas Aquinas. If one wishes to take a deeper look in this area he can do so in *The Christian Philosophy of St. Thomas Aquinas* and in the *History of Christian Philosophy in the Middle Ages*, both by Etienne Gilson.

There are lots of kinds of theology, and we will put off some of them to another place: ascetical and mystical theology, for example, deal more with spiritual experience and with knowing and keeping the rules (pp. 80 and 84–85) than with reasoning. But anyone who hopes to keep his own thinking about God on the track should get acquainted with at least the main outlines of formal theology.

An easy and interesting book of basic Catholic theology is F. J. Sheed's *Theology and Sanity*. A deeper book, bearing directly upon the question of God's reality, is *God: His Existence and His Nature* by the Dominican theologian Father Reginald Garrigou-Lagrange, a thorough exposition of the traditional proofs of God's existence and the knowledge of God's nature and attributes from the Catholic point of view. A Protestant theology is ably presented in Reinhold Niebuhr's famous book *The Nature and Destiny of Man*. Another outstanding Protestant theologian, Paul Tillich, in his *Systematic Theology* goes extensively into the question of the reality of God and discusses fully the place of reason in the quest of that reality. An Anglican exposition of sacred doctrine is provided in *Theological Outlines* by Francis J. Hall, a condensation of Professor Hall's classic ten-volume work.

An approach to God sometimes called "natural theology" develops out of the questions "Is there evidence in nature and in natural science for the existence of God? Can we see God in nature?" Gerald Heard presents a contemporary essay in natural theology in *Is God Evident?* Other books in this area are *Human Destiny* by Lecomte Du Noüy, *Man Does Not Stand Alone* by A. Cressy Morrison, and *The Imprisoned Splendour* by Raynor Johnson, particularly Part I, entitled "The Data of Natural Science."

Reason may be used to seek evidence of God not only in nature and in science but also in history (a very important pursuit for Christians, whose religion is particularly historical). Gerald Heard follows this line of inquiry in *Is God in History?* See further *A Study of History* by Arnold J. Toynbee, *The End of the Modern*

World by the Roman Catholic philosopher and theologian Romano Guardini, and *The Crisis of Our Age* by Pitirim A. Sorokin. Note also *The Dignity of Man*, an inquiry into the historic spiritual crisis of modern man by a former editor of *Fortune* magazine, the late Russell W. Davenport.

Finally, for those who wish to explore the nature of the divine Reality and man's place in it with an Eastern mind of universality, brilliance, and depth, *The Life Divine* by Sri Aurobindo is suggested.

BOOKS RELEVANT TO THE WAY OF FAITH
See pp. 56–61.

One of the most helpful of all books on faith is still Harry Emerson Fosdick's well-known and well-loved *The Meaning of Faith*. Arranged for daily reading over a twelve-week period, it covers the ground thoroughly from practical, inspirational, and rational viewpoints. The problem of faith and its renewal in the present human situation is explored on a world-wide scale by Sarvepalli Radhakrishnan in *Recovery of Faith*, a sharp pointing up of man's need for faith and the ways to its acquisition as taught and demonstrated in the great living faiths of Hinduism, Taoism, Judaism, Christianity, and others.

Faith, the spiritual reality, has a basic common meaning in all religions. But, in addition, "faith" as a system of belief or consent has different meanings in different religions, and you should make your choice of books with this condition in mind. For a Roman Catholic, for instance (as for the great majority of Christians of the past and present), faith is "a theological virtue by which our intellect is disposed to assent firmly to all the truths revealed by God . . ."* and also "'a habit of mind by which eternal life is begun in us, in that it makes the mind assent to things which appear not . . .'" (St. Thomas Aquinas' comment on St. Paul's statement that "faith is the substance of things to be hoped for, the evidence of things that appear not"†). So far the Catholic and many other Christians could agree. But to the Catholic, "faith" also means "the sum of the truth taught by the Catholic religion." And "Catholic"

* *A Catholic Dictionary*, p. 196.
† *Ibid.*

here evidently means not simply "universal" and not Anglican and Eastern Orthodox and others who call themselves "Catholic" but specifically "Roman Catholic." "Faith," therefore, to a Roman Catholic, is belief in what the Roman Catholic Church teaches. *The faith*, in this view, *is* Roman Catholicism. For a succinct yet comprehensive presentation of what the Roman Catholic faith is, in both its general and its more particular sense, see *A Catholic Dictionary*. See also *The Faith of Millions* by Reverend John A. O'Brien.

To certain Evangelical Christian groups, "faith" means belief in the literal words of the Bible, literally understood. To Anglican and Eastern Orthodox Catholics, and to Protestants of various denominations likewise, "faith" has different and particular meanings in addition to its universal meaning of belief and trust in God.

There is a further particularity in which the word "faith" distinguishes a large part of Christianity from the rest of the God-seeking world: many Christian groups accept Jesus of Nazareth as the Messiah, the only Son of God, and the one incarnation of God. Other great world religious faiths—Judaism, Hinduism, Islam, and Buddhism, for example—do not share this viewpoint. So faith, as creedal or formal belief, has different meanings not only within Christianity but within the world-wide body of all those who believe in and seek to know the Supreme Reality.

The different shades of belief among the various Protestant denominations and other religions are described in the literature of each group, which is far too large for a listing to be attempted here. You can easily find the works you are interested in by contacting a minister, priest, or rabbi of the particular group whose faith you are studying. Among survey books in this area are *A Guide to the Religions of America*, edited by Leo Rosten, *Religion in the Twentieth Century* by Vergilius Ferm, and *The World's Great Religions* by the editors of *Life* magazine.

The following books, dealing with the faith from a broad Christian point of view, are by Protestant authors, but they treat the subject without provoking Protestant interdenominational issues or raising the Protestant-Catholic question: *Mere Christianity* by C. S. Lewis and *The Christian Faith* by David H. C. Read.

Finally, a particular modern view needs special attention. A movement of religious-psychological thought and practice has grown up around the fact that faith can produce increase in mental and physical well-being and success in daily undertakings and practical affairs. In this movement faith is emphasized as a means to some or all of these ends. Christian texts, such as Mark 11:24, are quoted in support of this view. Faith is cultivated by prayer, by optimistic attitudes ("positive thinking"), by disciplined affirmations of good and denials of evil, and by keeping watch over the mind so that desired thoughts are retained and undesired thoughts are rejected. In brief, this movement believes and demonstrates that man, by religious and psychological techniques, can influence his inner and outer circumstances for good. The movement can trace its origins to the work of Ralph Waldo Emerson, Phineas Parkhurst Quimby, and Thomas Troward.

It is recognized that certain of the groups within the pattern would not acknowledge their inclusion in any such over-all designation as a movement. The common denominators, however, are apparent. The term "movement" is used here for the sake of brevity, clarity, and convenience and not with any intention of grouping bodies which do not wish to be so grouped. The chief divisions within the movement are those which are known as New Thought, Christian Science, Mental Science, Metaphysics, and the Unity School of Christianity. Many individuals who share the movement's views are not associated with these divisions but are members of regular Christian denominations. Dr. Peale, for example, one of the most influential spokesmen of the movement, is a minister of the Dutch Reformed Church.

These particular techniques in the application of faith, or "mental science," or "divine science" to the human problems of health and supply have become widely popular, especially in the United States. Obviously they fill a deeply felt need and often are genuinely effective. In some quarters, however, they have been regarded as serious distortions of the religious and psychological facts of life. A great contribution of these doctrines lies in their ability to correct and relieve people who are suffering from unfounded and obsessive pessimism. Difficulties arise, however, from the fact that when the teaching is not applied with understanding and discrimination, it tends to produce unfounded and obsessive optimism.

BOOKS RELEVANT TO THE WAY OF EXPERIENCE
See pp. 61–74.

There are many books which describe in detail the traditional three ways to God (purgation, illumination, union). Among the best of these are Evelyn Underhill's *Mysticism*‡ and Father Garrigou-Lagrange's *The Three Ages of the Interior Life*. The following books about the experience of God as reported in terms of the Western traditions are also suggested: *The Dialogues of Plato* (these works are usually read for their literary and philosophic interest, but actually they are full of references to experience of higher Reality; note particularly *The Republic*, Book VII, the story of the prisoners in the cave); *The Mysteries*, edited by Joseph Campbell (the Greek, Egyptian, and other mysteries were techniques for introducing their subjects into direct experience of spiritual Reality; note particularly "The Meaning of the Eleusinian Mys-

---

‡ "Mysticism" is another one of those hot terms. It is a very old and universal concept, and no one studying empirical knowledge of God can afford to misunderstand it. Mysticism means experience of God. But the word has become muddled almost beyond recognition as our knowledge and valuation of spiritual experience have degenerated. Evelyn Underhill's book by that name is an excellent exposition of what mysticism really is. So also are the articles entitled "Mysticism" in the Encyclopaedia Britannica and in the Columbia Encyclopedia. At least look up and read these articles, so the next time you hear someone talking or writing as if a mystic were somebody with a crystal ball and a dunce cap you will be able to determine on whose head the dunce cap really belongs. See further *Mysticism in Religion* and *Christian Mysticism* by W. R. Inge.

Mysticism lies at the root of all religion. Aldous Huxley, in his introduction to the Bhagavad Gita, has written: "From this fact [that mystical knowledge is superior to the devotional practices which lead up to it] have arisen misunderstandings in plenty and a number of intellectual difficulties. Here, for example, is what Abbot John Chapman writes in one of his admirable *Spiritual Letters:* 'The problem of *reconciling* (not merely uniting) mysticism with Christianity is more difficult. The Abbot (Abbot Marmion) says that St. John of the Cross is like a sponge full of Christianity. You can squeeze it all out, and the full mystical theory remains. Consequently fifteen years or so I hated St. John of the Cross and called him a Buddhist. I loved St. Teresa, and read her over and over again. She is first a Christian, and only secondarily a mystic. Then I found I had wasted fifteen years, so far as prayer was concerned.' And yet, he concludes, in spite of its 'Buddhistic' character, the practice of mysticism (or, to put it in other terms, the realization of the Perennial Philosophy) makes good Christians. He might have added that it also makes good Hindus, good Buddhists, good Taoists, good Moslems and good Jews."

teries," pages 23, 24, 29, 30). *The Enneads of Plotinus* (writings of one who experienced God directly* and whose views deeply influenced Christian thought for many centuries).

Outstanding books by or about Western saints and mystics include: *The Confessions of St. Augustine; St. Francis of Assisi*, by G. K. Chesterton; *The Little Flowers of St. Francis of Assisi; The Treatise on Purgatory and the Dialogue* of St. Catherine of Genoa; *The Complete Works of St. Teresa of Jesus*, particularly in Vol. 1, the *Life; The Life of the Servant*, an autobiography by Henry Suso; *St. Ignatius' Own Story*, a short, direct biography of St. Ignatius of Loyola; *Brother Nicholas*, a biography of Nicholas of Flüe, "Bruder Klaus," by George Lamb; *The Curé d'Ars*, a biography of an amazing man, the patron saint of priests, by Abbé Francis Trochu; *Storm of Glory* by John Beevers, the story of St. Thérèse of Lisieux; *The Life and Doctrines of Jacob Boehme* by Franz Hartmann.

The Miracle of Lourdes by Ruth Cranston and *The Voyage to Lourdes* by Alexis Carrel are books which touch upon special aspects of spiritual experience: charismatic healing, the apparition of persons in a supernatural state to human beings, unaccountable physical phenomena or miracles, stigmatization, and so on. Note also: *Miracles* by C. S. Lewis, *The Physical Phenomena of Mysticism* by Herbert Thurston, S.J., *The Story of Therese Neumann* (the life of a contemporary stigmatist) by A. P. Schimberg, and *Our Lady of Fatima* (an account of the appearance of "a Lady made wholly of light" to three Portuguese shepherd children and the unaccountable solar phenomena witnessed by 70,000 people) by W. T. Walsh.

Experiment in Depth by P. W. Martin is a good introduction to spiritual experience from the standpoint of modern depth psychology, particularly the psychology of C. G. Jung. Freud's psychology basically is materialistic, mechanistic, and atheistic, and so he and his followers are bound by their most fundamental hypotheses not to understand spiritual experience as spiritual experience but rather as illness, superstition, or illusion (see *The Future of an Illusion* by Freud). Jung, on the other hand, is genuinely and profoundly open

---

* "Four times, during the period I passed with him, he achieved this Term, by no mere latent fitness but by the ineffable Act. To this God, I also declare, I Porphyry, that in my sixty-eighth year I too was once admitted and entered into Union" (*Enneads*, Vol. 1, p. 24).

to and interested in the reality of religious and spiritual experience. See *Psychology and Religion: West and East* by C. G. Jung. For a criticism of Jung's religious views see *Eclipse of God* by Martin Buber (pp. 78–92 and 133–137).

Two modern survey books which cover the field of spiritual experience very thoroughly are *The Ways and Power of Love* and *Forms and Techniques of Altruistic and Spiritual Growth* by Pitirim A. Sorokin.

Insight into spiritual experience may be gained by exposing oneself to the witness of contemporaries who have had such experience. Four books by widely different modern witnesses are suggested: *The Seven Storey Mountain* by Thomas Merton, a young man who became a Trappist monk and priest; *You Are Greater Than You Know* by Lou Austin, a businessman who discovered he had a Partner; *Alcoholics Anonymous Comes of Age* by "Bill," the anonymous co-founder whose spiritual experience has led to the recovery of three quarters of a million alcoholics; and *Release* by Starr Daily, the incorrigible criminal who was visited by Christ in prison and taught the Way of freedom.

Anthologies offer a very practical and enjoyable way to study spiritual experience. The following are suggested: *The Perennial Philosophy* by Aldous Huxley, *The Choice Is Always Ours* by Dorothy Berkeley Phillips, *A Year of Grace* and *From Darkness to Light* by Victor Gollancz, and *The Soul Afire* by H. A. Reinhold.

Of special interest to the world of today is the spiritual experience of the Russian people. For a historical survey, including many writings and accounts of the lives of Russian theocentric saints, see *A Treasury of Russian Spirituality* edited by G. P. Fedotov (note particularly the conversation of St. Seraphim of Sarov with Nicholas Motovilov, pp. 266–279, an interesting example of a theophany transmitted to one man by the power of another, an ability which Sri Ramakrishna also possessed). For an inquiry into the spiritual life of present-day Russia see *Visions Rise and Change* by Pierre Van Paassen.

The Eastern traditions of direct experience of God have much of interest, wisdom, and help to offer the seeker, whatever his religion. The literature of these traditions is very large. The following books would provide a rudimentary introduction to this great area of empirical knowledge: *How to Know God: The Yoga Aphorisms* of *Patanjali* translated by Prabhavananda and Isherwood; *The Gospel of Sri Ramakrishna* translated by Swami Nikhilananda; *The Essence of Buddhism* by D. T. Suzuki; *Tibet's Great Yogi, Milarepa* edited by W. Y. Evans-Wentz; *The Secret of the Golden Flower* translated by Richard Wilhelm. (The Eastern scriptures are of course most essential for an understanding of the matter in hand and should be consulted ahead of the books indicated immediately above.) Zen Buddhism, a strictly experiential school of spiritual awakening, has aroused increasing interest in the Western world. A good introduction is *The Way of Zen* by Alan Watts. See also *Introduction to Zen Buddhism* by D. T. Suzuki.

The experimental path to God has had an interesting history in Islam. Note *Readings from the Mystics of Islam* by Margaret Smith, *The Mathnawí of Jalálu'ddín Rúmí* edited by Reynold A. Nicholson, and *Muhammad's People* by Eric Schroeder.

Jewish experience of God is set forth in the Old Testament. For later developments see *Major Trends in Jewish Mysticism* by Gershom Scholem; *Tales of the Hasidim* and *The Legend of the Baal-Shem* by Martin Buber; *God in Search of Man* by Abraham J. Heschel; and *The Zohar*.

BOOKS RELEVANT TO THE PRACTICE OF PRAYER
See pp. 127–170.

Useful books on prayer cover a very wide range. One must be careful not to read too many different kinds at anywhere near the same time, and not to read deep books too soon. To do so can lead to either pride or confusion or both; or it can give you a bad taste for books which, taken in right time, would be wonderfully good for you. On the other hand certain people, without vanity or gagging, are able to get help from even the deepest sources (from Meister Eckhart, for instance) quite early in their work. As you must find your own way in the Way, so you must find your own books.

The following listing is arranged in four divisions. These are necessarily somewhat arbitrary, and experts on prayer might easily rank some of the books differently. Our purpose, however, is not scholarly but strictly practical. The present grouping can serve as a rough but functional guide by which you may select books according to your present condition and need. These books are listed not chronologically but in the estimated order of their usefulness and interest to a working pray-er.

BEGINNERS' BOOKS

Prayer Works by Austin Pardue. Written in the simplest of language by the Episcopal Bishop of Pittsburgh, this is an excellent primer for anyone who wants to start prayer and really work at it, without getting into complications or intellectual problems right away.

Prayer by Dr. Alexis Carrel. A simple, powerful essay on prayer by a world-famous scientist, surgeon, and physiologist, "for those of little faith or none at all" as well as for more mature Christians.

The Meaning of Prayer by Harry Emerson Fosdick. Written back in 1915, this book remains to this day one of the classic practical introductions to prayer for the ordinary person. It is simple but thorough and quite complete in covering what you need to know in the first few years of work in prayer.

The Way of a Pilgrim. Anonymous. This book is discussed elsewhere (pp. 157–166), but it must be included in any list of beginners' books on prayer, because it is the only introduction in Christian terms to one of the most powerful of all methods of prayer—a method which, for all its depth, is within the range of the rankest novice.

WORKING BOOKS

A Preface to Prayer by Gerald Heard. A penetrating working inquiry into the meaning and practice of low, middle, and high prayer, by a man who has devoted a lifetime to the search for such meaning.

How to Pray by Jean-Nicolas Grou. This book consists of the chapters on prayer from Père Grou's outstanding work, *The School of Jesus Christ*. A working outline of prayer based on the view that God alone teaches to pray, including discussions of various ways of prayer and a spiritual commentary on the Lord's Prayer.

Spiritual Letters by Dom John Chapman, O.S.B. These letters, written to individuals who were involved in specific problems in prayer, are a mine of skilled and sensitive counsel, particularly in abandonment and in those phases of prayer in which "dryness" and lack of consolation are encountered. Abbot Chapman was one of the most understanding of near-contemporary directors of prayer. He taught that "the simplest kind of prayer is best" and "the more you pray the better it goes."

The Way to Christ by Jacob Boehme. The famous collection of prayers and instruction in prayer by the God-illuminated shoemaker of Goerlitz, Germany, written in the years 1622–1623 and containing six tracts as follows: "Of True Repentance," "Of True Resignation," "Of Regeneration or the New Birth," "Of the Supersensual Life," "Dialogue Between an Enlightened and Unenlightened Soul," and "Of Divine Contemplation." Boehme is not for everyone, but those who can hear him find him a very great help.

Contemplative Prayer by Shirley C. Hughson, O.H.C. "The only object [of this book] is, in a humble way, to introduce souls who desire to love God to that higher, simplified mode of prayer which St. Francis de Sales calls contemplation, and which he describes as 'no other than a loving, simple and permanent attention of the spirit to divine things.'"

The Book of English Collects by John Wallace Suter, Jr. The collect is a peculiarly useful and powerful form of short prayer. "Often it consists of one sentence; usually it expresses a single main thought, which is either a petition or a thanksgiving." A few favorite collects committed to memory can serve as a backlog and working resource in the life of prayer. This book is an outstanding compilation of collects from traditional sources.

The Book of Common Prayer. The Episcopal Prayer Book is listed here for both particular and general reference. It is understood, of course, that each one will find the greatest usefulness in the Prayer Book or books of his own particular denomination. Prayer books are prime aids in the study and practice of communion with God, incorporating as they do the wisdom of great bodies of praying men and women over the centuries.

ADVANCED BOOKS

Holy Wisdom by Augustine Baker. The famous book of "directions for the prayer of contemplation" written by "a monk of the English Congregation of the Holy Order of S. Benedict" who lived from 1575 to 1641. It is one of the most complete, most thorough, most respected, and most useful of all works on prayer. Although it is certainly not a beginners' book, nevertheless many beginners are able to get real help from it. As in the case of all advanced books, *Holy Wisdom* should be used judiciously and if at all possible with experienced counsel. It is among the very greatest treasures in the whole field of the work of prayer.

The Cloud of Unknowing. Anonymous. This book is discussed elsewhere (pp. 153-154). It is included here as a basic, lucid, powerful, and traditionally revered guide in a difficult and critical area of the soul's ascent to direct experience of God: the passage from sensible and mental images of any and all kinds into the tremendous realm beyond the senses and beyond the mind wherein lies the "cloud" which is the last veil between man and his Lord. Since in our time it is very widely assumed that there are no realms of consciousness beyond the mind, this book establishes a point of departure for a kind of inquiry and experiment much needed today if our psychology is ever to rise out of the artificial and strangulating limits it has set for itself.

The Scale of Perfection by Walter Hilton. A gentle, charming, wise, and incisive survey of the ladder of prayer. Not much is known of Hilton beyond what his works reveal. He may have been a Carthusian monk, although it seems more probable that he was an Augustinian canon. However that may be, he "occupies a central position in the small group of English medieval mystics, being third in time of its four outstanding personalities." (The other three are Richard Rolle, Julian of Norwich, and the unknown author of *The Cloud.*)

The Graces of Interior Prayer by A. Poulain, S.J. Possibly this is the greatest work of its particular kind on prayer. It is a comprehensive, technical, detailed, meticulous, scholarly, and at the same time deeply understanding and inspired treatise on the many aspects of mystical prayer. It is exactly the kind of book which most beginners, and certainly those with any tendency toward spiritual ambition or pride, should leave strictly alone. Also it is not for anyone who is unable or unwilling to study. But for those in whom experience of God actually is developing, it may serve as an invaluable source of knowledge.

Methods of Mental Prayer by Cardinal Lecaro. Like Poulain's book listed above, this is a technical, scholarly, and in a certain sense scientific work on prayer. It is concerned with method, degree, and structure in various Roman Catholic schools of mental prayer since the sixteenth century. It includes extensive and very helpful schemata of Ignatian, Salesian, Sulpician, and Carmelite prayer and of the prayer of St. Alphonsus and St. John Baptist de la Salle. The value of such a work as this is obvious for one whose conscious contact with God has been made and is developing, and who wishes to be guided not only by inspiration but by the most careful mental and rational use of traditional resources. For anyone else the dangers and difficulties of so highly intellectualized and strictly formalized an approach are also obvious.

The Complete Works of St. Teresa of Jesus. St. Teresa (of Avila) was a person who combined tremendous experience in prayer with great insight into her own states and encounters in divine communion and with a talent for expression. She deals particularly with techniques, problems, and stages of prayer in "The Way of Perfection" and "Interior Castle," both in Vol. II of *The Complete Works.*

The Ascent of Mount Sion by Bernardino de Laredo. This was the book upon which St. Teresa of Jesus leaned for help during the most critical years of her spiritual life. It is a systematic but heart-centered guide to the union of the soul with God. Bernardino de Laredo was a Spanish physician of the sixteenth century who became a lay brother in the Franciscan order.

On Contemplating God by William of St. Thierry. A short, beautiful, and intellectually limpid treatise on the deepest love of God, by a Benedictine contemplative by whom St. Bernard was influenced. This is a first translation of a twelfth-century manuscript which is a mirror of profound simplicity in the prayer of transforming love.

Of Cleaving to God by St. Albert the Great. St. Albert for his own use made this compilation, as he calls it, from the thought of such authorities in prayer as Cassian, St. Bernard, and St. Thomas Aquinas. It is an explorer's and guide's book on prayer which pays particular attention to abandonment and clinging to God in all the circumstances of life, in and out of the set periods of prayer. Strict and demanding but uncomplicated, warm, and genial.

Letters of Spiritual Direction by Bossuet. This brief collection of letters reflects the mastery of a man so evolved and so skilled in the inner life that he expresses his insight in terms of great simplicity. Although this is certainly an advanced book, it seems to me that many beginners might be able to use it as well as those who have been working for some years. Bossuet, who was tutor to the Dauphin at the time of Louis XIV, knew the life of prayer in juxtaposition to the life of this world as few men do, and his letters show this knowledge wonderfully.

On Prayer by J. P. de Caussade, S.J. Those who are looking for the fire and joy of Père de Caussade's writings on abandonment will not find them in this book. Its usefulness lies in another direction. It is a careful, restrained, and balanced study of a question which greatly disturbed the time in which it occurred, the so-called quietist controversy. Anyone hoping to understand the prayer life of European Christianity in the past several hundred years should inform himself as to what "quietism" is (and is not) and why it became so hard an issue. Caussade's work, subtitled "spiritual instructions on the various states of prayer according to Bossuet, Bishop of Meaux," seems to me an excellent presentation of the viewpoints of those who opposed the quietists. For the viewpoints of the quietists themselves, see *The Life of Madame Guyon* by Thomas C. Upham and *The Spiritual Guide* by Michael de Molinos.

A Testament of Devotion by Thomas Kelly. This is not only a book that people who are new to prayer might find helpful; it is a beginners' book par excellence. Nevertheless I have included it here among advanced books because that is where, in my opinion, it belongs. The gift of communication which enabled this beloved Quaker to convey his knowledge of God in terms nearly everyone can understand and accept should not be permitted to blind us to the height and depth of Thomas Kelly's place in the spiritual life. I believe that his book is directly comparable to *The Practice of the Presence of God* in that its beauty and its simplicity serve both to reveal and to conceal a master's experience and a master's way of prayer. Remember that most of the writings which comprise this short book represent the latter few years of Kelly's life, a period following a long time of hard work and struggle in prayer. In these years just before his death, he broke through into the singing, all-embracing, keen-seeing, seldom-interrupted love of God which is so powerfully and tenderly mediated in his *Testament*. For beginners, for old-timers, for all—here is great fare, and nothing to worry about by way of reservations, unless your heart is still so hard that the very exuberance and lyric quality of this man's song of God is unassimilable to you.

DEEP-WATER BOOKS

Enneads of Plotinus. "It is the secret of the power of Plotinus that in him the mystic's impulse to the finding of his own Soul and the scientific impulse to criticize and understand experience are so completely united" (*The System of Plotinus*, Shrine of Wisdom ed.). Plotinus is what Meister Eckhart would call a "heathen authority." He was a native of Egypt (born in A.D. 205) of unknown race. He had direct, personal, experimental knowledge of the ineffable and unutterable heights of communion with God, and he had real genius in communicating, so far as is possible in words, what he knew. He is both very deep and very balanced, very sane. His influence upon the history of thought, and upon Christian experience of God in the centuries following his death, is incalculable.

The Mystical Theology of Dionysius the Areopagite. (See also *The Celestial Hierarchies* and *The Divine Names*.) Here is a man, writing obviously (particularly in *The Mystical Theology*) from direct experience, who stands as the fountainhead, the first and probably the greatest single influence, of the whole stream of Christian experiential knowledge of God, after the apostles and Jesus Christ himself. Again and again he probes the (to human eyes) dark and terrible threshold of God's very Being and man's experience of that Being. And he plunges beyond the level of Being into kinds of knowledge of God in which words, including the word "knowledge," simply collapse in any of their usual senses and can be used only negatively, and doubly and triply negatively. This is very far from a speculative or a semantic exercise; it is what happens to the human tongue and the human mind when they have quite literally exceeded themselves. It is what happens when God and man have entered into a relationship (which is no longer "relationship") beyond all telling. And yet something *can* be told, and Dionysius has told it in a way that has nourished and inspired Christian Godseekers, the greatest and the least, ever since. Who he was is entirely unknown. He writes obviously under a pseudonym (that of St. Dionysius, St. Paul's Athenian convert), and his work was done probably some time around the end of the fifth century.

The Philokalia. A very large compilation of writings of the Fathers and the greatest saints and mystics of the Eastern Christian Church, from the third to the fourteenth centuries. Books of extracts from *The Philokalia* are now available, as noted and discussed on page 160. This basic work is listed here because it must be considered among any essential grouping of great charts of the deepest waters of prayer. The actual experience and the inspired expression of that experience among the Eastern Christian masters is of such authenticity, clarity, and power that it cannot very well be ignored by anyone who hopes to enter these waters, or who finds himself even now, by God's leading, drawn into them.

Selected Writings of Richard of Saint-Victor. Richard is the one whom Dante described as "more than a man" in his relationship to God. He is a disciplined and profoundly experienced teacher of contemplative prayer. He is outstanding, and in his era perhaps unique, in his knowledge of the psychological aspects of deep prayer. Contemplatives of all times owe a great debt to him who first showed clearly the reasons for the infirmities and difficulties which accompany the understanding of these things. Richard often is studied from the standpoint of his influence upon later currents and schools of Christian mysticism, but our interest in him here is as a great, sound, and currently available guide in experimental knowledge of God.

On the Song of Songs by St. Bernard. The relationship of the soul to God changes (from the soul's standpoint) at various stages of the regenerate life—from that of an outcast rebel, profligate, scorner—to that of a servant—to that of a friend—to that of a child—and finally, highest and most intimate of all, to that of a spouse. God as bridegroom of the soul is not merely a pious or poetic thought; it is a fiery and hair-raising truth at the very summit of the spiritual life. The recognition of this truth is universal; you will find it in the Old Testament (particularly in the Song of Songs), the New Testament, in the teaching of the Sufis, the Baal Shem Tov, John of the Cross, John of Ruysbroeck, and very widely elsewhere. Among the greatest of the traditional interpreters of this relationship is St. Bernard of Clairvaux. Nothing but confusion can come from a merely curious reading of his writings on the subject. But if you are beginning to come alive to the reality of the Supreme Person, and if you are being inwardly drawn to understand the awful mystery of his true relationship to your own soul, you may read St. Bernard *On the Song of Songs* with profit.

Before this area of knowledge can be touched with real insight, the intelligence first must have been purged of such sick notions as that which sees in mystical union a deviated or "sublimated" sexuality. The ignorant pruriency represented in such an attitude is very widespread and even naïvely respected and taught today, and it is not healed by argument. It is seen through only when the soul finally is beginning to open to the radiant and penetrating Truth.

Meister Eckhart, a modern translation, by Raymond Blakney. At first respected and beloved, and then mistrusted and rejected, in his own time (1260–1328), Meister Eckhart is one of the most deeply God-experienced and God-inspired of all Christian teachers after Christ himself. Meister Eckhart was that rare kind of man, a great scholar, a consummate and technically disciplined thinker, who at the same time was God-saturated and God-intoxicated. This condition led to a head-on encounter with the authorities of that day, but it also left one of the great intellectual and mystical teaching legacies of all time. It is said very truly that "Eckhart now emerges as a pivotal figure in the making of the modern religious mind." And Raymond Blakney writes of the enigmatic Dominican of Cologne: "It was in his doctrine of God that Meister Eckhart went beyond the tolerance of his time and perhaps beyond the capacity of ours . . . certainly he lifted Christianity above any parochial conception and revealed its inner relation to the great, universal spiritual movements which have found expression in many forms. . . ."

Eckhart's teaching was estimated as dangerous in his own era, and perhaps those who so regarded it were not all knaves. Maybe it was dangerous, and maybe it still is. His doctrine later was abused, and it still may be abused. But if you have got your feet on the ground, if you are working seriously in prayer, and if you are open to teaching of great originality, great boldness and sweep, great depth, and utter authenticity, Meister Eckhart is a man whose acquaintance you should make.

The Spiritual Espousals by John of Ruysbroeck. Spiritual history is full of key men named John. This one was the greatest of the Flemish mystics, born in the little village of Ruysbroeck, between Hal and Brussels, in 1293. In his long and lovely lifetime of eighty-eight years he became one of the earth's most lucid teachers of the spiritual espousals and the spiritual marriage. From the viewpoint of clarity he is perhaps even greater than St. Bernard and St. John of the Cross in this regard. His first biographer, Pomerius, describes him as "a simple, quiet, rather shabby-looking person who went about the streets of Brussels with his mind lifted up to God." John of Ruysbroeck is noted above all for his direct experience in mystical communion, and then for his shrewd common sense, his great intellectual power well based in profound intellectual humility, and his transparent genius in logical, sane, methodical exposition of the deepest and highest experience of the soul in the Uncreated Light. His writings are distinguished by their order, balance, and symmetry. He was a homely, humble, wise, and kind man who loved the forest and the birds. Indeed, he lived in the forest for a long time, and he wrote in the forest, under a beloved lime tree. This tender and heavenly man was at the same time a surgically ruthless exposer of the vagaries of the "Brethren of the Free Spirit" and other false twists in the spiritual life of his time. His very purity and sanctity are obstacles to reading him in some cases; but otherwise he is a wonderful friend and guide.

Complete Works of St. John of the Cross. (Note particularly "The Ascent of Mount Carmel" in Vol. I and "The Living Flame of Love" in Vol. II.) Juan de Yepes was born in Fontiveros, near Avila, in old Castile, in 1542. He spent all of his adult life in a strict monastic order, and he died at the age of forty-nine. He was later called St. John of the Cross. He understood communion with God as few men ever have, and he taught what he knew with a master's skill. His teaching technique ranges from bold and ecstatic poetry of immense depth and beauty to the most meticulous and many-sided prose. He is strictly for work, not for entertainment. He may be helpful to beginners, but they must be serious, well-balanced, and not-easily-discouraged beginners, because this man wades right in where the going is tough, and he does not admit any pious prettiness before the true beauty is touched.

John's beginners must already have reached some kind of end. Before you come to John of the Cross you must be, within your capacity, given up to God. He assumes that much, and he shows you where the path goes from there. He is particularly noted for his teaching of the "dark nights" (of the senses, of the soul, and of the spirit) through which the soul passes in her journey toward the Spouse, "the living Flame of Love."

Like Meister Eckhart, and no doubt for some of the same reasons, John of the Cross heavily strained the tolerance of his contemporaries, by whom he was imprisoned and disgraced. His works, however, have survived to establish him as among the greatest and soundest teachers of all ages and "Doctor of the Church Universal."

May we close with a practical note: the record (as given by Bucke) of John's escape from prison:

"When his imprisonment was drawing to its close, he heard our Lord say to him, as it were out of the soft light that was around him, 'John, I am here; be not afraid; I will set thee free.'

"A few moments later, while making his escape from the prison of the monastery, it is said he had a repetition of the experience as follows:

"He saw a powerful light, out of which came a voice, 'Follow me.' He followed, and the light moved before him toward the wall which was on the bank, and then, he knew not how, he found himself on the summit of it without effort or fatigue. He descended into the street, and then the light vanished. So brilliant was it, that . . . his eyes were weak, as if he had been looking at the sun in its strength."

May our Lord and Savior thus set us all free. And may the Truth nourish and keep us forever. Amen.

APPENDIX A

A Sampler of Some of Our Schoolmasters' Teachings in the Lifesavers Way of Life

C.S. Lewis—page 210

Lev Shestov—page 216

Hermes Trismegistus—page 226

Ernst Lehrs—page 230

Robert Mendelsohn—page 240

Harry M. Tiebout—page 244

O. Hobart Mowrer—page 254

Maurice Nicoll—page 262

Martin Gross—page 270

Arthur Machen—page 278

C. S. Lewis *on what space is really like when you get off the planet*

(From "Out of the Silent Planet")

When Ransom came to his senses he seemed to be in bed in a dark room. He had a pretty severe headache, and this, combined with a general lassitude, discouraged him at first from attempting to rise or to take stock of his surroundings. He noticed, drawing his hand across his forehead, that he was sweating freely, and this directed his attention to the fact that the room (if it was a room) was remarkably warm. Moving his arms to fling off the bedclothes, he touched a wall at the right side of the bed: it was not only warm, but hot. He moved his left hand to and fro in the emptiness on the other side and noticed that there the air was cooler—apparently the heat was coming from the wall. He felt his face and found a bruise over the left eye. . . . At the same time he looked up and recognized the source of the dim light in which, without noticing it, he had all along been able to see the movements of his own hands. There was some kind of skylight immediately over his head—a square of night sky filled with stars. It seemed to Ransom that he had never looked out on such a frosty night. Pulsing with brightness as with some unbearable pain or pleasure, clustered in pathless and countless multitudes, dreamlike in clarity, blazing in perfect blackness, the stars seized all his attention, troubled him, excited him, and drew him up to a sitting position. At the same time they quickened the throb of his headache, and this reminded him that he had been drugged. He was just formulating to himself the theory that the stuff they had given him might have some effect on the pupil and that this would explain the unnatural splendour and fullness of the sky, when a disturbance of silver light, almost a pale and miniature sunrise, at one corner of the skylight, drew his eyes upward again. Some minutes later the orb of the full

Appendix A

moon was pushing its way into the field of vision. Ransom sat still and watched. He had never seen such a moon—so white, so blinding and so large. "Like a great football just outside the glass," he thought, and then, a moment later, "No—it's bigger than that." By this time he was quite certain that something was seriously wrong with his eyes: no moon could possibly be the size of the thing he was seeing.

The light of the huge moon—if it was a moon—had by now illuminated his surroundings almost as clearly as if it were day. . . . The room was walled and floored with metal, and was in a state of continuous faint vibration—a silent vibration with a strangely life-like and unmechanical quality about it. But if the vibration was silent, there was plenty of noise going on—a series of musical raps or percussions at quite irregular intervals which seemed to come from the ceiling. It was as if the metal chamber in which he found himself was being bombarded with small, tinkling missiles. Ransom was by now thoroughly frightened—not with the prosaic fright that a man suffers in a war, but with a heady, bounding kind of fear that was hardly distinguishable from his general excitement: he was poised on a sort of emotional watershed from which, he felt, he might at any moment pass either into delirious terror or into an ecstasy of joy. He knew now that he was not in a house, but in some moving vessel. It was clearly not a submarine: and the infinitesimal quivering of the metal did not suggest the motion of any wheeled vehicle. A ship then, he supposed, or some kind of airship . . . but there was an oddity in all his sensations for which neither supposition accounted. Puzzled, he sat down again on the bed, and stared at the portentous moon.

An airship, some kind of flying-machine . . . but why did the moon look so big? It was larger than he had thought at first. No moon could really be that size. . . .

At that moment the sound of an opening door made him turn his head. An oblong of dazzling light appeared behind him and instantly vanished as the door closed again, having admitted the bulky form of a man whom Ransom recognized as Weston. No reproach, no demand for an explanation, rose to Ransom's lips or even to his mind; not with that monstrous orb above them. The mere presence of a human being, with its offer of at least some companionship, broke down the tension in which his nerves had long been resisting a bottomless dismay. He found, when he spoke, that he was sobbing.

"Weston! Weston!" he gasped. "What is it? It's not the moon, not that size. It can't be, can it?"

"No," replied Weston, "it's the Earth."

Ransom's legs failed him, and he must have sunk back upon the bed, but he only became aware of this many minutes later. At the moment he was unconscious of everything except his fear. He did not even know what he was afraid of: the fear itself possessed his whole mind, a formless, infinite misgiving. He did not lose consciousness, though he greatly wished that he might do so. Any change—death or sleep, or, best of all, a waking which should show all this for a dream—would have been inexpressibly welcome. None came. Instead, the lifelong self-control of social man, the virtues which are half hypocrisy or the hypocrisy which is half a virtue, came back to him and soon he found himself answering Weston in a voice not shamefully tremulous.

"Do you mean that?" he asked.

"Certainly."

"Then where are we?"

"Standing out from Earth about eighty-five thousand miles."

"You mean we're—in space." Ransom uttered the word with difficulty as a frightened child speaks of ghosts or a frightened man of cancer. . . .

The period spent in the space-ship ought to have been one of terror and anxiety for Ransom. . . . The odd thing was that it did not very greatly disquiet him. It is hard for a man to brood on the future when he is feeling so extremely well as Ransom now felt. There was an endless night on one side of the ship and an endless day on the other: each was marvellous and he moved from the one to the other at his will, delighted. In the nights, which he could create by turning the handle of a door, he lay for hours in contemplation of the skylight. The Earth's disk was nowhere to be seen; the stars, thick as daisies on an uncut lawn, reigned perpetually with no cloud, no moon, no sunrise to dispute their sway. There were planets of unbelievable majesty, and constellations undreamed of: there were celestial sapphires, rubies, emeralds and pin-pricks of burning gold; far out on the left of the picture hung a comet, tiny and remote: and between all and behind all, far more emphatic and palpable than it showed on Earth, the undimensioned, enigmatic blackness. The lights trembled: they seemed to grow brighter as he looked. Stretched naked on his bed, a second Danaë, he found it night by night more difficult to believe in

Appendix A

old astrology: almost he felt, wholly he imagined, "sweet influence" pouring or even stabbing into his surrendered body. All was silence but for the irregular tinkling noises. He knew now that these were made by meteorites, small, drifting particles of the world-stuff that smote continually on their hollow drum of steel; and he guessed that at any moment they might meet something large enough to make meteorites of ship and all. But he could not fear. He now felt that Weston had justly called him little-minded in the moment of his first panic. The adventure was too high, its circumstance too solemn, for any emotion save a severe delight. But the days—that is, the hours spent in the sunward hemisphere of their microcosm—were the best of all. Often he rose after only a few hours' sleep to return, drawn by an irresistible attraction, to the regions of light; he could not cease to wonder at the noon which always awaited you however early you went to seek it. There, totally immersed in a bath of pure ethereal colour and of unrelenting though unwounding brightness, stretched his full length and with eyes half closed in the strange chariot that bore them, faintly quivering, through depth after depth of tranquility far above the reach of night, he felt his body and mind daily rubbed and scoured and filled with new vitality. Weston, in one of his brief, reluctant answers, admitted a scientific basis for these sensations: they were receiving, he said, many rays that never penetrated the terrestrial atmosphere.

But Ransom, as time wore on, became aware of another and more spiritual cause for his progressive lightening and exultation of heart. A nightmare, long engendered in the modern mind by the mythology that follows in the wake of science, was falling off him. He had read of "Space": at the back of his thinking for years had lurked the dismal fancy of the black, cold vacuity, the utter deadness, which was supposed to separate the worlds. He had not known how much it affected him till now—now that the very name "Space" seemed a blasphemous libel for this empyrean ocean of radiance in which they swam. He could not call it "dead"; he felt life pouring into him from it every moment. How indeed should it be otherwise, since out of this ocean the worlds and all their life had come? He had thought it barren: he saw now that it was the womb of worlds, whose blazing and innumerable offspring looked down nightly even upon the earth with so many eyes—and here, with how many more! No: Space was the wrong name. Older thinkers had been wiser when they named it simply the heavens—the heavens which declared the glory—the

> "happy climes that ly
> Where day never shuts his eye
> Up in the broad fields of the sky."

He quoted Milton's words to himself lovingly, at this time and often.

From C. S. Lewis, *Out of the Silent Planet*

From the standpoint of both Catholics and Protestants, C. S. Lewis is undoubtedly one of the greatest teachers of the 20th century. He used his surpassing gifts as a scholar and an inspired creative writer (along with an obviously deep fund of personal spiritual experience) to communicate real religion.

Lewis was born in Belfast, Ireland, on November 29, 1898. After preparatory study in Irish and English schools, he attended Malvern College in England for a year, and then studied for Oxford under the tutor T. Kirkpatrick. By this time (he was sixteen), he had become an inveterate reader, developed into a habitual walker, and turned into an atheist.

Shortly after his nineteenth birthday, Lewis was wounded in action in the battle of the Somme. Before enlisting he had attended University College, Oxford, and after the war he returned to complete his studies. In 1925 Lewis became a Fellow at Magdalen College, Oxford. Four years later he was converted to Christianity—in his own view the most important event of his life. He remained at Oxford until 1954 when he was elected to the Chair of Medieval and Renaissance English at Cambridge University, a post he held until a few weeks before his death in November 1963.

Lewis wrote in many modes, but perhaps his greatest genius lay in his ability to teach by means of narrative. The first books you might want to read are the so-called children's stories, the Chronicles of Narnia (*The Lion, the Witch, and the Wardrobe; Prince Caspian; The Voyage of the Dawn Treader; The Silver Chair; The Horse and His Boy; The Magician's Nephew; The Last Battle*). Next, the Space Trilogy (*Out of the Silent Planet; Perelandra; That Hideous Strength*). *The Screwtape Letters* is Lewis's most popular book, and it stands in a class by itself for good fun and brilliant Christian apologetics. Other superb fiction: *Till We Have Faces, The Great Divorce,* and *The World's Last Night.*

In the front rank of Lewis's non-fiction works are: *Mere Christianity, Miracles, The Abolition of Man, The Problem of Pain, The Discarded Image,* and *The Four Loves.*

Lev Shestov *on why cry halt before Necessity?*

(From "Athens and Jerusalem")

We live surrounded by an endless multitude of mysteries. But no matter how enigmatic may be the mysteries which surround being, what is most enigmatic and disturbing is that mystery in general exists and that we are somehow definitely and forever cut off from the sources and beginnings of life. Of all the things that we here on earth are the witnesses, this is obviously the most absurd and meaningless, the most terrible, almost unnatural, thing—which forces us irresistibly to conclude either that there is something that is not right in the universe, or that the way in which we seek the truth and the demands that we place upon it are vitiated in their very roots.

Whatever our definition of truth may be, we can never renounce Descartes' *clare et distincte* (clarity and distinctness). Now, reality here shows us only an eternal, impenetrable mystery—as if, even before the creation of the world, someone had once and for all forbidden man to attain that which is most necessary and most important to him. What we call the truth, what we obtain through thought, is found to be, in a certain sense, incommensurable not only with the external world into which we have been plunged since our birth but also with our own inner experience. We have sciences and even, if you please, Science, which grows and develops before our very eyes. We know many things and our knowledge is a "clear and distinct" knowledge. Science contemplates with legitimate pride its immense victories and has every right to expect that nothing will be able to stop its triumphant march. No one doubts, and no one can doubt, the enormous importance of the sciences. If Aristotle and his pupil Alexander the Great were brought back to life today, they would believe themselves in the country of the gods and not of men. Ten lives would not suffice Aristotle to assimilate all the knowledge that has been accumulated on earth since his death, and Alexander would perhaps be able to realize his dream and conquer the world. The *clare et distincte* has justified all the hopes which were founded upon it.

But the haze of the primordial mystery has not been dissipated. It has rather grown denser. Plato would hardly need to change a single word of his myth of the cave.* Our knowledge would not be able to furnish an answer to his anxiety, his disquietude, his "premonitions." The world would remain for him, "in the light" of our "positive" sciences, what it was—a dark and sorrowful subterranean region—and we would seem to him like chained prisoners. He would again have to make superhuman efforts, "as in a battle," to break open for himself a path through the truths created by the sciences which "dream of being but cannot see it in waking reality." In brief, Aristotle would bless our knowledge while Plato would curse it. And, conversely, our era would receive Aristotle with open arms but resolutely turn away from Plato.

But it will be asked: What is the force and power of the blessings and curses of men, even if these men be such giants as Plato and Aristotle? Does truth become more true because Aristotle blesses it, or does it become error because Plato curses it? Is it given men to judge the truths, to decide the fate of the truths? On the contrary, it is the truths which judge men and decide their fate and not men who rule over the truths. Men, the great as well as the small, are born and die, appear and disappear—but the truth remains. When no one had as yet begun to "think" or to "search," the truths which later revealed themselves to men already existed. And when men will have finally disappeared from the face of the earth, or will have lost the faculty of thinking, the truths will not suffer therefrom. It is from this that Aristotle set out in his philosophical researches. He declared that Parmenides was "constrained to follow the phenomena." In another

---

*The myth of the cave is presented in *The Republic* by Plato as a dialogue between Socrates and Glaucon, his pupil:

[Socrates] And now, I said, let me show in a figure how far our nature is enlightened or unenlightened:—Behold! human beings living in an underground den, which has a mouth open towards the light and reaching all along the den; here they have been from their childhood, and have their legs and necks chained so that they cannot move, and can only see before them, being prevented by the chains from turning round their heads. Above and behind them a fire is blazing at a distance, and between the fire and the prisoners there is a raised way; and you will see, if you look, a low wall built along the way, like the screen which marionette players have in front of them, over which they show the puppets.

[Glaucon] I see.

And do you see, I said, men passing along the wall carrying all sorts of vessels, and statues and figures of animals made of wood and stone and various materials, which appear over the wall? Some of them are talking, others silent.

place, speaking of the same Parmenides and of other great Greek philosophers, we wrote, they were "constrained by the truth itself." This Aristotle knew definitely: the truth has the power to force or constrain men, all men alike, whether it be the great Parmenides and the great Alexander or Parmenides' unknown slave and the least of Alexander's stable-men.

Why does the truth have this power over Parmenides and Alexander, and not Parmenides and Alexander who have power over the truth? This is a question that Aristotle does not ask. If someone had asked it of him, he would not have understood it and would have explained that the question is meaningless and obviously absurd, that one can say such things but one cannot think them. And this is not because he was an insensible being who was indifferent to all and to whom everything was the same, or that he would have been able to say of himself, like Hamlet, "I am pigeon-livered and lack gall to make oppression bitter." For Aristotle oppression *is* bitter. In another passage of the same *Metaphysics* he says that it is hard to bow down before Necessity: "everything which constrains is called necessary and that is why the necessary is bitter, as Evenus says: 'every necessary thing is always painful and bitter.' And constraint is a form of necessity—as Sophocles also says: 'But an invincible force necessitates me to act thus.'" Aristotle, we see, feels pain and bitterness at ineluctable Necessity, but, as he himself adds immediately, he distinctly knows that "Necessity does not allow itself to be persuaded." And since it does not listen to persuasion and is not to be overcome, one must submit to it—be this bitter or not, painful or not—submit

---

You have shown me a strange image, and they are strange prisoners.

Like ourselves, I replied; and they see only their own shadows, or the shadows of one another, which the fire throws on the opposite wall of the cave?

True, he said; how could they see anything but the shadows if they were never allowed to move their heads?

And of the objects which are being carried in like manner they would only see the shadows?

Yes, he said.

And if they were able to converse with one another, would they not suppose that they were naming what was actually before them?

Very true.

And suppose further that the prison had an echo which came from the other side, would they not be sure to fancy when one of the passers-by spoke that the voice which they heard came from the passing shadow?

No question, he replied.

and henceforth renounce useless struggle: *anankê stênai*, "cry halt before Necessity."

Whence comes this "cry halt before Necessity?" Here is a question of capital importance which contains, if you wish, the *alpha* and *omega* of philosophy. Necessity does not allow itself to be persuaded, it does not even listen. The injustice cries to heaven, if there is no longer anyone here to whom one can cry. It is true that in certain cases and even very often, almost always, the injustice will cry and protest only to end up by becoming silent; men forget both their sorrows and their cruel losses. But there are injustices that one cannot forget. "If I forget thee, O Jerusalem . . . let my tongue cleave to the roof of my mouth." For two thousand years we have all repeated the Psalmist's oath. But did the Psalmist not "know" that Necessity does not allow itself to be persuaded, that it does not listen to oaths or prayers, that it hears nothing and fears nothing? Did he not know that his voice was and could be only the voice of one crying in the wilderness? Of course he knew it, he knew it quite as well as Aristotle. But, doubtless he had something more than this knowledge. Doubtless when a man feels the injustice as deeply as did the Psalmist, his thought undergoes, in a way that is completely unexpected, incomprehensible and mysterious transformations in its very essence. He cannot forget Jerusalem, but he forgets the power of Necessity, the omnipotence of this enemy so terribly armed—one does not know by whom or when or why; and, without thinking of the future, he begins a terrible and final battle against this enemy. This is surely the meaning of Plotinus' words: "A great and final battle awaits human souls." And these words of Plato have the same meaning: "If it

---

To them, I said, the truth would be literally nothing but the shadows of the images. That is certain.

And now look again, and see what will naturally follow if the prisoners are released and disabused of their error. At first, when any of them is liberated and compelled suddenly to stand up and turn his neck round and walk and look towards the light, he will suffer sharp pains; the glare will distress him, and he will be unable to see the realities of which in his former state he had seen the shadows; and then conceive some one saying to him, that what he saw before was an illusion, but that now, when he is approaching nearer to being and his eye is turned towards more real existence, he has a clearer vision,—what will be his reply? And you may further imagine that his instructor is pointing to the objects as they pass and requiring him to name them,—will he not be perplexed? Will he not fancy that the shadows which he formerly saw are truer than the objects which are now shown to him?

Far truer.

And if he is compelled to look straight at the light, will he not have a pain in his eyes

is necessary to dare everything, should we not dare to defy all shame?" Man decides to take up the struggle against all-powerful Necessity only when there awakens in him the readiness to dare everything, to stop before nothing. Nothing can justify this boundless audacity; it is the extreme expression of shamelessness. One has only to look at Aristotle's *Ethics* to be convinced of this. All the virtues are placed by him in the middle zone of being, and everything which passes beyond the limits of "the mean" is an indication of depravity and vice. "Cry halt before Necessity" rules his *Ethics* as well as his *Metaphysics*. His final word is the blessing of Necessity and the glorification of the spirit which has submitted to Necessity.

Not only the good but the truth as well wishes man to bow down before it. All who have read the famous Twelfth Book, especially the last chapter, of the *Metaphysics* and the Ninth and Tenth Books of the *Ethics* know with what fervor Aristotle supplicated Necessity which does not allow itself to be persuaded and which he had not the power to overcome. What irritated him or, perhaps, disturbed him most in Plato was the latter's courage or rather, to use his own expressions, Plato's audacity and shamelessness, which suggested to him that those who adore Necessity only dream of reality but are powerless to see it in the waking state. Plato's words seemed to Aristotle unnatural, fantastic, deliberately provoking. But how to silence Plato, how to constrain him not only to submit to Necessity in the visible and

---

which will make him turn away to take refuge in the objects of vision which he can see, and which he will conceive to be in reality clearer than the things which are now being shown to him?

True, he said.

And suppose once more, that he is reluctantly dragged up a steep and rugged ascent, and held fast until he is forced into the presence of the sun himself, is he not likely to be pained and irritated? When he approaches the light his eyes will be dazzled, and he will not be able to see anything at all of what are now called realities.

Not all in a moment, he said.

He will require to grow accustomed to the sight of the upper world. And first he will see the shadows best, next the reflections of men and other objects in the water, and then the objects themselves; then he will gaze upon the light of the moon and the stars and the spangled heaven; and he will see the sky and the stars by night better than the sun or the light of the sun by day?

Certainly.

Last of all he will be able to see the sun, and not mere reflections of him in the water, but he will see him in his own proper place, and not in another; and he will contemplate him as he is.

Certainly.

Appendix A 221

empirical world but also to render to it in thought the honors to which, Aristotle was convinced, it is entitled? Necessity is Necessity, not for those who sleep but for those who are awake. And the waking who see Necessity see real being, while Plato, with his audacity and shamelessness, turns us away from real being and leads us into the domain of the fantastic, the unreal, the illusory, and—by that very fact—the false. One must stop at nothing in order finally to extinguish in man that thirst for freedom which found expression in Plato's work. "Necessity" is invincible. The truth is, in its essence and by its very nature, a truth that constrains; and it is in submission to the constraining truth that the source of all human virtues lies. "Constrained by the truth itself," Parmenides, Heraclitus and Anaxagoras accomplished their work. It has always been so, it will always be so, it must be so. It is not the great Parmenides who rules over the truth but the truth that is the master of Parmenides. And to refuse obedience to the truth that constrains is impossible. Still more: to do other than bless it, whatever be the thing to which it constrains, is impossible. Herein lies the supreme wisdom, human and divine; and the task of philosophy consists in teaching men to submit joyously to Necessity which hears nothing and is indifferent to all.

Let us stop and ask ourselves: why does the truth that constrains need men's blessing? Why does Aristotle put himself to so much trouble to obtain for his Necessity men's blessing? Can it not get along without this blessing? If Necessity does not listen to reason, is it more

---

He will then proceed to argue that this is he who gives the season and the years, and is the guardian of all that is in the visible world, and in a certain way the cause of all things which he and his fellows have been accustomed to behold?

Clearly, he said, he would first see the sun and then reason about him.

And when he remembered his old habitation, and the wisdom of the den and his fellow-prisoners, do you not suppose that he would felicitate himself on the change, and pity them?

Certainly, he would.

And if they were in the habit of conferring honours among themselves on those who were quickest to observe the passing shadows and to remark which of them went before, and which followed after, and which were together; and who were therefore best able to draw conclusions as to the future, do you think that he would care for such honours and glories, or envy the possessors of them? Would he not say with Homer,

"Better to be the poor servant of a poor master,"

and to endure anything, rather than think as they do and live after their manner?

Yes, he said, I think that he would rather suffer anything than entertain these false notions and live in this miserable manner.

receptive to praises? There is no doubt that constraining Necessity listens no more to praises than to prayers or curses. The stones of the desert have never replied "Amen" to the inspired sermons of the saints. But this is not necessary. What is necessary is that to the silence of the stones—is not Necessity, like the stones, indifferent to everything?—the saints should sing hosannas.

I would recall in this connection the chapters already mentioned of the *Metaphysics* and *Ethics* of Aristotle, the high priest of the visible and the invisible church of "thinking" men. We are asked not only to submit to Necessity but to adore it: such always has been, and such is still, the fundamental task of philosophy. It is not enough that philosophy should recognize the force and power, in fact, of such or such an order of things. It knows and it fears (the beginning of all knowledge is fear) that empirical force, that is, the force that manifests itself in constraining man only once, may be replaced by another force that will act in a different way. Even the scientist, who refuses to philosophize, has, finally, no need of facts; the facts by themselves give us nothing and tell us nothing. There has never been a genuine empiricism among men of science, as there has never been a genuine materialism. What scientist would study facts merely for the sake of facts? Who would wish to observe this drop of water suspended from a telegraphic wire, or this other drop that glides over the windowpane after a rain? There are millions of such drops and these, in and of themselves, have never concerned the scientists and could not concern them. The scientist wishes to know what a water-drop in general is or what water in general is. If, in his laboratory, he decomposes into

---

Imagine once more, I said, such an one coming suddenly out of the sun to be replaced in his old situation; would he not be certain to have his eyes full of darkness?
To be sure, he said.
And if there were a contest, and he had to compete in measuring the shadows with the prisoners who had never moved out of the den, while his sight was still weak, and before his eyes had become steady (and the time which would be needed to acquire this new habit of sight might be very considerable), would he not be ridiculous? Men would say of him that up he went and down he came without his eyes; and that it was better not even to think of ascending; and if any one tried to loose another and lead him up to the light, let them only catch the offender, and they would put him to death.
No question, he said.
This entire allegory, I said, you may now append, dear Glaucon, to the previous argument; the prison-house is the world of sight, the light of the fire is the sun, and you will not misapprehend me if you interpret the journey upwards to be the ascent of the soul into the intellectual world according to my poor belief, which, at your desire, I have expressed—whether rightly or wrongly God knows. But whether true or false, my opinion is that in the world of knowledge the idea of good appears last of all, and is seen

its constituent elements some water drawn from a brook, it is not in order to study and know what he has at this moment in his hands and under his eyes but in order to acquire the right to make judgments about all the water that he will ever have occasion to see or never will see, about that which no one has ever seen and no one ever will see, about even that which existed when there was not a single conscious being or even any living being on earth. The man of science, whether he knows it or not (most often, obviously, he does know it), whether he wishes it or not (ordinarily he does not wish it), cannot help but be a realist in the medieval sense of the term. He is distinguished from the philosopher only by the fact that the philosopher must, in addition, explain and justify the realism practiced by science. In a general way, since empiricism is only an unsuccessful attempt at philosophical justification of the scientific, i.e., realistic, methods of seeking the truth, its work has, in fact, always led to the destruction of the principles on which it was based. It is necessary to choose: if you wish to be an empiricist, you must abandon the hope of founding scientific knowledge on a solid and certain basis; if you wish to have a solidly established science, you must place it under the protection of the idea of Necessity and, in addition, recognize this idea as primordial, original, having no beginning and consequently no end—that is to say, you must endow it with the superiorities and qualities that men generally accord to the Supreme Being. As we have seen, that is what was done by Aristotle, who thus deserves to be the consecrated pope or high priest of all men who think scientifically.

From Lev Shestov, *Athens and Jerusalem*
(For Lev Shestov biog, see next page)—

---

only with an effort; and, when seen, is also inferred to be the universal author of all things beautiful and right, parent of light and of the lord of light in this visible world, and the immediate source of reason and truth in the intellectual; and that this is the power upon which he who would act rationally either in public or private life must have his eye fixed.

I agree, he said, as far as I am able to understand you.

Moreover, I said, you must not wonder that those who attain to this beatific vision are unwilling to descend to human affairs; for their souls are ever hastening into the upper world where they desire to dwell; which desire of theirs is very natural, if our allegory may be trusted.

Yes, very natural.

And is there anything surprising in one who passes from divine contemplations to the evil state of man, misbehaving himself in a ridiculous manner; if, while his eyes are blinking and before he has become accustomed to the surrounding darkness, he is compelled to fight in courts of law, or in other places, about the images or the shadows

Invitation to a Great Experiment

Lev Shestov was born in 1866. Two years before, Dostoevsky had published *Notes from the Underground*. One year before, Tolstoy had published *War and Peace*. Nietzsche was then twenty-two and was as yet unpublished. Darwin had completed *The Origin of Species* seven years earlier. Marx was to loose *Das Kapital* upon the world a year later.

Shestov died in 1938, just a year before Hitler's tanks rolled into Poland. During his lifetime the world simply turned upside down. Wars and rumors of wars appear only marginally in Shestov's writings, but in one important sense the many volumes of his lifework are a monumental answer to the question: Why did the comfortable, optimistic, secular, scientific, and materialist European world of the mid-nineteenth century turn into the nightmare it had become by the middle of the twentieth?

Shestov is a giant, a true shaker of the earth, and his books are tracts for our most turbulent times. They make a positive contribution to the strength of mind of anyone who has set a personal goal of standing against the inhumanizing tendencies of this age. Shestov delivers one message above all others, emphasized over a lifetime with a striking insistence and constancy: the nightmare world of violence and unbelief we modern human beings live in is a direct product of 2500 years of rationalist, mechanistic, and egotistical philosophy, and it is a world shorn of hope and truth, a world which effectively denies God. A godless point of view holds the whole world in fee, and nothing but a return to the God of our Fathers, to the God of Abraham, Isaac, and Jacob, will do us any lasting good (speaking of "us" as individuals in a teetering world culture).

Lev Shestov's basic book is *Athens and Jerusalem*. Other Shestov books currently available are: *All Things Are Possible & Penultimate Words and Other Essays; Dostoevsky, Tolstoy and Nietzsche; In Job's Balances;*

---

of images of justice, and is endeavouring to meet the conceptions of those who have never yet seen absolute justice?

Anything but surprising, he replied.

Any one who has common sense will remember that the bewilderments of the eyes are of two kinds, and arise from two causes, either from coming out of the light or from going into the light, which is true of the mind's eye, quite as much as of the bodily eye; and he who remembers this when he sees any one whose vision is perplexed and weak, will not be too ready to laugh; he will first ask whether that soul of man has come out of the brighter life, and is unable to see because unaccustomed to the dark, or having turned from darkness to the day is dazzled by excess of light. And he will count the one happy in his condition and state of being, and he will pity the other; or, if he have a mind to laugh at the soul which comes from below into the light, there will be more reason in this than in the laugh which greets him who returns from above out of the light into the den.

Kierkegaard and the Existential Philosophy; Potestas Clavium. These books are in print now in English largely owing to the work and devotion of Professor Bernard Martin, who holds the Abba Hillel Silver Chair of Jewish Studies at Case Western Reserve University, and to the dedication to the public good of Ohio University Press.

That, he said, is a very just distinction.

But then, if I am right, certain professors of education must be wrong when they say that they can put a knowledge into the soul which was not there before, like sight into blind eyes.

They undoubtedly say this, he replied.

Whereas, our argument shows that the power and capacity of learning exists in the soul already; and that just as the eye was unable to turn from darkness to light without the whole body, so too the instrument of knowledge can only by the movement of the whole soul be turned from the world of becoming into that of being, and learn by degrees to endure the sight of being, and of the brightest and best of being, or in other words, of the good.

Very true.

Hermes Trismegistus on
why philosophy is hard to understand in modern times

(From "The Crowning Discourse")

[The following is a dialogue between Hermes Trismegistus and his student Asclepius. Trismegistus is the first to speak.]

... Since the world is God's handiwork, he who maintains and heightens its beauty by his tendance is co-operating with the will of God, when he contributes the aid of his bodily strength, and by his care and labour day by day makes things assume that shape and aspect which God's purpose has designed. What shall be his reward? Shall it not be that which our fathers have received, and which we pray with heartfelt piety that we too may receive, if God in his mercy is pleased to grant it? And that is, that when our term of service is ended, when we are divested of our guardianship of the material world, and freed from the bonds of mortality, he will restore us, cleansed and sanctified, to the primal condition of that higher part of us which is divine.—*Ascl.* Right and true, Trismegistus.—*Trism.* Yes, such is the reward of those who spend their lives in piety to God above, and in tendance of the world around them. But those who have lived evil and impious lives are not permitted to return to heaven. For such men is ordained a shameful transmigration into bodies of another kind, bodies unworthy to be the abode of holy mind.—*Ascl.* According to your teaching then, Trismegistus, souls have at stake in this earthly life their hope of eternity in the life to come.—*Trism.* Yes. But some cannot believe this; and some regard it as an empty tale; and to some, perhaps, it seems a thing to mock at. For in our bodily life on earth, the enjoyment derived from possessions is a pleasant thing; and the pleasure which they yield grips the soul by the throat, so to speak, and holds it down to earth, compelling it to cleave to man's mortal part.

Moreover, there are some whose ungenerous temper grudges men the boon of immortality, and will not suffer them to get knowl-

Appendix A

edge of that in them which is divine. For speaking as a prophet speaks, I tell you that in after times none will pursue philosophy in singleness of heart. Philosophy is nothing else than striving through constant contemplation and saintly piety to attain to knowledge of God; but there will be many who will make philosophy hard to understand, and corrupt it with manifold speculations.—*Ascl.* How so?—*Trism.* In this way, Asclepius; by a cunning sort of study, in which philosophy will be mixed with diverse and unintelligible sciences, such as arithmetic, music, and geometry. Whereas the student of philosophy undefiled, which is dependent on devotion to God, and on that alone, ought to direct his attention to the other sciences only so far as he may thereby learn to see and marvel how the returns of the heavenly bodies to their former places, their halts in pre-ordained positions, and the variations of their movements, are true to the reckonings of number; only so far as, learning the measurements of the earth, the depth of the sea, (the . . . of air,) the force of fire, and the properties, magnitudes, workings, and natures of all material things, he may be led to revere, adore, and praise God's skill and wisdom. And to know the science of music is nothing else than this,—to know how all things are ordered, and how God's design has assigned to each its place; for the ordered system in which each and all by the supreme Artist's skill are wrought together into a single whole yields a divinely musical harmony, sweet and true beyond all melodious sounds. I tell you then that the men of after times will be misled by cunning sophists, and will be turned away from the pure and holy teachings of true philosophy. For to worship God in thought and spirit with singleness of heart, to revere God in all his works, and to give thanks to God, whose will, and his alone, is wholly filled with goodness,—this is philosophy unsullied by intrusive cravings for unprofitable knowledge.

From Hermes Trismegistus, *The Crowning Discourse*

(For Hermes Trismegistus biog, see next page)—

Hermes Mercurius Trismegistus—called Thrice-Greatest Hermes—was a contemporary of Moses. He was known everywhere to be a God-sent and God-illuminated teacher of the very highest rank, and he was held in the greatest of respect by the Hebrews, the Egyptians, the Greeks, the Muslims, and the Christians through all ages until the present.

Writing in 1554, the Christian scholar Vergicius gives this account of the life of Trismegistus: "They say that this Hermes left his own country, and traveled all over the world . . . and that he tried to teach men to revere and worship one God alone; and that he lived a very wise and pious life, occupied in intellectual contemplation, and giving no heed to the gross things of the material world; and that having returned to his own country, he wrote at that time many books of mystical philosophy and theology."

The chief collection of writings attributed to Hermes Trismegistus is the so-called Corpus Hermeticum, which is currently available in four volumes entitled *Hermetica*, translated and with commentaries by Walter Scott. The place of Hermetic teaching in primitive Christianity is epitomized in the Apostolic writing entitled "The Shepherd of Hermas," found in *The Fathers of the Church: The Apostolic Fathers*, see listing, page 179.

Regarding the picture of Hermes shown above, Walter Scott has this to say: "Hermes Trismegistus is depicted in one of the designs with which the pavement of the cathedral of Siena is decorated. These designs are pictures incised in slabs of white marble, and filled in with black or red marble. The date of the Hermes-group is 1488. It is placed in the middle of the floor at the west end of the Duomo, so that it is the first thing that meets the eye as one enters."

Ernst Lehrs *on a spiritual understanding of natural science, on the basis of Goethe's method of training observation and thought*

(From "Man or Matter")

When I first made acquaintance with Rudolf Steiner and his work, I was finishing my academic training as an electrical engineer. At the end of the 1914–18 war my first thought had been to take up my studies from where I had let them drop, four years earlier. The war seemed to imply nothing more than a passing interruption of them. This, at any rate, was the opinion of my former teachers; the war had made no difference whatever to their ideas, whether on the subject-matter of their teaching or on its educational purpose. I myself, however, soon began to feel differently. It became obvious to me that my relationship to my subject, and therefore to those teaching it, had completely changed. What I had experienced through the war had awakened in me a question of which I had previously been unaware; now I felt obliged to put it to everything I came across.

As a child of my age I had grown up in the conviction that it was within the scope of man to shape his life according to the laws of reason within him; his progress, in the sense in which I then understood it, seemed assured by his increasing ability to determine his own outer conditions with the help of science. Indeed, it was the wish to take an active part in this progress that had led me to choose my profession. Now, however, the war stood there as a gigantic social deed which I could in no way regard as reasonably justified. How, in an age when the logic of science was supreme, was it possible that a great part of mankind, including just those peoples to whom science had owed its origin and never-ceasing expansion, could act in so completely unscientific a way? Where lay the causes of the contradiction thus revealed between human thinking and human doing?

Pursued by these questions, I decided after a while to give my studies a new turn. The kind of training then provided in Germany at the so-called Technische Hochschulen was designed essentially to give students a close practical acquaintance with all sorts of technical appliances; it included only as much theory as was wanted for understanding the mathematical calculations arising in technical practice. It now seemed to me necessary to pay more attention to theoretical considerations, so as to gain a more exact knowledge of the sources from which science drew its conception of nature. Accordingly I left the Hochschule for a course in mathematics and physics at a university, though without abandoning my original idea of preparing for a career in the field of electrical engineering. It was with this in mind that I later chose for my Ph.D. thesis a piece of experimental research on the uses of high-frequency electric currents.

During my subsequent years of study, however, I found myself no nearer an answer to the problem that haunted me. All that I experienced, in scientific work as in life generally, merely gave it an even sharper edge. Everywhere I saw an abyss widening between human knowing and human action. How often, for instance, was I not bitterly disillusioned by the behaviour, both in private and in public, of men for whose ability to think through the most complicated scientific questions I had the utmost admiration!

On all sides I found this same bewildering gulf between scientific achievement and the way men conducted their own lives and influenced the lives of others. I was forced to the conclusion that human thinking, at any rate in its modern form, was either powerless to govern human actions, or at least unable to direct them towards right ends. In fact, where scientific thinking had done most to change the practical relations of human life, as in the mechanisation of economic production, conditions had arisen which made it more difficult, not less, for men to live in a way worthy of man. At a time when humanity was equipped as never before to investigate the order of the universe, and had achieved triumphs of design in mechanical constructions, human life was falling into ever wilder chaos. Why was this?

The fact that most of my contemporaries were apparently quite unaware of the problem that stirred me so deeply could not weaken my sense of its reality. This slumber of so many souls in face of the vital questions of modern life seemed to me merely a further symptom of the sickness of our age. Nor could I think much better of those who, more sensitive to the contradictions in and around them, sought refuge in art or religion. The catastrophe of the war had shown me that this departmentalising of life, which at one time I had myself considered a sort of ideal, was quite inconsistent with the needs of today. To make use of art or religion as a refuge was a sign of their increasing separation from the rest of human culture. It implied a cleavage between the different spheres of society which ruled out any genuine solution of social problems.

I knew from history that religion and art had once exercised a function which is today reserved for science, for they had given guidance in even the most practical activities of human society. And in so doing they had enhanced the quality of human living, whereas the influence of science has had just the opposite effect. This power of guidance, however, they had long since lost, and in view of this fact I came to the conclusion that salvation must be looked for in the first place from science. Here, in the thinking and knowing of man, was the root of modern troubles; here must come a drastic revision, and here, if possible, a completely new direction must be found.

Such views certainly flew in the face of the universal modern conviction that the present mode of knowledge, with whose help so much insight into the natural world has been won, is the only one possible, given once for all to man in a form never to be changed. But is there any need, I asked myself, to cling to this purely static notion of man's capacity for gaining knowledge? Among the greatest achievements of modern science, does not the conception of evolution take a foremost place? And does not this teach us that the condition of a living organism at any time is the result of the one preceding it, and that the transition implies a corresponding functional enhancement? But if we have once recognised this as an established truth, why should we apply it to organisms at every stage of development except the highest, namely the human, where the organic form reveals and serves the self-conscious spirit?

Putting the question thus, I was led inevitably to a conclusion which science itself had failed to draw from its idea of evolution. Whatever the driving factor in evolution may be, it is clear that in the kingdoms of nature leading up to man this factor has always worked on the evolving organisms from outside. The moment we come to man himself, however, and see how evolution has flowered in his power of conscious thought, we have to reckon with a fundamental change.

Once a being has recognised itself as a product of evolution,

Appendix A 233

it immediately ceases to be that and nothing more. With its very first act of self-knowledge it transcends its previous limits, and must in future rely on its own conscious actions for the carrying on of its development.

For me, accordingly, the concept of evolution, when thought through to the end, began to suggest the possibility of further growth in man's spiritual capacities. But I saw also that this growth could no longer be merely passive, and the question which now beset me was: by what action of his own can man break his way into this new phase of evolution? I saw that this action must not consist merely in giving outer effect to the natural powers of human thinking; that was happening everywhere in the disordered world around me. The necessary action must have inner effects; indeed, it had to be one whereby the will was turned upon the thinking powers themselves, entirely transforming them, and so removing the discrepancy between the thinker and the doer in modern man.

Thus far I could go through my own observation and reflection, but no further. To form a general idea of the deed on which everything else depended was one thing; it was quite another to know how to perform the deed, and above all where to make a start with it. Anyone intending to make a machine must first learn something of mechanics; in the same way, anyone setting out to do something constructive in the sphere of human consciousness—and this, for me, was the essential point—must begin by learning something of the laws holding sway in that sphere. But who could give me this knowledge?

Physiology, psychology and philosophy in their ordinary forms were of no use to me, for they were themselves part and parcel of just that kind of knowing which had to be overcome. In their various accounts of man there was no vantage point from which the deed I had in mind could be accomplished, for none of them looked beyond the ordinary powers of knowledge. It was the same with the accepted theory of evolution; as a product of the current mode of thinking it could be applied to everything except the one essential—this very mode of thinking. Obviously, the laws of the development of human consciousness cannot be discovered from a standpoint within the contemporary form of that consciousness. But how could one find a view-point outside, as it were, this consciousness, from which to discover its laws with the same scientific objectivity which it had itself applied to discovering the laws of physical nature?

It was when this question stood before me in all clarity that

234   *Invitation to a Great Experiment*

destiny led me to Rudolf Steiner and his work. The occasion was a conference held in 1921 in Stuttgart by the anthroposophical movement; it was one of several arranged during the years 1920–22 especially for teachers and students at the Hochschulen and Universities. What chiefly moved me to attend this particular conference was the title of a lecture to be given by one of the pupils and co-workers of Rudolf Steiner—'The Overcoming of Einstein's Theory of Relativity'.

The reader will readily appreciate what this title meant for me. In the circles where my work lay, an intense controversy was just then raging round Einstein's ideas. I usually took sides with the supporters of Einstein, for it seemed to me that Einstein had carried the existing mode of scientific thinking to its logical conclusions, whereas I missed this consistency among his opponents. At the same time I found that the effect of this theory, when its implications were fully developed, was to make everything seem so 'relative' that no reliable world-outlook was left. This was proof for me that our age was in need of an altogether different form of scientific thinking, equally consistent in itself, but more in tune with man's own being.

What appealed to me in the lecture-title was simply this, that whereas everyone else sought to prove Einstein right or wrong, here was someone who apparently intended, not merely to add another proof for or against his theory—there were plenty of those already—but to take some steps to *overcome* it. From the point of view of orthodox science, of course, it was absurd to speak of 'overcoming' a theory, as though it were an accomplished fact, but to me this title suggested exactly what I was looking for.

Although it was the title of this lecture that drew me to the Stuttgart Conference (circumstances prevented me from hearing just this lecture), it was the course given there by Rudolf Steiner himself which was to prove the decisive experience of my life. It comprised eight lectures, under the title: 'Mathematics, Scientific Experiment and Observation, and Epistemological Results from the Standpoint of Anthroposophy'; what they gave me answered my question beyond all expectation.

In the course of a comprehensive historical survey the lecturer characterised, in a way I found utterly convincing, the present mathematical interpretation of nature as a transitional stage of human consciousness—a kind of knowing which is on the way from a past pre-mathematical to a future post-mathematical form of cognition. The importance of mathematics, whether as a discipline of the human spirit or as an instrument of natural science, was not for a moment undervalued. On the contrary, what Rudolf Steiner said about Projective (Synthetic) Geometry, for instance, its future possibilities and its role as a means of understanding higher processes of nature than had hitherto been accessible to science, clearly explained the positive feelings I myself had experienced—without knowing why—when I had studied the subject.

Through his lectures and his part in the discussions—they were held daily by the various speakers and ranged over almost every field of modern knowledge—I gradually realised that Rudolf Steiner was in possession of unique powers. Not only did he show himself fully at home in all these fields; he was able to connect them with each other, and with the nature and being of man, in such a way that an apparent chaos of unrelated details was wrought into a higher synthesis. Moreover, it became clear to me that one who could speak as he did about the stages of human consciousness past, present and future, must have full access to all of them at will, and be able to make each of them an object of exact observation. I saw a thinker who was himself sufficient proof that man can find within the resources of his own spirit the vantage ground for the deed which I had dimly surmised, and by which alone true civilisation could be saved. Through all these things I knew that I had found the teacher I had been seeking.

Thus I was fully confirmed in my hopes of the Conference; but I was also often astonished at what I heard. Not least among my surprises was Rudolf Steiner's presentation of Goethe as the herald of the new form of scientific knowledge which he himself was expounding. I was here introduced to a side of Goethe which was as completely unknown to me as to so many others among my contemporaries, who had not yet come into touch with Rudolf Steiner's teachings. For me, as for them, Goethe had always been the great thinker revealing his thoughts through poetry. Indeed, only shortly before my meeting with Rudolf Steiner, it was in his poetry that Goethe had become newly alive to me as a helper in my search for a fuller human experience of nature and my fellow men. But despite all my Goethe studies I had been quite unaware that more than a century earlier he had achieved something in the field of science, organic and inorganic alike, which could help modern man towards the new kind of knowledge so badly needed today. This was inevitable for me, since I shared the modern conviction that art and science were fields of activity essentially strange to one another. And so it was again left to Rudolf Steiner to open the way for me and others to Goethe as botanist, physicist and the like.

I must mention another aspect of the Stuttgart Conference which belongs to this picture of my first encounter with Anthroposophy, and gave it special weight for anyone in my situation at that period. In Stuttgart there were many different activities concerned with the practical application of Rudolf Steiner's teachings, and so one could become acquainted with teachings and applications at the same time. There was the Waldorf School, founded little more than a year before, with several hundred pupils already. It was the first school to undertake the translation into educational practice of the knowledge of man gained through Spiritual Science; later it was followed by others, in Germany and elsewhere. There was one of the clinics, where qualified doctors were applying the same knowledge to the study of illness and the action of medicaments. In various laboratories efforts were made to develop new methods of experimental research in physics, chemistry, biology and other branches of science. Further, a large business concern had been founded in Stuttgart in an attempt to embody some of Rudolf Steiner's ideas for the reform of social life. Besides all this I could attend performances of the new art of movement, again the creation of Rudolf Steiner and called by him 'Eurythmy', in which the astounded eye could see how noble a speech can be uttered by the human body when its limbs are moved in accordance with its inherent spiritual laws. Thus, in all the many things that were going on besides the lectures, one could find direct proof of the fruitfulness of what one heard in them.

Under the impression of this Conference I soon began to study the writings of Rudolf Steiner. Not quite two years later, I decided to join professionally with those who were putting Spiritual Science into outer practice. Because it appeared to me as the most urgent need of the time to prepare the new generation for the tasks awaiting it through an education shaped on the entire human being, I turned to Rudolf Steiner with the request to be taken into the Stuttgart School as teacher of natural science. On this occasion I told him of my general scientific interests, and how I hoped to follow them up later on. I spoke of my intended educational activity as something which might help me at the same time to prepare myself for this other task. Anyone who learns so to see nature that his ideas can be taken up and understood by the living, lively soul of the growing child will thereby be training himself, I thought, in just that kind of observation and thinking which the new science of nature demands. Rudolf Steiner agreed with this, and it was not long afterwards that I joined the school where I was to work for eleven years as a science master in the senior classes, which activity I have since continued outside Germany in a more or less similar form.

This conversation with Rudolf Steiner took place in a large hall where, while we were talking, over a thousand people were assembling to discuss matters of concern to the anthroposophical movement. This did not prevent him from asking me about the details of my examination work, in which I was still engaged at that time; he always gave himself fully to whatever claimed his attention at the moment. I told him of my experimental researches in electrical high-frequency phenomena, briefly introducing the particular problem with which I was occupied. I took it for granted that a question from such a specialised branch of physics would not be of much interest to him. Judge of my astonishment when he at once took out of his pocket a notebook and a huge carpenter's pencil, made a sketch and proceeded to speak of the problem as one fully conversant with it, and in such a way that he gave me the starting point for an entirely new conception of electricity. It was instantly borne in on me that if electricity came to be understood in this sense, results would follow which in the end would lead to a quite new technique in the use of it.

From that moment it became one of my life's aims to contribute whatever my circumstances and powers would allow to the development of an understanding of nature of this kind.

From Ernst Lehrs, *Man or Matter*

(For Ernst Lehrs biog, see next page)—

Invitation to a Great Experiment

A native Berliner, Ernst Lehrs spent much of his adult life in England. He was a physicist and an electrical engineer by training, and was for many years a science master at Hawkwood College, a Rudolf Steiner Center for Adult Education in England. Dr. Lehrs also taught and lectured extensively in the United States for some years before his death in 1979.

His lifework was to demonstrate the validity and critical importance of a world view that sanely balances the values of the humanities—traditional vehicles of spiritual wisdom and teaching—and science. This is a viewpoint originally articulated by Goethe, and subsequently developed by Dr. Steiner.

Ernst Lehrs's basic book is *Man or Matter* (subtitle: *Introduction to a Spiritual Understanding of Nature, on the Basis of Goethe's Method of Training Observation and Thought*). Other books by Dr. Lehrs are: *The Language of the Clouds* and *Spiritual Science, Electricity, and Michael Faraday*.

Robert Mendelsohn on the escalation of the AIDS controversy and the gamma globulin fiasco

(From "The People's Doctor Newsletter")

A wire service story dated August 30, 1986, begins with the words, "Turmoil among AIDS experts at the Federal Centers for Disease Control."

In case your newspaper did not carry this important article, CDC's AIDS squad has been plagued by personality conflicts, firings of eminent scientists, an exodus of researchers, and delayed studies of ways to halt the deadly epidemic. The intensity of infighting in the CDC research laboratories has been demonstrated by experts sabotaging each other's experiments and suppressing research to combat the deadly disease. Virus cultures have turned up missing or contaminated. There have been petty squabbles over authorship of papers. Top scientific officials have ordered that their names be added to studies they never worked on.

While this sorry state of affairs at the top level of U.S. government health agencies may come as a shock to many people, it should come as no surprise to regular readers of this Newsletter. A decade ago, I brought you early warnings about what was to become the CDC's swine flu fiasco. Later, I revealed how that same bunch fumbled the ball on Legionnaire's disease. More recently, the CDC vaccine enthusiasts have forced mandatory immunizations on this country's children, without telling parents the risks of the vaccines and without requiring doctors to report vaccine reactions. So why should we expect any different behavior when it comes to AIDS?

I often have referred to the personnel at the CDC as second-rate doctors. Now, reporter Steve Sternberg, who wrote this article for Knight-Ridder Newspapers, supports my evaluation by pointing out that those scientists who have been forced to leave the CDC rank among the nation's most prestigious researchers. Indeed, few of the laboratory's original scientists remain. Perhaps these remaining lesser lights in medicine account for the strange behavior of the CDC in giving gay rights priority over public health.

Lest you think that the CDC is unique in the world of medicine because it places personality conflicts over scientific progress, ask your own doctor how often he angrily has watched scientists in his own medical schools and hospitals graft their own names onto published research with which they had practically nothing to do.

What's the point of government-funded research if the researchers have no integrity?

(From the same Newsletter)

Question, from M.R.: My doctor suggests I have a gamma globulin shot before I travel overseas. I know this shot is made from blood, and I wonder whether, in view of the AIDS epidemic, it's safe for me to take it.

Answer, from Dr. Mendelsohn: Many doctors still are using gamma globulin to ameliorate chicken pox in children and to protect Americans traveling abroad.

If your doctor assures you this human blood product is safe, ask him if he has read the February 7, 1986, issue of the *Journal of the American Medical Association*. That issue contains the information that the entire supply of gamma globulin available in the United States is positive for the AIDS (HTLV-III) antibody.

Donald Steele, M.D., of Newport Beach, California, comments: "I am appalled that the Food and Drug Administration, the Centers for Disease Control, local health services or the drug companies have not informed physicians throughout the United States that administration of gamma globulin to their patients or employees may entail the risk of converting them to a false-positive reaction for the HTLV-III antibody. . . . Without advance knowledge, however, the liability imposed on each of us is potentially enormous. Each of us can envision innumerable scenarios that might put us at grave risk if we fail to inform the patient in advance. . . ."

While I am all in favor of giving patients information, perhaps a simpler solution would be to dump all gamma globulin down the drain.

From Robert Mendelsohn, *The People's Doctor Newsletter*

(For Robert Mendelsohn biog, see next page)—

Robert Mendelsohn, M.D., was a life-long faithful and responsible servant of modern medicine. He was at the same time a life-long faithful and fair critic of modern medicine.

Dr. Mendelsohn practiced medicine for over thirty-five years. He was Chairman of the Medical Licensing Committee for the State of Illinois. He was National Director of the Medical Consultation Service of Project Head Start. And he was the recipient of numerous awards for excellence in medicine and medical teaching. At the time of his death in 1988 he was Associate Professor of Preventive Medicine and Community Health in the School of Medicine of the University of Illinois.

He was also a stoutly self-proclaimed medical heretic. Dr. Mendelsohn believed that the greatest danger to your health was usually your own doctor. Modern medicine's methods, he argued, are rarely effective, and in many instances are more dangerous than the diseases they are designed to diagnose and treat.

Mendelsohn's basic book is *Confessions of a Medical Heretic*. Equally important are the monthly newsletters which he wrote beginning in 1977. You can get any or all of the newsletters from *The People's Doctor Newsletter,* 1578 Sherman Avenue, Suite 318, Evanston, Illinois 60201.

Harry M. Tiebout *on how psychotherapists and psychiatrists can learn something from Alcoholics Anonymous*

(From "Psychological Factors Operating in Alcoholics Anonymous")

In recent years AA has been shining brightly if at times unevenly in the firmament of psychotherapy. No one can as yet be sure whether it is a meteor, a comet, or a star of some considerable magnitude, but it should be observed with respect and interest, and assayed for the light it may shed upon the therapeutic process. As with other new and striking phenomena, investigators initially tend to examine it from the perspective of known or relatively proved principles of psychotherapy. Hence there is a flood of explanations as to what makes AA tick—explanations which run from homosexual outlet, dependency upon a father person, opportunity to exploit exhibitionistic, narcissistic trends, through to vague and rather pontifical assertions about the therapeutic influence of the group. No one professes to be quite clear about his opinion, and everyone generally concedes that there must be an X factor, the presence of which is assumed by conjecture.

Now the strange fact in all this picture of uncertainty and conjecture is that very few of the investigators have studied AA carefully, nor have they availed themselves of opportunities to talk to members who have made the grade over a sufficient period to have achieved a long-term slant on what goes on and what is essential. If they had, they would have learned what that X factor is. They would have discovered that a religious component, a spiritual development, a belief in a God, was considered by AAs the one cardinal element without which there could be no permanent sobriety.

Failure to accept repeated testimony of the more experienced AAs is in itself an interesting phenomenon and attests to the stranglehold which Freud and his dicta have upon current psychotherapeutic thinking. Fairly early in his career, for reasons best known to himself and his own unconscious, Freud took the position

Appendix A

that religious beliefs and feelings were signs of dependency and immaturity, sedulously to be avoided and decried. This "opiate-for-the-masses" attitude he maintained unflinchingly to the day of his death, and it is this attitude which has influenced present-day psychiatry to the point of excluding the possibility of religion and religious forces having any valid therapeutic effect or function. It is my belief that here, as in his insight into feminine psychology, Freud suffered from certain blind spots and biases which prevented him from seeing the role of religion in human affairs. It is my further belief that the phenomenon of AA can never be understood until more insight is gained into the phenomenon of religion and spiritual growth.

In this paper, therefore, I plan to present some material plucked from AA which supports pretty conclusively the AA conviction that this religious factor is the essential X quantity. I shall then set forth my own tentative explanation as to why such is the case.

In offering you the following account of AA experience, I wish first to express my indebtedness to some of the older members who have provided the information on which these stories are based.

Some six or seven years ago there was a new member who, according to reports, was one of the toughest-minded men ever to enter AA. However, he became quickly enthusiastic about the program, at the same time violently opposing the "spiritual angle." "Damn this God business" was his constant cry, to the consternation of the others in the group who felt he was a disturbing influence in that he seemed to prove that sobriety could be maintained without God. He remained dry for many months, got his family together, worked hard and successfully with other alcoholics. He finally felt secure enough to leave AA work and go back into his old business of selling on the road. Within three weeks he began drinking, and after a terrific bat, while writhing with an awful hangover in a cheap hotel, "something cracked," as he put it, and "I gave in and admitted that the boys must have something with their God stuff," as he later reported. This man has since stayed sober and five years ago founded one of the most successful and active current AA groups.

Many other individual members have been through similar experiences, but it is also true of groups, as the history of one in a Western city clearly indicates. This group was started by an AA member who was one of the very few able to stay dry without the "spiritual angle." In other respects this man is a most enthusiastic member with a sobriety record running at least six years. Some five years ago, while taking a business trip through this community, he assembled a group of alcoholics and sold them the idea of AA minus the need for a belief in "a power greater than themselves." This he insisted was not necessary. After he left the group hung together and got in quite a few new members, but a year later, when they numbered perhaps twenty, they were, with one exception, all drunk at the AA Christmas party.

Later, and largely on the basis of AA literature and letters from the central office in New York, the group went straight AA, accepting the necessity of the religious or spiritual slant. Now, four years later, there are a dozen groups in this area numbering several hundred members with a record of seventy-five percent sober.

The third illustration is perhaps even more telling, as it concerns the efforts of a psychiatrist to use most of the AA program but without any emphasis on the "God angle." Club houses, group activities, discussions were all offered, but the record over a considerable period of time was far from satisfactory until some of the men surreptitiously visited the local AA group and started to spread straight AA among the others. Before the "higher power" idea was introduced, the secretary reports, the results were small. Although everyone who wanted to stop drinking felt he had been much helped by the instruction received from the doctor, and although the doctor personally was both popular and respected professionally, the alcoholics with one or two exceptions could not seem to stay dry on his regimen. After the contact with AA, progress was much greater. Now about twenty men who could do nothing with the club program are AAs and are progressing far more satisfactorily.

These examples, which are typical of AA experience, lend solid support to the opinion that the religious element is essential.

What the religious element may be, therefore, becomes the real nub of the question as to why AA succeeds where others fail. In attempting to determine the answer to this question I have developed certain speculations which seem to some extent to supply the answer sought for.

Before detailing the facts on which my speculations are based, one source of confusion must be eliminated, namely, the distinction between religious practice and religious feeling. Religious practice frequently produces religious feeling, but it does not inevitably do so. In order to avoid two such conflicting usages of the word "religious,"

Appendix A

the word "spiritual" will be employed to refer to the feeling which may arise during the course of religious observance. In other words, a spiritual feeling should result from religious practice.

The question now reads, "What is a spiritual feeling?" The answer to this question, an essential preliminary to any discussion of AA, is most difficult. It cannot be stated directly, but it must be attempted, because it is only by appreciating the nature of a spiritual feeling that one can arrive at an understanding of what goes on in AA.

The first series of facts which focused my attention upon the spiritual factor sprang from observations made upon what I have come to call conversion experiences. Differing slightly from more customary usage, I define a conversion experience as a psychological event in which there is a major shift in inner response or affectivity. Whereas, before, the patient was swayed by a set of predominantly hostile, negative attitudes, after the conversion process the patient is swayed by a set of predominantly positive, affirmative ones. This change is generally although not necessarily religious both in inspiration and in expression. It may take place with sweeping, almost cataclysmic suddenness, or it may occur slowly over a period of time. The important fact for the purpose of this paper is that as a result of this change there develops a new type of inner response. This new type is spiritual in quality.

To date, I have been in a position to study at least thirteen patients who have exhibited this response. Incidentally, not all of these patients were alcoholic. From these observations, I have gathered a picture of the new feelings which arise and how they affect the individual.

It is these new, positive, affirmative feelings, spiritual in nature, which I must now attempt to describe even though to describe a feeling kills it and in no way creates it. Unfortunately, also, the feeling I must discuss has to be seen or felt before it can be realized and, therefore, thought about in all its aspects.

The outstanding quality to appear is a frame of mind for which patients use words such as "peaceful," "quiet," "contented," "calm," "serene," "tranquil," and the like. Pressed further, they fall back on words and phrases which show that the tense, roused, anxious state so characteristic of the alcoholic has gone without a trace. Characteristically they report, "I feel different; I'm not tense and nervous like I used to be. I don't have to get everything settled at once, I'm not so impatient. Things don't bother me like they used to. I now don't think that when things don't go my way, it's aimed at me." Some will say further, "It's astonishing what it [the new emotional viewpoint] does to your outlook on life. Before I used to think about the future and how I could enjoy that. Now I enjoy the present and let the future take care of itself. It's much simpler that way because your thinking does not have to be all clogged with what may happen in the future. You don't ignore the future but it isn't a burden any more." One patient carried this point further by adding, "If you're not so full of demands as to what you should get out of life, you can live in the present because you're satisfied with it. You're not always hoping that the future will bring you what you want; even though you know that, when you get it, you won't be satisfied long." The tense, driving, goal-pushed person has disappeared and in his place there is an individual who can be patient, relaxed, and much more tolerant.

Along with this new type of inner feeling response go changes in many of the personality or character attributes formerly in the ascendancy. For instance, there may be a loss, temporary or lasting, of most of the overt signs of what may be designated as "automatic hostility." As an example, patients are frequently victims of what may be called the "sucker" complex. They will complain of a sense of isolation and loneliness which they frequently offer as an explanation for their drinking. They then proceed to explain their loneliness as follows: They are basically friendly, trusting souls who have tried to get close to other people, but they have always been disappointed sooner or later so that now they are cautious about really going "all out" for anyone. They have been "suckers" too often and now they are going to wait until they see what is real underneath. The interesting fact is that, with the changed emotional status, the problem of hostility and its associated mechanisms drops out; the "sucker" fear vanishes and patients remark, "I feel easier with people; I'm not so suspicious, and I realize they do things because they are themselves and it is not directed against me. I can like them and I think they can like me and I don't get all upset when I find that there are things about them that I don't like. I don't fear that my feelings will change because I don't go all out for people in the same way. I know they have faults, but that's because they are human. I don't fear being a sucker any more."

Fully as striking is the disappearance of the perfectionistic drive.

Appendix A

The mechanism for this disappearance is easy to decipher and interestingly clear. During the automatically negative phase the patient projects the feeling of hostility into the world about him and, therefore, finds it filled with hostility, for which the world always affords plenty of factual support. When the new phase comes up, instead of automatic hostility there is an automatic positive note which in turn projects a friendly feeling into the environment. It is then possible to view the bad with kindlier eyes and call it a human tendency to err. Furthermore, the good is seen as real and genuine and not as a hypocritical mask which covers a basic hostility and selfishness.

With the submergence of the hostility components and the consequent disappearance of the perfectionistic drive, there is also a corresponding dimming of the idealistic overtones. In retrospect, it becomes apparent that the search for the true, the good and the perfect is a naïve, unconscious effort to neutralize the projected hostility. The unconscious thinking seems to run as follows: "If the world is perfect or I can find enough perfection in it, then the badness (or hostility) of the world cannot continue to prevail."

Along with the cessation of the idealistic pressures, there is a corresponding shift in the feelings of guilt. Whereas prior to the conversion change the patient is burdened by a sense of guilt which can be called truly sadistic and punishing, after the change the individual acknowledges guilt and wrongdoing but accepts his own human tendency to err as he does that of other people. One patient pointed up this particular aspect when she said, "Before I always knew what was right and wrong. I would always be trying to live up to ideals. I was sort of blank about what I *wanted* to be. I would have doubts. I would put on a front to be what I wanted to be. Then something came along and I had to stay up there; that's when I became tense. Now I know I have been doing right and wrong all my life but I don't have to be so virtuous about being good or guilty about being bad." Commenting on her former sense of righteousness, she said, "Before if there were any Ten Commandments, I had to be at the bottom of them. I was a queen without a kingdom." Her final thought on her perfectionism was, "It made me sit on many things which would have helped me to grow."

Along with the amelioration of the hostility component, there is an equally striking loss of the egocentric power drive. Prior to the shift, happiness is the goal and happiness is pictured as independence, freedom, and doing what you please. Happiness, it is unconsciously assumed, can only be achieved through being strong enough to get what one wants. It can never be attained by a weakling who is doomed to unhappiness because he must always be frustrated. Since the feeling of inner strength automatically implies the opposite weakness, the individual involved in the dilemma of securing happiness through power inevitably suffers from a superiority-inferiority conflict. When he feels strong, he feels superior; when he feels weak, he feels inferior.

Logically, if the power drive is diminished or changed in quality, the goal of happiness disappears and so does the striving for superiority with its accompanying inferiority reaction. Instead of happiness as a goal, patients find contentment in the present. Furthermore, with the departure of the pressure for power, the superiority-inferiority issue sinks into a proper recognition of the fact that some people are better in one thing, others in another. The patient can then add, "I have my weaknesses and my own good points or strengths."

Another and quite unexpected feature of the new state is the change which comes in the capacity to work. Before, work had been resented as duty, put up with as a boring, cramping routine, entered into with a competitive drive for power and superiority. Characteristically, alcoholics work either under the relentless pressure of superior attainment or in spurts as an outlet for their inner tension states. Once a goal has been reached and an outside incentive is lacking, the drive for work promptly vanishes and in its place their so-called "lazy streak" makes its appearance. At this point they demand fun, amusement, and freedom from responsibility.

After the conversion shift, the work picture is quite different. With the absence, or at least marked decline, of the drive for superiority and the concern for what the job can do for and with the ego, there comes an interest in the job itself. The job is viewed more objectively, it becomes "my responsibility, which I assume without question because it is one place where I fit into life and am a part of things." With the development of this attitude, work habits become steadier and more predictable.

Patients themselves are surprised at this change and comment as follows: "Before I used to be busy, now I am just occupied." Another, a student and in no way alcoholic, said, "Now I can plug at my lessons [her work] and not mind it." Asked to define plugging, she replied, "Plugging is working without lift." Still another patient said, "I guess I've got to revamp my ideas about myself. I thought I was a hard worker. I was, but only to get what I wanted. Now I can see there is fun in doing the job, not so I can outshine anybody else but so I know inside I've been doing my honest best." The shift to a more consistent, even output of energy is always an unexpected increment.

The last attribute of the change is a markedly greater degree of objectivity. This has already been hinted at, first by the patient who remarked concerning her perfectionism, "It made me sit on many things which would have helped me to grow." It was also noted in the new attitude toward work.

The change which makes the objectivity possible is a basic switch from nonreceptivity to receptivity. The nonreceptive egocentric individualist is too busy maintaining his own status, too wrapped in his own affairs, to be able to perceive what is going on about him. Instead he must impose his own thoughts and feelings upon circumstances. When the shift takes place and the individual is no longer dominated either by idealistic demands or hostile presumptions, a receptivity to experience, to one's self appears. The individual can accept facts without inner argument or resistance; he can remain open-minded about ideas, neither totally excluding them nor wholly accepting them and then not being able to alter them as the facts require.

The difference in response is most notable in the learning situation, and it is here that the patients' remarks are the most pointed. As one patient put it, "Learning is after all a matter of cooperation, and I don't believe I've ever cooperated in any thing all my life. I've thought I had, but I always did it with reservations." Another said, "I now pray to let my mind see and hear all and to let my mind stay open. I want to find out what's wrong. I want to know the facts, but I now know there are many different outlets from a fact." Her final comment, made as her ability to think became more firmly ingrained, was, "The deterioration of me was the inability to think. There were times when I couldn't will myself to think. Before I used to plan, now I can think without planning. Before it was to let me think of what I could do."

To sum up, the change in emotional state which follows the conversion experience is characterized primarily by altered response in which quiet and serenity predominate. It was also pointed out that associated with that altered response are other changes, the following of which were mentioned and discussed: (1) the loss of automatic hostility; (2) the disappearance of the perfectionistic drive; (3) the disappearance of the egocentric power drive; (4) the appearance of a better response to work demands; and finally, (5) the appearance of a much greater capacity for objectivity.

Other changes in attitude accompany the new state. I have, however, perhaps described enough to give you some slant as to what follows after the conversion shift has taken place. The new feelings which appear are distinctly spiritual in quality and alter the psychic picture in the direction of what it must be conceded are healthier reactions. Experience has furthermore demonstrated that these reactions furnish a substantial base for continued sobriety.

Having pointed out and described the true nature and extent of spiritual feelings, I am now in a position to answer the original question, "What is the X factor which the program of AA contains above and beyond that of other therapeutic efforts?" The answer is that the program supplies through its religious emphasis a source of spiritual strengthening, a conversion, if you will, either quick or gradual, which, coupled with the rest of the activities, provides a new basis of emotional orientation in which the former egocentric hostile pattern is supplanted by a more object-centered approach in which positive and affirmative attitudes prevail.

Obviously, this answer leaves much unsaid. There is no discussion of what causes a conversion which, in turn, brings out the spiritual manifestations; neither is there any explanation of the altered psychology which appears with the conversion switch. Moreover, I have said nothing about the permanence or impermanence of these reactions. These are questions with which, naturally, I have been much occupied, but in this paper I have limited myself to stressing the significance of the spiritual development in members of Alcoholics Anonymous. I have also tried through a description of the changed personality attributes to indicate that along with the development of the spiritual feelings there are new features in personality make-up which are decidedly healthier attitudes.

In conclusion, therefore, I can only reiterate what I initially set forth: namely, that the success of the AA program may be understood only in the light of a recognition of the religious practices it encourages and the consequent spiritual awakening. All the other parts of the AA program are valid and important, but I am convinced that a true understanding of its effectiveness depends upon insight into the source and nature of what has been called the X factor, or "spiritual feeling."

> From Harry M. Tiebout, *Psychological Factors Operating in Alcoholics Anonymous*

Harry M. Tiebout, M.D., was the first psychiatrist to endorse Alcoholics Anonymous as a means of recovery from alcoholism, even though AA's methods were directly opposed to much of psychoanalytic theory. Recognizing the soundness and effectiveness of AA's methods, Dr. Tiebout altered his entire professional approach to the treatment of alcoholism and other behavior disorders, in conformity to the AA model. He laid special stress on the need for ego deflation and reliance upon God.

Dr. Tiebout was born in Brooklyn in January 1896. He received a B.S. degree from Wesleyan University in 1917, was married in 1920, and completed his medical and psychiatric training at Johns Hopkins University in 1922. He was associate professor of psychiatry at Cornell Medical College from 1932 to 1935, medical director of Blythewood Sanitarium in Greenwich, Connecticut, from 1935 to 1950, and a member of the advisory panel on mental health and alcoholism for the World Health Organization in Geneva from 1954 to 1959. Dr. Tiebout was president and chairman of the board of the National Committee on Alcoholism from 1950 to 1952, and chairman of the American Psychiatric Association's committee on alcoholism. He was a trustee of Alcoholics Anonymous from 1957 until his death in 1966.

Dr. Tiebout's best-known article is "Surrender Versus Compliance in Therapy." A listing of the numerous articles he published in medical, scientific, and psychiatric journals is available from *The Quarterly Journal of Studies on Alcohol* (Rutgers University, P.O. Box 969, Piscataway, New Jersey).

O. Hobart Mowrer *on the place of sin in modern religion and modern psychiatry*

(*From "The Crisis in Psychiatry and Religion"*)

As long as one adheres to the theory that psychoneurosis implies no moral responsibility, no error, no misdeed on the part of the afflicted person, one's vocabulary can, of course, remain beautifully objective and "scientific." But as soon as there is so much as a hint of personal accountability in the situation, such language is, at the very least, wide of the mark and, conceivably, quite misleading. Therefore, if "moral judgment" does enter the picture, one might as well beard the lion and use the strongest term of all, *sin*. . . .

But there is also a deeper objective here. "Sickness" is a concept which generates pervasive pessimism and confusion in the domain of psychopathology; whereas sin, for all its harshness, carries an implication of promise and hope, a vision of new potentialities. Just so long as we deny the reality of sin, we cut ourselves off, it seems, from the possibility of radical redemption ("recovery").

In some ways it is perhaps not surprising that we are . . . [exploring] the question of whether real guilt, or sin, is relevant to the problem of psychopathology and psychotherapy. For half a century now we psychologists, as a profession, have very largely followed the Freudian doctrine that human beings become emotionally disturbed, not because of their having *done* anything palpably wrong, but because they instead *lack insight*. Therefore, as would-be therapists we have set out to oppose the forces of repression and to work for *understanding*. And what *is* this understanding, or insight, which we so highly prize? It is the discovery that the patient or client has been, in effect, *too* good; that he has within him impulses, especially those of lust and hostility, which he has been quite unnecessarily inhibiting. And health, we tell him, lies in the direction of recognizing and expressing these impulses.

But there are now widespread and, indeed, ominous signs that this logic and the practical strategies it seems to demand are ill-founded. The situation is, in fact, so grave that we are even willing to consider the possibility that misconduct may, after all, have something to do with the matter and that the doctrine of repression and insight are more misleading than helpful.

However, as soon as we psychologists get into a discussion of this problem, we find that our confusion is even more fundamental than might at first appear. We find that not only have we disavowed the connection between manifest misconduct and psychopathology; we have, also, very largely abandoned belief in right and wrong, virtue and sin, in general.

On other occasions when I have seen this issue under debate and anyone has proposed that social deviousness is causal in psychopathology, there is always a chorus of voices who clamor that sin cannot be defined, that it is culturally relative, that it is an unscientific concept, that it is a superstition—and therefore not to be taken seriously, either in psychopathology or in ordinary, everyday experience. And whenever an attempt is made to answer these objections, there are always further objections—often in the form of reductions to absurdity—which involve naivety or sophistry that would ill-become a schoolboy. Historically, in both literate and non-literate societies, human beings are supposed to have reached the age of discretion by early adolescence; yet here we have the spectacle of grown men and women soberly insisting that, in effect, *they* cannot tell right from wrong—and that no one else can.

Now I realize how futile it is to try to deal with this kind of attitude in a purely rational or logical way. The subversive doctrine that we can have the benefits of orderly social life without paying for it, through certain restraints and sacrifices, is too alluring to be counteracted by mere reason. The real answer, I believe, lies along different lines. The unassailable, brute fact is that personality disorder is the most pervasive and baffling problem of our time; and if it *should* turn out that persons so afflicted regularly display (or rather *hide*) a life of too *little*, rather than too much, moral restraint and self-discipline, the problem would take on an empirical urgency that would require no fine-spun argument.

Sin used to be—and, in some quarters, still is—defined as whatever one does that puts him in danger of going to Hell. Here was an assumed cause-and-effect relationship that was completely metaphysical and empirically unverifiable; and it is small wonder that it has fallen into disrepute as the scientific outlook and method have steadily gained in acceptance and manifest power. But there is a very tangible and very present Hell-on-this-earth which science has not yet helped us understand very well; and so I invite your attention to the neglected but very real possibility that it is *this* Hell—the Hell of neurosis and psychosis—to which sin and unexpiated guilt lead us and that it is *this* Hell that gives us *one* of the most, perhaps *the* most realistic and basic criteria for defining sin and guilt. If it proves empirically true that certain forms of conduct characteristically lead human beings into emotional instability, what better or firmer basis would one wish for labeling such conduct as destructive, self-defeating, evil, sinful?*

If the Freudian theory of personality disorder were valid, one would expect neurotic and psychotic individuals to have led exemplary, yea saintly lives—to have been just too good for this world. The fact is, of course, that such individuals typically exhibit lives that have been disorderly and dishonest in extreme degree. In fact, this is so regularly the case that one cannot but wonder how so contrary a doctrine as that of Freud ever gained credence. Freud spurned The Wish and exalted Reality. What he regarded as Reality may yet prove to have been the biggest piece of wishfulness of all.

Or, it may be asked, how is it if sin and psychic suffering are correlated that not *all* who sin fall into neurosis or psychosis? Here the findings of the Kinsey studies are likely to be cited, showing that, for example, many persons have a history of sexual perversity who are later quite normal. In other words, the argument is that since sin and persistent suffering do not always go hand-in-hand, there is perhaps no relationship at all. The answer to this question is surely obvious. *Some* individuals, alas, simply do not have enough character, or conscience, to be bothered by their sins. These are, of course, the world's psychopaths. Or an individual may have been *caught* in his sin

---

*There is, admittedly, an element of circularity in the above argument. If it is maintained that mental illness is caused by unacknowledged and unexpiated sin, or real guilt, then it adds nothing to our knowledge to *define* sin as that which causes mental illness. In fact, there is a sense in which such a definition is not only circular but misleading. Obviously, what is needed is an *independent criterion* for identifying sin or guilt.

Appendix A

and punished for it. Or it may have weighed so heavily on his conscience that he himself has *confessed* it and made appropriate expiation. Or, quite conceivably, in some instances the individual, without either detection or confession, may have set upon a program of service and good works which has also brought him peace and redemption. In other words, there is, surely, no disposition on the part of anyone to hold that sin, as such, necessarily dooms a person to interminable suffering in the form of neurosis or psychosis. The presumption is rather that sin has this effect only where it is acutely felt but not acknowledged and corrected.

Also, it is sometimes contended that individuals who eventually come to the attention of psychotherapists have, to be sure, been guilty of major errors of conduct; but, it is held, the illness was present first and the misconduct was really just an expression or symptom thereof. If this were true, where then would we draw the line? Is there no such thing as moral responsibility and social accountability at all? Is every mean or vicious thing that you or I, as ordinary individuals, do not sin but rather an expression of "illness"? Who would seriously hold that a society could long endure which consistently subscribed to this flaccid doctrine?

Then there is, of course, the view that, in the final analysis, all psychopathology—or at least its profounder forms—have a constitutional or metabolic basis. One must, I believe, remain open-minded with respect to this possibility—indeed, perhaps even somewhat hopeful with respect to it; for how marvelous it would be if all the world's madness, stupidity, and meanness could be eliminated through biochemistry. But over the years we have seen one approach after another of this kind come into prominence, with much heralding as the long-awaited break-through on the problem of mental disease, only to fade out as manifestly not quite the panacea we had imagined it to be. Some of us may, at this point, even suspect that today the main incentive for keeping the biochemical hypothesis alive is not so much the supporting empirical evidence, which is meager enough, but instead the fact that it at least obliquely justifies the premise that the whole field of mental disorder is the proper and exclusive domain of medicine. Also, and again somewhat obliquely, it excuses the clergy from facing squarely the responsibilities that would devolve among them if neurosis and psychosis should indeed turn out to be essentially *moral* disorders.

The conception of personality disturbance which attaches major etiological significance to moral and interpersonal considerations thus faces formidable resistance, from many sources; but programs of treatment and prevention which have been predicated on these other views have gotten us nowhere, and there is no clear reason to think they ever will. Therefore, in light of the total situation, I see no alternative but to turn again to the old, painful, but also promising possibility that man is preeminently a *social* creature and that he lives or dies, psychologically and personally, as a function of the openness, community, relatedness, and integrity which by good action he attains and by evil action destroys.

As long as we could believe that the psychoneurotic's basic problem was not evil but a kind of ignorance, it did not seem too formidable a task to give him the requisite enlightenment or insight. But mental hospitals are now full of people who have had this kind of therapy, in one guise or another, and found it wanting; and if we are thus forced to reconsider the other alternative, the therapeutic or redemptive enterprise, however clear it may be in principle, is by no means simple in practice. If the problem is genuinely one of morality, rather than pseudo-morality, most of us in the secular healing professions, of psychology, psychiatry, or social work, find ourselves reduced to the status of laymen, with no special training or competence for dealing with or even approaching the problem in these terms. We know something, of course, about procedures for getting disturbed persons to talk about themselves, free-associate, "confess"; but the whole aim of this strategy has been insight, not redemption and personal reformation. And clergymen themselves have so often been told, both by their own leaders and by members of the secular healing professions, that they must recognize their own "limitations" and know when to "refer" that they, too, lack the necessary confidence and resources for dealing with these problems adequately.

Many present-day psychoanalysts will offer no serious objection to the way in which classical Freudian theory and practice have been evaluated in this paper; but they will insist that many "advances" have been made since Freud's time and that these put the whole problem in a very different light. If we ask, "Precisely what *are* these advances?" we are told that they have to do with the new emphasis upon "ego psychology" rather than upon "the unconscious." But what did Emalian Gutheil (1958) tell us at our convention last year in Wash-

Appendix A

ington about ego psychology? He said that although analysts now recognize the ego as much more important than formerly, they know next to nothing about the conditions for modifying or strengthening it; and the same position has been voiced earlier by Lawrence Kubie (1956) and in one of his last papers (1937) even by Freud himself.

Therefore, I do not see how we can avoid the conclusion that at this juncture we are in a real crisis with respect to the whole psychotherapeutic enterprise. But I do not think we are going to remain in this crisis, confused and impotent, indefinitely. There is, I believe, growing realism with regard to the situation on the part of both psychologists and psychiatrists, on the one hand, and ministers, rabbis, and priests, on the other; and I am hopeful and even confident that new and better ways of dealing with the situation are in the making.

What, precisely, these ways will be I do not know; but I venture the impression that Alcoholics Anonymous provides our best present intimation of things to come and that the therapeutic programs of the future, whether under religious or secular auspices, will, like AA, take guilt, confession, and expiation seriously and will involve programs of *action* rather than mere groping for "insight."

From O. Hobart Mowrer, *The Crisis in Psychiatry and Religion*

O. Hobart Mowrer's lifework was to correct, both in theory and in practice, the failure of professional religion and professional psychiatry to deal effectively with the problems of mental and emotional disturbances in modern times. He was quoted by *Time* Magazine in 1976 as summing up his vision of a new direction in psychic healing, in the following terms: "Future treatment of the emotionally disturbed will, like Alcoholics Anonymous, take guilt, confession, and expiation seriously and will involve programs for action rather than mere groping for insights."

Hobart Mowrer was born in 1907 in Unionville, Missouri. He received an A.B. degree from the University of Missouri in 1929, was married in 1931, and received a Ph.D. from Johns Hopkins University in 1932. Between 1932 and 1948 he served on the faculties of Northwestern, Yale, and Harvard Universities. He was research professor of psychology at the University of Illinois from 1948 to 1975. A dean in the field of psychology, Dr. Mowrer was a member of the board of directors of the American Psychological Association from 1952 through 1955 and was president of that organization in 1953 and 1954. From 1951 through 1954 he was a consultant to the National Institute of Mental Health. He died in June, 1982.

Dr. Mowrer published hundreds of articles over the years in professional journals. His basic books are *The Crisis in Psychiatry and Religion, The New Group Therapy,* and *Morality and Mental Health.*

Maurice Nicoll *on*
false personality and self-love

(From "Psychological Commentaries")

Questions are asked at different times in which the term "self-love" is used. I have explained that this term "self-love" is not used in this system of teaching and when I use it myself I have usually added that it is not a technical Work expression. In the early days of the Work in London we often discussed among ourselves why this word was not used and I remember someone saying that perhaps it was because it was either a worn out word or it did not contain any clear meaning. On one occasion, at a private talk among a few of us, Mr. Ouspensky said that if we could find another term for it, it might be of some use to describe False Personality. [Mr. Ouspensky's understanding of what psychology really is was quite different from what recent and current notions hold it to be.*] Various words were suggested such as "self-esteem," "self-admiration," "self-importance," and others, but when the term "self-liking" was suggested, he said that perhaps it came nearest to what he had in mind. He added that the whole question lay in the emotional reactions of False Personality in a man or woman. He said man, or woman, must be shaken to their depths to get rid of False Personality. We are easily offended and upset because False Personality is our feeling of ourselves and it is an imaginary

---

*From *The Psychology of Man's Possible Evolution*, by P. D. Ouspensky:

I shall speak about the study of psychology, but I must warn you that the psychology about which I speak is very different from anything you may know under this name.

To begin with I must say that practically never in history has psychology stood at *so low a level* as at the present time. It has lost all touch with its *origin* and its *meaning* so that now it is even difficult to define the term "psychology": that is, to say what psychology is and what it studies. And this is so in spite of the fact that never in history have there been so many psychological theories and so many psychological writings.

Psychology is sometimes called a new science. This is quite wrong. Psychology is, perhaps, the *oldest science*, and, unfortunately, in its most essential features a *forgotten science*.

In order to understand how psychology can be defined it is necessary to realize that psychology except in modern times has never existed under its own name. By one reason or another psychology always was suspected of *wrong or subversive tendencies*, either religious or political or moral, and had to use different disguises.

thing, an acquired artificial mask, a pretended person that we like to imagine ourselves to be and are not. This False Personality takes itself as a unity and this is how Imaginary 'I' arises; it borrows, so to speak, the idea that it is a real person and so says 'I'. The keeping up of the False Personality takes a great deal of force. It makes us internally consider: it exhausts us. Mr. Ouspensky said that the False Personality always justifies itself in order to maintain its existence. This wastes force. In regard to the False Personality, which in my case is called Nicoll, he said that one has to be able to see that it is not really 'I'. He said it was composed of a certain grouping of rolls in centres and groups of 'I's which may shift from time to time in regard to their composition according to the environment in which one happens to be, and yet at the same time it always has the same quality of falseness, of something kept up—some invention. A man, for example, may amongst lower class people assume a certain pretence of himself and amongst higher class people assume another pretence of himself, and yet at the same time it is all the same thing—that is, it is False Personality. He said that we have come to the point of being able to say to ourselves internally "this is not really I". He said that this inner separation—in my case from Nicoll—was the most important point in the Work, and was connected with making the Personality as a whole passive. He said that the study of False Personality was almost a life task and eventually could only be understood through the development of inner taste which led into Real Conscience. He said that Real Conscience part from Acquired Conscience

---

For thousands of years psychology existed under the name of philosophy. In India all forms of *Yoga*, which are essentially psychology, are described as one of the six systems of philosophy. *Sufi teachings*, which again are chiefly psychological, are regarded as partly religious and partly metaphysical. In Europe, even quite recently, in the last decades of the nineteenth century, many works on psychology were referred to as philosophy. And in spite of the fact that almost all subdivisions of philosophy such as logic, the theory of cognition, ethics, æsthetics, referred to the work of the human mind or senses, psychology was regarded as inferior to philosophy and as relating only to the lower or more trivial sides of human nature.

Parallel with its existence under the name of philosophy, psychology existed even longer connected with one or another religion. This does not mean that religion and psychology ever were one and the same thing, or that the fact of the connection between religion and psychology was recognized. But there is no doubt that almost every known religion—certainly I do not mean modern *sham religions*—developed one or another kind of psychological teaching connected often with a certain practice, so that the study of religion very often included in itself the study of psychology.

There are many excellent works on psychology in quite orthodox religious literature of different countries and epochs. For instance, in early Christianity there was a

was one of our greatest internal senses, and that unless it had been given us, no one could awaken. Acquired Conscience is, of course, merely a matter of how we have been brought up and what we have been taught is right or wrong. He said that Acquired Conscience is different in every nation. It could be anything. It was a matter of imitation. Some people are taught by imitation and education that it is right to have many wives and others are taught that it is right to have one wife, and so on, in a thousand different ways, but Real Conscience is the same in all people, but it is buried beneath the surface of the False Personality. He said further that no one of course could ever act without some admixture of self—that is, in the sense of self-interest—but that usually it was *all* self-interest. People did not externally consider. He said that we are told to love our neighbours as ourselves and that one meaning is that we could not do things completely without self-interest or self-liking, but that half of it should be self and half love of neighbour.

I asked him to speak about the stages of emotional development—that is, the development of the Emotional Centre to its highest receptive powers—as it was formulated in the Gospels—namely, "love of oneself, love of one's neighbour, and love of God". It is recorded that Christ, when he was asked by one of the Pharisees which was the great commandment replied: "Thou shalt love thy neighbour as thyself" (Matthew 22:37). It is only possible to attempt to give a summary of what Mr. O.'s answer was. He began by saying: "False Personality loves itself only and all that flatters it or agrees with it. Unless a man can find something to love greater than himself he

---

collection of books of different authors under the general name of *Philokalia*, used in our time in the Eastern Church, especially for the instruction of monks.

During the time when psychology was connected with philosophy and religion it also existed in the form of art. Poetry, drama, sculpture, dancing, even architecture, were means for transmitting psychological knowledge. For instance, the Gothic cathedrals were in their chief meaning works on psychology.

In the ancient times before philosophy, religion, and art had taken their separate forms as we now know them, psychology had existed in the form of *Mysteries*, such as those of Egypt and of ancient Greece.

Later, after the disappearance of the Mysteries, psychology existed in the form of *Symbolical Teachings* which were sometimes connected with the religion of the period and sometimes not connected, such as astrology, alchemy, magic, and the more modern Masonry, occultism, and Theosophy.

And here it is necessary to note that all psychological systems and doctrines, those that exist or existed openly and those that were hidden or disguised, can be divided into two chief categories.

can never modify this inner state. Nowadays," he said, "people have got a very strange view of the Universe and take it all for granted as if it created itself and see nothing marvellous in it. How can a thing create itself? Scientists ascribe every discovery to themselves, not understanding that they are studying a Universe already given them which existed long before they were born. They even call stars by their own names. It is absurd. But False Personality ascribes everything to itself. In more ancient times when a man had sense of the miraculous and worshipped God as the Creator, both of himself and of the Universe, he was emotionally in a far better state than exists nowadays in the average human outlook. His understanding was better. He could stand *under* himself. In regard to what is said in the Gospels about love, you must realize that this is said in a very big sense, on a very big scale, and has meaning within meaning in it. These meanings destroy False Personality because when they begin to be understood by a man or a woman then the sense of the smallness of themselves in comparison with the great mystery of Creation begins to affect them emotionally. All greater emotions destroy the small self-emotions which arise from the narrow contracted sphere of the False Personality and its own minute self-liking and self-importance." He said, in so many words: "You know already that all sayings and parables in the Gospels contain immense density of meaning which reveals itself as we change in level of Being. To argue about whether Christ existed or not as an historical fact has little sense. In fact He did, and carried out his rôle deliberately. The point is that any man with any kind of discrimination and understanding who reads the Gospels for the first time knows at once that these brief records, these words, are completely different from anything that has ever been written since that time. But people read the Gospels mechanically; they do not understand what they read. They read about the Phar-

---

First: systems which study man *as they find him, or such as they suppose or imagine him to be*. Modern "scientific" psychology, or what is known under that name, belongs to this category.

Second: systems which study man not from the point of view of what he is, or what he seems to be, but from the point of view of what he may become; that is, from the point of view of his *possible evolution*.

These last systems are in reality the original ones, or in any case the oldest, and only they can explain the forgotten origin and the meaning of psychology.

When we understand the importance of the study of man from the point of view of *his possible evolution*, we shall understand that the first answer to the question, what is psychology, should be that psychology is the study of the principles, laws, and facts of man's possible evolution.

isees and Christ's continual condemnation of them, but they do not see that it applies to themselves—to their own False Personality. The Pharisee in you is your False Personality; it is always pretending to be what it is not. It is the Pharisee living in you. People even think sometimes that it is easy to understand that one must love God with all one's heart, with all one's soul, and with all one's mind, and imagine they do. They do not understand that this means first making Personality passive—a long task. They must give up completely the idea that they are their own creators, realize practically, blow after blow, that something infinitely greater than themselves exists and that they are nothing. The trouble is that they think they understand what Christ said, and even quite religious people profess that they love God and do not observe that they insist on their own opinions and are a mass of False Personality so that really in the long run they love themselves". He added: "For example, they are liable to judge and condemn everyone who behaves in a way they do not like. That is, they hate in secret. Now what does "love of neighbour" mean? Who is one's neighbour? Some people perhaps think it means the person who happens to live next door. Psychologically it has to do with those nearest you in Being, those near you in understanding, in what they seek, or who are going along the same road. That is why we must make a conscious relation to those in the Work—the second line of work. And then what does love of self mean? *Which self?* We have many selves. And finally, how can we understand what "love of God" means? It is something tremendous, something we may imagine we know about, but cannot know yet. Yes, people say they love God and then go and kill one another or hate each other, or talk evilly. How can that be love of God? Perhaps No. 7 man knows what "love of God" means—that is, a man belonging to the highest development possible to Man—certainly ordinary mechanical Man cannot know what it means. He may love his *own opinion* of God, the God he supposes he worships, but that is subjective, and if someone disagrees with him, he will be angry and even persecute him and wish to kill him. A state of *objective consciousness* (i.e., the fourth state of consciousness) would have to be reached before the meaning of Christ's words became fully understandable. All we can say of ourselves is that we do not know how to love others or God. That is the first thing. We must see that it is so. What we call love can turn to dislike, suspicion, jealousy or hate in a moment. Love means positive emotion and we do not know positive emotions. Their characteristic is that they never turn into opposites because they include all opposites. We only know emotions that turn readily into their opposites, and do so often in a flash. We call it love but it is not love. It is self-love. The term *love* is used in the Gospels in a special way. It is conscious love, conscious relation, not mechanical love, that is meant. That is clear enough. When a man begins to realize he cannot love as he is, then at least he is nearer truth. He is no longer a fool. He has at least got rid of some imagination, some part of False Personality, got rid of some make-up, and so is nearer the possibility of conscious love. What passes as love in mechanical life is chiefly imagination. What people call love is usually satisfied self-love. To love is to work. Love is work."

Some people, of course, disagreed with these words and were sure they knew what love was even though they were unhappy or sad in appearance, I noticed. At another time Mr. O. said that we could not form any conception of a "development of love" without a development of consciousness. He said: "This Work speaks mainly of a possible development of consciousness in Man; as Man is he is not yet properly conscious. Love must become conscious, not passion. Man is asleep. Everything in him is mixed with dreams, with imagination, and with negative emotions, to which he clings most of all. Most of his life takes place in his imagination. He is subjective and especially governed by False Personality—this false person he has to obey which is not himself. He cannot see anything as it is. But a man who reaches the highest state of consciousness is in a quite different state. While in that state he sees what everything really is. He is no longer in personal subjective meanings. He is objective and so universal. He can include all things in himself. This happens when a man becomes conscious in the highest or most real part of him—that is, in "Real I" in him. Such a man would understand what love of God is. But a man living in False Personality in which only small one-sided self-emotions occur, cannot do so. How could such a man, so prejudiced, so small-souled, so selfish, so negative, understand what love of God is— a man who even looks down on others if they do not belong to the same club, and utterly rejects a man of a different religion or nation?"

From Maurice Nicoll, *Psychological Commentaries on the Teaching of Gurdjieff and Ouspensky*

(For Maurice Nicoll biog, see next page)—

Maurice Nicoll was born in England in 1884. He completed his training as a medical doctor in 1910. In 1912 he went to Vienna to study Freud's system of psychology. Then he went to Zurich, where he studied directly with Dr. Carl G. Jung, whose teachings awoke in him an interest in the spiritual side of psychic healing, and changed the direction of his career completely.

When World War I broke out, Dr. Nicoll was commissioned in the R.A.M.C., serving in Gallipoli and Mesopotamia until 1917. On his return to England he joined the staff of Empire Hospital as a neurologist. Using largely Jungian methods, he did critical pioneering work in the new field of psychological treatment of shell-shock.

He had been in practice for some years as a Harley Street neurologist when he met P. D. Ouspensky in 1921. This encounter exposed him to a powerful system of teaching on the awakening of higher consciousness, a system known as the Fourth Way. Once again his life's direction changed completely. Dr. Nicoll retired from his medical practice and underwent a year's training in France under Ouspensky's teacher, G. I. Gurdjieff.

Returning to London he resumed his medical practice and continued to study under Ouspensky until 1931, when he received permission from Ouspensky to teach Gurdjieff's system. He continued his teaching right through World War II and up until his death in 1953. He is best known for his commentaries on the Gurdjieff-Ouspensky system and for his writings on the New Testament from the viewpoint of the Fourth Way.

Nicoll's basic work is his five-volume communication of the Fourth Way, entitled *Psychological Commentaries on the Teaching of Gurdjieff and Ouspensky*. Recently, the Gurdjieff Society of Washington, D.C., has issued a one-volume index to Nicoll's *Commentaries*. This is a remarkably useful book for anyone studying Maurice Nicoll's psychology. It enables one quickly and easily to track basic subjects—such as Self-Love, Lying, Imagination, Self-Observation, Self-Remembering—throughout the entire body of the *Commentaries*. Nicoll's other books are *Living Time*, *The Mark*, and *The New Man*. An excellent biography—*Maurice Nicoll: A Portrait*—is available, written by Beryl Pogson, Nicoll's long-time friend and secretary.

Martin Gross *on the alteration of the nature of our civilization brought about by modern psychology*

(From "The Psychological Society")

Much has been said about the awesome *external* transformation in our modern world. These changes are obvious. But the *internal* shift in man's psyche has altered both our actions and expectations more than any technological force. This change in inner man has taken place quietly, yet it has altered the nature of our civilization beyond recognition.

The major agent of change has been modern psychology. At the time of Sigmund Freud's visit to Clark University in Massachusetts in 1909, psychology was an infant discipline. Today, psychology is an art, science, therapy, religion, moral code, life style, philosophy and cult. It sits at the very center of contemporary society as an international colossus whose professional minions number in the hundreds of thousands.

Its ranks include psychiatrists, psychoanalysts, clinical psychologists, psychotherapists, social workers, psychiatric nurses, school psychologists, guidance counselors, marriage and family therapists, educational psychologists, Sensitivity T-Group and Encounter leaders, and assorted lay therapists. Recently, it has added a number of newly hyphenated professionals including psycholinguists, biopsychologists and psychobiographers.

Its experimental animals are an obliging, even grateful human race. We live in a civilization in which, as never before, man is preoccupied with *Self*. We have become fascinated with our madness, motivations and our endless, sometimes wearying search for normality. Modern psychology and psychiatry seek to satisfy that fascination by offering us a full range of systems, from the serious to the whimsical, with which we can understand our confused psyche, then seek to heal it.

The contemporary Psychological Society is the most vulnerable culture in history. Its citizen is a new model of Western man, one who is dependent on others for guidance as to what is real or false. In the unsure state of his mind, he is even doubtful of the authenticity of his own emotions. As the Protestant ethic has weakened in Western society, the confused citizen has turned to the only alternative he knows: the psychological expert who claims there is *a new scientific standard of behavior* to replace fading traditions.

In the 1950s, David Riesman spoke of the "other directed" man as receiving his life cues from outside sources. Today, we can see a new *psychologically directed* man in operation. His antennae are thrust continually outward for hints from experts who are handsomely paid to tell him what to make of himself and others, how best to live, even feel.

The citizen-patient has been told, and usually believes, that his tormenting doubts about love, sex, work, interpersonal relations, marriage and divorce, child raising, happiness, loneliness, even death, will yield to the new technology of the mind. Mouthing the holy name of *science*, the psychological expert claims to know all.

This new truth is fed to us continuously from birth to the grave. Childhood, once a hardy time of adventure, is now seen as a period of extreme psychological fragility. A U.S. Senate subcommittee warns us that premature emotional disturbance will strike one in ten of our children. The nation's child guidance clinics have trebled in number over the last twenty years. One physician, Dr. Arnold Hutschnecker, even suggests a grand scheme to screen all the nation's children to find those who need preventive psychotherapy.

The schoolhouse has become a vibrant psychological center, staffed not only by schoolteachers trained in "educational psychology" but by sixty thousand guidance workers and seven thousand school psychologists whose "counseling" borders on therapy. In one case, virtually an entire first-grade class at P.S. 198 in New York City has been given free psychotherapy at nearby Mount Sinai Hospital.

The need for psychological expertise follows us doggedly through life. Erik Erikson's *identity crisis* has become a symbol for millions of adolescents, an age group which is increasingly concerned about its psyche. A CBS-TV special on youth reported that uppermost in the minds of those interviewed were nagging doubts about mental health. The college-age population is also heavily into its psyches as "drop-in" counseling centers handle record numbers of anguished youth. Columbia University reports a threefold increase in student use of psychological services in a decade.

The adult is, of course, the mainstay of the new Society, for his anxieties are endless. The enormity of that need is only hinted at in a George Washington University study which showed that Americans ingest tons of psychochemicals, mainly minor tranquilizers, in a continuous search for tranquillity.

This frenetic quest is part of modern man's search for the elusive goal of normality. It is a state which Freud once called an *ideal fiction* and which society hopelessly confuses with happiness and peace of mind. "The quest for peace of mind—or good mental health, which is another name for it—is universal," the National Association of Mental Health informs an eager public.

Modern psychological-mindedness springs from many origins, one of which is the breakdown in the separation between health and sickness when applied to the mind. Historically, insanity was an affliction that struck the few. The remainder felt spared. They may have been mean, or unhappy, or even eccentric, but they were considered sane.

Today, that boundary between the well and the sick has been blurred by psychology and psychiatry. Emotional illness is now seen as an ugly but natural manifestation that strikes us all in varying degrees. "Now every normal person is only approximately normal," Freud reminded us shortly before his death. "His ego resembles that of the psychotic in one point or another, in a greater or lesser degree." In modern parlance, we are all, to some extent, *sick*.

Impressionable citizens of the Society have even falsely equated mental health with the usually unreachable *idea* state which combines success, love and lack of anxiety. The Psychological Society thus creates its own self-fulfilling prophecy. *We are all sick, for normality is almost unattainable.*

This might be called *the theory of universal madness*. We have increasingly directed suspicion of mental instability against our friends, family and, eventually, ourselves. In New York City, a ten-year study, *Mental Health in the Metropolis*, claimed that approximately 80 percent of adults showed some symptoms of mental illness, with one in four actually impaired.

In 1977 the President's Commission on Mental Health confirmed these dire diagnoses. It concluded that the state of our psyches is worse than believed, and that one-quarter of all Americans suffer from severe emotional stress. They warn that up to 32 million Americans are in need of professional psychiatric help.

A National Institute of Mental Health psychologist even portrays universal madness as a statistical certainty. "Almost no family in the nation is entirely free of mental disorders," he stated in a recent federal study. The NIMH psychologist estimates that in addition to the 500,000 schizophrenics in hospitals, there are 1.75 million psychotics not hospitalized, and up to *60 million Americans who exhibit deviant mental behavior related to schizophrenia*. He speaks of the "psychological turbulence that is rampant in an American society that is confused, divided and concerned about its future."

Despite these warnings, mental illness has not increased significantly since 1955, when complete records first began. The annual mental hospitalization rate of 8.5 per 1000 population is remarkably steady and consistent throughout much of the developed world. What the Psychological Society has done is to redefine *normality*. It has taken the painful reactions to the normal vicissitudes of life—despair, anger, frustration—and labeled them as maladjustments.

The semantic trick is in equating happiness with normality. By permitting this, we have given up our simple right to be both *normal and suffering* at the same time. Instead, we have massively redefined ourselves as *neurotic*, even as incipient mental cases, particularly when life plays its negative tricks. It is a tendency which gives modern America, and increasingly much of the Western world, the tone of a giant psychiatric clinic.

This is only one legacy of modern psychology. Its pervasiveness in the fabric of our culture has become near total as it absorbs new disciplines each year. Armed with what it claims are the hidden truths about man's behavior, it has impressed its philosophical stamp on virtually all of contemporary life: mental health and illness, the arts, education, religion, medicine, the family, child care, business, the social sciences, history, government, language, advertising, law, crime and punishment, even architecture and economics.

Its most obvious impact is on what are now collectively called *the helping professions*, a mental health team that includes perhaps a dozen professionals headed by the psychiatrist. Much as the ministry did for years, the superprofessionals of psychology and psychiatry have now assumed the supreme watchdog role. Not only have we entrusted them with the care of so-called neurotics and our mentally ill, but delinquents, drug addicts, the low-achieving student, the stutterer, the confused collegian, the suicidal, the homosexual, the criminal, the alcoholic, even the aged and the poor are all considered their natural patients.

In the Psychological Society, human problems are no longer seen as normal variations or unseemly twists of fate. We now view them as the products of internal psychological maladjustments. We are even encouraged to believe that there would be no failure, no crime, no malevolence, no unhappiness if man could only understand his psyche, then set it for a metaphysical condition called *adjustment*. As more of us find that ideal state defeated by life's pressures, psychology offers its ultimate remedy—*psychotherapy*.

"The demand for psychotherapy is non-ending. It's unbelievable," states Dr. Donald M. Kaplan, a New York teaching and practicing psychologist-analyst. "Individual psychotherapy was once an elitist privilege, but it has now been democratized. The general population now feels entitled to it, and is seeking it out. In prior times, people would take care of ordinary life crises by themselves, or with the help of their families. Now they all want psychotherapy."

Millions receive psychotherapy each year in a multitude of forms, from psychoanalysis to simple supportive therapy, in groups or alone. Others seek the Nirvana in the new wave of *humanistic* therapies including scores of imaginative ideas from Gestalt Therapy to nude marathons. We are offered almost a hundred different psychotherapies for every healing taste. Each proclaims a somewhat different method, sworn to be the superior key.

The outpatient psychiatric clinics are busy sites of this new therapy rush. In 1955 they treated a total of 233,000 people. Since then, the number has risen dramatically to 2.4 million patients annually. This figure does not include another 1.5 million patients treated each year in the 570 federally supported Community Mental Health Centers.

The establishment bases of psychotherapy are the psychiatrists, the majority of whom see patients in their private offices, clinical psychologists and the psychiatric social workers (M.S.W. degree), the burgeoning third rung of the helping professions. Judging from a 1973 American Psychiatric Association study of private practice, and a more recent report on health services from the American Psychological Association, we can estimate that one and a half million Americans take their psychic repair in the private offices of these practitioners.

In all, some six million Americans each year receive psychotherapy in clinics and hospitals and from private therapists. To find the total number in therapy, however, we must also look at the growing legions of *lay therapists* who offer a psychological inventory from *est* to primal workshops and encounter. At least a million more Americans take their therapy from these sources, or a total of seven million who receive psychological intervention annually.

This balm is not evenly distributed, for the therapy professions have a geographic bias. Almost half the psychiatrists, for example, practice in New York, California, Illinois, Pennsylvania or Massachusetts. Nearly one-third are in New York and California alone. But the profession is expanding rapidly into the rest of the country. Once psychologically isolated Nebraska now boasts over a hundred psychiatrists.

Psychology is now an international movement which cuts across national and class boundaries. With the demise of the belief in immortality and the end of absolute morality, it is becoming the most generally accepted substitute. Its power level in each nation varies with how well its theme of magical human improvement matches the indigenous ethic.

It has not yet gained a strong hold in southern Europe, but its strength increases as one progresses northward into France, Germany, Holland, Scandinavia and Britain. Even the Soviet Union, a consistent critic of Western insight psychology, has begun to recant. In *Kommunist*, the official ideological journal, Soviet psychologists have recently called for more research into applications of the unseen *unconscious*.

America, however, has been the warm, natural host for modern psychology. It has nurtured the young colossus from its infancy to its current adulthood. In fact, the American sponsorship of psychology may be setting a pattern for world society as definitive as America's earlier leadership in industrial technology.

Psychology has taken hold in the Protestant world mainly because both the psychological and Protestant ethics insist that a method be found for the perfectibility of men. That perfectibility was once sought through the intervention of God, but is now accomplished by supposed scientific adjustment of the psyche. Long before the Psychological Society, the nineteenth-century social historian

Alexis de Tocqueville saw this urgent need for perfectibility in the American character. "Aristocratic nations are liable to narrow the scope of human perfectibility; democratic nations to expand it beyond reason," he observed.

This democratic hope has encouraged our desperate search for psychic understanding and repair. Instead of increasing our stability as a culture, that search has paradoxically accelerated man's tendency toward anxiety and insecurity, shaking the very underpinnings of Western civilization. It is now apparent that the Judeo-Christian society in which psychology began its ascendancy is atrophying under the massive impact of several forces, particularly that of modern psychology. In its place stands a new culture of a troubled and confused citizenry, the Psychological Society.

For many, this Society has all the earmarks of a potent new religion. When educated man lost faith in formal religion, he required a substitute belief that would be as reputable in the last half of the twentieth century as Christianity was in the first. Psychology and psychiatry have now assumed that special role. They offer mass belief, a promise of a better future, opportunity for confession, unseen mystical workings and a trained priesthood of helping professionals devoted to servicing the paying-by-the-hour communicants.

Not only is the new Society attempting to fill the void left by Christianity, but it has created images that parallel older spiritual ones. The traditional religious idea of *sin* is becoming obsolete. But the medico-psychological concept of *sick* has replaced it almost intact. We now speak glibly of murderers, addicts, even the personality-distorted as being "sick" or "neurotic" as effortlessly as neighbors once gossiped about the sinfulness of the local alcoholic.

Even though psychology and psychiatry are at the core of this new Society, surprisingly they have been the least analyzed of all disciplines. While attention has been focused on their customers, psychology and psychiatry themselves have escaped outside scrutiny, leaving their extraordinary control over our lives less than understood.

This book [*The Psychological Society*] hopes to correct that oversight and explain the psychologization of our culture. It will probe the Psychological Society, its operations, origins, claims, manifestations, customs, mores, shortcomings, validity, aspirations and ultimate significance. *This evaluation has become essential, for not an idea, not a*

Appendix A 277

style, not a personal or cultural relationship exists which has not been drastically affected by the new supremacy of the Psychological Society.

From Martin Gross, *The Psychological Society*

Martin Gross is a foremost defender of our rights to protection against professional arrogance, incompetence, and error in the fields of medicine and psychiatry. His first book, *The Brain Watchers*, was such an effective critique of the abuses of psychological testing that it triggered a Congressional investigation which resulted in the Civil Service Commission's discontinuing the use of psychological tests.

Martin Gross was born and brought up in New York City. He received his undergraduate degree from City College of New York, and completed two years of graduate study at Columbia University. He served in the Air Corps as a navigator and radar operator during World War II. Gross has published more than 250 articles in national magazines, most of them critical commentaries on psychology, medicine, education, and national affairs.

Martin Gross's three basic books are:

The Doctors, which is an incisive, fair, understanding, appreciative, and practically very helpful critique of modern medicine;

The Psychological Society, which is an incisive, fair, understanding, appreciative, and practically very helpful critique of modern psychology and modern psychiatry;

The Brain Watchers, which is an incisive, fair, understanding, appreciative, and practically very helpful critique of modern psychological testing techniques.

Arthur Machen *on the healing of Olwen Phillips by the vision of the Holy Graal*

(From "The Great Return")

The well-to-do and dignified personages who left their pews in the chancel of Llantrisant church and came hurrying into the nave could give no explanation of what they had done. They felt, they said, that they "had to go," and to go quickly; they were driven out, as it were, by a secret, irresistible command. But all who were present in the church that morning were amazed, though all exulted in their hearts; for they, like the sailors who saw the rose of fire on the waters, were filled with a joy that was literally ineffable, since they could not utter it or interpret it to themselves.

And they too, like the sailors, were transmuted, or the world was transmuted for them. They experienced what the doctors call a sense of *bien être,* but a *bien être* raised to the highest power. Old men felt young again, eyes that had been growing dim now saw clearly, and saw a world that was like paradise, the same world, it is true, but a world rectified and glowing, as if an inner flame shone in all things, and behind all things. . . .

It was on that Sunday night that Olwen Phillips of Croeswen dreamed her wonderful dream. She was a girl of sixteen, the daughter of small farming people, and for many months she had been doomed to certain death. Consumption, which flourishes in that damp, warm climate, had laid hold of her; not only her lungs but her whole system was a mass of tuberculosis. As is common enough, she had enjoyed many fallacious brief recoveries in the early stages of the disease, but all hope had long been over, and now for the last few weeks she had seemed to rush vehemently to death. The doctor had come on the Saturday morning, bringing with him a colleague. They had both agreed that the girl's case was in its last stages. "She cannot possibly last more than a day or two," said the local doctor to her mother. He came again on the Sunday morning and found his patient perceptibly

Appendix A

worse, and soon afterwards she sank into a heavy sleep, and her mother thought that she would never wake from it.

The girl slept in an inner room communicating with the room occupied by her father and mother. The door between was kept open, so that Mrs. Phillips could hear her daughter if she called to her in the night. And Olwen called to her mother that night, just as the dawn was breaking. It was no faint summons from a dying bed that came to the mother's ears, but a loud cry that rang through the house, a cry of great gladness. Mrs. Phillips started up from sleep in wild amazement, wondering what could have happened. And then she saw Olwen, who had not been able to rise from her bed for many weeks past, standing in the doorway in the faint light of the growing day. The girl called to her mother: "Mam! mam! It is all over. I am quite well again."

Mrs. Phillips roused her husband, and they sat up in bed staring, not knowing on earth, as they said afterwards, what had been done with the world. Here was their poor girl wasted to a shadow, lying on her death-bed, and the life sighing from her with every breath, and her voice, when she last uttered it, so weak that one had to put one's ear to her mouth. And here in a few hours she stood up before them; and even in that faint light they could see that she was changed almost beyond knowing. And, indeed, Mrs. Phillips said that for a moment or two she fancied that the Germans must have come and killed them in their sleep, and so they were all dead together. But Olwen called out again, so the mother lit a candle and got up and went tottering across the room, and there was Olwen all gay and plump again, smiling with shining eyes. Her mother led her into her own room, and set down the candle there, and felt her daughter's flesh, and burst into prayers and tears of wonder and delight, and thanksgivings, and held the girl again to be sure that she was not deceived. And then Olwen told her dream, though she thought it was not a dream.

She said she woke up in the deep darkness, and she knew the life was fast going from her. She could not move so much as a finger, she tried to cry out, but no sound came from her lips. She felt that in another instant the whole world would fall from her—her heart was full of agony. And as the last breath was passing her lips, she heard a very faint, sweet sound, like the tinkling of a silver bell. It came from far away, from over by Ty-newydd. She forgot her agony and listened, and even then, she says, she felt the swirl of the world as it came back to her. And the sound of the bell swelled and grew louder, and it thrilled all through her body, and the life was in it. And as the bell rang and trembled in her ears, a faint light touched the wall of her room and reddened, till the whole room was full of rosy fire. And then she saw standing before her bed three men in blood-coloured robes with shining faces. And one man held a golden bell in his hand. And the second man held up something shaped like the top of a table. It was like a great jewel, and it was of a blue colour, and there were rivers of silver and of gold running through it and flowing as quick streams flow, and there were pools in it as if violets had been poured out into water, and then it was green as the sea near the shore, and then it was the sky at night with all the stars shining, and then the sun and the moon came down and washed in it. And the third man held up high above this a cup that was like a rose on fire; "there was a great burning in it, and a dropping of blood in it, and a red cloud above it, and I saw a great secret. And I heard a voice that sang nine times: 'Glory and praise to the Conqueror of Death, to the Fountain of Life immortal.' Then the red light went from the wall, and it was all darkness, and the bell rang faint again by Capel Teilo, and then I got up and called to you."

The doctor came on the Monday morning with the death certificate in his pocket-book, and Olwen ran out to meet him. I have quoted his phrase in the first chapter of this record: "A kind of resurrection of the body." He made a most careful examination of the girl; he has stated that he found that every trace of disease had disappeared. He left on the Sunday morning a patient entering into the coma that precedes death, a body condemned utterly and ready for the grave. He met at the garden gate on the Monday morning a young woman in whom life sprang up like a fountain, in whose body life laughed and rejoiced as if it had been a river flowing from an unending well.

From Arthur Machen, *"The Great Return"*
(Tales of Horror and the Supernatural)

Appendix A

Arthur Machen was born on March 3, 1863, at Caerleon-on Usk, Wales. The only child of a clergyman, Machen began his education in 1874 at Hereford Cathedral School, where for several years he was at the top of his class in both divinity and classics. But instead of pursuing a career in medicine as his father had expected, Machen began writing. His first published work was a long poem entitled *Eleusinia*, which appeared in 1880. Thereafter he never stopped writing until shortly before his death in 1947. He was at various times a poet, an essayist, a novelist, a translator, and a reporter for *The London Evening News*.

Like C. S. Lewis and J. R. R. Tolkien, Machen frequently taught in the narrative mode. His own knowledge and experience obviously included the reality of other worlds existing alongside, or superimposed upon, the ordinary world. His life's vocation was communicating that reality.

The basic Machen book is *Tales of Horror and the Supernatural*, a collection of his writings about white and black magic. The book is a classic and has been in print for nearly sixty years in the U.S. and in England. The best account of Machen's remarkable life is Wesley D. Sweetser's *Arthur Machen: A Biography*.

*The Lifesavers Groups
Are Self-Help Groups
Based on the Motto:
In God We Trust*

Lifesavers Associates, Box 75, White Lake, NY 12786

APPENDIX B

The Lifesavers Way of Life

With the coming of Alcoholics Anonymous, millions of alcoholics, otherwise hopeless, have found their way back to sanity. But there is far greater lifesaving power in the AA principles than has yet been widely recognized, because what is involved is *the practice of the ethical and spiritual principles common to all mankind,* and applicable to all mankind.

The original program of Alcoholics Anonymous consisted of the Four Absolutes and the Twelve Steps (see below). The Absolutes were in use several years before the Steps were formulated. In a real sense, the Absolutes were the foundation on which the Steps were built. The Absolutes and the Steps together constituted the primitive program, and it was a world-shaker. This is the program by which co-founders Bill W. and Dr. Bob S. got sober, by which the first hundred AAs recovered, by which the whole movement was launched.

This original program—applied not only to alcohol problems but to a wide range of other problems—is called the Lifesavers way of life. It is so called because in many cases it is the only means by which people who are floundering in deep trouble can get their heads above water and keep them above water.

The following are statements of Lifesavers principles as practiced in effective Lifesavers groups in our critical times:

The Four Absolutes: Used in the Oxford Group and in the pioneering years of Alcoholics Anonymous, these life-transforming principles in one form or another have been the foundation of the spiritual life in all ages and all cultures. They were the basis, for example, upon which Gandhi's ashram operated; they are among the essentials of the first of the traditional eight limbs of yoga (the *yamas*); and they are clearly the principles to which a life in Christ requires adherence:

1. Absolute honesty—non-lying to oneself or others; fidelity to the truth in thought, word, and actions.
2. Absolute purity—purity of mind, purity of body, purity of the emotions, purity of heart, sexual purity.
3. Absolute unselfishness—seeking what is right and true in every situation above what I want.
4. Absolute love—loving God with all your heart, all your soul, all your mind, and all your strength, and your neighbor as yourself.

The Absolutes, of course, are not claims of attainment. They are *aims, levels of commitment* for daily conduct. When they are maintained faithfully as *goals,* they become powerful transformers of conduct, character, and consciousness.

The Twelve Steps: One of the most effective and most widely applied statements of the Lifesavers principles in modern times, and one of the great working statements of the spiritual life of all times, this fundamental version of the program of Alcoholics Anonymous was in general use throughout the AA Fellowship even before the publication of the "Big Book" (*Alcoholics Anonymous,* AA's basic text) in April 1939. The shorter statements which had preceded it are now forgotten, and the Twelve Steps have become the universally accepted and only generally known version of the AA program.

These Steps are a lifeline for alcohol addicts, many of whom, lacking opportunity to contact an AA group, have recovered by the mere knowledge and application of these twelve principles. From the standpoint of the whole world of recovery from addiction, it is impossible to exaggerate the importance of the Twelve Steps of Alcoholics Anonymous. If an addict who is sincerely seeking a way out had no other tool than a working knowledge of these Steps, he would have a very good chance of recovery. Do not let the simple language in which they are stated fool you. They are a spiritual powerhouse to which

Appendix B

hundreds of thousands of addicts, now walking the streets as free men and women, owe their lives and their liberty.

Adapted versions of the Steps have been used by non-alcoholics for many years—by the Al-Anon Family Groups, Neurotics Anonymous, Narcotics Anonymous, Gamblers Anonymous, Overeaters Anonymous, and many others. The original version of the Steps, for use by alcoholics only, may be found in the Big Book, *Alcoholics Anonymous* (1976: Alcoholics Anonymous World Services, Inc.). The Steps as adapted here can be used by anyone:

1. We admitted we were powerless, that our lives had become unmanageable.
2. Came to believe that a Power greater than ourselves could restore us to sanity.
3. Made a decision to turn our will and our lives over to the care of God as we understood him.
4. Made a searching and fearless moral inventory of ourselves.
5. Admitted to God, to ourselves, and to another human being the exact nature of our wrongs.
6. Were entirely ready to have God remove all these defects of character.
7. Humbly asked him to remove our shortcomings.
8. Made a list of all persons we had harmed and became willing to make amends to them all.
9. Made direct amends to such people wherever possible, except when to do so would injure them or others.
10. Continued to take personal inventory and when we were wrong promptly admitted it.
11. Sought through prayer and meditation to improve our conscious contact with God as we understood him, praying only for knowledge of his will for us and the power to carry that out.
12. Having had a spiritual awakening as the result of these Steps, we tried to carry this message to others, and to practice these principles in all our affairs.

Altogether (leaving aside the commentaries) there is not a lot of material here. In the entire Lifesavers program—the Four Absolutes

286   *Invitation to a Great Experiment*

and the Twelve Steps—there are only sixteen things to remember. The Lifesavers way of life is based on an astonishingly simple program. *But it embodies the very power of life over death.*

As a matter of experience it has been found that these sixteen principles produce recovery not only from addiction but also from a broad spectrum of the spiritual ills of life.

The Lifesavers experience proves that *anyone* who is suffering from hopelessness, resentment, depression, fear, burnout, or loss of direction in life—can attain spiritual awakening, self-control, freedom, peace, and joy if he or she will go to sufficient lengths in adopting these principles as a way of life.

How to get going on the Lifesavers way of life

If you are in real trouble—if you are more or less permanently hung up in worry, fear, discouragement, resentment, or crazy behavior; if you are an addictive liar or thief; or if you are addicted to alcohol, food, sex, work, or drugs—if you want to recover; if you are willing to accept and act on suggestions from people who themselves have recovered—the outlook for you is good. Do not let anybody tell you that recovery from the worst spiritual troubles of this life is impossible, or even unusual. Many hundreds of thousands, in the past 150 years, have recovered—fully, beautifully, and permanently.

The people who clutter up the recovery scene and make it seem like a big deal are those (all of us, at one stage of the game) who do not really want to recover and who are still horsing around with the situation and mainly playing games. However—when you yourself reach the point of *really wanting* to recover and *becoming willing* to do what recovered lifesavers tell you to do, the battle is more than half won.

The recovery program of the Lifesavers groups is based on a set of sixteen principles which are easy to understand and easy to apply.

In the beginning of your recovery, you are so weak physically and so bombed out mentally that you are easily confused and easily put off. Therefore you have to make "first things first" a rule and stick to it. What do you do?

The first thing you do is to learn the *first principles of recovery* (see pages 284–285) from someone who knows them and practices them, and to begin to practice them yourself. If you approach them with a little humility, they are not hard to understand, and it is not an impossible task to follow them. These principles, and the company of people who practice them, are your lifeline. You simply cannot afford to argue about them. You merely have to *do* them, one day at a time.

The way to recovery begins with a few simple, uncomplicated first principles, which come to you as suggestions. Maybe you will not like some of these recommendations, but the thing to remember is that they work, and none of them should be left out. The whole way to go is to *hang on* while you are coming out of the fog, and these suggestions tell you what (and what not) to hang on to.

Hang on to God

The first source of help you need to turn to—first in the order of time and first in the order of importance—is God. This is not a matter of religion or philosophy, but simply a matter of fact. It is the power of God which enables addicts to recover. Without that power, there are very few recoveries.

Now there are a lot of different opinions about God, but we are not talking about God as an opinion but as a living power. Do not waste time theorizing about God. What you do is *get in touch* with God by the simple and direct means of talking to God, that is, by plain, old, ordinary prayer. Every nitwit knows how to pray; the knack here is to *do* it. No preliminary ducking or bobbing is necessary. Just do it.

All real recovery begins here. It makes no difference whether you are a believer or not. If you are not, start by praying to the God you don't believe in. Just park your objections for a while, and do it as an experiment.

Hang on to the truth

You connect with God by means of the truth. And you connect with the truth by stopping lying. All addicts are liars. Please do not resent this. It is just a statement of fact. Some of us lie in gross ways, some in subtle ways; but all of us are ferocious liars.

As a starter, stop lying to yourself about your condition. Stop pretending it is better than it is.

If you have any real addiction—which is merely a really bad habit which you find it impossible to break—you are into a condition which is apt to ruin your life and kill you. On the record, the chances are that you will not be able to do anything about it—not by yourself and not with the best scientific, psychiatric, or medical help in the world. Addiction—the unbreakable really bad habit—is often beyond help except through spiritual conversion. If you face that fact, your chances for recovery are good. If you ignore it, your chances are poor.

Next, stop lying to get out of jams or to smooth off the rough edges of life. Don't lie for the sake of peace; don't lie when common sense invites you to do so; don't lie to cover up your past; don't lie on job applications, expense accounts, or tax returns; don't lie to your boss; don't lie to your husband or wife. Just don't lie. When you fail in this resolve (as you will), admit it promptly. And don't indulge failure; that is, don't fail any oftener than you have to.

This policy of non-lying takes real courage if you have a messy past, as many of us do. It feels like it is going to cause problems for you, rather than solve them. But in actual practice it is a life-saver and a life-transformer. Try it, and you will find that non-lying simplifies life and makes it easier to deal with. And it does something else of greatest importance: When you take truth-telling seriously, you put yourself in direct touch with God. God *is* truth, and throughout the day every decision you make to be honest opens you up to the healing light of his presence. This is not just a pretty thought; it is something real, like electricity, only alive. Work for the truth, as best you can, and the living truth—God—will work for you. He will give you the strength which you yourself lack, the strength to take the next step.

Hang on to total abstinence

If you are a liar, abstain totally from lying. If you are a thief, abstain totally from stealing. If you are an addict, one day at a time, stay away from alcohol, drugs, crazy eating, crazy work, crazy sex—or whatever it is that you are addicted to. *Total* abstinence is the key. That means *none*—not even a little bit, not even one or two, under any circumstances, for any reason, ever.

One day at a time, with the help of God and the truth, *you can do it*. It is the first lie or the first theft or the first drink or pill to which you must say no. One day at a time, stay away from the first lie or drink or drug or whatever, and you will never have to worry about all those disastrous ones that follow. "One day at a time" is not a trick with words; it is a thoroughly practical, well-proven formula for success. No addictive person can face the prospect of a whole lifetime of total abstinence. It is too big an order. But any of us, with God's help, can stay away from the first lie, the first drink, the first pill, the first shot, or the first whatever, for twenty-four hours. Do not underestimate the power of this principle.

*Hang on to your recovering
brothers and sisters*

You cannot recover alone. It is a deadly mistake to think that you can. In our times God has chosen to speak to addicts through brothers and sisters who are ahead of them on the road to freedom. These brothers and sisters are the people who can show you how to recover. Find them. Learn from them. Work with them. Join their group, and go to their meetings. If you cannot locate a group, do what the pioneers in this field did: Dig up a couple of people who are also looking for recovery, and start your own group. Start having meetings once a week to share experience, strength, and hope, and to talk about how to work the program. Practice the 16-principle program in all your affairs, twenty-four hours at a time. Work with others who are on the program, too. It really is that simple.

The Upstate Lifesavers Group—located in Hankins, New York, 120 miles northwest of New York City—offers sponsoring help to anyone, anywhere, who wants to get started on the Lifesavers way of life. To get in touch, write: Upstate Group, Box 225, Hankins, NY 12741. Or call 914-887-5499, ask for Trudy, and just say you want some information about the Lifesavers way of life.

Working with a group is necessary; you cannot sustain a recovery alone. But the group is not God; it is only a vehicle through which he works. The principles are what communicate the power. Recovery begins with getting in touch with God. *He* gives us the courage to get honest; *he* gives us the strength to stay away from the first lie, the first drink or pill or shot or whatever, one day at a time; and *he* puts us in touch with the people we need to work with.

At the same time, do not use trust in God as an excuse to avoid people or to try to get around any of the other factors in the basic equation. Hanging on to God, hanging on to honesty, staying away from alcohol or drugs (or whatever your addiction is), and working with your recovering brothers and sisters—these constitute the formula for recovery, and they go together. You probably cannot work successfully with any of them unless you are working with all of them.

By doing these few simple things, hundreds of thousands of previously desperate and hopeless men and women have had their lives, their freedom, and their strength restored through the Lifesavers way of life.

The Lifesavers way of life, essentially, consists of the Four Absolutes of the Oxford Group and the Twelve Steps of Alcoholics Anonymous, as adapted for anyone (see pages 283–285). Seven pioneers, with a couple of hundred close associates, did the major work in formulating these principles for effective rescue work in the modern world. Here they are—

Pioneers in the Lifesavers Way of Life

Frank Buchman, former Dutch Reformed minister, founder and director of the Oxford Group—which was the basic intellectual and practical ground in which Bill and Dr. Bob developed the principles and practices of Alcoholics Anonymous.

William G. Wilson—"Bill" to his innumerable friends—former New York stockbroker, and co-founder of Alcoholics Anonymous.

Robert H. Smith, M.D.—"Dr. Bob" to his innumerable friends—physician and surgeon, and co-founder of Alcoholics Anonymous.

Father Edward Dowling, S.J., the Roman Catholic priest who worked closely with Bill and Bob in formulating the Steps and the Traditions of Alcoholics Anonymous.

Dr. Harry M. Tiebout, the psychiatrist who understood the spiritual and medical aspects of Alcoholics Anonymous and presented them to modern medicine (see page 244).

Dr. William D. Silkworth, the physician who understood Bill's spiritual experience and its practical relationship to modern medicine.

Father Samuel Shoemaker, the Episcopal priest and Oxford Group leader who worked closely with Bill and Bob in formulating the principles and practices of Alcoholics Anonymous.

A further word about the pioneers—

The Lifesavers way of life was pioneered by deeply religious men and women, and the Lifesavers way—although in itself in no sense a religion—is necessarily a deeply religious way of life. The pioneers, although working in different schools, were agreed upon one source for faith and basic help—the Bible.

The pioneers and early members looked to certain key Bible texts (see below) for inspiration and comfort—

Frank Buchman found the following particularly useful: Psalm 23 (p. 299), Psalm 32 (p. 299), Psalm 103 (p. 300), Psalm 121 (p. 301), John 17 (p. 311), and II Timothy 2 (p. 315).

Bill found the following particularly useful: the Sermon on the Mount (p. 305), I Corinthians 13 (p. 314), and the Epistle of James (p. 317).

Dr. Bob found the following particularly useful: the Sermon on the Mount (p. 305), I Corinthians 13 (p. 314), and the Epistle of James (p. 317).

Father Dowling found the following particularly useful: John 19:25–27 (p. 313).

Dr. Tiebout found the following particularly useful: Psalm 1 (p. 297), Psalm 23 (p. 299), and Proverbs 1:2–7 (p. 301).

Dr. Silkworth found the following particularly useful: II Kings 6:8–17 (p. 297).

Father Shoemaker found the following particularly useful: John 17:1–26 and 19:25–27 (p. 311–13).

These key texts are given in full on the following pages.

Appendix B

Excerpt from

THE SECOND BOOK OF THE KINGS

CHAPTER 6:8–17

Elisha reveals Ben-hadad's plans.

8 Then the king of Syria warred against Israel, and took counsel with his servants, saying, In such and such a place shall be my camp.

9 And the man of God sent unto the king of Israel, saying, Beware that thou pass not such a place; for thither the Syrians are come down.

10 And the king of Israel sent to the place which the man of God told him and warned him of, and saved himself there, not once nor twice.

11 Therefore the heart of the king of Syria was sore troubled for this thing; and he called his servants, and said unto them, Will ye not shew me which of us is for the king of Israel?

12 And one of his servants said, None, my lord, O king: but Elisha, the prophet that is in Israel, telleth the king of Israel the words that thou speakest in thy bedchamber.

Elisha at Dothan.

13 And he said, Go and spy where he is, that I may send and fetch him. And it was told him, saying, Behold, he is in Dothan.

14 Therefore sent he thither horses, and chariots, and a great host: and they came by night, and compassed the city about.

15 And when the servant of the man of God was risen early, and gone forth, behold, an host compassed the city both with horses and chariots. And his servant said unto him, Alas, my master! how shall we do?

16 And he answered, Fear not: for they that be with us are more than they that be with them.

17 And Elisha prayed, and said, Lord, I pray thee, open his eyes, that he may see. And the Lord opened the eyes of the young man; and he saw: and, behold, the mountain was full of horses and chariots of fire round about Elisha.

Excerpts from

THE BOOK OF PSALMS

PSALM 1

Psalm of the two ways: introductory to entire Psalter.

Blessed is the man that walketh not in the counsel of the ungodly, nor standeth in the way of sinners, nor sitteth in the seat of the scornful.

2 But his delight is in the law of the Lord; and in his law doth he meditate day and night.

3 And he shall be like a tree planted by the rivers of water, that bringeth forth his fruit in his season; his leaf also shall not wither; and whatsoever he doeth shall prosper.

4 The ungodly are not so: but

are like the chaff which the wind driveth away.

5 Therefore the ungodly shall not stand in the judgment, nor sinners in the congregation of the righteous.

6 For the Lord knoweth the way of the righteous: but the way of the ungodly shall perish.

PSALM 22

To the chief Musician upon Aijeleth Shahar, A Psalm of David.

My God, my God, why hast thou forsaken me? why art thou so far from helping me, and from the words of my roaring?

2 O my God, I cry in the daytime, but thou hearest not; and in the night season, and am not silent.

3 But thou art holy, O thou that inhabitest the praises of Israel.

4 Our fathers trusted in thee: they trusted, and thou didst deliver them.

5 They cried unto thee, and were delivered: they trusted in thee, and were not confounded.

6 But I am a worm, and no man; a reproach of men, and despised of the people.

7 All they that see me laugh me to scorn: they shoot out the lip, they shake the head, saying,

8 He trusted on the Lord that he would deliver him: let him deliver him, seeing he delighted in him.

9 But thou art he that took me out of the womb: thou didst make me hope when I was upon my mother's breasts.

10 I was cast upon thee from the womb: thou art my God from my mother's belly.

11 Be not far from me; for trouble is near; for there is none to help.

12 Many bulls have compassed me: strong bulls of Bashan have beset me round.

13 They gaped upon me with their mouths, as a ravening and a roaring lion.

14 I am poured out like water, and all my bones are out of joint: my heart is like wax; it is melted in the midst of my bowels.

15 My strength is dried up like a potsherd; and my tongue cleaveth to my jaws; and thou hast brought me into the dust of death.

16 For dogs have compassed me: the assembly of the wicked have inclosed me: they pierced my hands and my feet.

17 I may tell all my bones: they look and stare upon me.

18 They part my garments among them, and cast lots upon my vesture.

19 But be not thou far from me, O Lord: O my strength, haste thee to help me.

20 Deliver my soul from the sword; my darling from the power of the dog.

21 Save me from the lion's mouth: for thou hast heard me from the horns of the unicorns.

22 I will declare thy name unto my brethren: in the midst of the congregation will I praise thee.

Appendix B

23 Ye that fear the Lord, praise him; all ye the seed of Jacob, glorify him; and fear him, all ye the seed of Israel.

24 For he hath not despised nor abhorred the affliction of the afflicted; neither hath he hid his face from him; but when he cried unto him, he heard.

25 My praise shall be of thee in the great congregation: I will pay my vows before them that fear him.

26 The meek shall eat and be satisfied: they shall praise the Lord that seek him: your heart shall live for ever.

27 All the ends of the world shall remember and turn unto the Lord: and all the kindreds of the nations shall worship before thee.

28 For the kingdom is the Lord's: and he is the governor among the nations.

29 All they that be fat upon earth shall eat and worship: all they that go down to the dust shall bow before him: and none can keep alive his own soul.

30 A seed shall serve him; it shall be accounted to the Lord for a generation.

31 They shall come, and shall declare his righteousness unto a people that shall be born, that he hath done this.

PSALM 23

A Psalm of David.

The Lord is my shepherd; I shall not want.

2 He maketh me to lie down in green pastures: he leadeth me beside the still waters.

3 He restoreth my soul: he leadeth me in the paths of righteousness for his name's sake.

4 Yea, though I walk through the valley of the shadow of death, I will fear no evil: for thou art with me; thy rod and thy staff they comfort me.

5 Thou preparest a table before me in the presence of mine enemies: thou anointest my head with oil; my cup runneth over.

6 Surely goodness and mercy shall follow me all the days of my life: and I will dwell in the house of the Lord for ever.

PSALM 32

A Psalm of David, Maschil.

Blessed is he whose transgression is forgiven, whose sin is covered.

2 Blessed is the man unto whom the Lord imputeth not iniquity, and in whose spirit there is no guile.

3 When I kept silence, my bones waxed old through my roaring all the day long.

4 For day and night thy hand was heavy upon me: my moisture is turned into the drought of summer. Selah.

5 I acknowledged my sin unto thee, and mine iniquity have I not hid. I said, I will confess my transgressions unto the Lord; and thou forgavest the iniquity of my sin. Selah.

6 For this shall every one that is

godly pray unto thee in a time when thou mayest be found: surely in the floods of great waters they shall not come nigh unto him.

7 Thou art my hiding place; thou shalt preserve me from trouble; thou shalt compass me about with songs of deliverance. Selah.

8 I will instruct thee and teach thee in the way which thou shalt go: I will guide thee with mine eye.

9 Be ye not as the horse, or as the mule, which have no understanding: whose mouth must be held in with bit and bridle, lest they come near unto thee.

10 Many sorrows shall be to the wicked: but he that trusteth in the Lord, mercy shall compass him about.

11 Be glad in the Lord, and rejoice, ye righteous: and shout for joy, all ye that are upright in heart.

PSALM 46:1–7

To the chief Musician for the sons of Korah, A Song upon Alamoth.

God is our refuge and strength, a very present help in trouble.

2 Therefore will not we fear, though the earth be removed, and though the mountains be carried into the midst of the sea;

3 Though the waters thereof roar and be troubled, though the mountains shake with the swelling thereof. Selah.

4 There is a river, the streams whereof shall make glad the city of God, the holy place of the tabernacles of the most High.

5 God is in the midst of her; she shall not be moved: God shall help her, and that right early.

6 The heathen raged, the kingdoms were moved: he uttered his voice, the earth melted.

7 The Lord of hosts is with us: the God of Jacob is our refuge. Selah.

PSALM 103

A Psalm of David.

Bless the Lord, O my soul: and all that is within me, bless his holy name.

2 Bless the Lord, O my soul, and forget not all his benefits:

3 Who forgiveth all thine iniquities; who healeth all thy diseases;

4 Who redeemeth thy life from destruction; who crowneth thee with lovingkindness and tender mercies;

5 Who satisfieth thy mouth with good things; so that thy youth is renewed like the eagle's.

6 The Lord executeth righteousness and judgment for all that are oppressed.

7 He made known his ways unto Moses, his acts unto the children of Israel.

8 The Lord is merciful and gracious, slow to anger, and plenteous in mercy.

9 He will not always chide: neither will he keep his anger for ever.

10 He hath not dealt with us after our sins; nor rewarded us according to our iniquities.

11 For as the heaven is high

above the earth, so great is his mercy toward them that fear him.

12 As far as the east is from the west, so far hath he removed our transgressions from us.

13 Like as a father pitieth his children, so the Lord pitieth them that fear him.

14 For he knoweth our frame; he remembereth that we are dust.

15 As for man, his days are as grass: as a flower of the field, so he flourisheth.

16 For the wind passeth over it, and it is gone: and the place thereof shall know it no more.

17 But the mercy of the Lord is from everlasting to everlasting upon them that fear him, and his righteousness unto children's children;

18 To such as keep his covenant, and to those that remember his commandments to do them.

19 The Lord hath prepared his throne in the heavens; and his kingdom ruleth over all.

20 Bless the Lord, ye his angels, that excel in strength, that do his commandments, hearkening unto the voice of his word.

21 Bless ye the Lord, all he his hosts; ye ministers of his, that do his pleasure.

22 Bless the Lord, all his works in all places of his dominion: bless the Lord, O my soul.

PSALM 121

A Song of degrees.

I will lift up mine eyes unto the hills, from whence cometh my help.

2 My help cometh from the Lord, which made heaven and earth.

3 He will not suffer thy foot to be moved: he that keepeth thee will not slumber.

4 Behold, he that keepeth Israel shall neither slumber nor sleep.

5 The Lord is thy keeper: the Lord is thy shade upon thy right hand.

6 The sun shall not smite thee by day, nor the moon by night.

7 The Lord shall preserve thee from all evil: he shall preserve thy soul.

8 The Lord shall preserve thy going out and thy coming in from this time forth, and even for evermore.

Excerpts from

THE PROVERBS

CHAPTER 1

Part I. Instruction and exhortation to sons.

The proverbs of Solomon the son of David, king of Israel;

2 To know wisdom and instruction; to perceive the words of understanding;

3 To receive the instruction of wisdom, justice, and judgment, and equity;

4 To give subtilty to the simple, to the young man knowledge and discretion.

5 A wise man will hear, and will increase learning; and a man of un-

derstanding shall attain unto wise counsels:

6 To understand a proverb, and the interpretation; the words of the wise, and their dark sayings.

7 The fear of the Lord is the beginning of knowledge: but fools despise wisdom and instruction.

8 My son, hear the instruction of thy father, and forsake not the law of thy mother:

9 For they shall be an ornament of grace unto thy head, and chains about thy neck.

10 My son, if sinners entice thee, consent thou not.

11 If they say, Come with us, let us lay wait for blood, let us lurk privily for the innocent without cause:

12 Let us swallow them up alive as the grave; and whole, as those that go down into the pit:

13 We shall find all precious substance, we shall fill our houses with spoil:

14 Cast in thy lot among us; let us all have one purse:

15 My son, walk not thou in the way with them; refrain thy foot from their path:

16 For their feet run to evil, and make haste to shed blood.

17 Surely in vain the net is spread in the sight of any bird.

18 And they lay wait for their own blood; they lurk privily for their own lives.

19 So are the ways of every one that is greedy of gain; which taketh away the life of the owners thereof.

20 Wisdom crieth without; she uttereth her voice in the streets:

21 She crieth in the chief place of concourse, in the openings of the gates: in the city she uttereth her words, saying,

22 How long, ye simple ones, will ye love simplicity? and the scorners delight in their scorning, and fools hate knowledge?

23 Turn you at my reproof: behold, I will pour out my spirit unto you, I will make known my words unto you.

24 Because I have called, and ye refused; I have stretched out my hand, and no man regarded;

25 But ye have set at nought all my counsel, and would none of my reproof:

26 I also will laugh at your calamity; I will mock when your fear cometh;

27 When your fear cometh as desolation, and your destruction cometh as a whirlwind; when distress and anguish cometh upon you.

28 Then shall they call upon me, but I will not answer; they shall seek me early, but they shall not find me:

29 For that they hated knowledge, and did not choose the fear of the Lord:

30 They would none of my counsel: they despised all my reproof.

31 Therefore shall they eat of the fruit of their own way, and be filled with their own devices.

32 For the turning away of the simple shall slay them, and the prosperity of fools shall destroy them.

33 But whoso hearkeneth unto me shall dwell safely, and shall be quiet from fear of evil.

CHAPTER 3:5–6

5 Trust in the Lord with all thine heart; and lean not unto thine own understanding.

6 In all thy ways acknowledge him, and he shall direct thy paths.

CHAPTER 8

Part II. In praise of wisdom.

Doth not wisdom cry? and understanding put forth her voice?

2 She standeth in the top of high places, by the way in the places of the paths.

3 She crieth at the gates, at the entry of the city, at the coming in at the doors.

4 Unto you, O men, I call; and my voice is to the sons of man.

5 O ye simple, understand wisdom: and, ye fools, be ye of an understanding heart.

6 Hear; for I will speak of excellent things; and the opening of my lips shall be right things.

7 For my mouth shall speak truth; and wickedness is an abomination to my lips.

8 All the words of my mouth are in righteousness; there is nothing froward or perverse in them.

9 They are all plain to him that understandeth, and right to them that find knowledge.

10 Receive my instruction, and not silver; and knowledge rather than choice gold.

11 For wisdom is better than rubies; and all the things that may be desired are not to be compared to it.

12 I wisdom dwell with prudence, and find out knowledge of witty inventions.

13 The fear of the Lord is to hate evil: pride, and arrogancy, and the evil way, and the froward mouth, do I hate.

14 Counsel is mine, and sound wisdom: I am understanding; I have strength.

15 By me kings reign, and princes decree justice.

16 By me princes rule, and nobles, even all the judges of the earth.

17 I love them that love me; and those that seek me early shall find me.

18 Riches and honour are with me; yea, durable riches and righteousness.

19 My fruit is better than gold, yea, than fine gold; and my revenue than choice silver.

20 I lead in the way of righteousness, in the midst of the paths of judgment:

21 That I may cause those that love me to inherit substance; and I will fill their treasures.

22 The Lord possessed me in the beginning of his way, before his works of old.

23 I was set up from everlasting, from the beginning, or ever the earth was.

24 When there were no depths, I was brought forth; when there were no fountains abounding with water.

25 Before the mountains were settled, before the hills was I brought forth:

26 While as yet he had not made the earth, nor the fields, nor the highest part of the dust of the world.

27 When he prepared the heavens, I was there: when he set a compass upon the face of the depth:

28 When he established the clouds above: when he strengthened the fountains of the deep:

29 When he gave to the sea his decree, that the waters should not pass his commandment: when he appointed the foundations of the earth:

30 Then I was by him, as one brought up with him: and I was daily his delight, rejoicing always before him;

31 Rejoicing in the habitable part of his earth; and my delights were with the sons of men.

32 Now therefore hearken unto me, O ye children: for blessed are they that keep my ways.

33 Hear instruction, and be wise, and refuse it not.

34 Blessed is the man that heareth me, watching daily at my gates, waiting at the posts of my doors.

35 For whoso findeth me findeth life, and shall obtain favour of the Lord.

36 But he that sinneth against me wrongeth his own soul: all they that hate me love death.

CHAPTER 9

(The praise of wisdom, continued.)

Wisdom hath built her house, she hath hewn out her seven pillars:

2 She hath killed her beasts; she hath mingled her wine; she hath also furnished her table.

3 She hath sent forth her maidens: she crieth upon the highest places of the city.

4 Whoso is simple, let him turn in hither: as for him that wanteth understanding, she saith to him,

5 Come, eat of my bread, and drink of the wine which I have mingled.

6 Forsake the foolish, and live; and go in the way of understanding.

7 He that reproveth a scorner getteth to himself shame: and he that rebuketh a wicked man getteth himself a blot.

8 Reprove not a scorner, lest he hate thee: rebuke a wise man, and he will love thee.

9 Give instruction to a wise man, and he will be yet wiser: teach a just man, and he will increase in learning.

10 The fear of the Lord is the beginning of wisdom: and the knowledge of the holy is understanding.

11 For by me thy days shall be multiplied, and the years of thy life shall be increased.

12 If thou be wise, thou shalt be wise for thyself: but if thou scornest, thou alone shalt bear it.

13 A foolish woman is clamorous: she is simple, and knoweth nothing.

14 For she sitteth at the door of her house, on a seat in the high places of the city,

15 To call passengers who go right on their ways:

16 Whoso is simple, let him turn

in hither: and as for him that wanteth understanding, she saith to him,

17 Stolen waters are sweet, and bread eaten in secret is pleasant.

18 But he knoweth not that the dead are there; and that her guests are in the depths of hell.

Excerpts from

ECCLESIASTES or THE PREACHER

CHAPTER 5:18

18 Behold that which I have seen: it is good and comely for one to eat and to drink, and to enjoy the good of all his labour that he taketh under the sun all the days of his life, which God giveth him: for it is his portion.

CHAPTER 12:12–13

12 And further, by these, my son, be admonished: of making many books there is no end; and much study is a weariness of the flesh.

13 Let us hear the conclusion of the whole matter: Fear God, and keep his commandments: for this is the whole duty of man.

Excerpt from

THE SONG OF SOLOMON

CHAPTER 3:1–5

By night on my bed I sought him whom my soul loveth: I sought him, but I found him not.

2 I will rise now, and go about the city in the streets, and in the broad ways I will seek him whom my soul loveth: I sought him, but I found him not.

3 The watchmen that go about the city found me: to whom I said, Saw ye him whom my soul loveth?

4 It was but a little that I passed from them, but I found him whom my soul loveth: I held him, and would not let him go, until I had brought him into my mother's house, and into the chamber of her that conceived me.

5 I charge you, O ye daughters of Jerusalem, by the roes, and by the hinds of the field, that ye stir not up, nor awake my love, till he please.

Excerpts from

THE GOSPEL ACCORDING TO ST. MATTHEW

CHAPTER 5

The sermon on the mount.
The beatitudes.

And seeing the multitudes, he went up into a mountain: and when he was set, his disciples came unto him:

2 And he opened his mouth, and taught them, saying,

3 Blessed are the poor in spirit: for theirs is the kingdom of heaven.

4 Blessed are they that mourn: for they shall be comforted.

5 Blessed are the meek: for they shall inherit the earth.

6 Blessed are they which do hunger and thirst after righteousness: for they shall be filled.

7 Blessed are the merciful: for they shall obtain mercy.

8 Blessed are the pure in heart: for they shall see God.

9 Blessed are the peacemakers: for they shall be called the children of God.

10 Blessed are they which are persecuted for righteousness' sake: for theirs is the kingdom of heaven.

11 Blessed are ye, when men shall revile you, and persecute you, and shall say all manner of evil against you falsely, for my sake.

12 Rejoice, and be exceeding glad: for great is your reward in heaven: for so persecuted they the prophets which were before you.

Similitudes of the believer.

13 Ye are the salt of the earth: but if the salt have lost his savour, wherewith shall it be salted? it is thenceforth good for nothing, but to be cast out, and to be trodden under foot of men.

14 Ye are the light of the world. A city that is set on an hill cannot be hid.

15 Neither do men light a candle, and put it under a bushel, but on a candlestick; and it giveth light unto all that are in the house.

16 Let your light so shine before men, that they may see your good works, and glorify your Father which is in heaven.

Relation of Christ to the law.

17 Think not that I am come to destroy the law, or the prophets: I am not come to destroy, but to fulfil.

18 For verily I say unto you, Till heaven and earth pass, one jot or one tittle shall in no wise pass from the law, till all be fulfilled.

19 Whosoever therefore shall break one of these least commandments, and shall teach men so, he shall be called the least in the kingdom of heaven: but whosoever shall do and teach them, the same shall be called great in the kingdom of heaven.

20 For I say unto you, That except your righteousness shall exceed the righteousness of the scribes and Pharisees, ye shall in no case enter into the kingdom of heaven.

21 Ye have heard that it was said by them of old time, Thou shalt not kill; and whosoever shall kill shall be in danger of the judgment:

22 But I say unto you, That whosoever is angry with his brother without a cause shall be in danger of the judgment: and whosoever shall say to his brother, Raca, shall be in danger of the council: but whosoever shall say, Thou fool, shall be in danger of hell fire.

23 Therefore if thou bring thy gift to the altar, and there rememberest that thy brother hath ought against thee;

24 Leave there thy gift before the altar, and go thy way; first be recon-

ciled to thy brother, and then come and offer thy gift.

25 Agree with thine adversary quickly, whiles thou art in the way with him; lest at any time the adversary deliver thee to the judge, and the judge deliver thee to the officer, and thou be cast into prison.

26 Verily I say unto thee, Thou shalt by no means come out thence, till thou hast paid the uttermost farthing.

27 Ye have heard that it was said by them of old time, Thou shalt not commit adultery:

28 But I say unto you, That whosoever looketh on a woman to lust after her hath committed adultery with her already in his heart.

29 And if thy right eye offend thee, pluck it out, and cast it from thee: for it is profitable for thee that one of thy members should perish, and not that thy whole body should be cast into hell.

30 And if thy right hand offend thee, cut if off, and cast it from thee: for it is profitable for thee that one of thy members should perish, and not that thy whole body should be cast into hell.

Jesus and divorce.

31 It hath been said, Whosoever shall put away his wife, let him give her a writing of divorcement:

32 But I say unto you, That whosoever shall put away his wife, saving for the cause of fornication, causeth her to commit adultery: and whosoever shall marry her that is divorced committeth adultery.

33 Again, ye have heard that it hath been said by them of old time, Thou shalt not forswear thyself, but shalt perform unto the Lord thine oaths:

34 But I say unto you, Swear not at all; neither by heaven; for it is God's throne:

35 Nor by the earth; for it is his footstool: neither by Jerusalem; for it is the city of the great King.

36 Neither shalt thou swear by thy head, because thou canst not make one hair white or black.

37 But let your communication be, Yea, yea; Nay, nay: for whatsoever is more than these cometh of evil.

38 Ye have heard that it hath been said, An eye for an eye, and a tooth for a tooth:

39 But I say unto you, That ye resist not evil: but whosoever shall smite thee on thy right cheek, turn to him the other also.

40 And if any man will sue thee at the law, and take away thy coat, let him have thy cloke also.

41 And whosoever shall compel thee to go a mile, go with him twain.

42 Give to him that asketh thee, and from him that would borrow of thee turn not thou away.

43 Ye have heard that it hath been said, Thou shalt love thy neighbour, and hate thine enemy.

44 But I say unto you, Love your enemies, bless them that curse you,

do good to them that hate you, and pray for them which despitefully use you, and persecute you;

45 That ye may be the children of your Father which is in heaven: for he maketh his sun to rise on the evil and on the good, and sendeth rain on the just and on the unjust.

46 For if ye love them which love you, what reward have ye? do not even the publicans the same?

47 And if ye salute your brethren only, what do ye more than others? do not even the publicans so?

48 Be ye therefore perfect, even as your Father which is in heaven is perfect.

CHAPTER 6

Sermon on the mount, continued: mere externalism in religion condemned.

Take heed that ye do not your alms before men, to be seen of them: otherwise ye have no reward of your Father which is in heaven.

2 Therefore when thou doest thine alms, do not sound a trumpet before thee, as the hypocrites do in the synagogues and in the streets, that they may have glory of men. Verily I say unto you, They have their reward.

3 But when thou doest alms, let not thy left hand know what thy right hand doeth:

4 That thine alms may be in secret: and thy Father which seeth in secret himself shall reward thee openly.

5 And when thou prayest, thou shalt not be as the hypocrites are: for they love to pray standing in the synagogues and in the corners of the streets, that they may be seen of men. Verily I say unto you, They have their reward.

6 But thou, when thou prayest, enter into thy closet, and when thou hast shut thy door, pray to thy Father which is in secret; and thy Father which seeth in secret shall reward thee openly.

7 But when ye pray, use not vain repetitions, as the heathen do: for they think that they shall be heard for their much speaking.

The new revelation concerning prayer.

8 Be not ye therefore like unto them: for your Father knoweth what things ye have need of, before ye ask him.

9 After this manner therefore pray ye: Our Father which art in heaven, Hallowed be thy name.

10 Thy kingdom come. Thy will be done in earth, as it is in heaven.

11 Give us this day our daily bread.

12 And forgive us our debts, as we forgive our debtors.

13 And lead us not into temptation, but deliver us from evil: For thine is the kingdom, and the power, and the glory, for ever. Amen.

14 For if ye forgive men their trespasses, your heavenly Father will also forgive you:

15 But if ye forgive not men their trespasses, neither will your Father forgive your trespasses.

Externalism again rebuked.

16 Moreover when ye fast, be not, as the hypocrites, of a sad countenance: for they disfigure their faces, that they may appear unto men to fast. Verily I say unto you, They have their reward.
17 But thou, when thou fastest, anoint thine head, and wash thy face;
18 That thou appear not unto men to fast, but unto thy Father which is in secret: and thy Father, which seeth in secret, shall reward thee openly.

The kingdom law of riches.

19 Lay not up for yourselves treasures upon earth, where moth and rust doth corrupt, and where thieves break through and steal:
20 But lay up for yourselves treasures in heaven, where neither moth nor rust doth corrupt, and where thieves do not break through nor steal:
21 For where your treasure is, there will your heart be also.
22 The light of the body is the eye: if therefore thine eye be single, thy whole body shall be full of light.
23 But if thine eye be evil, thy whole body shall be full of darkness. If therefore the light that is in thee be darkness, how great is that darkness!

24 No man can serve two masters: for either he will hate the one, and love the other; or else he will hold to the one, and despise the other. Ye cannot serve God and mammon.

The cure of anxiety: trust in the Father's care.

25 Therefore I say unto you, Take no thought for your life, what ye shall eat, or what ye shall drink; nor yet for your body, what ye shall put on. Is not the life more than meat, and the body than raiment?
26 Behold the fowls of the air: for they sow not, neither do they reap, nor gather into barns; yet your heavenly Father feedeth them. Are ye not much better than they?
27 Which of you by taking thought can add one cubit unto his stature?
28 And why take ye thought for raiment? Consider the lilies of the field, how they grow; they toil not, neither do they spin:
29 And yet I say unto you, That even Solomon in all his glory was not arrayed like one of these.
30 Wherefore, if God so clothe the grass of the field, which to day is, and to morrow is cast into the oven, shall he not much more clothe you, O ye of little faith?
31 Therefore take no thought, saying, What shall we eat? or, What shall we drink? or, Wherewithal shall we be clothed?
32 (For after all these things do the Gentiles seek:) for your heav-

enly Father knoweth that ye have need of all these things.

33 But seek ye first the kingdom of God, and his righteousness; and all these things shall be added unto you.

34 Take therefore no thought for the morrow: for the morrow shall take thought for the things of itself. Sufficient unto the day is the evil thereof.

CHAPTER 7

Sermon on the mount, continued: *judgment of others forbidden.*

Judge not, that ye be not judged.

2 For with what judgment ye judge, ye shall be judged: and with what measure ye mete, it shall be measured to you again.

3 And why beholdest thou the mote that is in thy brother's eye, but considerest not the beam that is in thine own eye?

4 Or how wilt thou say to thy brother, Let me pull out the mote out of thine eye; and behold, a beam is in thine own eye?

5 Thou hypocrite, first cast out the beam out of thine own eye; and then shalt thou see clearly to cast out the mote out of thy brother's eye.

6 Give not that which is holy unto the dogs, neither cast ye your pearls before swine, lest they trample them under their feet, and turn again and rend you.

Encouragements to pray.

7 Ask, and it shall be given you; seek, and ye shall find; knock, and it shall be opened unto you:

8 For every one that asketh receiveth; and he that seeketh findeth; and to him that knocketh it shall be opened.

9 Or what man is there of you, whom if his son ask bread, will he give him a stone?

10 Or if he ask a fish, will he give him a serpent?

11 If ye then, being evil, know how to give good gifts unto your children, how much more shall your Father which is in heaven give good things to them that ask him?

Summary of O.T. righteousness.

12 Therefore all things whatsoever ye would that men should do to you, do ye even so to them: for this is the law and the prophets.

The two ways.

13 Enter ye in at the strait gate: for wide is the gate, and broad is the way, that leadeth to destruction, and many there be which go in thereat:

14 Because strait is the gate, and narrow is the way, which leadeth unto life, and few there be that find it.

*Warning against false
teachers: the test.*

15 Beware of false prophets, which come to you in sheep's clothing, but inwardly they are ravening wolves.

16 Ye shall know them by their fruits. Do men gather grapes of thorns, or figs of thistles?

17 Even so every good tree bringeth forth good fruit; but a corrupt tree bringeth forth evil fruit.

18 A good tree cannot bring forth evil fruit, neither can a corrupt tree bring forth good fruit.

19 Every tree that bringeth not forth good fruit is hewn down, and cast into the fire.

20 Wherefore by their fruits ye shall know them.

*The danger of profession
without faith.*

21 Not every one that saith unto me, Lord, Lord, shall enter into the kingdom of heaven; but he that doeth the will of my Father which is in heaven.

22 Many will say to me in that day, Lord, Lord, have we not prophesied in thy name? and in thy name have cast out devils? and in thy name done many wonderful works?

23 And then will I profess unto them, I never knew you: depart from me, ye that work iniquity.

The two foundations.

24 Therefore whosoever heareth these sayings of mine, and doeth them, I will liken him unto a wise man, which built his house upon a rock:

25 And the rain descended, and the floods came, and the winds blew, and beat upon that house; and it fell not, for it was founded upon a rock.

26 And every one that heareth these sayings of mine, and doeth them not, shall be likened unto a foolish man, which built his house upon the sand:

27 And the rain descended, and the floods came, and the winds blew, and beat upon that house; and it fell: and great was the fall of it.

28 And it came to pass, when Jesus had ended these sayings, the people were astonished at his doctrine:

29 For he taught them as one having authority, and not as the scribes.

Excerpts from

THE GOSPEL
ACCORDING TO ST. JOHN

CHAPTER 17

The prayer of intercession.

These words spake Jesus, and lifted up his eyes to heaven, and said, Father, the hour is come; glorify thy Son, that thy Son also may glorify thee:

2 As thou hast given him power over all flesh, that he should give eternal life to as many as thou hast given him.

3 And this is life eternal, that they might know thee the only true God, and Jesus Christ, whom thou hast sent.

4 I have glorified thee on the earth: I have finished the work which thou gavest me to do.

5 And now, O Father, glorify thou me with thine own self with the glory which I had with thee before the world was.

6 I have manifested thy name unto the men which thou gavest me out of the world: thine they were, and thou gavest them me; and they have kept thy word.

7 Now they have known that all things whatsoever thou hast given me are of thee.

8 For I have given unto them the words which thou gavest me; and they have received them, and have known surely that I came out from thee, and they have believed that thou didst send me.

9 I pray for them: I pray not for the world, but for them which thou hast given me; for they are thine.

10 And all mine are thine, and thine are mine; and I am glorified in them.

11 And now I am no more in the world, but these are in the world, and I come to thee. Holy Father, keep through thine own name those whom thou hast given me, that they may be one, as we are.

12 While I was with them in the world, I kept them in thy name: those that thou gavest me I have kept, and none of them is lost, but the son of perdition; that the scripture might be fulfilled.

13 And now come I to thee; and these things I speak in the world, that they might have my joy fulfilled in themselves.

14 I have given them thy word; and the world hath hated them, because they are not of the world, even as I am not of the world.

15 I pray not that thou shouldest take them out of the world, but that thou shouldest keep them from the evil.

16 They are not of the world, even as I am not of the world.

17 Sanctify them through thy truth: thy word is truth.

18 As thou hast sent me into the world, even so have I also sent them into the world.

19 And for their sakes I sanctify myself, that they also might be sanctified through the truth.

20 Neither pray I for these alone, but for them also which shall believe on me through their word;

21 That they all may be one; as thou, Father, art in me, and I in thee, that they also may be one in us: that the world may believe that thou hast sent me.

22 And the glory which thou gavest me I have given them; that they may be one, even as we are one:

23 I in them, and thou in me, that they may be made perfect in one; and that the world may know that thou hast sent me, and hast loved them, as thou hast loved me.

24 Father, I will that they also, whom thou hast given me, be with me where I am; that they may behold my glory, which thou hast given me: for thou lovedst me before the foundation of the world.

25 O righteous Father, the world hath not known thee: but I have known thee, and these have known that thou hast sent me.

26 And I have declared unto them thy name, and will declare it: that the love wherewith thou hast loved me may be in them, and I in them.

CHAPTER 19:25-27

The scene at the foot of the cross.

25 Now there stood by the cross of Jesus his mother, and his mother's sister, Mary the wife of Cleophas, and Mary Magdalene.

26 When Jesus therefore saw his mother, and the disciple standing by, whom he loved, he saith unto his mother, Woman, behold thy son!

27 Then saith he to the disciple, Behold thy mother! And from that hour that disciple took her unto his own home.

Excerpts from

THE FIRST EPISTLE OF PAUL THE APOSTLE TO THE CORINTHIANS

CHAPTER 11:23-29

The order and meaning of the Lord's table.

23 For I have received of the Lord that which also I delivered unto you, That the Lord Jesus the same night in which he was betrayed took bread:

24 And when he had given thanks, he brake it, and said, Take, eat: this is my body, which is broken for you: this do in remembrance of me.

25 After the same manner also he took the cup, when he had supped, saying, This cup is the new testament in my blood: this do ye, as oft as ye drink it, in remembrance of me.

26 For as often as ye eat this bread, and drink this cup, ye do shew the Lord's death till he come.

27 Wherefore whosoever shall eat this bread, and drink this cup of the Lord, unworthily, shall be guilty of the body and blood of the Lord.

28 But let a man examine himself, and so let him eat of that bread, and drink of that cup.

29 For he that eateth and drinketh unworthily, eateth and drinketh damnation to himself, not discerning the Lord's body.

CHAPTER 13

The ministry gifts must be governed by love.

Though I speak with the tongues of men and of angels, and have not charity, I am become as sounding brass, or a tinkling cymbal.

2 And though I have the gift of prophecy, and understand all mysteries, and all knowledge; and though I have all faith, so that I could remove mountains, and have not charity, I am nothing.

3 And though I bestow all my goods to feed the poor, and though I give my body to be burned, and have not charity, it profiteth me nothing.

4 Charity suffereth long, and is kind; charity envieth not; charity vaunteth not itself, is not puffed up,

5 Doth not behave itself unseemly, seeketh not her own, is not easily provoked, thinketh no evil;

6 Rejoiceth not in iniquity, but rejoiceth in the truth;

7 Beareth all things, believeth all things, hopeth all things, endureth all things.

8 Charity never faileth: but whether there be prophecies, they shall fail; whether there be tongues, they shall cease; whether there be knowledge, it shall vanish away.

9 For we know in part, and we prophesy in part.

10 But when that which is perfect is come, then that which is in part shall be done away.

11 When I was a child, I spake as a child, I understood as a child, I thought as a child: but when I became a man, I put away childish things.

12 For now we see through a glass, darkly; but then face to face: now I know in part; but then shall I know even as also I am known.

13 And now abideth faith, hope, charity, these three; but the greatest of these is charity.

Excerpt from

THE SECOND EPISTLE OF PAUL THE APOSTLE TO THE CORINTHIANS

CHAPTER 4

The ministry: honesty.

Therefore seeing we have this ministry, as we have received mercy, we faint not;

Because the truth taught is commended by the life.

2 But have renounced the hidden things of dishonesty, not walking in craftiness, nor handling the word of God deceitfully; but by manifestation of the truth commending ourselves to every man's conscience in the sight of God.

Because not self but Christ Jesus as Lord is preached.

3 But if our gospel be hid, it is hid to them that are lost:

4 In whom the god of this world hath blinded the minds of them which believe not, lest the light of the glorious gospel of Christ, who is the image of God, should shine unto them.

5 For we preach not ourselves, but Christ Jesus the Lord; and ourselves your servants for Jesus' sake.

6 For God, who commanded the light to shine out of darkness, hath shined in our hearts, to give the light of the knowledge of the glory of God in the face of Jesus Christ.

Because the power is of God alone.

7 But we have this treasure in earthen vessels, that the excellency of the power may be of God, and not of us.

The ministry: suffering.

8 We are troubled on every side, yet not distressed; we are perplexed, but not in despair;

9 Persecuted, but not forsaken; cast down, but not destroyed;

10 Always bearing about in the body the dying of the Lord Jesus, that the life also of Jesus might be made manifest in our body.

11 For we which live are alway delivered unto death for Jesus' sake, that the life also of Jesus might be made manifest in our mortal flesh.

12 So then death worketh in us, but life in you.

13 We having the same spirit of faith, according as it is written, I believed, and therefore have I spoken; we also believe, and therefore speak;

14 Knowing that he which raised up the Lord Jesus shall raise up us also by Jesus, and shall present us with you.

15 For all things are for your sakes, that the abundant grace might through the thanksgiving of many redound to the glory of God.

16 For which cause we faint not; but though our outward man perish, yet the inward man is renewed day by day.

17 For our light affliction, which is but for a moment, worketh for us a far more exceeding and eternal weight of glory;

18 While we look not at the things which are seen, but at the things which are not seen: for the things which are seen are temporal; but the things which are not seen are eternal.

Excerpt from

THE SECOND EPISTLE OF PAUL THE APOSTLE TO TIMOTHY

CHAPTER 2

Part II. The path of a good soldier in the time of apostasy.

Thou therefore, my son, be strong in the grace that is in Christ Jesus.

2 And the things that thou hast heard of me among many witnesses, the same commit thou to faithful men, who shall be able to teach others also.

3 Thou therefore endure hardness, as a good soldier of Jesus Christ.

4 No man that warreth entangleth himself with the affairs of this life; that he may please him who hath chosen him to be a soldier.

5 And if a man also strive for masteries, yet is he not crowned, except he strive lawfully.

6 The husbandman that laboureth must be first partaker of the fruits.

7 Consider what I say; and the Lord give thee understanding in all things.

8 Remember that Jesus Christ of the seed of David was raised from the dead according to my gospel:

9 Wherein I suffer trouble, as an evil doer, even unto bonds; but the word of God is not bound.

10 Therefore I endure all things for the elect's sakes, that they may also obtain the salvation which is in Christ Jesus with eternal glory.

11 It is a faithful saying: For if we be dead with him, we shall also live with him:

12 If we suffer, we shall also reign with him: if we deny him, he also will deny us:

13 If we believe not, yet he abideth faithful: he cannot deny himself.

14 Of these things put them in remembrance, charging them before the Lord that they strive not about words to no profit, but to the subverting of the hearers.

15 Study to shew thyself approved unto God, a workman that needeth not to be ashamed, rightly dividing the word of truth.

16 But shun profane and vain babblings: for they will increase unto more ungodliness.

17 And their word will eat as doth a canker: of whom is Hymenaeus and Philetus;

18 Who concerning the truth have erred, saying that the resurrection is past already; and overthrow the faith of some.

19 Nevertheless the foundation of God standeth sure, having this seal, The Lord knoweth them that are his. And, Let every one that nameth the name of Christ depart from iniquity.

20 But in a great house there are not only vessels of gold, and of silver, but also of wood and of earth; and some to honour, and some to dishonour.

21 If a man therefore purge himself from these, he shall be a vessel unto honour, sanctified, and meet for the master's use, and prepared unto every good work.

22 Flee also youthful lusts: but follow righteousness, faith, charity, peace, with them that call on the Lord out of a pure heart.

23 But foolish and unlearned questions avoid, knowing that they do gender strifes.

24 And the servant of the Lord

must not strive; but be gentle unto all men, apt to teach, patient,

25 In meekness instructing those that oppose themselves; if God peradventure will give them repentance to the acknowledging of the truth;

26 And that they may recover themselves out of the snare of the devil, who are taken captive by him at his will.

THE GENERAL EPISTLE OF JAMES

CHAPTER 1

Part I. The testings of faith.
The purpose of testings.

James, a servant of God and of the Lord Jesus Christ, to the twelve tribes which are scattered abroad, greeting.

2 My brethren, count it all joy when ye fall into divers temptations;

3 Knowing this, that the trying of your faith worketh patience.

4 But let patience have her perfect work, that ye may be perfect and entire, wanting nothing.

5 If any of you lack wisdom, let him ask of God, that giveth to all men liberally, and upbraideth not; and it shall be given him.

6 But let him ask in faith, nothing wavering. For he that wavereth is like a wave of the sea driven with the wind and tossed.

7 For let not that man think that he shall receive any thing of the Lord.

8 A double minded man is unstable in all his ways.

9 Let the brother of low degree rejoice in that he is exalted:

10 But the rich, in that he is made low: because as the flower of the grass he shall pass away.

11 For the sun is no sooner risen with a burning heat, but it withereth the grass, and the flower thereof falleth, and the grace of the fashion of it perisheth: so also shall the rich man fade away in his ways.

12 Blessed is the man that endureth temptation: for when he is tried, he shall receive the crown of life, which the Lord hath promised to them that love him.

Solicitation to do evil
is not of God

13 Let no man say when he is tempted, I am tempted of God: for God cannot be tempted with evil, neither tempteth he any man:

14 But every man is tempted, when he is drawn away of his own lust, and enticed.

15 Then when lust hath conceived, it bringeth forth sin: and sin, when it is finished, bringeth forth death.

16 Do not err, my beloved brethren.

17 Every good gift and every perfect gift is from above, and cometh down from the Father of lights, with whom is no variableness, neither shadow of turning.

18 Of his own will begat he us with the word of truth, that we

should be a kind of firstfruits of his creatures.

19 Wherefore, my beloved brethren, let every man be swift to hear, slow to speak, slow to wrath:

20 For the wrath of man worketh not the righteousness of God.

21 Wherefore lay apart all filthiness and superfluity of naughtiness, and receive with meekness the engrafted word, which is able to save your souls.

The test of obedience.

22 But be ye doers of the word, and not hearers only, deceiving your own selves.

23 For if any be a hearer of the word, and not a doer, he is like unto a man beholding his natural face in a glass:

24 For he beholdeth himself, and goeth his way, and straightway forgetteth what manner of man he was.

25 But whoso looketh into the perfect law of liberty, and continueth therein, he being not a forgetful hearer, but a doer of the work, this man shall be blessed in his deed.

The test of true religion.

26 If any man among you seem to be religious, and bridleth not his tongue, but deceiveth his own heart, this man's religion is vain.

27 Pure religion and undefiled before God and the Father is this, To visit the fatherless and widows in their affliction, and to keep himself unspotted from the world.

CHAPTER 2

The test of brotherly love.

My brethren, have not the faith of our Lord Jesus Christ, the Lord of glory, with respect of persons.

2 For if there come unto your assembly a man with a gold ring, in goodly apparel, and there come in also a poor man in vile raiment:

3 And ye have respect to him that weareth the gay clothing, and say unto him, Sit thou here in a good place; and say to the poor, Stand thou there, or sit here under my footstool:

4 Are ye not then partial in yourselves, and are become judges of evil thoughts?

5 Hearken, my beloved brethren. Hath not God chosen the poor of this world rich in faith, and heirs of the kingdom which he hath promised to them that love him?

6 But ye have despised the poor. Do not rich men oppress you, and draw you before the judgment seats?

7 Do not they blaspheme that worthy name by the which ye are called?

8 If ye fulfil the royal law according to the scripture, Thou shalt love thy neighbour as thyself, ye do well:

9 But if ye have respect to persons, ye commit sin, and are convinced of the law as transgressors.

10 For whosoever shall keep the whole law, and yet offend in one point, he is guilty of all.

11 For he that said, Do not com-

mit adultery, said also, Do not kill. Now if thou commit no adultery, yet if thou kill, thou art become a transgressor of the law.

12 So speak ye, and so do, as they that shall be judged by the law of liberty.

13 For he shall have judgment without mercy, that hath shewed no mercy; and mercy rejoiceth against judgment.

The test of good works.

14 What doth it profit, my brethren, though a man say he hath faith, and have not works? can faith save him?

15 If a brother or sister be naked, and destitute of daily food,

16 And one of you say unto them, Depart in peace, be ye warmed and filled; notwithstanding ye give them not those things which are needful to the body; what doth it profit?

17 Even so faith, if it hath not works, is dead, being alone.

18 Yea, a man may say, Thou hast faith, and I have works: shew me thy faith without thy works, and I will shew thee my faith by my works.

19 Thou believest that there is one God; thou doest well: the devils also believe, and tremble.

20 But wilt thou know, O vain man, that faith without works is dead?

The illustration of Abraham.

21 Was not Abraham our father justified by works, when he had offered Isaac his son upon the altar?

22 Seest thou how faith wrought with his works, and by works was faith made perfect?

23 And the scripture was fulfilled which saith, Abraham believed God, and it was imputed unto him for righteousness: and he was called the Friend of God.

24 Ye see then how that by works a man is justified, and not by faith only.

25 Likewise also was not Rahab the harlot justified by works, when she had received the messengers, and had sent them out another way?

26 For as the body without the spirit is dead, so faith without works is dead also.

CHAPTER 3

Part II. A true faith will control the tongue.

My brethren, be not many masters, knowing that we shall receive the greater condemnation.

2 For in many things we offend all. If any man offend not in word, the same is a perfect man, and able also to bridle the whole body.

3 Behold, we put bits in the horses' mouths, that they may obey us; and we turn about their whole body.

4 Behold also the ships, which though they be so great, and are driven of fierce winds, yet are they turned about with a very small helm, whithersoever the governor listeth.

5 Even so the tongue is a little member, and boastest great things.

Behold, how great a matter a little fire kindleth!

6 And the tongue is a fire, a world of iniquity: so is the tongue among our members, that it defileth the whole body, and setteth on fire the course of nature; and it is set on fire of hell.

7 For every kind of beasts, and of birds, and of serpents, and of things in the sea, is tamed, and hath been tamed of mankind:

8 But the tongue can no man tame; it is an unruly evil, full of deadly poison.

9 Therewith bless we God, even the Father; and therewith curse we men, which are made after the similitude of God.

10 Out of the same mouth proceedeth blessing and cursing. My brethren, these things ought not so to be.

11 Doth a fountain send forth at the same place sweet water and bitter?

12 Can the fig tree, my brethren, bear olive berries? either a vine, figs? so can no fountain both yield salt water and fresh.

13 Who is a wise man and endued with knowledge among you? let him shew out of a good conversation his works with meekness of wisdom.

14 But if ye have bitter envying and strife in your hearts, glory not, and lie not against the truth.

15 This wisdom descendeth not from above, but is earthly, sensual, devilish.

16 For where envying and strife is, there is confusion and every evil work.

17 But the wisdom that is from above is first pure, then peaceable, gentle, and easy to be intreated, full of mercy and good fruits, without partiality, and without hypocrisy.

18 And the fruit of righteousness is sown in peace of them that make peace.

CHAPTER 4

Part III. The rebuke of worldliness.

From whence come wars and fightings among you? come they not hence, even of your lusts that war in your members?

2 Ye lust, and have not: ye kill, and desire to have, and cannot obtain: ye fight and war, yet ye have not, because ye ask not.

3 Ye ask, and receive not, because ye ask amiss, that ye may consume it upon your lusts.

4 Ye adulterers and adulteresses, know ye not that the friendship of the world is enmity with God? whosoever therefore will be a friend of the world is the enemy of God.

5 Do ye think that the scripture saith in vain, The spirit that dwelleth in us lusteth to envy?

6 But he giveth more grace. Wherefore he saith, God resisteth the proud, but giveth grace unto the humble

7 Submit yourselves therefore to God. Resist the devil, and he will flee from you.

8 Draw nigh to God, and he will draw nigh to you. Cleanse your hands, ye sinners; and purify your hearts, ye double minded.

9 Be afflicted, and mourn, and weep: let your laughter be turned to mourning, and your joy to heaviness.

10 Humble yourselves in the sight of the Lord, and he shall lift you up.

11 Speak not evil one of another, brethren. He that speaketh evil of his brother, and judgeth his brother, speaketh evil of the law, and judgeth the law: but if thou judge the law, thou art not a doer of the law, but a judge.

12 There is one lawgiver, who is able to save and to destroy: who art thou that judgest another?

13 Go to now, ye that say, To day or to morrow we will go into such a city, and continue there a year, and buy and sell, and get gain:

14 Whereas ye know not what shall be on the morrow. For what is your life? It is even a vapour, that appeareth for a little time, and then vanisheth away.

15 For that ye ought to say, If the Lord will, we shall live, and do this, or that.

16 But now ye rejoice in your boastings: all such rejoicing is evil.

17 Therefore to him that knoweth to do good, and doeth it not, to him it is sin.

CHAPTER 5

Part IV. The rich warned.

Go to now, ye rich men, weep and howl for your miseries that shall come upon you.

2 Your riches are corrupted, and your garments are motheaten.

3 Your gold and silver is cankered; and the rust of them shall be a witness against you, and shall eat your flesh as it were fire. Ye have heaped treasure together for the last days.

4 Behold, the hire of the labourers who have reaped down your fields, which is of you kept back by fraud, crieth: and the cries of them which have reaped are entered into the ears of the Lord of sabaoth.

5 Ye have lived in pleasure on the earth, and been wanton; ye have nourished your hearts, as in a day of slaughter.

6 Ye have condemned and killed the just; and he doth not resist you.

Part V. Exhortations in view of the coming of the Lord.

7 Be patient therefore, brethren, unto the coming of the Lord. Behold, the husbandman waiteth for the precious fruit of the earth, and hath long patience for it, until he receive the early and latter rain.

8 Be ye also patient; stablish your hearts: for the coming of the Lord draweth nigh.

9 Grudge not one against another, brethren, lest ye be condemned: behold, the judge standeth before the door.

10 Take, my brethren, the prophets, who have spoken in the name of the Lord, for an example of suffering affliction, and of patience.

11 Behold, we count them happy which endure. Ye have heard of the patience of Job, and have seen the end of the Lord; that the Lord is very pitiful, and of tender mercy.

12 But above all things, my brethren, swear not, neither by heaven, neither by the earth, neither by any other oath: but let your yea be yea; and your nay, nay; lest ye fall into condemnation.

13 Is any among you afflicted? let him pray. Is any merry? let him sing psalms.

14 Is any sick among you? let him call for the elders of the church; and let them pray over him, anointing him with oil in the name of the Lord:

15 And the prayer of faith shall save the sick, and the Lord shall raise him up; and if he have committed sins, they shall be forgiven him.

16 Confess your faults one to another, and pray one for another, that ye may be healed. The effectual fervent prayer of a righteous man availeth much.

17 Elias was a man subject to like passions as we are, and he prayed earnestly that it might not rain: and it rained not on the earth by the space of three years and six months.

18 And he prayed again, and the heaven gave rain, and the earth brought forth her fruit.

19 Brethren, if any of you do err from the truth, and one convert him;

20 Let him know, that he which converteth the sinner from the error of his way shall save a soul from death, and shall hide a multitude of sins.

Index

Abandonment; *see* Surrender to God
Addiction, recovery from, 282–290
Adultery and fornication, contra-
 indicated, 81–82, 130
Adversary (Monkey, *Shaitan,
 Mephiztophel*), 13, 29, 31, 54, 65–
 66, 118, 129, 136, 137–138, 141
 Ahriman and Lucifer, 137
Alcoholics Anonymous, xv, 8, 16, 244–
 253, 259, 283–295
Alive, spiritually, 102–106, 125
Aristotle, 216–224
Asleep, spiritually, 92, 102–114
Atheism, 49, 50 n.*, 132
Athens and Jerusalem, 216–225
Attachment; *see* Concupiscence; *see also*
 Bhagavad Gita (for non-attachment)
Attention, 108, 109, 110, 164, 165; Prayer
 of, 167–169
Aurobindo, Sri, 192
Austin, Lou, 197
Avalokitesvara, 160, 162
Avesta, 43
Awake, spiritually, 102–107
Awakening (conversion), 68–71, 80, 149,
 247, 251, 252
Awareness of God, sustained, 90, 92

Baal Shem Tov, xvii, 206
Baker, Augustine, 201
Bar Hebraeus, 64
Beevers, John, 196
Benedictines, the, 16
Benoit, Hubert, 110
Bhagavad Gita, 37, 39–40, 45, 79, 82, 97,
 172 (bibliog.), 195n.‡
Bhakti (devotion), 159 n.‡, 168

Bible, 35–36, 44, 50 n.*, 173 (bibliog.)
 and spiritual experience, 71
 favorite passages of Lifesavers pioneers,
 296–322
Bible reading, 43–45
Blakney, Raymond, 206
Body, physical, 47, 98
 position of, in prayer, 146–148
 spiritual, 99–101
Boehme, Jacob, xviii, 118, 196, 200
Boisen, Anton, 72 n.†
Book of Changes, 43, 55
Book of Common Prayer, The, 200
Book of English Collects, The, 200
Book of Tao (Tao Te Ching), 40–41, 45
Books, bibliography, 171–189
 as helps in spiritual life, 29–46, 51, 66
 special listings, 190–208
Brahmananda, 61, 64, 161
Breathing; *see* Prayer
Brianchaninov, Bishop Ignatius, 160, 165
Buber, Martin, xvii, 64, 96, 197, 198
Buchman, Frank, 292, 296
Bucke, R.M., 29, 208
Buddha, xvii, 41, 78, 108, 111, 160 n.*
Buddhism, 3, 41–42, 108, 152, 160 n.*,
 193, 195 n.‡, 198
 Zen, 42, 108, 198
Buddhist Bible, A, 43, 60, 83
Buddhist Guiding Principles, 83, 84

Campbell, Donald L., xv
Carrel, Alexis, 195
Catton, Bruce, xviii
Chaitanya, 72
Chapman, Dom John, O.S.B., 165,
 195n.‡, 200

Chesterton, G.K., 196
Christ, and Christ Jesus, ii, xvii, 3, 20, 26, 43, 45, 47, 58, 71, 74, 94, 99–108, 111, 119, 123, 155, 193, 197, 204, 305–322
Christianity, Christian religion, 3, 68 n.*, 97, 127, 158, 192, 194, 203, 204, 207, 305–322
  Eastern Orthodox, 85, 109, 156, 160, 167, 193, 205
Christians, 3–4, 155, 159, 160, 195
  and books, 34, 44, 45
Christian Science, 194
Cleckley, Hervey, M.D., 13
Cloud of Unknowing, The, 134, 153–154, 201
Collin, Rodney, 80
Concupiscence (craving, attachment), 84
Confucius, 40
Conversation with God, 88–91
Conversion; *see* Awakening
Coomaraswamy, Ananda K., 99
Cosmic Consciousness; *see* Mysticism
Cousins, Norman, xviii
Cranston, Ruth, 196
Craving; *see* Concupiscence
Crisis in Psychiatry and Religion, The, 254–260
Cross, the, 100, 135
Curé d'Ars, 196

Daily, Starr, 197
Davenport, Russell, 192
Dead, spiritually, 103–104, 125
Death, of the ego, 98, 99
  and resurrection of Jesus, 99
Decalogue, the, 81
De Caussade, J.P., xvii, 39, 138–142, 203
De Laredo, Bernardino, 202
Desert Fathers, the, 16, 160, 162
Dhammapada, The, 42
Dionysius the Areopagite, 34, 68 n.*, 152 n.‡, 204
Divine Comedy, The, 34, 174
Dostoevsky, Fyodor, xviii
Dowling, Fr. Edward, 294, 296
Du Noüy, Lecomte, 191
Durant, Will and Ariel, xviii, 54–55

Eckhart, Meister, 34, 96, 198, 206, 208
Ego, and egotism, 68, 84, 94–102, 114, 128, 137, 170

Ellul, Jacques, xvii
Emerson, Ralph Waldo, 194
Emmerich, Anne Catherine, xviii
Essenes, 16
Evil, 123
Evola, 108
Exman, Eugene, 51 n.†
Experience, books about, 195–198
  and psychosis, 61, 62, 72 n.†
  spiritual, 61–74

Faith, as help in spiritual life, 56–61, 64
  books about, 192–194
Fénelon, 79
Ferm, Vergilius, 193
First Questions on the Life of the Spirit, viii, xiv
Fischer, Louis, 21
Fosdick, Harry Emerson, 192, 199
Four Absolutes, 283–284
Fox, George, 72 n.†
Freud, Sigmund, 196, 244, 256, 270

Gamblers Anonymous, 8, 285
Gandhi, M.K., xvii, 21, 97, 159, 166, 284
Garrigou-Lagrange, Father Reginald, 89, 191, 195
Gilson, Etienne, 191
God, existence, and reality of, 3, 7–11, 71, 86
  grace of, 118–126, 141
  knowledge of, 19, 22, 23, 28, 49, 74, 120–122, 204–208
  the Way and ways to, 77–80
  will of, 118–126, 140
Gollancz, Victor, 197
Gospel According to St. John, The, 20, 296, 311–313
Grace, of God, *see* God; Prayer of, 167–170
Great Return, The, 278–281
Gregoreite (wake up! watch!), 81, 105, 111, 112
Gross, Martin L., xviii, 209, 270–277
Grou, Jean-Nicolas, 141 n.†, 155–156, 199
Groups, spiritual or growth, 7–10, 136–137, 282–290
Guardini, Romano, 192
Guatama Sakyamundi; *see* Buddha
Gurdjieff, G.I., 79, 80, 109, 112, 113, 121, 268

Hahnemann, Samuel, xviii
Hall, Francis J., 191
Hartmann, Franz, 196
Healing, 114, 166, 278–280, 283–290
Heard, Gerald, 93, 94, 191, 199
Heart, the, 166, 167
Hermes, xvii, xviii, 209, 226–228
Heschel, Abraham J., 108, 198
Hesychast tradition, 16, 156, 160, 199, 205
Hilton, Walter, 201
Hinduism, 3, 158, 163, 192, 193
Hippocrates, xviii
Honesty, 10–16, 20, 21, 51, 53, 68, 70, 80, 83, 107, 118, 131, 153
  absolute, 284, 287
Householder (man or woman in the world), 77–80, 87, 144–145
Hughson, Shirley C., O.H.C., 85, 200
Humility, 14, 20, 53
Huxley, Aldous, 121 n.‡, 195 n.‡, 197

I Ching; see Book of Changes
Identity, one's own, "Who am I?", 47–48; see also Self
Illumination, 69, 195
"Illuminism," 68, 117 n.*
Inge, W.R., 195 n.‡
Islam, 3, 72 n.†, 159 n.†, 193, 198

James, William, 62
John of Ruysbroeck, 206, 207
Johnson, Raynor C., 191
Judaism, 108, 192, 198
Jung, C.G., xviii, 55–56, 73, 196, 268

Kant, Immanuel, 50 n.*, 53
Karma yoga, 79
Kavanah (attentiveness to God), 108–109
Kelly, Thomas, 34, 203, 204
Ko Hung, xvii
Koran, 36, 37, 181 (bibliog.)
Krishna, xvii, 111
Kristol, Irving, xviii

Lamb, George, 196
Lao Tse, xvii, 40, 78
Lawrence, Brother, 87–94
Learning, 17–18, 20, 26
Lecaro, Cardinal, 202
Lehrs, Ernst, xviii, 209, 230–237

Lewis, C.S., xvii, xviii, 125, 196, 209, 210–214
Lifesavers way of life, xvii, 282–322
Lin Yutang, 40
Love, 49, 126–131, 153, 168
  absolute, 284
  and truth, 14
Lying, 10–13
  contra-indicated, 81, 82, 130–131

MacDonald, George, xvii, xviii
Machen, Arthur, xviii, 209, 278–281
Maharshi, Bhagavan Sri Ramana, 33, 48, 160
Manchester, William, xviii
Man or Matter, 230–237
Mantram, 159, 163
Maritain, Jacques, 190
Marmion, Abbot, 195 n.‡
Martin, Malachi, xvii
Martin, P.W., 196
Mary of Agreda, xviii
Materialism, 53, 124
Medicine, xviii, 2 n.*, 240–242
Meditation, 168
Mendelsohn, Dr. Robert S., xviii, 2 n.*, 209, 240–242
Mental Science, 194
Mephiz-Tophel; see Adversary
Merton, Thomas, 197
Metanoia ("repent," change your mind, change your state), 81, 107
Metaphysics, 194
Miracles, 196
Monkey; see Adversary
Moral disciplines, pre-yogic, 82–83
Morals, moral clean-up, 129–133
Morrison, A. Cressy, 191
Moses, xvii, 71
Mowrer, O. Hobart, xviii, 209, 254–259
Muhammad, xvii, 72 n.†, 78
Murder, contra-indicated, 81, 82, 83
Musto, David F., xviii
Mysteries, the, 195
Mysticism, mystical insight, 152, 195, 204–208
Myth of the Cave, The, 217 n.*

Narcotics Anonymous, 285
Neumann, Theresa, 78, 196
Neurotics Anonymous, 8, 285
New Thought, 194

Nicephorus the Solitary, 109
Nicholas of Flüe, 196
Nicoll, Maurice, xviii, 80, 109, 113, 209, 262–268
Niebuhr, Reinhold, 191
Novak, Robert, xviii

O'Brien, Rev. John A., 193
Osborne, Arthur, 48
Ouspensky, P.D., 1, 80, 109, 262 n.*, 264, 268
Out of the Silent Planet, 210–214
Overeaters Anonymous, 8, 285
Oxford Group, 16, 283, 284, 292–295

Paracelsus, xviii
Pardue, Bishop Austin, 11, 167, 199
Pascal, 29
Patanjali, The Yoga Aphorisms of, 85, 161, 197
Peale, Norman Vincent, 194
People, as helps in spiritual life, 2, 7–8, 20, 22–29, 51–52, 67, 289
People's Doctor, The, 240–242
Phillips, Dorothy Berkeley, 197
Philo Judaeus, 34
Philokalia, The, 26, 34, 110, 160, 205
Pilgrim, the, xvii, 157, 158, 160, 162, 163, 166, 199
Pilgrim Continues His Way, The, 157
Plato, 50 n.*, 195, 217 n.*, 218, 221–222
Plotinus, xvii, xviii, 34, 196, 204
Positive thinking, 193, 194
Poulain, A., 201
Prabhavananda, 85, 161, 162, 198
Practice of abandonment, the; *see* Surrender to God
Practice of continuous prayer, the, 154–160, 170
Practice of ego-reduction, the, 94–102
Practice of penetrating the cloud, the, 142–154, 170
Practice of the Presence of God, the, 87–94, 102, 110, 114, 140, 167
Practice of watching, the, 102–114, 140, 167
  commanded by Christ, 81, 103, 105
Praos ("meek," trained, tractable), 82
Prayer, 103, 106, 114, 127–133, 142–170
  and the body, 145–147
  books about, 198–208
  and breathing, 147, 148
  commanded by Christ, 82, 155
  continuous, 154–167
  of Jesus, 155–156, 162–167
  "making the mind blank," in, 151–153
  map of, 168
  place of, 144
  time of, 142–144
  and visions, 150
Protestants and faith, 193
Psychiatry, xviii, 243–253, 254–260
Psychic phenomena, 149–150
Psychological Commentaries, 262–268
Psychological Society, The, 270–277
Psychology, xviii, 262–268, 270–277
  effect of, on modern civilization, 270–277
Psychology of Man's Possible Evolution, The, 262 n.*
Psychopathic personalities, 13
Purgation, 68–69, 131, 195
Purity, absolute, 284

Questions, as helps in spiritual life, 1, 2
Quietism, 203
Quimby, Phineas Parkhurst, 194

Radhakrishnan, Sarvepalli, 192
Rama, 78, 158, 159 n.‡, 162
Ramakrishna, Sri, 32, 72 n.†, 78, 98, 160, 198
Ramanama, 158, 159, 160, 166
Ramayana of Tulasidas, 159 n.‡
Read, David H.C., 193
Reason, as help in spiritual life, 49–56, 59–61, 64
  books about, 190–192
Recollection of God, 88–89; *see also* Remembering
Recovery from addiction, 282–322
Remembering, importance of, 136–138, 141, 169; *see also* Recollection
Rheinhold, H. A., 197
Richard of St. Victor, 205
Roman Catholics, and faith, 192–193
Rosten, Leo, 193
Roueché, Berton, xviii
Rules, of spiritual life, 80–85, 87
Rumi Jalálúddin, 34, 198

St. Albert the Great, 202
St. Anselm, 50 n.*
St. Augustine, 29, 53, 196

St. Bernard, 67, 203, 205, 207
St. Catherine of Genoa, 196
St. Francis de Sales, 79
St. Francis of Assisi, 72 n.†, 78, 196
St. Gregory of Sinai, 60
St. Ignatius of Loyola, 196
St. Isaac, 109
St. John of the Cross, 34, 150, 195 n.‡, 207
St. John of the Ladder, 109
St. Paul, 72 n.†, 99, 192, 313–317
St. Seraphim of Sarov, 197
St. Simeon, 109
St. Teresa of Jesus, 195 n.‡, 196, 202
St. Therese of Lisieux, 196
St. Thomas Aquinas, xviii, 50 n.*, 53, 56, 191, 192, 203
Satori (sudden awakening), 108
Schaer, Hans, 73
Schimberg, A.P., 196
Scholem, Gershom, 198
Schoolmasters, xvii, 209–281
Schroeder, Eric, 198
Schuon, Frithjof, xvii, 160
Schweitzer, and rational thought, 51 n.†
Science, xviii, 230–238
Scupoli, Lorenzo, 85
Secret of the Golden Flower, The, 198
Self, the Higher and the lower, 99–101
Shaitan; see Adversary
Shankaracharya, 34, 65
Sheean, Vincent, 21
Sheed, F.J., 191
Shestov, Lev, xvii, 209, 216–225
Shoemaker, Fr. Samuel, 295, 296
Silkworth, Dr. William D., 295, 296
Sin, 254–259
    the seven capital sins, 84
Sincerity, 16, 17, 68
Smith, Margaret, 198
Smith, Dr. Robert H., 293, 296
Song of Songs, The, 205, 305
Sorokin, Pitirim, A., 192, 197
Stealing, contra-indicated, 81–83
Steiner, Rudolf, 230, 234–237
Suffering (pain, loss, sickness, accidents), as helps in spiritual life, 82, 83, 133–135, 166
Sufis, xvii, 206
Surrender to God (abandonment), 83, 102
    practice of, 133–142, 167, 170
Suso, Henry, 196

Suzuki, D.T., 198
Szasz, Thomas, xviii

Tales of Horror and the Supernatural, 278–281
Tanquerey, Adolphe, 85
Tao Te Ching; *see* Book of Tao
Tauler, John, 152
Theologica Germanica, 101, 102, 152
Theology, books about, 191
Therapeutae, 16
Thurston, Herbert, 196
Tibet's Great Yogi, Milarepa, 198
Tiebout, Dr. Harry M., xviii, 209, 244–253, 294, 296
Tillich, Paul, 191
Tolkien, J.R.R., xvii
Toynbee, Arnold J., 191
Treasury of Russian Spirituality, A, 197
Trochu, Abbé Francis, 196
Troward, Thomas, 194
Trueblood, Elton, 190
Truth, 11, 13, 14, 20, 26–27, 70, 80, 85, 118–119, 123, 128, 150, 152, 170, 208, 284, 287
Twelve Steps, The, 283–286

Underhill, Evelyn, 195
Union with God, 69, 70, 195, 204–208
Unity School of Christianity, 194
Unselfishness, absolute, 284
Upanishads, 37–39, 45, 48, 99

Van Paassen, Pierre, 197
Vedas, the, 37, 38
Virtue (holy power), 130

Wachsmuth, Guenther, xviii
Waite, A.E., xviii, 63, 70
Walsh, W.T., 196
Watching; *see* Practice of watching
Watts, Alan, 198
Way of a Pilgrim, The, 157, 199
Weatherhead, Leslie, 122, 123
William of St. Thierry, 202
Wilson, William G., 293, 296
Work, necessity of, 17–20, 46, 80, 85
    place of, 46–48

Zarathustra, xvii

Acknowledgments

Acknowledgment is made for permission to reprint extracts from some of our Schoolmasters' teachings (see pages 209–281):

Out of the Silent Planet, by C. S. Lewis. Copyright © 1946. Reprinted with the permission of the Estate of C. S. Lewis.

Athens and Jerusalem, by Lev Shestov. Copyright © 1966. Reprinted with the permission of The Ohio University Press/Swallow Press, Athens.

Man or Matter, by Ernst Lehrs. Copyright © 1958. Reprinted with the permission of Rudolf Steiner Press, London.

The People's Doctor Newsletter, by Robert S. Mendelsohn. Copyright © 1986. Reprinted with the permission of The People's Doctor Newsletter, 1578 Sherman Avenue, Evanston, Illinois 60201 (annual subscription $24.00).

"Psychological Factors Operating in Alcoholics Anonymous," by Harry M. Tiebout. Copyright © 1946. Reprinted with the permission of Grune & Stratton, Inc., Orlando, Florida.

Psychological Commentaries on the Teaching of Gurdjieff and Ouspensky, by Maurice Nicoll. Copyright © 1952. Reprinted with the permission of Robinson's Books Ltd. 1951/Shambhala Publications Inc. 1983.

The Psychological Society, by Martin L. Gross. Copyright © 1978 by Martin L. Gross. Reprinted with the permission of Random House, Inc.

2-4 meditation $10
6-8 emotion
8-10 dance & chanting } $30

Ruth Gaskins
 984-2317 Laurence

Ask if   Science & Creation
  tell if wants her to check out
     again   by Sat.